MAFIA WIPEOUT

MAFIA WIPEOUT

How the Feds Put Away an Entire Mob Family

Donald W. Cox

Shapolsky Publishers, Inc.
New York

A Shapolsky Book

For any additional information, contact:
Shapolsky Publishers, Inc.
136 West 22nd Street, NY, NY 10011
(212)-633-2022

9 8 7 6 5 4 3 2 1

Library of Congress Cataloging-in-Publication Data

Cox, Donald W. 1921-
Mafia Wipeout:
How the Law Put an Entire Mob Family in Prison
Donald W. Cox. -- 1st ed.
p.   cm.
Includes bibliographical references.
ISBN 0-944007-52-X
1. Mafia--Pennsylvania--Philadelphia Metropolitan Area--Case studies.
2. Scarfo, Nicodemo Domenic, 1929-   . I. Title.

HV6452.P4M343 1989   364.1'06'0974811--dc20   89-10770 CIP

Manufactured in the United States of America

The author is indebted to the Federal Bureau of Investigation for the photographs reproduced on pages 199 through 210.

To the hardworking prosecutors and staffs of the U.S. Attorney's Office, the U.S. Organized Crime Strike Force of the Eastern District of Pennsylvania, and of the Philadelphia District Attorney's Office, who never gave up on their quarry — to see that justice was done, despite early acquittals, hung juries, and other setbacks...and to the long-suffering, anonymous, and sequestered 18 members of the Scarfo-RICO jury who deliberated for over two months, but in the end, rendered the just decision.

Contents

Introduction
by John H. Davis

One of the continuing sins of the American Establishment has been a marked proclivity to indulge in self-deception when confronted by some of the more unacceptable evils that afflict the nation. There is a canon of beliefs by which the Establishment lives and works that the consensus considers beyond challenge. Included in this catechism are sacred dogmas of the uniqueness of American freedom and democracy: that "only in America," as the Bruce Springsteen song goes, can an individual rise from poverty and obscurity to great wealth and prominence and that the various forms of tyranny and oppression that have afflicted most other nations on earth "can't happen here."

Yet it is precisely because the self-deceivers blindly insist that a given social evil "can't happen here" that it often *does* happen here — by default because of the absence of concern and action that would have prevented the evil from flourishing.

The power and influence of the Mafia in the United States is a case in point. No less a member of the Establishment than J. Edgar Hoover, who ran the Federal Bureau of Investigation for forty-eight years, publicly proclaimed time and again that there was no such thing as organized crime in America. It was not until a 'made' member of a Mafia crime family, Joseph Valachi, broke his vow of silence in September, 1963, by testifying before a Senate committee about the structure, code, and criminal activities of the Mafia in America, that Hoover came reluctantly to admit that such a phenomenon as organized crime did exist in the United States.

Until recently few Americans in positions of leadership could face the affront to their cherished beliefs that the Mafia's rise to vast power and influence represented. It could not happen here — but it did: the emergence of a brutal criminal tyranny within American society based on the willingness to commit murder to achieve its ends, and powerful enough to oppress and damage millions of Americans in countless ways. Yes, it happened here, but who would admit it?

Who among our leaders in government, finance, business, education, and communications in the early sixties was prepared to accept the fact that the Mafia boss of the Gulf States underworld controlled the political machinery of an entire state?

Who among our leaders then was prepared to accept the fact that another Mafia boss exercised absolute control over certain voting districts in Chicago and thus was in a position to deliver the electoral votes of the state of Illinois to the presidential candidate of his choice?

And who was prepared to believe, prior to 1979, that there was a high probability an American President was executed as a result of a Mafia conspiracy? (It was not until 1979 that an official investigation of the murder of President Kennedy — that conducted by the House Select Committee on Assassinations — suggested that, on the basis of evidence available to it, organized crime may well have been involved in a conspiracy to assassinate the President.)

One of the merits of Donald Cox's book, *Mafia Wipeout*, is that it squarely faces reality and painfully affronts the belief system of the self-deceivers who keep chanting, "it can't happen here."

This work focuses on the appalling corruption in the city of Philadelphia, William Penn's City of Brotherly Love, the site of the proclamation of the Declaration of Independence and of the drafting and adoption of the Constitution of the United States.

As Mr. Cox vividly demonstrates, this shrine of American Democracy had become, by the dawn of the 1980's, perhaps the most corrupt municipality in the nation. A member of Philadelphia's City Council had become a mere tool of the Mafia and its city streets had degenerated into battlegrounds of drug dealers and of contending factions within the leading Mafia organization. In the six years following the assassination of long-time boss Angelo Bruno in 1980, the City of Brotherly Love witnessed the murders of no fewer than twenty-eight would-be heirs to Bruno's tarnished crown.

It is a supreme irony that the Constitution born in Philadelphia protected the Mafia organization that had so corrupted the city. How many times had television audiences witnessed alleged Mafia leaders refusing to answer questions posed by congressional committees and invoking their constitutional rights under the First, Fourth, Fifth, and Fourteenth Amendments?

The Constitution, which established as a *sine qua non* the doctrine of presumption of innocence until proven guilty, had made it illegal for law enforcement authorities to detain a suspect in a crime without first obtaining an indictment from a grand jury, and had established the right of a criminal suspect to refuse to testify to authorities on the grounds that his testimony might tend to incriminate him. With such protection of the rights of the individual against the demands of the state, secret criminal brotherhoods such as as the Mafia were able to grow and prosper with little interference from the law.

That the Mafia had thoroughly corrupted America's cradle of liberty is indeed depressing. After delineating the extent of this corruption, however, *Mafia Wipeout* does not leave us in despair. Rather, Mr. Cox ultimately provides us with nothing less than heroic redemption.

The main body of Donald Cox's book presents a long and brutal struggle between law enforcement authorities — federal, state and city — against the powerful Philadelphia crime family headed by Nicodemo ('Nicky') Scarfo that gloriously resulted in one of the most decisive and total victories over a Mafia family in the nation's history.

Through the combined efforts of the offices of the U.S. Organized Crime Strike Force, the United States Attorney for the Eastern District of Pennsylvania, the Pennsylvania Crime Commission, and the District Attorney of Philadelphia, the entire leadership of a major Mafia family has been eliminated. No fewer than seventeen 'made' members of the Scarfo family — boss, underbosses, lieutenants, and soldiers — have been convicted on charges of racketeering, conspiracy, and murder, and sent off to federal prison to serve sentences of from thirty to fifty-five years each.

It was, as Mr. Cox aptly terms it, a complete wipeout. Having sunk over the years into a morass of corruption, the city in which the nation's most sacred testaments of freedom and democracy were born had finally been redeemed.

JOHN H. DAVIS
New York
1989

John Davis is the author of several best selling books including *MAFIA KINGFISH, THE KENNEDYS: DYNASTY & DISASTER, THE GUGGENHEIMS* and *THE BOUVIERS*. A *cum laude* graduate of Princeton, he studied in Italy on a Fulbright scholarship and served as a naval officer with the Sixth Fleet.

Foreward
by Ronald D. Castille

Don Cox provides a comprehensive look at the South Jersey/ Philadelphia La Cosa Nostra. His account of the history and leadership of the regional Mafia organization is interesting and revealing.

Especially gratifying from my perspective is the fact that the book documents the unprecedented cooperation between local law enforcement which served to end the brutal reign of terror of Mob Boss Nicky Scarfo Sr. This effort — by my office, the New Jersey State Police, the FBI, the U.S. Attorney's Office, the Organized Crime Strike Force and state and local police — decimated the Scarfo criminal organization.

The author's chapter on the murder convictions won by Philadelphia D.A. prosecutors of Scarfo (the *first* time a state won a first-degree murder conviction of a reigning Mob boss) and seven of his associates is, indeed, the final chapter for Nicky's criminal enterprise.

RONALD D. CASTILLE
District Attorney of Philadelphia
1989

Acknowledgements

I wish to personally thank my three typists, Phyllis Fertik, Louisa Zullo and Denise Nicholson for their ability to transcribe my rough draft of this book over a two-year period. I also wish to thank Eileen Eckstein for giving me the necessary professional photographer's tips on how to properly shoot the Scarfo family photos from those made available to me from the FBI files.

I am also deeply indebted to the cooperation shown to me by the Lead Prosecutor of the U.S. Organized Crime Strike Force, Louis Pichini, for his making the RICO trial photos, indictments and transcripts available for my use in the book, enhancing its credibility. My daughter, Heather, gets special thanks for lending me her Minolta camera to take many of the photos included here when my Model T camera failed.

The team of *Philadelphia Inquirer* court reporters, particularly Emilie Lounsberrry, Susan Caba, Robin Clark, Dan Biddle and George Anastasia, were all most helpful, both directly and indirectly, with the filing of well-researched professional news stories of the nine trials that I attended over a two-year period (1987-1989).

Rich Kirkner, Associate Editor of *Focus* Magazine, helped me with Chapter #30, 'The Enterprise' to smooth out its organization and content of how the Mafia runs its business.

Barbara Cowan and a person very close to me gave many untiring hours in copyreading and editing the final copy of the manuscript.

I also wish to exend my appreciation to Ms. Barbara Christie, the head of the Homicide Unit in the Philadelphia D.A.'s Office, who read and edited the chapters concerning her office's two major trials and to Douglas and Lois Olena of West Chester, Pennsylvania for re-editing my work. Thanks also to Betty Guardiani for help with indexing.

I am particularly indebted to John H. Davis, author of the recently-published *Mafia Kingfish*, who read the entire manuscript and gave me some valuable insights into needed restructuring, cutting and editing of the book as well as writing a perceptive introduction.

Finally, to my wife, Jane, who stood by me throughout the gestation period of this book, despite her many misgivings during the long struggle from the initial spark to birth, I owe a deep debt of gratitude.

If this first narrative history of the contemporary Mafia crime family in the Philadelphia area manages to become an accepted standard work, it is because of all the people named above who played a vital role in helping me to complete this writing effort that stretched between January 1987 and June 1989 — covering nine crime trials which I attended in their entireties.

Donald Cox
Philadelphia, Pa.
1989

Voltaire thought there was no religious bigotry or fanaticism in England: even the Quakers had subsided into comfortable businessmen. He visited one of them and was pleased to be told that Pennsylvania was a utopia without classes, wars or enemies. (1720)

-Will and Ariel Durant[*]

Prologue

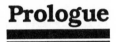

PHILADELPHIA: THE CITY OF BROTHERLY LOVE AND OF UNBROTHERLY GREED

In the past decade, two Philadelphia Congressmen and three Councilmen (including the Council President, George X. Schwartz) have each been convicted and served prison terms for taking monetary bribes from a mythical Arab potentate in the Abscam scandal. (One other Councilman, Isadore Bellis, the former Majority Leader, had been convicted several times over for extorting up to $500,000 from numerous concessionaires during the Philadelphia International Airport expansion operations. He wiggled off the judicial hook, however, by making an appeal to the Pennsylvania Supreme Court.

Elected officials were not the only ones to get themselves into legal troubles in recent Philadelphia history. By August, 1987, 34 local police officers had been convicted and sent to jail after being found guilty of various Federal criminal charges, from extortion to drug dealing. Almost three dozen crooked cops were caught in the net of the law as a result of a four-year investigation into rampant corruption in the Philadelphia Police Department.

Simultaneously, 15 Common Pleas Court and Municipal

---

[*] *The Age Of Voltaire*, p. 247 (one of the books in their 11 volume STORY OF CIVILIZATION)

Court Judges were relieved of their duties. One was convicted of bribery and several others were indicted on various State and Federal charges.

With scandals hitting high-level officials in all three governmental departments — executive, legislative and judicial — the political atmosphere in the City of Brotherly Love had become severely polluted.

A PREVIEW OF THINGS TO COME:

THE MILLION DOLLAR SCAM AT PENN'S LANDING

The main subplot in this book covers the escapades of one legislator who became involved in a million dollar extortion plot aimed at the Number One local real estate developer, Willard Rouse III. Mr. Rouse had successfully built two twin downtown multi-story shopping malls, Gallerys' I and II plus the massive #1 Liberty Place, the tallest skyscraper in the city.

Rouse had been the successful bidder to redevelop the abandoned Penn's Landing dock areas along the Delaware River where the founder of Pennsylvania first stepped down onto the riverbank back in 1683 from his sailing ship, *Welcome*. But by mid-1986, after Rouse had been designated as the prime contractor to erect a modern waterfront mini-city consisting of marinas, hotels, condos, restaurants, office buildings and even the possibility of a Disneyland North, a group of modern day buccaneers, masquerading under the mantle of the Mafia, decided to squeeze a slice of the billion-dollar planned development from Rouse and Co.

They planned to cajole a small cut of a mere $1 million (or 1/1000th) of the total construction package from Mr. Rouse for 'protection' and to guarantee the builder that he "would not have any major labor troubles on the project." The intrigue and twisted shenanigans that occurred during the mounting of this complex scam involved both the head of the local Mafia and the richest member of the City Council. This loose-knit group of piranhas felt they would have no trouble with their projected extortion scheme since Mr. Rouse had just been promised a $20 million Federal grant to underwrite the project.

The central concern of this book is the story and analysis of the gyrations of the largest Mafia-dominated crime family in Southeastern Pennsylvania and Southern New Jersey. Nicodemo Scarfo and the leaders of his crime family have seen their Rogue's Gallery portraits emblazoned in local area newspapers and broadcast on television during the past year as a result of their involvement in a series of nine show trials covering the mob's illegal operations.

This legal skewering of the inner parts of the Mafia hopefully lays bare one of the motivating forces that guided the interplay of actors in this melodrama: human greed. This character trait was best explained by a little-known political advisor who served on Vice President George Bush's finance committee during his 1980 Presidential campaign. Arthur Dubow, a venture capitalist, summed up the nation's pulse in mid-1987 when he said: "Cynicism is the mood of the day and greed the dominating force. We are simultaneously selling our souls and our children's futures." His astute observation may explain why the leading characters in the tragi-comic drama surrounding the Penn's Landing redevelopment project acted the way they did. Strangely, they all felt they could succeed in their million dollar scam — until they all got caught.

A MOB ASSOCIATE ATTEMPTS A GREAT ESCAPE

While serving his long, second prison term in the Lewisburg Federal Penitentiary, Steven 'Steakie' Vento, an associate of Scarfo in the drug business, brazenly tried to engineer a dramatic escape. He had acknowledged arranging several profitable drug deals in methamphetamine, cocaine and marijuana from behind the prison walls, for which he was never charged. He told the jury that his various prison terms "had brought about his rehabilitation" but that he had earned "better than a million and a half dollars" on one drug deal alone, consummated while he was behind bars.

Vento, who had quadruple heart bypass surgery in prison, explained to the jury how he used $700,000 of the $1,500,000 that he had made operating the illegal coke and methamphetamine operation to try to escape. He felt because of his failing health he had nothing to lose in the dramatic gamble of asking his son to arrange for a private helicopter firm to send in a whirlybird and a pilot to scoop him up from the open prison yard at a pre-arranged time and date, July 15, 1986.

However, the copter company got cold feet and went to the Feds and spilled the beans about the plots. When the attempted rescue mission was faked by the Feds with the copter swooping low over the prison yard and Vento waving to those he believed were his rescuers, the prison guards who had been alerted, moved in and rearrested him. He and his son were each given a five-year prison term for the botched effort. His son is also awaiting a separate trial on a murder charge.

THE RITES OF A MOB CHRISTENING

One of the most riveting bits of testimony repeated over and over again in seven of the eight Mafia trials that are covered here, was the description of the process of a mob initiation ceremony, as told to the jury, judge and court by Nicholas 'Nicky Crow' Caramandi, a former 'made member' of the Scarfo family. Caramandi vividly described the steps in the secret ceremony held in unlikely places where the law was least likely to have surveillance apparatus.

The sites of the secret underworld passage into membership in the South Jersey, Southeastern Pennsylvania Mafia family rotated from a room above the Pizzateria Restaurant on lower South Street in Philadelphia to Merighi's Savoy Inn in Buena Vista Township, New Jersey to Sam La Russa's Whitemarsh Township home in Montgomery County, just north of Philadelphia. (La Russa was the owner of the well-known La Cucina Restaurant in South Philadelphia.)

Caramandi was inducted in La Russa's home, several years after the Spirito killing. The ceremony of 'the making' of him as a mob member took place in the presence of 35 Scarfo Mafia family members. Three prospective members, Caramandi, Charles Iannece, and Charles Grande, were taken to the house by Thomas Del Giorno and Frank Iannarella and were ushered into a bedroom, Caramandi said. Iannece was called in first, then he was told to come in. "We entered into a large room, where the other members were sitting around a large table on top of which was a knife and a gun. Scarfo presided at the head of the table and was surrounded by several *capos*. I stood in front while Scarfo made a little speech, stating that I deserved to become a member because 'he done a good job for us, the last couple of years,'" Caramandi told the Scarfo trial jury on April 30, 1987, staring down at the imprisoned Little Napoleon Mafia leader as he related his story.

Caramandi said Scarfo then told him: "We would like you to become one of us. If you don't want to join, you can walk out of here and we'll show you respect." After giving his assent to the boss, Scarfo told him to look around the room and then said: "I want you to do a couple of things (pointing to a knife and a gun on the table). Would you use this knife and gun for any one of your friends around the table?"

"Yes," responded Caramandi.

Scarfo then handed him a piece of facial tissue, lit it with a cigarette lighter and told him to hold it, which Caramandi did. He was then ordered to extinguish it with his own hands. He complied and dropped the blackened piece of tissue on the table. Scarfo then said to Caramandi: "May I burn like the saints in Hell if I betray one of my friends."

According to government surveillance, at this moment, all of the 35 members around the table joined hands while Scarfo mumbled something in Italian (that Caramandi did not understand.)

Scarfo then concluded the so-called *christening* of Caramandi with a bizarre added ritual that included the substitution of blood for holy water. As part of the rigamarole, Scarfo ordered the inductee's trigger-finger to be *pinched* until it bled. The new inductee's blood would then be mixed with that of his Mafia sponsor and Scarfo said something more in Italian after which Caramandi went around the table and kissed each member. "You are now a member," said a proud Scarfo and they all shook hands.

As the ceremony ended, Scarfo gave the new inductee a friendly warning: "You can't fool with drugs, bonds or counterfeit money," he said, "but you can shake any drug dealers down, since we are the only mob in Philadelphia."

They aren't anymore, and the rest of this book tells why.

*...I haven't seen *any* evidence of the Mafia. There is *no* Italian Mafia, but there *is* organized crime...in America.*

1

-Bruce Cutler, Defense Lawyer for John Gotti[*]

THE BLOODY MAFIA WARS
OF THE 20TH CENTURY

A LTHOUGH Scarfo wasn't home at the time of the search, the investigators found him the next morning at the nearby home of a woman whom he described as a 'friend.' They arrested him for the murder of the Margate cement contractor, Vincent Falcone, who also was described as a 'friend.' Scarfo's nephew, Philip 'Crazy Phil' Leonetti, and Lawrence 'Yogi' Merlino, two of his constant companions in crime, were also arrested and charged with the murder of Falcone in December 1979.

The law had what seemed to be a pretty good case against the three men, pinpointing the young, handsome Leonetti as the alleged triggerman in the murder. The government's case was based largely on the testimony of a man named Joe Salerno, Jr., a down-and-out plumber, who was befriended by the three and moved into the Scarfo apartment house at a time of personal and financial difficulty. Salerno told the lawmen that he had hoped to get some plumbing work from Scarf Inc. through its contacts with construction contractors. He was also drawn to them because of their rich and exotic lifestyle where money and women were always available.

One night at the Brajole Cafe in Atlantic City, Scarfo told Salerno: "You know Joe, I like you, 'cause you're like me...you got the same bloodlines that I have. We are Calabrese people... That's good. We are good people."

Salerno revealed to prosecutors that Falcone made the mistake

---

[*] Reputed head of Mafia organized crime families in New York, spoken live on the "Sons of Scarface: The New Mafia," a nationally syndicated TV documentary, August 17, 1987.

of bad-mouthing Scarfo, calling him crazy to Salvatore 'Chuckie'
Merlino, 'Yogi's' brother. 'Chuckie' relayed this denigrating remark to Nicky when the two were on a trip to Italy. Falcone,
who was jealous of the fact that Phil Leonetti had been dating a
woman who had formerly gone out with him, made disparaging
remarks against Leonetti, allegedly saying that "Phil shouldn't be
in the concrete business."

Salerno discovered that these were two sufficient reasons for
Scarfo and his lieutenants to 'wipe out' Falcone. At a dinner
Salerno attended in Scarfo's apartment after the murder, Scarfo
remarked that, "if it hadn't been messy he would have cut out
Falcone's tongue."

Salerno testified that Scarfo lured him unwittingly to Falcone's apartment. While there he observed the following sequence of events.

Falcone had been mixing drinks at the kitchen sink when
Leonetti shot him in the back with a pearl-handled antique pistol.
Leonetti was four feet away from Falcone when he fired the gun.
The dying man "turned halfway around, slid down and sort of sat
with his hand on his stomach and stared." Then Leonetti "looked
right into my eyes" and said, "Vincent Falcone was a no good
motherfucker, Joe!"

Scarfo knelt down and put his head against Falcone's chest,
then stood and said: "I think we should give him another one...
do you want me to do it?" Leonetti walked over as Scarfo
opened Falcone's leather jacket, while Leonetti shot the dying
man once again in the chest. "The gun was almost touching
him," Salerno related.

Scarfo then ordered both Leonetti and Merlino to go home,
take showers and change their clothes. Merlino was told to use
Falcone's car and come back to the murder scene. Salerno, who
had a sinking feeling that he might be the next man marked to be
killed, was approached by Scarfo, who grabbed him by the arms
and said, "You are one of us now!"

Scarfo then got a blanket and some twine and said to Salerno:
"Let's turn him over. We're going to tie him up, like old times,
tie him like a cowboy...I love this! I love this! The big shot is
dead!"

Scarfo then lifted Falcone's head, closed the dead man's
eyes, and covered his face with a blanket. Scarfo then dispatched
Salerno to a nearby payphone to check on Merlino, telephoning

his home in nearby Brigantine....

According to Salerno, the cold calculated murder was treated as an everyday affair by Scarfo and his cohorts. Salerno clearly did not feel like "one of us." He felt threatened enough to go to the authorities and spill his guts.

Who are these people who hold themselves above the law? Are they a law unto themselves? If there is organized crime then these men must be part of it—lieutenants must have a captain, or as it is in this instance a boss. We must ask, however, what the origin of this organization is if we are to understand the traditions it carries like a badge of honor. It appears that what Mr. Bruce Cutler, cited at the beginning of this chapter, does not tell us the whole truth about the existence of the Mafia.

THE ORIGINS OF THE MAFIA . . . OVER THERE AND HERE

The Mafia originated in Italy during feudal times, when lords hired rough brigands to guard their estates in exchange for protection from the royal authority. Then, in the 19th and 20th centuries, a number of organized bands of Sicilian brigands arose to plunder the countryside by infiltrating regular businesses on the island. Unlike the Camorra of nearby Naples in southern Italy, the Mafia had no hierarchic organization in the beginning. Each group operated on its own.

The justification the Mafia used to perpetuate their existence was that legal authorities were useless and that justice must be obtained directly, through the use of vigilantes and the vendetta. The existence of political corruption gave the Mafia tremendous influence in early 20th Century Italy. Benito Mussolini, the late Italian dictator, even tried to suppress the Mafia in a vigorous campaign, but failed.

Immigrants from these two sister Mediterranean countries, Italy and Sicily which were combined into one nation in 1881, established their family connections in the New World, where the Mafia was sometimes called 'The Black Hand.' This organization caused much trouble in Louisiana in the late 19th Century and allegedly controlled many illegal operations, i.e., trade in narcotics, prostitution, gambling, loan sharking and labor union racketeering, particularly in the blue-collar trade unions like the Teamsters and the Roofers.

'AL' AND 'LUCKY' TAKE OVER IN AMERICA

'Scarface Al' Capone was the first bigtime mob leader in America. He reigned over the Chicago family in the 1920's and 30's which combined the organized discipline of the old country with his new U.S. connections. But Elliott Ness and other Federal authorities convicted him on income tax evasion and he spent most of the rest of his life in prison, dying of syphilis in 1947.

After the Second World War, the loose-knit organization grew rapidly in Italy, Sicily, and particularly in the United States where the heirs of the late Al Capone violently fought each other for power.

In 1931, New York's ruthless mob leader, 'Lucky' Luciano, organized the first American Mafia (control) Commission to end the gang warfare that had wiped out at least 40 mobsters in just two days in September of the same year. He partly succeeded, at least lowering the rate of assassinations of mob members in the ensuing years.[*]

For two decades, the Mafia managed to keep its board of directors hidden from the outside world until it held a convention in Apalachin, New York, November, 1957. More than 60 of the alleged Mafia leaders from around the country met at this so-called 'Summit' meeting where they were surprised by law enforcement authorities in a celebrated raid. About one-third of them were convicted in December, 1959, for obstructing justice, but the convictions were reversed on appeal almost a year later. This situation led to the continued mushrooming growth of other families, particularly on the Eastern seaboard.

'Lucky' Luciano started his heroin drug traffic operations in the New World from the Hotel De Palma in Sicily, marketing his underground product to the poor minorities located mainly in the Northeastern cities of the USA. After his death, a succession of Mafioso overlords, like the late Vito Genovese and Albert Anas-

---

[*] Before 1930, top Mafia gangsters like Salvatore Marazano had managed to shoot their way into becoming the *capo di tutti capi* (Boss of Bosses). Marazano, who organized New York's immigrant Sicilian gangsters into five families, became the first casualty of Luciano's new order.

tasia, reigned supreme in the New York area until they were gunned down by rivals.[*]

Strangely, the late, longtime FBI Director, J. Edgar Hoover, for many years refused to believe that the Mafia existed. The power of the Mafia to perpetuate the myth of its non-existence in recent years was best displayed by the pressure exerted by Joe Columbo on the producers of the famed series of *Godfather* films. The name Mafia was not mentioned even once in the dialogue. Hoover finally believed the Mafia was real when the ex-mob informer, Joe Valachi, exposed his cohorts in a celebrated series of (televised) Congressional hearings in 1963.[†]

THE STATUS OF THE 'NEW' MAFIA

According to New York's chief FBI agent, Tom Sheer, the new breed of Mafia leaders now imitate the sophisticated business leaders of corporate America, which enables them to move swiftly into profitable moneymaking arrangements, i.e., legitimate businesses, such as transportation, and unions. The new smooth-running mob operations have global contacts and high-paid legal advisers to help them over the hurdles as the mob attempts to penetrate these legitimate enterprises to supplement its regular base income from gambling, extortion and loansharking.

They move into legitimate businesses and eventually take them over, and compete with other businesses in the same field. When they get the gut feeling that they are losing out, "they will revert to breaking legs," said Sheer. "True American corporate competition does not include breaking legs."

The 'breaking of legs' could actually be only in the form of threats to other corporations to 'join the club' before they are ruined by the Mafia. In the real estate industry, this threat would usually take the form of extorting a flat 2 or 3 percent from contractors on a project and/or allocating all construction contracts of $2 million or more to the mob-controlled organization in the area.

Mr. Alan Cohen, one of the Federal prosecutors who brought charges against various top Mafia members in the New York area

---

[*] Genovese had Anastasia shot in a New York barbershop in 1958.
[†] He and Frank Costello broke the sacred Mafia pledge of promising never to squeal on the organization and their colleagues. They both ratted on friends and associates to save their own hides.

in April, 1987, stated that the Mafia was "a criminal organization that has two principal goals — money and power...It infiltrated major industries and unions by operating through greedy businessmen and corrupt labor leaders."

The Mafia thrives on urban scandals, giving birth to them, and feeding off them while they are still in the latent stage. When so-called honest, low-grade graftees cross the line into big-time racketeering, a major scandal soon erupts and the law and order officials are usually able to unearth a Mafia connection somewhere along the line.

"Scandals are commonplace in American politics," wrote Martin Shefter, Professor of Government at Cornell University, "They should not, however, be taken at face value. Rather, scandals should be recognized as political events — an important technique in the struggle for power in American cities." He believes that the roots of the current scandals (like those which have erupted recently in Philadelphia and which are the main subject of this book) have their roots in the fiscal crisis of the 1970's that befell most of our large cities.

To prevent bankruptcies and a sharp rise in the city taxes, many urban politicians took shortcuts to find new ways to 'get the show on the road.' The Mafia has always been in the wings, ready to help out, as long as it got its share of the pie and a chance to control the action.

THE NEW YORK MOB

The main muscle of organized crime during the past half century has been centered in New York City, where the Mafia's grip on many underworld-controlled operations, such as building contracting, transportation, gambling, drug trafficking and sports betting, still remains formidable, even though it has been seriously wounded.

The mob has even infiltrated the porn film industry, with Anthony 'Tony' Perino, a member of the Columbo crime family acting as the producer of the successful and highly lucrative porn classic, *Deep Throat*, starring Linda Lovelace. In her autobiography, the 'star' of that film noted that several .45 caliber pistols and an M-16 machine gun were pointed at her as she was forced to perform unconventional sexual acts before the cameras.

Perino and his brother, known as 'the Sultans of Smut,' were later convicted on obscenity charges for making pornographic films using children.

Two of the current, big-time national, New York-based Mafia leaders, 'Fat Tony' Salerno, 76, and 'Tony Ducks' Corrallo, 74, of the Genovese family still control an empire worth between $200 and $300 million. Like many Mafia dons, they put down their income as 'miscellaneous' but it is gained from illegal gambling, sports betting, slot machines, and other operations. Both of these two senior dons are in prison now for long terms.

Their fate differed from that of one of today's younger mob leaders, John Gotti, age 46, the 'wolf' who drives a custom car, and has a fancy second home in Florida. Known as the 'Dapper Don,' he wears tailored $1,800 suits and has his hair carefully coiffed.

Gotti, who escaped conviction on a technicality in the spring of 1987 in a New York mob-related trial, claims that he is a self-employed plumbing salesman and spends most of his afternoons in select New York City social clubs.

It has been alleged that former crime boss, Paul Castellano, was murdered in 1985 in a 'hit' engineered by Gotti in his power move to take over the remnants of the Gambino family and its gambling, loansharking, and heroin drug-trafficking operations.

Castellano, 70, was gunned down along with his top aide, Thomas Billoti, in Manhattan on December 16, 1985. Since that double slaying, the 5 foot, 10 inch tall, 200 pound Gotti has slowly forged a growing reputation within both New York and national Mafia ranks as an omnipotent mob boss of bosses.

He and his wife live in a split-level, brick and white clapboard house in a middle-class section of Howard Beach, Queens. The only signs of real affluence are the presence of a huge satellite TV dish on the roof of his home and a bevy of fancy cars forming a metal phalanx around the house. (They include three Mercedes Benzes, a Lincoln Continental, and a Cadillac.) One of the Mercedes was registered in the name of the Arc Plumbing Co., with Gotti stating on an arrest sheet in 1985 that he was "an Arc salesman."

On most days, surrounded by Mafia bodyguards, Gotti is chauffeured in a black Mercedes Benz, first to a social or sports club — like the Bergen Hunt and Fish Club for morning meetings, and then is driven to Manhattan's Little Italy. While there he has frequently been observed by federal agents conducting arm-in-arm sidewalk conversations with several of his henchmen, or sipping Espresso coffee on Mulberry St. with other well-known reputed mobsters.

THE MAFIA + CONSTRUCTION = CORRUPTION

In September, 1987, a report made for the Cuomo Administration by New York State's Organized Crime Task Force, and released to the *New York Times*, concluded that a large segment of New York City's construction industry willingly accepted domination by organized crime as a 'necessary evil' that helped to promote stability and profits for many construction companies and union officials. This devastating report marked the first time in modern America that a government agency criticized important management and labor elements in the city's multi-billion-dollar construction industry for accommodating themselves willingly to the Mafia's corruption and racketeering practices in order to do business and survive.

"By controlling the activities of desperate groups of racketeers preying on the industry," the report stated, "syndicates can assure contractors that they will only have to pay off once for a specified result, that the amount to be paid will be 'reasonable' and the 'services' paid for, will be delivered." The report acknowledged that the corruption in the building industry had been "long standing and deep rooted" and that since 1922, numerous law enforcement agencies and legislative groups had periodically warned about corruption and organized crime's expanding role within the private and public construction industry.

But these warnings seemed to have passed through deafened ears, since the report concluded: "Public construction is an easier and more lucrative target" than private construction for racketeers to muscle in on, because city and state agencies have lacked the resources to verify whether builders have met the contract specifications. Furthermore, corruption costs are more easily passed along by builders to the public through inferior building materials and workmanship and bribery of public inspectors. Needless to say, this increases safety hazards through poorly constructed buildings.

Finally, the industry's reputation (in New York, Philadelphia and elsewhere) for corruption and racketeering discourages out-of-town contractors from bidding for public and private work, which through lack of competition further increases the costs to the city.

THE WITNESS PROTECTION PROGRAM, RICO, AND ELECTRONIC SURVEILLANCE

The series of Federal investigations leading to trials in 1986-89 in New York and elsewhere, featuring turncoat underworld informers plus Federal agents who risked their lives to penetrate and expose the Mafia, has resulted in a severe crippling of to-day's Mafia leadership. The targets were no longer single figures like the late Al Capone or Lucky Luciano, but a whole bevy of aging Mafia leaders.

The inner workings of this underworld organization with its many tentacles into both legitimate and illegitimate businesses have been laid bare. The old mob families have been split psychologically as well as by the generation gap. An investigative reporter of the *New York Times*, Robert McFadden, wrote of the modern Mafia in early 1987: "Its hand [is] in the corporate glitz of the 1980's and its heart is in the sentimental sepia of a bygone era."

The national crime struggle against the Mafia overlords is being fought on many fronts at the same time by area law enforcement officials. Although New York gets the big play in the media, events generating the smaller headlines in cities like Chicago, New Orleans, and Philadelphia are also important in the fight to bring the Mafia into the halls of justice and successfully prosecute them.[*]

The successful infiltrations of the Mafia by courageous federal undercover agents posing as thieves and thugs (including one who served as a Mafia mole for seven years) have provided law and order officials with a wealth of information on murder plots, leadership moves, and mob-connected drug operations.

The Feds successfully used the dual lures of the Witness

---

[*] From 1981 through 1985, federal prosecutors brought 1,025 indictments against 2,554 Mafiosi and won convictions against 809 Mafia members and their associates. The Mafia is the largest criminal organization in the country, even larger than the motorcycle gangs and Latin American, Jamaican and Asian drug traffickers.

Protection Program (where the mob turncoats were guaranteed a new name, family security and a monthly stipend) coupled with the offer of lighter prison sentences to get many former hard-nosed Mafia members to break the once sacred code of silence and testify in court against their former friends.

After the Mafia had been romanticized in books, TV series and movies like *The Godfather*, *Wiseguy*, *Married to the Mob* and *The Untouchables*, some mob members became quite brazen about their affairs. In 1983, former mob boss, Joe Bonanno even published an autobiography, *A Man of Honor*, about his years with the Mafia.

After Rudolph Giuliani, the former U.S. Attorney in the Southern District of New York, read that book he came to recognize that the little-understood RICO Act could be used as an even more potent weapon than it previously had been against the Mafia and its ruling commission. Bonanno had written a whole chapter about the power of the commission, and Giuliani reasoned that RICO provided excellent grounds for prosecuting this ruling elite.

When they were hauled into court, many Mafia leaders adopted an unusual defense. Rather than fighting government efforts to prove the existence of the Mafia, they admitted it. Recently one Mafia defense attorney, Samuel Dawson, conceded this point, but then argued to various juries that "just because a person is a member of the Mafia doesn't mean that he had committed the charged crime or even agreed to commit the charged crime."

Dawson depicted the Mafia Commission as a sort of underworld businessmen's round table that approves the Mafia members and arbitrates disputes "to avoid conflict. That is its main purpose."

Floyd Clark, the Assistant FBI Director in charge of criminal investigations, noted that the books written by top mob figures such as James Fratiano's *The Last Mafioso*, the confession of the 72-year-old acting boss of the Los Angeles crime family, means that the Mafia is losing a "tremendous asset: fear and intimidation."

He asserts that this former iron-gloved grip that the Mafia formerly had over its family members is now being removed, due to the willingness of some hoodlums, hangers-on and victims to defy the mob's long-standing Code of Silence. This turn of events had been aided by the existence of the Federal Witness Security Program, which since it started in 1970 has helped 4,889 people move safely to different locations in the country and acquire new identities, Social Security numbers, and most important, jobs.

This program has so far cost the government about $100,000 a year for each protected person — totalling almost half a billion dollars ($490 million). This staggering figure has fortunately resulted in a conviction rate of 78 percent in the cases where such witnesses were used by the prosecution to help pin the guilt on the Mafia.*

The success in getting younger Mafia members to turn to this program to 'give up' their former colleagues has resulted in a major breakdown in Mob discipline. The new generation of Mafia family members is not as dedicated as the older Sicilian-bred members. Many who have gotten themselves in trouble with their Mafia families for some minor infraction begin to fear that they might be killed if they don't turn themselves in to the government.

Some feel that the spectre of a long prison sentence is too stiff a price to pay for continued family loyalty if they are caught doing mob business. The younger ones are more Americanized than the old boys, more crass, less respectful, more individualisic, and easier to flip, according to government observers.

The Feds have also made effective use of the formerly little-known RICO —the Racketeer-Influenced and Corrupt Organization Act authored by G. Robert Blakey to bring Mafia members into court on various criminal charges.†

Under the RICO statute, Federal prosecutors have been suc-

---

* For some former gangsters, however, this life has not been a bed of roses. Leading a conventional life in a small town, hundreds of miles away from their former urban haunts, families and friends, has turned out to be more than difficult. Many have run up fresh debts and some have even returned to a life of crime.

†This act, formerly known as Title 18 of the U. S. Code, passed Congress and was signed by President Nixon as Public Law 91-452 on October 15, 1970. In the 19 years since this law has been on the books, prosecutors have found that it has carried greater criminal penalties than the earlier laws, and allowed the government to seize records and corporate assets to buttress the criminal indictments handed down against top Mafia figures.

cessful in convincing juries that the leaders of Mafia families should be imprisoned for long terms and that in some cases their ill-gotten gains should be confiscated. RICO has become the favorite and most potent weapon to destroy Mafia families as prosecutors harp on the point that their very existence is a crime.

Success in most of the 1986-89 New York cases (only Gotti slipped off the hook), plus new indictments affecting at least 17 of the 24 American Mafia families across the country, has depleted the hopes of expanding mob operations. As a result of this, the oath-taking membership in the families has been severely curtailed.*

On August 11, 1987, the U.S. Attorney for the Southern District of New York announced the arrest of 58 people, including 44 municipal officials in New York City and its suburbs, as the result of a year long 'sting' operation on urban corruption. An FBI agent posing as an undercover salesman of steel products convinced 105 officials — ranging from highway superintendents to purchasing directors — to accept bribes and kickbacks in rigged bids for the products offered for sale.

"On 106 occasions, bribes were offered or discussed," said Rudolph Giuliani, the U.S. Attorney. "On 105 of those occasions, the public official involved accepted the bribe. And on the other occasion, *he turned it down because he didn't think the amount was enough*." (emphasis added)

The investigation highlighted the corruption problem in the whole state that extended as far north as Canada, to show that the corruption scandals were not restricted to New York City alone. The same could be said for the public officials involved in the Philadelphia-Atlantic City axis who succumbed to Mafia overtures in return for a piece of the action.

Besides the Witness Protection Program and the greater use of RICO, officials on state and federal levels have made extensive use of modern eavesdropping and surveillance techniques, including audio and video taping of key mobsters engaging in illicit acts.

Wiretaps provided the major evidence in the 1987 Gotti case. The job was done by a Mafia soldier of the Gambino family

---

* It has been estimated that there are presently some 4,000 to 5,000 Mafioso members in the USA, with approximately half belonging to the five New York clans, each of which is larger and more effective than those in any other city — including the Philadelphia-Atlantic City Scarfo family.

named Dominick Lofaro. Lofaro consented to cooperate after he was arrested in upstate New York on heroin charges and chose the option of becoming a government informant instead of facing a certain 20-year jail sentence. In 1984 he agreed to be wired with a tiny microphone taped to his chest and a miniature cassette recorder, no bigger than two packs of gum fitted into the small of his back.

Equipped with a magnetic switch on a cigarette lighter, which was used to activate the recorder, Lofaro was able to discuss Gambino family affairs freely with the unsuspecting Gotti brothers, who never caught on to his double-dealing. After he recorded a conversation Lofaro would place the tapes inside folded copies of the Business Section of *The New York Times* and then drop them in a pre-selected trash bin where government agents would later pick them up. Lofaro was able to provide the Government with more than 50 of these tapes over a two-year period, which brought this comment from one admiring U.S. investigator: "You can't help wondering how many sleepless nights he (Lofaro) spent knowing that if caught he would get a slow cutting job by a knife expert."

A top federal investigator said that the increased use of wiretaps and tapes has been "like the opening of a Pandora's box of the Mafia's top secrets, letting them all hang out in the open."

The FBI's bugging has increased sharply in recent years, from just 90 court-approved taps in 1982 to more than 400 in 1984-85. Investigating agencies (local, state and federal) have found novel places to hide their bugs aimed at suspected mobsters. According to a *Time* magazine cover story, "The Mafia on Trial," (September 29, 1986), some of these intriguing hiding places included: "a Perrier bottle, a stuffed toy, a pair of binoculars, shoes, an electric blanket, and a horse's saddle. Agents even admitted to dropping snooping devices into a confessional at a Roman Catholic Church frequented by mobsters, as well as in a church candlestick holder and a church men's room." The agents who planted these bugs all claimed that they did it with the local court's permission.

One agent, posing as a street vendor in a New York Mafia neighborhood, soon discovered which nearby public telephone was being used by local gangsters to call sources in Sicily about heroin shipments coming into the USA. The phone was quickly

tapped, and the evidence which it produced was used successfully in several 'pizza parlor connection' heroin trials that snared
numerous U.S. and Sicilian mobsters.

HOW THE MOB OPERATES IN THE 80'S

In recent years, the younger, more reckless and flamboyant
mobsters who talk glibly of killing and making big money,
operate by a different set of rules than their elders, most of whom
still require honor and loyalty above all else. The elders still re-
vere friendship, respect, and the 'code of silence' and would
rather die than compromise these values.

The constant series of indictments and convictions against the
elder Mafioso leaders has reduced many of the once powerful
families to the status of the other street gangs that need constant
surveillance. Thomas L. Sheer, the head of the New York Office
of the FBI and an expert on organized crime, recently said that:
"the government of the mob, the ability to make secret agreements and to set up spheres of influence, has been weakened.
The [crime] families have been driven apart." The damage
wrought on the Genovese, Gambino, Lucchese, Bonnano and
Columbo families by younger mobsters and government prosecution has been extensive.

Unlike the Mafia dons of fiction, who lived in swanky man-
sions surrounded by machine-gun-toting bodyguards, most of
the current younger mob leaders lead surprisingly modest lives,
living in unpretentious row houses in the suburbs.

Recent revelations at various Mafia trials around the country
have given the public a fascinating inside look at various Mafia
family operations. Life in the Mafia is no longer just a series of
photos of bullet-riddled bodies, of accounts of Godfathers and
their ring-kissing coteries of obedient soldiers. But we have seen
for the first time a picture of the organizational structures used by
the mob families to run their operations.

Prosecutors in several of the recent New York Mafia trials
have used elaborate charges and testimony of mobsters-turned-
informants to show that there is a loose-knit national Mafia commission that rules most mob activities in this country. The New
York-based commission divides up the pie on the Eastern
seaboard — with the Philadelphia-South Jersey mob apparently

being subservient to its dictates.

There have been hints that a second major Mafia commission operates out of Chicago with jurisdiction over the western parts of the country. But the consensus among most law enforcement officials is that the New York-based commission is the supreme mob authority in the nation. This commission is composed of the top five crime family leaders which constitute the policy-making body that carves up the territory in the Eastern USA and decides what rackets to pursue, then parcels them out among the member families. The commission also acts as a de-facto Mafia Supreme Court with the power to resolve disputes 'peacefully' between families and on occasion orders the executions of those members who refuse to cooperate.

A vivid example of this power was the order given by 'Fat Tony' Salerno (on tape in 1984) to mobsters from Buffalo and Cleveland at the Palma Boys Social Club in New York that the commission would settle a raging dispute over mob control in Buffalo, saying that the commission "wants it straightened out. Tell them they are dealing with the big boys now." They were told, and obeyed the ruling.

Below the commission level, each family operates along semi-military lines to facilitate proper communication, secrecy and planned actions. There is a boss, underboss, a *consigliere* or counselor, a number of captains or *capos*, lieutenants, and hundreds of 'made' soldiers on the bottom rungs who do the dirty work. Below these are those who are labeled 'associates' or 'with' the Mafia, who either wish to become members or are willing to do business with the mob.

THE ADVANTAGES OF A MAFIA NICKNAME

A taped discussion between two Mafia members of one of the New York crime families highlighted the reasons why a distinctive nickname could be most helpful in becoming a member of the Mafia. The two Mafia members, Anthony 'Fat Tony' Salerno and Matthew 'Matty the Horse' Ianniello, were on trial in New York during December, 1987, charged with being leaders of the Genovese crime family. They were taped discussing the rival Bonanno family boss, Philip 'Rusty' Rastelli, who wished to induct some new members.

"Rusty wanted to know if it's O.K. to 'make' these guys," Ianniello said to Salerno. "He gave me a list to check them out."

"I don't know none of them," Salerno complained after looking at the list. "They don't put the nicknames down there."

"They should have the nicknames down [on the list]," 'Matty the Horse' agreed. "Rusty wants to be sure he don't put nobody in there that a guy has got something against."

Most of the Mafia mobsters' nicknames seemed to have been acquired in the innocence of their youth, but once they have acquired such a name — even before induction into the Mafia — it usually sticks as a badge of identification and respect. (The main cast of characters in the succeeding chapters, comprising the the heart of the Philadelphia-South Jersey Scarfo Mafia family, ALL have nicknames — which they seem to be proud of.)

And incidentally, these nicknames make for colorful coverage of their shenanigans in the press, radio and TV.

The remainder of this book is an analysis of a crime organization during a series of Mafia operations and subsequent trials in Southern New Jersey and Southeastern Pennsylvania. No attempt will be made to examine the inner workings of the larger New York crime families. But this description of the Nicky Scarfo family should give readers a dramatic insight into the life of the Mafia in the late Eighties.

Philadelphia — the City of Brotherly Love — founded by William Penn in a spirit of philanthropy, the birthplace of the Declaration of Independence, the memorable spot where was drafted and adopted the Constitution of the United States, now holds beyond possibility of dispute the ignoble palm of being the most corrupt city in the world.

The Philadelphia thieves were never more powerful than they are today: and the end of the domination is apparently still remote. Well may the world contemplate this "City of Brotherly Love" with justifiable disgust and horror.

-Editorial, from *Living Age*[*]

2 THE 20-YEAR MOB REIGN OF ANGELO BRUNO

THE RISE AND FALL OF ANGELO BRUNO ANNALORO

IN the late 1950s, Angelo Bruno, (born Angelo Bruno Annaloro in the village of Villalba, Caltamisetta in Sicily, in 1910) took over a disorganized gang of thugs and extortionists in South Philadelphia, and soon transformed them into one of the most profitable crime families in the USA.

Although Bruno had become a millionaire, you couldn't tell it from his lifestyle or his estate. Bruno dressed immaculately and expensively, but he owned no yachts, country homes, or fancy cars or any signs of his real wealth. He lived in a modest brick row house on Snyder Avenue in South Philadelphia. His two children, Jeanne, married to a real estate man, and Michael, who

[*] A Weekly Magazine of Contemporary Literature and Thought, Feb. 20, 1904. (reprinted in "The Scene" column by Clark DeLeon, *The Philadelphia Inquirer*, Aug. 9, 1987)

was in the exterminating business, grew up, married and set out
to make a legitimate living in upper-middle-class society.

Bruno started out as a salesman for a cigarette vending machine company, reporting modest earnings of $50,000 a year.
But when the casino gambling referendum was passed in 1976 in
Atlantic City, his firm took over a $500,000 account that had
been controlled for years by a competitor. He was a master at
hiding his assets. According to law enforcement authorities, his
main holdings over the years consisted of several legitimate and
illegitimate business enterprises, including gambling casinos in
London and the Dominican Republic, a hotel in the Netherlands
Antilles, travel-junket clubs in Philadelphia and New York, a
trucking firm in New Jersey and assorted real estate holdings in
Florida, New Jersey and Pennsylvania.

He didn't drink, smoke or gamble, or even have a telephone
in his home. But he knew how to communicate persuasively
with his underlings.

The hammer that he used to keep his Mafia family in line was
the threat of violence rather than the manifestation of it. As the
most revered Mafia leader in Philadelphia's history of organized
crime, Bruno stood up to his egomaniacal subordinates, who
criticized him for being reactionary, old-fashioned and loath to
admit new 'made' men into the inner circle.

BRUNO AND THE DRUG RACKET

Bruno always cautioned his new mob members to stay away
from drug running, yet he managed to profit from the flood of
heroin that devastated the inner-city neighborhoods beginning in
the late 1960's. Most of the heroin that filtered into Philadelphia
was brought in from New York. Although he opposed narcotics
trafficking and forbade his men to become involved in it on moral
grounds, Bruno was able to profit from the fringes of the lucrative drug business.

Even though he preferred to make most of his money from
extortion and the numbers rackets, Bruno did become involved
with drugs in a 'rational' way that he could justify to his personal
code. It started in 1959, when Dominick Pollina, who was then
head of the Philadelphia Mafia, put out a contract on Bruno's life.
He had become suspicious that Bruno was trying to dethrone

him. But when the would-be hit man informed Bruno of the assassination plot, the future mob boss hopped a train to New York where he met secretly with Carlo Gambino, the "boss of bosses" and the head of the Mafia's powerful National Commission.

This commission created back in 1933, had never been effective in 'organizing' organized crime nationally. But it still wielded a lot of muscle on the East Coast, where it has usually been able to name the leaders of the weaker mobs in the region. So in 1981, when Nicky Scarfo wanted to become the boss in Philadelphia, first he went to New York to obtain the commission's blessing.

Bruno felt he could get help from Gambino since they had been close friends from the era of the early 1930's, when they had both invested in Florida land together. They were also both Sicilians, whereas Pollina was an Italian. Everyone in the mob business knew that bad blood had long existed between these two regional groups and had been a direct cause of several mob murders. Gambino, who was in charge of the commission at the time, named Angelo Bruno the new boss of the Philadelphia crime family and gave him his official permission to get rid of Pollina.

However, Bruno took pity on his predecessor, probably because he felt deep down that if he killed Pollina, the latter's followers would feel obliged to avenge their murdered boss. He gambled, by letting Pollina live, that his gang of followers would not wish to test Gambino's power, and would eventually join the new Bruno family. He guessed right and for the next 20 years, Bruno ruled the Philadelphia Mafia family.[*]

At the moment Gambino anointed Bruno as head of the Philadelphia Mafia, he was gearing up for a major mob marketing thrust into the drug trafficking business. He had already lined up important Black drug dealers in Harlem, including the now fabled Leroy 'Big Bad Leroy Brown' Barnes. Gambino informed Bruno that he planned to expand his drug sales southward shortly after making him the don of the Philadelphia family, but knowing of Bruno's moral compunction against selling drugs directly, Gambino came up with a scheme that the greedy Bruno could live with.

---

[*] Ironically, Pollina, who has always denied that he was ever a member of the Mafia, was still alive at age 97 in 1989 — long after his successor, Bruno, had been replaced.

Instead of 'invading' Philadelphia directly with their heroin and other drugs, Gambino's 'salesmen' would make their stuff available to Bruno's chief lieutenants. By the early 1970's, the price of heroin to the Philadelphia mob was $20,000 a kilo, leaving a clear profit to the New York members of the Gambino family of $15,000 a kilo.

The participating Bruno lieutenants would not sell the drugs, but would loan money to white 'contractors' in South Philadelphia, so the contractors could use the money to buy the heroin from the mobsters. These contractors would eventually sell the drug to Black pushers after being first required to borrow the money to buy the heroin from Bruno's chosen men.

If the contractors did not agree to this 'money laundering' scheme, they wouldn't get a loan to buy the drugs in the first place. So, the Bruno middlemen profited in two ways: they made big money selling heroin and they made a double profit by forcing the contractors to borrow from them at sky-high loan shark rates.

Bruno, in turn, profited by loaning his own money to his lieutenants to lend out. He would charge them 20% interest, and they in turn would charge the contractors 30% interest. This shuffling of underground money was part of the pyramid of traditional Mafia economics in which profits flowed from the bottom to the top through a 'street tax' system of mob muscle.

The contractor would not only pay back the loans but also a tax on profits. The collector would keep a portion of both, depending on the volume of business and what they thought the traffic could bear. Each collector would then turn over a portion of his collections to his superiors (the bosses and the *capos*).

Because of inexact bookkeeping, a certain amount of cheating pervaded the passing of the tribute money up the ladder to Bruno. However, the old fashioned 'carrot and stick' device was always available to help make the system work fairly efficiently. The 'stick' was the threat to life and limb if any cheater was discovered. One Bruno enforcer even carried a ballpeen hammer with him, with which he knocked out the teeth of any recalcitrant 'taxpayer' to send a message to other would-be cheaters.

The 'carrot' came in the form of expanded drug territories and the opportunities for honest taxpayers to move into other lucrative crime territories having established their credibility with the mob hierarchy.

During the Federal RICO trial held in the Fall of 1988 in Philadelphia, the government played dozens of tapes to dramatize the true flavor of the Mafia organization and life of the mob. Federal Prosecutor Louis Pichini emphasized the importance of these tapes both in the trial and during his closing arguments to the jury.[*]

THE 'BIG FOUR' MAFIA TAPE OF MID- 1980

This tape-recorded conversation of four high-ranking mob members of the Angelo Bruno family takes one 'into the inner sanctum of the mob,' according to Pichini. The four voices belong to Philip 'Chickenman' Testa, Harry 'The Hunchback' Riccobene, Frank Narducci, Sr. and Nicodemo Scarfo, who was then a *capo*.

Pichini noted that this tape and an earlier one recorded on November 4, 1977, related the "calm before the storm" and marked a series of "internal storm warnings" of dissatisfaction with the rule of the aged mob boss, Bruno. Two of the four, (Narducci and Testa) are "voices from the grave," since both were assassinated later by other mob members.

(Note: When the four Mafiosos speak of 'that guy,' they are usually referring to Boss Bruno. When Scarfo addresses one of them as 'Chick,' he is speaking to 'Chickenman' Testa.

HARRY
RICCOBENE: I have spoken to no one!

FRANK
NARDUCCI: I want this motherfucker! Hah!

RICCOBENE: Well, let's get to the bottom of that...

PHIL TESTA: We'll get to the bottom of it, that's all.

NARDUCCI: I will. I'll go grab him right away now.

RICCOBENE: I don't want these things, you know. Rumors get around!

TESTA: This is, this is dead right here, you know.

---

[*] This recording came from Book #G of the Scarfo-RICO trial.

NARDUCCI: Well, that's it.

TESTA: You know, we'll kill that guy over there, you know. We'll make sure he don't...

NARDUCCI: So how are you making out with your thing? You got any grief there?

RICCOBENE: And they are the guys that make the trouble for us.

NARDUCCI: You know how much they get you in trouble?

TESTA: That's why I'm against other guys being in business with me. When it comes to Rent, he says, well, like all these guys, do you protect them kind of guys? I think his phone is tapped.

NARDUCCI: Everybody's phone, his phone is tapped....Two bookmakers got on the phone, far off from me...."I got Chickie Narducci lending me fifteen hundred." "Yeah, do you think he'll lend me fifteen hundred?" "Well, he charged me time and a half for it, three hundred a week." They are getting tapped. Now they know that this guy borrowed something. Maybe they will go and pressure the guy!...Huh? They got him on the tape. And, under pressure...

RICCOBENE: Not only that.

NICODEMO
SCARFO: And they get a guy they talk them into putting, ah...

NARDUCCI: The wire!

SCARFO: The wire, and listen.

RICCOBENE: Then they come and talk to you.

NARDUCCI: I've had that done to me already!

TESTA: That's why I say, when you hear something you should go right to the source. Then straighten it out and forget about it. Because it could be nothing. It could be something sometimes.

             [Scarfo, Testa, Narducci and Riccobene are discussing a meeting of the Mafia Commission to select a new boss.]

TESTA: See, I want to tell you something, Harry.

SCARFO: And sit there and listen!

TESTA: I'm gonna tell you something. I know who is qualified. I really do. This is my heart. I know who is qualified, but I know he'll never get it, because there is too much opposition right now. That's why he's qualified....He knows this fucking thing better than a lot of guys. I'm talking about the young, the young generation. He's got smarts. He's not a kid, you know.

RICCOBENE: I know it.

TESTA: He's forty-eight...How old do you have to be to, ah...get somewhere? I mean — How old are you, Nick?

NARDUCCI: Forty-seven? Forty-eight?

SCARFO: Forty-eight. I'll be forty-nine.

TESTA: I think you're old enough. I don't know...understand. They [Bruno] look at us like we was kids. What's wrong with it?

RICCOBENE: Nothing, as long as the man's got it on his brains.

NARDUCCI: No, nothing, if he's got it on the ball. What the hell has the age got to do with it?

RICCOBENE: Not a thing.

NARDUCCI: You know what I mean? There's people are smart at twenty.

RICCOBENE: That's right.

NARDUCCI: And they get smarter as they get older, with it...

RICCOBENE: Well, see, nobody can take the initiative in this thing.

TESTA: Why not?

RICCOBENE: Because you can get ostracized, ostracized!

TESTA: Ostracized? What the hell is that? That word I don't understand.

RICCOBENE: [Laughs]...You become an outlaw.

TESTA: Oh?

RICCOBENE: You know what I mean?

SCARFO: But if you could, ah....If you disagree with certain things...

RICCOBENE: You need, you need backing though! You need, ah...

SCARFO: A little construction behind it.

RICCOBENE: You see, it isn't like it used to be, where everybody was invited. Today, it's not gonna be that way. They are only gonna invite certain people. And the certain people are gonna be the ones that are gonna give him the vote.

TESTA: Right.

RICCOBENE: You follow me?

SCARFO: Uh huh.

RICCOBENE: If it could be like the old days, then you could go around him a little, a, be, ah... you know, use the power. You talk to all your potential close associates. Then you get the names, nominate somebody. You propose him. I propose this guy. And somebody seconds the motion. And then there is a vote between them. If nobody goes against the guy that is selected, it's all over.

NARDUCCI: Over here, he's not even bounded by the cigars [the bosses]. He just proposes "A" and that's it. Whatever he says.

RICCOBENE: That's right, that's what it is!

SCARFO: Right.

TESTA: I figure he's the guy that's gonna get it. But guess what?

NARDUCCI: Because he's up there. He's no kid. He's about seventy-five, ain't he? He's, he's not a young man.

SCARFO: Well, that's just it. I mean, just keep...keeps it up
              in the old-age bracket.

TESTA: Yeah.

NARDUCCI: Yeah.

SCARFO: I mean, not that I'm against old age, but I know
              now, if I lived to be seventy-five, I don't think I
              want no headaches. I'd leave it to the younger
              generation.

RICCOBENE: You know who wants it?

TESTA: Who?

RICCOBENE: Mr. Migo. He wants...

SCARFO: He's got to be ninety!

TESTA: Oh, I know he wants it! I spoke to...he spoke to
              me about it. And I talked against him. You know.
              I says, you gotta be crazy to want it. What the fuck
              do you want that for?...They are gonna knock it
              down. They are gonna louse it up. He's gonna
              ah...he ain't gonna go....But, and I told him, "I
              ain't gonna help you."...I hate to say anything and
              louse him up like that.

RICCOBENE: Yeah. It's gonna be an embarrassment. I told him,
              "Number one. You're too old! You're sick!"

TESTA: No, he shouldn't be it.

RICCOBENE: He should forget about it.

NARDUCCI: He's eighty-six years old, that guy.

RICCOBENE: Eighty-five!

NARDUCCI: Eighty-five?

SCARFO: You gotta have somebody that's gotta come out of
              the house...Not this other shit! Like this guy, he
              used to stay home and you had to go see him....All
              that stuff....Let them put a guy...

RICCOBENE: Yeah. That's able to get around.

SCARFO: That's out on the street and he's gonna show up.

SCARFO: He won't get no opposition! I don't know whose idea it was to make the other guy *consigliere*. I don't know whose brainstorm that was, but that was the most unbalanced...

RICCOBENE: Which one?

SCARFO: Joe, Joe...I think he was like this. He...he was way off the scale, Phil! I saw it and...

TESTA: Oh! He was more this way than anything else! A...guy in that position, see, a guy in that position? He's supposed to be the guy that tries to save your life!

NARDUCCI: Save you, save you, right!

TESTA: You know, it's got to be a guy that can really...

SCARFO: You need, you need...a thinking guy!

NARDUCCI: Out to save you!

TESTA: You know a guy that's got a, a little head...

NARDUCCI: Out to save you.

TESTA: ...don't get excited, you know. "Take it easy here..." [All four talking at once.]...

TESTA: We're talking about a life here, you know.... But he couldn't get around to get satisfied. This guy, geez, he was a very vindictive person! Yeah.

NARDUCCI: Right.

TESTA: He was very vindictive!

SCARFO: Right.

RICCOBENE: Who has no, you know, he makes no enemies.

SCARFO: Right.

TESTA: He was too vindictive, that guy.

SCARFO: Too vindictive! Prejudice! And our friend allowed him to go too far, Harry!

TESTA: Christ. Look, look at the hatred he carried for this kid, for Christ sake!

RICCOBENE: Right.

TESTA: He tried every way in the world to kill him!

SCARFO: He tried for twenty years, fifteen years now.

TESTA: Guess what, if I...

SCARFO: He tried to kill me!

TESTA: If I wasn't around a couple of times, you would have went!

SCARFO: Yeah, sure!

NARDUCCI: And after what I seen, huh...

SCARFO: Oh yeah, Chick. He was really bad!

TESTA: He even tried after I was "away," Chickie! [Laughs]

NARDUCCI: Oh, he tried again when you was away?

TESTA: With Chickie! The original, the real beef? Because he wanted this kid to marry his daughter!

RICCOBENE: And he turned her down?

NARDUCCI: And he turned her down. He didn't want to go out with her.

TESTA: That was the real beef.

SCARFO: That started it! And then his association with me, and then me...this association with him.

TESTA: That didn't help it.

SCARFO: And the whole confrontation...It was an instigation of things...And the least little thing that would come up with me, or somebody close to me, he was ready to get on it....Trying to get back at me....

TESTA: He had, he had built-in liars!

SCARFO: Yeah.

TESTA: Built in to that Nicky Diamond, who is a two-face fucking liar. You know Nick? He's real treacherous!

SCARFO: Lie, he'll lie in your face!

TESTA: Geez, I could see a guy lie to help a guy....To cover a guy.

NARDUCCI: It helps a guy and in a little while a lie don't help nobody.

RICCOBENE: Not to lie to hurt somebody!...

SCARFO: A lie can kill somebody!...

TESTA: Yeah, he lied to me in my house. [Laughs]...

NARDUCCI: No, he would lie and believe it. After a day he believes that the fucking lie is true. That's the kind of liar he is.

BRUNO IS BLIND TO THE RUMBLINGS FROM BELOW

The complaints against Bruno were that he was too conservative, too fatherly, too insulated from the changing tastes of his underlings, and too strict in trying to keep the drug traffic to a minimum.

At age 69, Bruno strongly considered a semi-retirement in Florida since he was not interested in expanding his empire. He was personally financially secure, but he underestimated the depth of the discontent within his own crime family. This myopia would soon lead to his demise.

Bruno saw no reason to split the pie more ways than was absolutely necessary. He refused to relinquish his territorial claims to Atlantic City. The casino industry was just starting up at 'America's Playground' and the rackets there looked promising. As an old-time paternal Godfather, Bruno ruled his crime family with a tight fist, but his reluctance to change with the times led to his violent downfall. Bruno was marked for a 'hit' in 1980.

When he was assassinated on March 21, 1980, few suspected that either Phil Testa, the underboss, or Nicky Scarfo, who owed his life to Bruno, were the hit men. When Scarfo was pegged as a troublemaker back in the early '60s, it was Bruno who made sure nothing happened to him physically.

WHY NO ONE WAS EVER TRIED FOR BRUNO'S MURDER

It took nine years for the real story of the assassination of
Angelo Bruno to come to light. We now understand why no one
was ever indicted for his murder. In early March, 1989, in a
Newark, N.J., federal courtroom a mob informant, Vincent
'Fish' Cafaro, age 56, took the witness stand as a prosecution
witness in a trial of members of the Genovese crime family. The
defendants had been accused of trying to murder John Gotti, the
head of the rival Gambino family and his brother.

Cafaro had been the former right-hand man and confidant of
Anthony 'Fat Tony' Salerno, the Genovese family's mob boss
who had been sentenced to 100 years in prison in 1986 after
being convicted of serving with Bruno on the Mafia Commission.

The Genovese family in recent years had built up a reputation
as the most ruthless mob family in the country, according to government authorities. Its members routinely used murder, may-
hem, treachery and deceit as tools to advance the family's lucrative racketeering operations.

Cafaro and two Bruno-Scarfo family mob informants,
Thomas 'Tommy Del' Del Giorno and Nicholas 'Nicky Crow'
Caramandi, each pointed the finger at Anthony 'Tony Bananas'
Caponigro, 67, Bruno's *consigliere* or family adviser, as the man
behind the hit.

Caponigro was a Newark mob figure in charge of a small
North Jersey branch of the Bruno family. He was ambitious,
independent and fed up with Bruno's old-fashioned ways. On
his visits to Philadelphia, he began to complain openly that Bruno
was losing control of the mob. He then quietly started lining up
support for a coup.

Early in 1980, Caponigro went to New York to seek approval
from the leaders of the five New York based crime families (who
made up the ruling commission) to murder Bruno. He petitioned
Frank 'Funzi' Tieri, then head of the Genovese family, to be his
intermediary. It was a fatal mistake for Caponigro. Tieri, a wily
and ruthless mob chief led 'Tony Bananas' to believe that such
permission was granted.

Tieri (who died a year later in 1981 of natural causes) was
still smoldering over a dispute with Caponigro for control of the
Jersey City bookmaking operation that grossed "$2 million a

week.* This may be the reason why this guy (Tieri) set Tony up to kill Angie (Bruno)."

Tieri saw that the proposed plot to murder Bruno could also be used as a vehicle to remove Caponigro and gain sole control of the bookmaking operation, weakening the Bruno family's hold on Atlantic City.

So, Caponigro engineered the shooting of Bruno in March, 1980, in front of his Snyder Avenue row house in South Philly. He then planned to assume control of the Bruno organization in April. He walked into Del Giorno's South Philadelphia bar and boasted: "Everything is going to be all right. I'm going to be the boss!"

The next day, however, Caponigro and his brother-in-law, Alfred Salerno, age 64, went to New York to meet with high-ranking mob leaders to receive their blessings to take over Bruno's mantle. Caponigro and Bruno's underboss, Philip 'Chickenman' Testa, each met separately with Anthony Salerno, then the underboss of the Genovese family, about the murder. Testa told Salerno that 'Tony Bananas' was behind the Bruno killing. A short time later, Anthony Salerno sent Caponigro in to see the boss, Vincent 'The Chin' Gigante, who had 'Tony Bananas' and his brother-in-law Alfred Salerno 'banged out,' according to Cafaro's testimony. The justification for this was that the Bruno killing was 'unauthorized.'

Caponigro was stabbed, shot and beaten to death "a victim of a bloody triple cross orchestrated with Machiavellian precision by members of the Genovese organization."†

Edward S. D. Dennis, the former U.S. Attorney for the Eastern District of Pennsylvania and presently the head of the Criminal Division of the Department of Justice, described the bloody details of the Caponigro murder. "He had been tortured, beaten, strangled, and repeatedly stabbed and shot. His naked body was in a mortuary bag stuffed in the trunk of a car. Approximately $300 in $20 bills was found stuffed in various parts of his body."

According to law enforcement officials familiar with the

---

* According to Del Giorno's testimony at an earlier trial.

† According to George Anastasia, a crime reporter for *The Philadelphia Inquirer* years later.

mob's ritual, the money and its placement in the body were symbolic gestures indicating that it was Caponigro's greed that killed him. It was also a message to other mob members not to take it upon themselves to rub out a fellow Mafioso without the proper authorization from the commission.

Dennis said that Alfred Salerno was found on the same day (April 18th) about four miles away, stuffed in a similar mortuary bag. "He had been shot three times behind the right ear. Rope was tied around his neck. The autopsy report indicated rope burns on his neck, wrist and ankles. Also most of the bones in his face were broken."

A New Jersey State Police intelligence report later identified John DiGilio, a member of the North Jersey branch of the Genovese crime family, as a key suspect in both killings. In early 1988, before he could be indicted or brought to trial, he mysteriously disappeared — one of the latest victims in the ongoing power struggle with Gigante and his *consigliere*, Louis 'Bobby' Manna. DiGilio's bullet-riddled body was found in May floating in the Hackensack River in North Jersey...also stuffed inside a mortuary bag.

So, the killer of the killers of Angelo Bruno met a similar fate in the Mafia's continuing game of a modified form of Russian Roulette.

In the aftermath of the Bruno bloodbath, an internecine war broke out among the *capos* of the Bruno family to see who could gain control of the mob and keep it. In the following six years, the battle for control of this lucrative crime organization witnessed the killings of at least 28 senior Mafia members and associates, according to a report of the Pennsylvania Crime Commission. Carl P. Brown of the Commission indicated that these killings wiped out a whole generation of potential leaders and led to a "breakdown of the code of silence that was previously entrenched, enforced and inviolate."

"Nicky was in the doorway [of his Winter home, Casablanca South].
Several of the La Cosa Nostra men kissed Scarfo on the cheek. It is
a known showing of respect for persons who are higher up in the
organization. Just like — like I would salute my superior."

3

-Joe Moran, a Pennsylvania State Police Officer[*]

THE RISE OF 'LIL NICKY' SCARFO IN THE MOB

WHO IS NICKY SCARFO? HIS ORIGINS AND INTRODUCTION TO THE MOB

NICODEMO Domenic Scarfo was born in Brooklyn, N.Y., on March 8, 1929. The family soon moved to South Philadelphia in 1938 where the young Nicky enrolled in the now defunct Hawthorne Public Elementary School. From there, he went to the Campbell Public School and then to the Bartlett Junior High before graduating from the Benjamin Franklin High School in 1947 where the students voted him "the Most Talkative," "Loudest," "One of the Best Cutters" and "Out to Lick the World" in a senior class poll.

Several neighbors in South Philadelphia remember the Scarfos as good and regular churchgoers. One neighbor said, "His grandmother had 10-12 grandchildren and his mother was ambitious and devoted to the church." She worked in a local garment factory as a seamstress. His father was a quiet family man who worked days in the bakery at the Uneeda Biscuit Co. and stayed home at night.

Since his mother worked all day, the two children, Nicky and his older sister, Nancy, raised each other. They never gave the neighbors any trouble. When he grew to adulthood, he married

---

[*]Surveying a gathering of the mob in Fort Lauderdale, Florida on January 4, 1986.

young and had his first son, Nicky Jr. "Then things went bad," related a neighbor, "when he got into that fight in the diner."

Nicky was first introduced into the underworld by Nick Piccolo, a neighbor, who once owned and operated the 500 Club in the heart of South Philly with his two brothers, Mike and Joe. The Piccolos were uncles on his mother's side, and Nicky Scarfo soon discovered that Nick Piccolo had been a *capo* in the Bruno Mafia family, and was using the 500 Club as a front for an illegal gambling operation.

Nick Piccolo hired young Scarfo right out of high school in 1947 as a runner and bartender. He worked for his Uncle Nick into the early 1960's and accepted advice from him. Piccolo served as his *consigliere* into his late seventies.

Scarfo also served as a caretaker for an apartment building owned by his mother, Catherine. Later he was a salesman for a custom shirt company and was a representative for an entertainment booking agency. He apparently did very well in these businesses.

On June 4, 1963, Scarfo had his first serious run in with the law. He was accused of stabbing to death a longshoreman named Dugan in a fight over a booth in the Oregon Diner in South Philadelphia and served several months in prison after pleading guilty ('Chuckie' Merlino, who was later to become Scarfo's underboss, was also accused in that killing, but the charges against him were dropped.)

When Scarfo got out of jail, he got the 'word.' He heard through the grapevine that the head of the local Mafia family, Angelo Bruno, was displeased over the stabbing incident, and he (Scarfo) was exiled to Atlantic City — the Siberia of the underworld — as 'punishment' for his rash act. In the mid-1960's, Atlantic City was a town looking for a way out. Half of its 45,000 people were blue collar Blacks and Hispanics. It had a high unemployment rate and hundreds of families on welfare.

"As far as the potential for organized crime," observed Lt. Col. Justin Dintino of the New Jersey State Police, "there was little of it in those days except for loansharking, bookmaking, and prostitution, but on a mini-scale because there was no high population...and no one with money to blow."

When Nicky was sent to the run-down Elba, Atlantic City had degenerated into a gloomy, seedy seaside resort. There was no glimmer of the resurrection that was to come with the opening of the casinos and the roll of the dice in the mid 1970's that transformed wounded Atlantic City into the gambling capital of the East — comparable to Las Vegas.

Nicky Scarfo was described as a slight, middle-aged man, prone to motion sickness with nervous twitches in his facial jowls, who enjoyed Cutty Sark Scotch whiskey and sweet chocolates, and possessed an erratic personality.

He was considered by his friends and neighbors to be a charming, polite person to socialize with, long addicted to old movies and boxing. Relatively quiet in his conversations with others, to law enforcement officials he seemed a Napoleonic type seeking to compensate for his short five-foot-five stature. He acquired the monicker 'Lil Nicky', a title he abhors, because of his size.

He controlled his temper most of the time, but once he was seen yelling at an associate in a public restaurant, leading Scarfo observers to characterize 'Lil Nicky' as a Jekyll-Hyde type who can ooze charm one minute, then fly off the handle the next. One day at a big Sunday dinner for friends, Scarfo's wife brought in a large plate of spaghetti. He tasted it, winced and then threw the whole plate against the wall in an outburst of displeasure, saying that it tasted terrible.

NICKY'S RISE TO POWER IN ATLANTIC CITY

As Nicky Scarfo rose through the ranks of the Mafia, he needed a 'front.' He found a convenient one in the form of Scarf, Inc., a cement contracting business located near the Boardwalk in Atlantic City, which was owned by young Phil Leonetti, his nephew. In reality it became the headquarters of Scarfo's many illegal operations: loansharking, illegal gambling, building contractor shakedowns and narcotics. However, Scarfo's publicly claimed source of income was from his mother for doing maintenance jobs on the apartment house she owned.

He and his top deputies lived on North Georgia Avenue in the Ducktown section of Atlantic City. The modest housing on the block was interrupted only by a couple of beauty salons and Angeloni's Restaurant.

Scarfo lived upstairs at #26 Philip's Apartments, a dark brick and stucco affair with bay windows. It was owned by his mother and named for his late father, who was an immigrant from the Italian province of Calabria, where his mother was also born. His mother moved down to the ground floor apartment after her husband died, since the upstairs was "just too roomy for her."

A white concrete shed with a brown Liberty Bell symbol painted on its front door was located in the back yard with the words **GOD BLESS AMERICA** painted in red, white and blue colors. Scarfo's sister, Nancy Leonetti, and her son Phil, as well as Lawrence 'Yogi' Merlino, all lived next door in #28, conveniently located behind Scarf, Inc.

NICKY GETS EVEN CLOSER TO ANGIE

Although Scarfo already had been assigned by Bruno to be his 'man' in Atlantic City, he got even closer to him in 1971, after being sent to jail for almost three years for refusing to testify before the New Jersey Commission of Investigation. He did his time in the state prison in Yardville, New Jersey. According to inmates, on visiting days, Scarfo and Bruno took long walks together in the prison yard; Bruno talking and Scarfo listening.*

After being released from Yardville, Scarfo attended a meeting on April 20, 1976, at a dingy South Philly hangout called Frank's Cabana Steaks, where he heard the then underboss, Philip 'Chickenman' Testa, bad-mouthing Boss Bruno. He was angry because Bruno refused to 'make' new members of the family to do mob business.

A year and a half later, Testa once again raged about Bruno in a back room of a talent agency on South Broad Street which the FBI conveniently taped for evidence. Because Bruno failed to respond to any of his suggestions, Testa felt that something had to be done to prevent the old man from pocketing all of the money raked in from local loan sharks and bookies. The main purpose of this November 4, 1977, meeting, however, was to pick a new *consigliere*. No one in the room wanted to openly challenge

---

*Several members of the North Jersey branch of the Genovese family, Gerardo Catena, a much-feared *capo*, Anthony 'Little Pussy' Russ and Joseph 'Bayonne Joe' Ziccarelli, rivals of Bruno and the Gambino family, were also imprisoned in Yardville for refusing to testify.

Bruno, but Testa let it be known that he favored Scarfo for the post. No one knew who Bruno favored for the important counselor job. Although no decision was made that day, it marked a significant step up the ladder for Scarfo. This marked his arrival as a member of the inner circle of the Bruno family.

THE BLOODY BATTLE TO SUCCEED BRUNO

Soon after Bruno's demise, the clock started running out on John McCullough, a onetime ally of the old mob boss and the head of the area's rough and tough Roofer's Union. When Scarfo, Phil Testa and Raymond 'Long John' Martorano, all Mafia *capos* vying for the Number One job as Bruno's successor, sought a 'piece of the action' on roofers' contracts, McCullough resisted. Furthermore, he did not stop trying to organize the Atlantic City hotel and casino workers in direct competition to Local #54 of the Restaurant Workers in Atlantic City.

So Martorano and an associate, Albert Daidone, a vice president of Local #54, hired Willard Moran, a local hood, to wipe out McCullough. Moran appeared at the McCullough home in Philadelphia in December, 1980, posing as a deliveryman with a bunch of poinsettias, and shot the union leader six times with a .22 caliber pistol hidden in the flowers. Moran was tried, convicted and sentenced to death in the electric chair. To escape the 'hot seat,' he became a government informer and ratted on Martorano and Daidone, who were tried in 1984 and found guilty of conspiring to kill McCullough. They are still awaiting sentencing five years later.

Several months after McCullough's death, 'Chickenman' Testa (Bruno's successor) was blown up on the porch of his South Philadelphia home in 1981 by a homemade bomb packed with nails.

Testa's rule over the Bruno Mafia lasted just one year. Because of a growing feud within the family, Pete Casella, an old-time drug dealer who had taken a 40-year prison sentence for the family, arranged for two young men from Testa's own South Philly neighborhood to plant the bomb on his front porch. Casella resented the easy way Bruno's mantle had passed on to Testa and sought revenge. Casella got it. Testa died instantly.

After the Testa killing, Scarfo moved to center stage from his de facto position as head of what was left of the Bruno-Testa Mafia fiefdom. He had now moved from the minor leagues of the underworld to the majors. His new headquarters in Atlantic City now became the 'Mecca of the Mafia' for running the operations in New Jersey and Southeastern Pennsylvania.

Inside the small 10' X 10' room housing Scarf, Inc.'s main office, the walls were decorated with maps of the United States and the world. Two red plastic panels with lights in back of them were placed above an imitation walnut desk. On the opposite wall, a sign read: "THIS PLACE IS BUGGED."

When asked who had bugged the place, one Mafia soldier in the office replied nonchalantly: "By the FBI, who else?"

Many of the top Mafiosi in Scarfo's family spent much of their time just hanging around the mob's headquarters at Scarf, Inc., which some considered a 'boring and dull business,' whether Scarfo was in jail or out of it.

For many years of the Scarfo reign, his two top lieutenants, Phil Leonetti and Lawrence Merlino, were responsible for keeping an eye on the business in Atlantic City, while 'Chuckie' Merlino served as acting boss during Scarfo's absence. The day-to-day operations in Philadelphia were handled for many years by Chick Ciancaglini, a beefy former bodyguard who survived the shakeup after the death of Angelo Bruno.

These men were Italian-Americans, which is understandable, yet many mob observers often wonder why the great majority of the Mafia has been almost exclusively of Italian-Sicilian origin.

The answer may be found in the explanation given by several retired Italian-Americans:

Since many Italian-Americans found themselves working in the building trades, i.e., carpentry, plumbing, roofing and masonry, it was fairly obvious that the so-called smart ones who opted to work with their brains, instead of their hands and muscles, would try to take control of the union organizations and union relations with building contractors. The Mafia served as a conduit for acquiring that power.

Scarfo, with his Italian-American roots, had the correct ethnic background and had paid enough dues to claim leadership of the mob operations.

The key to Scarfo's success was the use of force. As one local investigator put it: "If you're doing anything illegal in

Philadelphia or South Jersey, you are going to have to pay tribute." And that 'tribute' went straight into the pockets of Scarfo and his cohorts.

THE MURDER OF VINCE FALCONE

Backed by a warrant and a tip, the Atlantic County prosecutor's office sent a group of investigators to Scarfo's home in Atlantic City, breaking into his apartment through a window one December night in 1979. They were met by a woman, Scarfo's wife, Domenica, wearing a pajama top and waving a large kitchen knife. (The investigators would later testify in court that they had both knocked and announced themselves before entering his apartment.) His wife swore later that she heard nothing until her young son screamed, which was the reason why she grabbed the kitchen knife.

Meanwhile, Catherine Scarfo, Nicky's mother, who lived downstairs, was aroused from her sleep by the sound of the breaking window glass, and quickly rushed upstairs to her son's abode. When she arrived, she found her grandson screaming on the kitchen floor, her daughter-in-law sitting in a chair wearing Nicky's pajama top, and a number of strange men going in and out of rooms like 'little rabbits.'

The investigators had come looking for an antique .32 Colt pistol with white pearl handles, some jogging pants, and Nicky Scarfo. They had a warrant to search Nicky's home, dated two days before Christmas in 1979, for some incriminating evidence that might help them find the killers of a local cement contractor from nearby Margate, Vincent Falcone. The body had been found earlier in the trunk of his own car. The searchers did not find any trace of the targeted evidence, but they did find a small .22 derringer which was definitely not the murder weapon. This seemingly innocuous find, however, was to be an important item for the law enforcement officials in their attempts to place Scarfo behind bars for the second time.

They found this weapon in a bedroom drawer. Scarfo had been forbidden to carry any kind of gun since he had served time for stabbing a longshoreman to death, so this tiny pistol, with its holster sewn inside an eyeglass case that could fit comfortably inside a breast coat pocket, was justification to arrest the owner — if he could be found.

Domenica Scarfo, trying to protect her missing husband, insisted that the derringer was hers, saying it had come from a

friend of Nicky's, named Cookie. She related that in the course
of doing Cookie's laundry, she found the gun in a pocket of his
shirt. "I put it in my underwear drawer away from my children,"
she said and was to keep it there until Cookie came back to claim
it. "But the guy never came back, and I remained with the gun."

Just before the December 23rd raid, she moved the gun from
one drawer to another, where the investigators found it nestled
among family birth certificates and the Scarfo's marriage license.
They also found and took away a bullet-proof vest with a .22
caliber slug lodged in it, a pair of jogging pants, and what proved
to be a real find — a coded telephone list that included the names
of several top mobsters connected with the notorious Genovese
crime family in New York City.

Although Scarfo wasn't home at the time of the search, the
investigators found him the next morning at the nearby home of a
woman whom he described as a 'friend.' They arrested him for
the murder of the Margate cement contractor, Vincent Falcone,
who also was described as a 'friend.' Scarfo's nephew, Philip
'Crazy Phil' Leonetti, and Lawrence 'Yogi' Merlino, two of his
constant companions were also arrested and charged. The law
had what seemed to be a pretty good case against the three men,
pinpointing Leonetti as the alleged triggerman.

According to one New Jersey investigator, Falcone planned
to return to his native Italy to "get away from these people."
Unfortunately, his passport came through in the mail two days
after he was shot dead.

Joe Salerno, Jr. spent three days on the witness stand telling
his story of the crime, but the jury was not convinced beyond a
reasonable doubt because of some controversial evidence that had
been introduced at the trial of the three mobsters about Salerno's
credibility.

Gary Breland, a detective sergeant from Margate with a
spotless record, testified that he and his girlfriend had been walking near the home where and when the murder was supposed to
be taking place. He also said that he did not see Scarfo's car, a
black, late model Cadillac that all Atlantic City area cops had been

trained to identify on sight. Salerno said that it had been there.*

Based on Breland's testimony on the whereabouts of Scarfo's Caddy, the jury acquitted all three defendants in September, 1980. Breland mysteriously resigned soon thereafter in the midst of a divorce and moved back home to Louisiana with his girlfriend. Salerno was relocated somewhere in the USA, in the Federal Witness Protection Program.

Nicky Scarfo praised the American jury system and threw a party. That's when Scarfo's Liberty Bell and the **GOD BLESS AMERICA** lettering were put on the concrete shed behind his mother's apartment house.

THE AFTERMATH OF THE FALCONE TRIAL ACQUITTAL

For Scarfo, who thought he was a free man, the discovery of the tell-tale derringer in his apartment soon came back to haunt him. Four months after his acquittal in the Falcone murder, he was arrested in January, 1981, and indicted for illegal possession of a firearm by a convicted felon. In July, 1981, he was convicted and sentenced to two years in prison.

After spending one year behind bars, Scarfo was released on bail in the summer of 1982 to appeal his conviction. Almost simultaneously, Joe Salerno, Sr., a Philadelphia court officer and father of Joe, Jr., was mysteriously shot in the neck in the family resort motel in Wildwood Crest, New Jersey.

Investigators believed that Scarfo was behind the shooting and had retaliated against the father for the sins of the son. A court hearing linked Scarfo to that incident, though there was no direct evidence associating Scarfo with that hit. But a connection was implied by statements that Scarfo was at the "very vortex" of the internecine gangland warfare that had claimed the lives of at least a dozen local Mafiosi since March, 1980.

This latest indictment meant that Scarfo's bail was revoked on the grounds that he had violated court-ordered terms to not asso-

---

*Breland did not state that he had been in the vicinity of the murder until months later when he was asked about it by one of Scarfo's defense attorneys. Then he said, the information had 'not struck him as significant' until he was asked about it.

ciate himself with known criminals. He failed in this miserably, having been seen with Joseph 'Chick' Ciancaglini, a Mafia lieutenant who had been previously convicted on loansharking, gambling, and mail fraud charges, as well as Saul Kane, a convicted attempted extortionist out on bail, and Nicholas 'Nick the Blade' Virgilio, a twice-convicted murderer and longtime Scarfo family friend.

For the oversight of hiding a small derringer in his apartment, which Scarfo's attorney designated as a 'howitzer' in sarcastic jest, Scarfo was sent off to a new prison.

He found himself placed behind bars in Anthony, Texas, where he was forced to share a dormitory with 70 Mexican men who had been assigned with him to the steamy laundry detail. He didn't like that job, not so much because it was beneath his former exalted position as a mob leader, but because the steam in the laundry room aggravated his sensitive sinus condition.

Eventually, he was released and went back to his old haunts in Atlantic City and Philadelphia to take back the reins of his mob and rule it once again. It is clear from the evidence that he was not going back just to supervise the maintenance of his mother's apartment house and to put out the daily garbage.

I only shot a gun twice in my criminal career...and that was in target practice.

-Nicholas 'Nicky Crow' Caramandi

4 THE MAKING OF A MAFIA MEMBER

In recent exposés of the operations of various branches of U.S. Mafia crime families, there has not been a more riveting and dramatic confession on the making of a Mafia mobster than that given by Nicholas 'Nicky Crow' Caramandi, age 52.[*]

He testified that he had been a member of the 'mob' for three years. The mob, a.k.a. 'The Mafia,' is also known as LCN which means La Cosa Nostra or 'This Thing of Ours' according to Caramandi, who never rose above the rank of common 'soldier.' He described the hierarchy of the local mob, with the Boss (Nicky Scarfo) overseeing the whole family and the Underboss ('Crazy Phil' Leonetti, Scarfo's nephew) handing out orders when the top man was not around.

The hierarchy of the typical Scarfo branch of the Mafia family had a rather rigid organization with the entire group being called a 'regime.' Twenty soldiers, like Caramandi, would report to a single *capo*, who in turn would report to the boss and the underboss, headquartered at Scarf Inc. "The soldier reports all family [Mafia] business to his *Capo*," Caramandi told the court in the first Beloff and Scarfo trials. He described how he and others became members of the mob, after first going through a long test period of loyalty.

"I was first proposed as a member by another soldier, Pat

---

[*] Testifying as a government witness at the Scarfo and Beloff-Rego extortion trials, 1987.

Spirito," he said. But first he had to prove himself in a variety of illegal Mafia operations — loansharking, collecting 'street taxes,' shakedowns of numbers operators and sports betting bookies who would be shot or hurt if they didn't pay a percentage of their take to the Mafia for being allowed to operate in a geographic area. This tax was also known as 'the elbow' and would be collected once a week.

The take from the shakedowns usually was split 50-50, with half of Caramandi's collections going to Scarfo and the other half to his first *capo*, Charles 'Charlie White' Iannece. (Caramandi would hand his share of the 'elbow' to the Scarfo designated middleman, Chuck Merlino or Frank Iannarella, for submission to headquarters.)

THE INCUBATION — TEST PERIOD BEGINS

To become a blood member of Scarfo's mob, Caramandi related, one had to participate in the murder of a targeted mobster who had aroused the ire of boss Scarfo. In his case, the target was Pat Spirito, a member of the Philadelphia Mafia family. 'Nicky Crow' was told that he would be taking his orders from 'Charlie White' Iannece — his 'guardian.' 'Crow' was first introduced to Spirito after he got out of jail in 1979 and together they started an extortion ring, garnishing over $2 million in 18 months (from the start of 1982 through April, 1983).

"I kept 10-15 percent of the four shakedowns that we engineered in that period," Caramandi related, "and 50% went to Scarfo. The rest was then split among a half-dozen members [which included himself and Spirito]. I did the collecting on a weekly basis.

"Then 15 of us went to the televised Jerry Cooney fight one night in the Atlantic City Convention Hall with both Nicky Scarfo and Phil Leonetti. After the fight, we went to a local bar and Scarfo called Pat Spirito aside and they conversed in private for one hour."

"On the drive back home, Pat tells us that Scarfo wants us to kill 'Lil Harry' or Robert 'Sonny' Riccobene, who were both members of the Angelo Bruno family and opposed to Scarfo's rule." In a gravelly voice 'Nicky Crow' recounted, "We started to prepare for the operation by getting some old cars and guns, and started to watch key spots where our quarry might appear over a six-month period. I did not kill either of these two targets.

"We had set up a plan when 'Sonny' Riccobene went to a funeral parlor to view his uncle Fred. We hid in an ambush, but the attempt to kill him never worked out. Pat got hell for it after we returned to the restaurant and when we were all questioned by 'Chuckie' Merlino and Sal Testa the next day, and I was asked: "What happened?" I answered: "I don't know, I just take orders!

"Pat then took us off the case, and Spirito found himself subpoenaed by a Grand Jury. Scarfo was irate. He said, "This is no good. It is treason!" Two weeks later, I was summoned to Joe Ciccholini's house at 921 Catherine Street. He was a *capo* in the Scarfo family who told us soldiers what to do.

"He told me and 'Charlie White' that 'Pat' Spirito has got to be killed because he failed to carry out the order to kill Sonny Riccobene. So me, 'Charlie White' Iannece and Joe DeCaprio went outside to find a secluded spot to kill Pat. We three participated in the murder. Charles Iannece shot him in a car. I'm in the car with a gun. We ran to DeCaprio in the getaway car, left the scene and changed our clothes. The body was left for the police to find."

Caramandi had passed the most important part of the gestation period for new Mafia members. He had participated in a murder on orders from on high. He was now ready to be inducted, since he had met the Mafia requirement that all full-fledged members prove themselves first by doing a killing.

After the Mafia membership ceremony, life within the crime family became more exhilarating and prestigious.

LIFE IN THE MOB — AFTER BEING 'MADE'

Following his initiation in Whitemarsh, Caramandi entered the construction business with a fringe member of the mob, John Pastorella. He also kept a side business of shakedowns, extorting a 'street tax' from drug traffickers, bookies, gamblers and loan sharks. "I extorted from over 100 people during a five-year period," Caramandi said. "I even took shakedown money from a minister, the Rev. Carmen DiBiase, who had gotten old ladies to leave him money when they died. He was a crook and got their money from the banks."

Every time he extorted money from one of these 'touches,' Caramandi had to report the take to his *capo*, who in turn reported it to the boss, Scarfo. Although he had agreed not to engage in the narcotics business when he became a member, 'Lil' Nicky' eventually gave him the green light. He also got into sports betting with his new gambling partner, Johnny 'Cupcakes' Nacelli in an operation that lasted for five years.

One of Caramandi's more intriguing underworld operations involved his confessed conspiracy with Nicky Scarfo and Caramandi's *capo*, Tommy Del Giorno, to import 100 gallons of P2P oil from Germany which was an essential ingredient used in the making of methamphetamine — speed.

"We were working with 'Junior' Staino [a South Philly mobster]. I told the government that we imported 100 gallons of the stuff but 'Junior' Staino robbed us of 50 gallons, so we actually imported only 47 gallons. I got $85,000 for the P2P and after the manufacturing, I got another $25,000, but Charles Iannece, my partner, stole it from me," related Caramandi.

Because of the constant fear of being overheard, either by wiretap or other means, members of the Mafia would constantly use doubletalk in their conversations with prospective customers. Scarfo was usually referred to as either 'the boss' or 'the Lil guy' and rarely ever as Nicky Scarfo. The Mafia was known as 'the union.'

Caramandi also stated that he only shot a gun twice in his underworld career and that "was just in target practice." He admitted to setting up the murder of his "friend and sponsor, Pat Spirito," by encouraging him to look for Sonny Riccobene on the night that had been picked for the killing. "He [Spirito] picked me up in a car, and then later we picked up Charlie Iannece," said Caramandi. When we reached Front and Mifflin Streets in South Philly down by the Delaware River, Charlie told him to pull over so we could exchange some money. Then he shot him twice in the head."

We've been through 10 Mayors and 10 Administrations and in 10 more years, we'll be a force here. The kings [Mayors] may come and go, but the Barons [Councilpersons] stay on forever.

-'Bobby' Rego, Assistant to Councilman Lee Beloff[*]

5 THE CROWNING OF THE BARON FROM SOUTH PHILLY

L eland Beloff is a son of a late local judge, whose forebears were Russian immigrants who settled in Philadelphia at the turn of the century. It was Judge Beloff who served as a model for his first offspring and who indirectly contributed to his son's eventual downfall as a Philadelphia Councilman.

THE RISE OF JUDGE BELOFF IN PHILADELPHIA POLITICS

Born in Philadelphia, Emanuel 'Manny' Beloff, the councilman's father, became a scholar/athlete at South Philadelphia High School where he was both captain and quarterback on the football team. He was elected class president in both his junior and senior years and then went on to study law at Temple University. He passed the bar before he was 21 and went right into the City Solicitor's office and then into the DA's office. He had plenty of political smarts and had the savvy to move ahead fast.

In 1949, when he was appointed as a judge in the Philadelphia Common Pleas Court bench, *The Philadelphia Inquirer* called the ascension "disappointing" because "political pressure

[*]At the trial of Beloff and Rego in the Philadelphia Federal Courthouse, April, 1987.

was decisive in getting him the post rather than merit."

It was no surprise when the Judge named his second son, Hardy Austin Beloff, after the Irish Republican Party boss, Sheriff 'Aus' Meehan. Naming his sons after local political cronies was a ploy by Emanuel to honor his benefactors in life and to generate a little positive publicity for himself.

In recent years, Hardy Austin Beloff, Leland's only sibling, has distanced himself from his more controversial political brother, living outside Philadelphia and pursuing real estate ventures and helping his widowed mother in running the family nursing home business.

While he was still an assistant District Attorney, 'Manny' Beloff, then 35, eloped with a Temple graduate, Jean Rosenwald, 22. After their marriage, Jean made headlines when she sued her father and her siblings, alleging that she had been denied a part of her late mother's estate that was due her. One of her brothers, Evan, whom she didn't sue, would later become a Philadelphia judge — like her husband.

Once, when 'Manny' Beloff was serving as Judge, he accused the then District Attorney Richardson Dilworth (who would later become Mayor) of not having his cases prepared properly or having his witnesses ready for trials. Ex-marine officer Dilworth, stormed into Beloff's courtroom in protest at these allegations. The Judge ejected him, shouting: "The court will not permit you to come in here and in a snide and sly way alibi your short-comings. Now get out!" Needless to say, Dilworth stayed out of the courtroom after the Judge's outburst.

Although Judge Beloff began his political-judicial career as a Republican, he was urged by leaders of the important political families like the Greenfields and the Greens to switch parties, as it became clear in the late Forties that the Democrats would eventually take over the corrupt Republican city machine. But 'Manny' Beloff stuck it out, since there was a lucrative legal sideline available to most judges in those days which offered him a tidy bonus.

A sitting judge could also act as an independent and binding arbitrator in civil cases, and obtain a set fee, such as $500, payable by each side in a dispute. Judge Beloff profited financially from this side practice and invested his money wisely, purchasing real estate, several nursing homes and a 30-acre summer camp in the Poconos, called Camp Pinecrest, which the family operated for several years.

BELOFF EMBARKS ON HIS FIRST CAREER OPPORTUNITIES

While sitting on the bench Beloff was often called upon to settle domestic matters, but was less successful at home counselling his son, Leland, to pursue a "proper" educational and professional career that would include college and hopefully the practice of law. Unfortunately, young Leland was not brainy or interested in getting good grades. He felt more comfortable hanging around local street corners with neighborhood kids.

After graduating from Southern High School, his first career opportunity ironically surfaced in the field of boxing, where he was good enough to score 16 knockouts in his first 18 fights — until his concerned, and influential, father stepped in and had his boxing license revoked. Leland enrolled at Temple for a semester and then decided to spend a summer in California.

In Los Angeles, Lee looked up Ernie Kovacs, the radio and TV comedian, who had become friendly with Judge Beloff during his pioneering days at a Philadelphia radio and television station. Kovacs felt young Beloff had the looks and possible talents for eventual stardom, so he took him under his wing to help get him a break in Hollywood. Lee said later that Kovacs was "showing me around. It was at the height of his career and he was a big box office draw, and he said I should take a screen test."

Beloff asked the comic: "What for?" and Kovacs answered: "For fun." Lee took it and he passed. He was put under a small contract to 20th Century Fox and sent to acting school at UCLA. For awhile, he lived in Kovac's house.

"I met everybody," said Beloff proudly, "Frank Sinatra, Dean Martin, Cary Grant. I was 19 and going to all of their houses for parties." He finally garnered a bit part as a uniformed orderly in the Kovac's comedy film *Wake Me When It's Over* (starring Dick Shawn, Jack Warden and Don Knotts) and later was given a role as an aircraft engineer in the spy plane thriller, "X-15," which was narrated by James Stewart and starred a young Charles Bronson and Mary Tyler Moore.

Meanwhile, he continued in acting school and performed a few small roles in local TV shows. Soon after Beloff's arrival in California, Kovacs met an untimely death in a car crash, wrapping his station wagon around a telephone pole on a rainy night. This tragedy to his friend and benefactor took the glitter out of Hollywood living. Beloff returned to Philadelphia, bringing back his first wife, a Californian named Susan Smith who had been a runner-up in a Miss America pageant. She was also under contract to Fox and according to Beloff, was a "hell of a singer." She had made a couple of records in the 1960's. But life in Philadelphia was not what she expected, and they soon split up.

LEE ENTERS THE POLITICAL ARENA

Lee then did a short stint in the Merchant Marine as a seaman. When it became apparent to his father that his son was not going to finish college, Manny Beloff decided that the best place for Leland was politics. So, he pulled the proper behind-the-scenes political strings and 'arranged' for his son to be elected to office as a State Representative in the legislature in Harrisburg.

This move was accomplished with a phone call to the right person, who just happened to be the rising star of South Philadelphia, Democratic State Senator, Henry 'Buddy' Cianfrani, a former member of Merrill's Marauders during the Burma Campaign in World War II.

Cianfrani would eventually rise to become the most powerful legislator in the state when he assumed the post of Chairman of the influential Senate Finance Committee. Although Judge Beloff was still a Republican, he and Buddy were able to cut a deal.*

When the Judge called 'Buddy' and said he was interested in his son's obtaining a House seat, the ex-Senator recalled later: "Manny explained that it might be advantageous for him and me to enter into some sort of agreement where I would help Lee and

---

* Buddy would eventually end up in Federal prison for two years for taking bribes to arrange medical and veterinary school admissions, as well as hiring dozens of people for "no show" jobs on the state payroll.

he would help me." Cianfrani, a gruff, rough politician, was the leader in a South Philly ward, but knew that the Judge had influence in the neighboring Ward #39 — so they backed each other. Both Buddy and young Beloff won, and soon became close friends.

"I became a sort of a second father to Lee," related Cianfrani, "because I promised his father I'd always look after him, politically and otherwise. We lived together [at the Holiday Inn] in Harrisburg during those sessions. And Lee always respected me, even after my troubles. He had a wonderful reputation as a politician because he is likable...and likes to serve people. He is one of the few people that never called me anything but 'Senator.' I protected him politically and he protected me. He likes to do a favor and doesn't stand on formality."

However, other South Philly politicians do not remember the Beloff-Cianfrani relationship as being so cozy. One ward leader commented: "I remember Buddy saying that Mrs. Jean Beloff was giving Lee $1,000 a week, a new car and a credit card to stay away from the family [nursing home] business. Behind his back, Buddy used to characterize Leland as a 'total waste of fucking human life,' and he would laugh about it.

"One time Buddy told Lee to do something that was totally off the wall. It was like, you gotta be crazy to do it — it was either illegal or just plain stupid. And Lee's retort was: 'Yeah, yeah, I'll do it,' and he ran out to go do it."

The ward leader had then turned to Buddy and said, "He's got fuckin' balls," and Buddy answered: "Let me teach you something. If a guy goes and does something and he's so fuckin' dumb that he doesn't know what the ramification is, that ain't balls, that's stupidity! If he knew what the fuck he was doin' and did it, then you can say he has balls." Cianfrani denied that these comments were true.

BELOFF'S RECORD IN THE STATE CAPITAL

At the age of 23, Beloff became the youngest person ever to be elected to the Pennsylvania House of Representatives in Harrisburg, where he served without distinction from 1966 to 1970 as a Republican and again as a Democrat from 1977 to 1984.

His 11 years in the State House were political blanks with the exceptions of a few public brawls: one which took place on the House floor during a budget deadlock, another at Frank Palumbo's famous South Philadelphia restaurant during a political function, and still another at the polls in 1972. This latter incident led to a vote fraud conviction — his first brush with the law.

In 1973, Beloff and seven others were charged with election fraud and irregularities, being accused of illegally barring poll watchers from visiting the polling places in the 39th Ward.

A year later the charges against three of the accused, including State Senator Vincent Fumo, the Co-Ward Leader, were dropped for insufficient evidence, but the charges against Beloff remained. He was later convicted in Municipal Court in 1974 and fined $500, but was acquitted on separate assault charges of pushing a camera in the face of a poll watcher. This incident marked a beginning brush with the law which set a pattern for his future high stakes scam.

THE BELOFF NURSING HOME SYNDROME

Before Emanuel Beloff died, he and his wife started three lucrative nursing homes which are the primary basis of the Beloff family's financial empire. They are still operated by Leland's widowed mother, Jean. Back in 1972 there was an embarrassing incident involving the Colonial Gardens Nursing Home, owned by Beloff's maternal uncle, David Rosenwald, which was later shut down by the state in 1978 as a 'killer home.'

Beloff's immediate family denied that they had anything to do with the Colonial Gardens home. However, when his mother, a sister of the defendant and a member of the state Nursing Home Administrators' Board of Examiners pleaded the Fifth Amendment when called upon by the investigating Grand Jury to testify, it raised a lot of eyebrows.

In 1972, Beloff was indicted for the first time by the District Attorney (now U.S. Senator) Arlen Specter, on a minor charge, but he looked upon "the whole thing as a joke. Anyone who didn't agree with Specter got indicted," he said. "It [his minor scuffle with the law] wasn't even a misdemeanor."

In 1979, State Representative Lee Beloff had seemed almost

too insignificant to criticize when he was instrumental in cutting state funding for the Pennsylvania Nursing Home Ombudsman's Office, that had blown the whistle in the first place on malpractices and gouging in the fast-growing business. It was this type of Beloff-sponsored legislation that caused the Editorial Board of the *Philadelphia Daily News* to label Beloff as a "lackluster hack."

By 1983, however, it became increasingly clear that Beloff was becoming more powerful. When local Congressman Michael 'Ozzie' Myers finally went to jail because of his Abscam conviction for accepting a $40,000 bribe from a phony Arab sheik, it was Lee Beloff who drove him to the Allenwood, Pennsylvania, Federal prison. Upon returning home, he took over 'Ozzie's' old Ward #39B.*

HOW BELOFF MADE IT INTO THE CITY COUNCIL

In early 1984, just after Jim Tayoun had been re-elected to the City Council for a third term, he met in a caucus with other South Philly ward leaders seeking party caucus support to run against the incumbent district Congressman Tom Foglietta. Both Beloff and State Senator Vincent Fumo, who were ward leaders in a split ward (39A and 39B), also wanted to run for Tayoun's seat in Harrisburg which was up for grabs. On the first vote, Tayoun abstained, whereupon an irate Beloff turned to his fellow ward leader, Tayoun, and shouted: "Vote, you son of a bitch!"

A chastened Tayoun, who owned the Middle East Restaurant which sported a slew of belly dancers to go along with the Lebanese cuisine, tried to calm the angry Beloff by offering him his Council seat, saying: "Now look, Leland, it's just not your time to be a State Senator."

A livid Beloff grabbed Tayoun by the throat and pushed him up against the wall of the back room where the meeting occurred and after hitting his head against the wall several times, shouted: "Whaddya mean, you Arab motherfucker? Vote for somebody, you mother!"

---

* It was Myers who was ousted from Congress for his role in Abscam, and who left an historic tombstone legacy on the government tapes that helped send him to jail — that "Money talks and Bullshit walks!"

Tayoun explained later that he had abstained because of pressure from Mayor Goode and because he was waiting to see how another ward leader would vote. Tayoun also denied that Beloff ever touched him, saying that there was no way that Beloff could have picked him up by the throat and survived. A few minutes later, a partially calmed down Beloff stormed back into the front room and told the caucus, "I vote for Vince."

Beloff got himself elected to the Philadelphia City Council in 1984 as the so-called "peace candidate" — sponsored by the just re-elected and recently resigned Councilman James Tayoun, who wanted to go up the political ladder by unseating the incumbent Congressman, Tom Foglietta.*

LEE'S EMPIRE EXPANDS

In South Philadelphia, the corner of Fifth and Ritner Streets has long been known as Lee Beloff's corner, when he was both out of and in the political limelight. Beloff had a district council office in the heart of South Philadelphia located there, which he shared with Joe Howlett, a former longshoreman, who succeeded Beloff in the state House of Representatives with a push from Lee. From this office, Beloff took care of neighborhood problems, like satisfying complaints about potholes and garbage.

Beloff knew that his continued success in local politics depended mainly on how well he doled out constituent services to his voters and not whether he ever received the endorsement of the Editorial Boards of either *The Philadelphia Inquirer* or *The Daily News*. Obtaining bouquets from the media did not concern Beloff as much as keeping his voters happy and practicing grass roots politics. This *quid pro quo* largesse was left over from the turn-of-the-century political practices in which neighborhood politicians traded continued constituent services for loyalty in the voting booths.

To Beloff, politics was not a profession but a 'hobby'. Unfortunately, he never mastered the hobby or learned the fine points of the rules of the game. In his role as Councilman in a

---

*Tayoun lost, not once but twice in his hopes of going to Washington, before he came back down the ladder in 1987 to run again for his old Council office.

(mixed) district, he envisioned his role as a mini-political boss who could wheel and deal as much as the traffic would bear. The traffic to him was not the typical row house voter, but the big real estate developers in Center City who were ripe for the picking.

When he was servicing local neighbors, Beloff liked to stay in the back room of his District Councilman's office near his home, dressed in a colorful blue or red velour running suit and Reebok sneakers. For some people, Beloff would put on an air of rakish charm, but to others he emitted a feeling of being uncomfortable with having to take time to handle the myriad of problems of his constituents.

Beloff has been known as one who thrived on Philadelphia's social and nightlife circuit long before he entered the political arena. He wooed the ladies, bought everyone at the bar drinks, and tried to make the bar crowds laugh at his contrived antics and corny jokes.

There was one lady who intrigued him as a young teenager. He became smitten with her and in time she would become the third Mrs. Leland Beloff.

THE THIRD MRS. BELOFF AND THE CROSS SHE HAS HAD TO BEAR

Diane Beloff's parents were divorced when she was young, so money in her family was sometimes tight when she was growing up in West Philadelphia. Determined to earn enough money as a teenager to pay for private school tuition, she worked as a waitress in a pizza restaurant, did some freelance modeling, and provided some publicity for the Philadelphia Boat Show. One time her job was to walk around in a bikini all day with Tug McGraw, the Phillies and Mets star relief pitcher.

When she met Lee at a poolside at Atlantic City's Strand Hotel where he owned a penthouse, Diane was only 15 and he was more than twice her age at 32. He was footloose at the time and out of office having just shucked his second wife, Trudy, whom he had dated for years but stayed married to for only a few weeks.

Beloff asked Diane out to dinner that evening, beginning a courtship that lasted four years. "In the years we were dating,"

Diane reminisced, "we went out to dinner every night, out to clubs. I knew all these people like Nicky Scarfo...We went to a barbecue at his house at the shore. It wasn't like I came to South Philadelphia and all of a sudden...shock...meeting all those people you read about in the newspapers. Lee had a fast lifestyle. If you're out every night in Center City and you go to these kinds of places, those are the people who were hanging out in them. Those were the fun people at the bar."

Diane noted that since they had been married she and Lee had been in Scarfo's company no more "than a half-dozen times." One of those times was Diane's wedding to Beloff, where Scarfo was present. The two late mob bosses, Philip 'Chickenman' Testa and Frank 'Chickie' Narducci, also attended, according to Beloff's own testimony at his extortion trial.

Diane Beloff has been devoted as a wife to Lee and mother to their two young children. She was supportive of her husband's political career and served willingly as a committeewoman in his ward, for which she later got into trouble with the law.

In attempting to explain the Councilman's brusqueness in dealing with others, Diane, 28, told a magazine reporter that "I guess Lee's money allows him a certain arrogance that other politicians can't afford. I don't think he changed with the rules."

BELOFF'S AND SCARFO'S DISTORTED VISION

Ironically, both Scarfo and Beloff rose to positions of power in their respective mob and political worlds when the legendary men who came before them, like the late mob boss Angelo Bruno and State Senator Henry 'Buddy' Cianfrani had been removed from the scene by violent methods and by the long hand of the law. But by the time these two men reached positions of power and authority, the worlds they hoped to rule became not only politically unacceptable but also dangerous. Yet both men moved blindly towards their courthouse confrontations with the law, consumed by individual greed and their belief in their own omnipotence.

Neither realized at the time of their dual rise up the ladders of criminal and political power, that one day they would be forming a conspiracy to extort a million dollars from the biggest real estate developer in Philadelphia. But that day was not too far away for either of them.

Diane Beloff assessed her husband's Achilles' Heel this way: "Lee has always been hardheaded and I guess that carries over into his lack of judgment politically. He was brought up that when you are friends with someone, that's it. He's still old-time South Philadelphia politics. And maybe the only reason he never changed is that he loves politics, but he can afford to live without it. Most politicians, if they lose office, they have no way to feed their family."

Democratic contrivances are quarantine measures against the ancient plague, the lust for power. As such, they are very necessary and boring.

-Friedrich Nietzsche

6 THE PRICE OF CLOSING ORIANA STREET

BELOFF'S MAN FRIDAY

WHEN Beloff was elected to the Council, he chose as his Administrative Assistant, Robert 'Bobby' Rego, age 43, a South Philadelphian who acted in the multiple roles of 'gofer', chief spokesman, negotiator, and trouble-shooter for his boss. Beloff did not like the nitty-gritty of politics and would often turn over the running of his office to Rego.

'Bobby' Rego parlayed a boyhood friendship with Beloff to a position of influence 20 years later as the powerful aid to a Councilman in the pantheon of 17 Councilpersons. He was the only Councilman's assistant with the power to speak at all times for his boss. The only difference in their behavior seemed to be Beloff's ability to introduce and vote upon legislation. Rego had no hesitation in speaking for his boss as his alter ego without consulting with him first.

Originally, he and Beloff were Republicans, but both quietly switched parties a dozen years ago. Rego even wangled a spot on the Democratic State Committee, though he never held an elected public office.

Before rising to power in the City Council, Rego had been a principal partner, along with a convicted counterfeiter and two others later convicted as major drug dealers, in a web of interlocking companies whose business records came under scrutiny later, in 1986, by the US DEA (Drug Enforcement

Administration). Four of the firms, according to a *Philadelphia Daily News* investigatory series, amassed more than $130,000 in debts and $8,100 in unpaid federal taxes during a four-year period.

Additionally, Rego failed to file his income tax returns between 1977 and 1984. When he finally filed, he listed $5,000 of income from selling rugs as consulting fees and the collection of bad debts.

Although Rego had rubbed shoulders with mobsters in his past, there was no evidence that he ever had become a 'blood member' of the Mafia. However, he seemed to have skirted a fine line on the fringes of the mob during his pre-council years.

WAS BOBBY'S BUSINESS RUGS OR DRUGS?

In the Fall of 1986, the *Philadelphia Daily News* reported in a series of exposé articles that the agents of the DEA were examining records of seven of the 10 companies that Bobby Rego had set up between 1980 and 1983 in a four-story building located at 116 North Broad Street. Most of the companies were listed as being in the rug-dealing business, but several were fronts for the manufacture and distribution of methamphetamine (or 'speed') — a powerful drug made from P2P.* Two of his associates in seven of the companies, Stephen McKernan from South Philadelphia and James Santonastasi of Cherry Hill, N.J., had been convicted between 1985-87 of both manufacturing and selling the drug.

Santonastasi pleaded guilty in April, 1986, in U.S. District Court in New Jersey for participating in a South Jersey drug operation that "involved millions of dollars worth" of illegal drugs and was sentenced to prison later. McKernan was sentenced to five years in prison in 1985 on similar charges and for the unlawful possession of a machine gun.

BOBBY SENDS A CLEAR MESSAGE

Dr. John Bennett, 36, a Philadelphia Center City developer (a medical doctor no longer in practice) met Beloff and Rego in the

---

* P2P, short for phenyl-2-propanone, is an essential ingredient used in the manufacture of methamphetamine, a powerful stimulant which is usually imported or smuggled into this country.

Councilman's City Hall office, on February 22, 1985. They met to discuss the fate of a bill that Bennett wanted passed involving a Redevelopment Authority owned building located at 117-125 North 8th Street, which Bennett wanted. "We expected to make $1,000,000 a year from our council seat," said Rego boastfully (immortalized on a hidden tape).

Soon after Bennett came into the City Hall office, Beloff left with the remark, "You two have some business to take care of." Rego, the alter ego, sitting behind Lee's desk, then said confidentially: "We have certified friends, and only our friends get to do their projects."

Bobby thereupon opened a drawer of Beloff's desk, and pointed down to a pile of papers, saying: "If you don't pay us $25,000, this is where your legislation will go."

Bennett didn't complain when Rego later tried to cover up his bribe demand by trying to convince the developer to buy carpet from him for his building at a $25,000 markup. Bennett rejected the idea, although he knew Rego was in the rug business, since Bennett bought his carpet from his own father who was also in the business.

But ultimately, Bennett succumbed to the scam and wrote checks for $5,000 and $20,000 made payable to the Carpet Market in Haddonfield, N.J., which was a company owned by Rego's half brother, Joseph DeChristofaro. DeChristofaro eventually wrote out checks, on his own account, to Rego for $22,000 — keeping $3,000 for himself as 'payment for a loan' from Rego.

Walking down a corridor of City Hall early in 1985, Bennett had an encounter with a local judge who surprised him by asking the developer to ask "Mr. Beloff if he could keep his job." Bennett's response two years later to this outright begging on the part of a high-ranking judicial official who was up for re-election was: "Unbelievable. I couldn't believe it. It was unbelievable."

But it happened and Bennett remembers that the same judge had been in Beloff's office earlier in the day, and the Councilman boasted to him that he "had 15 to 20 judges in the court system that were 'our judges'."

THE BELOFF INSURANCE CLAIM SCAM

In September, 1985, a cracked sewer pipe in the basement den of the Councilman's home in South Philadelphia leaked waste water. It allegedly did 'major' damage when it flooded the cellar area. Dr. Bennett had done most of the repair work 'for free' for the Beloffs, who had collected an additional $5,000 from the developer in return for 'legislative favors' from the Councilman.

Beloff countered this charge later by stating from the witness stand that he had 'thrown an envelope containing $5,000 in cash at Bennett in his refurbished basement, when the developer came to visit him.'

When the work was completed, the Beloffs submitted a bill to the St. Paul Insurance Co. for $17,432 to cover labor and materials purchased to repair the damaged basement den. After subtracting the $5,000 that he claimed he allegedly paid Bennett in cash, the Beloffs asked for and got $12,000 more from the insurance company, which did not send an investigator to process the claim before it was paid.

The claim amounted to at least a $7,000 rip-off of the insurance company (according to a government prosecutor). Bennett also stated that he had written off most of the labor and materials used on the Beloff job against other construction work in which he was involved.

So, what did the Beloffs do with the extra money? A very nervous Mrs. Beloff testified that she not only ordered new rugs and bookcases to replace the damaged ones, but also "floor to ceiling closets, with folding doors enclosed by fancy mirrors, buckets of paint to redo the walls" and to top it off, a complete set of new acoustical tiles for the ceiling. But how can a leaky sewer pipe defy the force of gravity and wet the ceiling as well as the floor?

The insurance company did not contest this obvious over-billing scam. They reimbursed the Beloffs in full.

THE FEDS FIND A DIRECT LINK TO THE MOB

John Pastorella, 51, liked to live high on the wrong side of the law. In the tiny coal town of Sheppton, in Northeastern Pennsylvania, when St. Peters Lutheran Church became vacant, he bought it, remodeled it and put a bedroom in the belfry and a new kitchen in front of a stained glass window. It made him the talk of the town. He was a street savvy, bright person who knew just how far to go and not to go.

John Pastorella, a bearded, sometime building contractor, was also a broker for the importation of $4.8 million worth of heroin from Turkey between 1980-1984. As the middleman, Pastorella arranged numerous sales of heroin between a group of Turks in Baltimore and Joseph Fama, described by Federal authorities as a major narcotics dealer in Brooklyn, N.Y. He had served time in the Allenwood, P.A., Federal penitentiary for a previous drug conviction in the 1970's. When caught this time, he pleaded guilty to conspiracy to import and distribute 52 pounds (25 kilos) of heroin in one of Baltimore's largest federal drug prosecutions.

He failed to be of any help to the DEA officials in Baltimore "after agreeing to cooperate" with the government in return for a promise of having to serve no more than 15 years of a maximum 30-year prison sentence. Pastorella then let it be known to government agents that he "knew people in Philadelphia." Initially, no one in the City of Brotherly Love was very optimistic that he could be helpful in burrowing into the Mafia. But after making contact with the FBI in that city and mentioning that he had done business with Nicholas Caramandi, a known Mafia soldier, he was put to work penetrating the local construction industry.

Philadelphia government officials agreed and place him under federal protective custody, paying him a lucrative stipend each month for his services. Pastorella, who had worked in the construction business in South Philadelphia years before, slid back into the business with great ease, especially when he renewed his old friendship with Nick Caramandi in May, 1985, whom he had met while doing time in prison in 1970. Pastorella had paid him $5,000 to fix a corrupt judge during that period.

Pastorella's instructions from the FBI were to report any organized crime activities affecting the construction trades in the Philadelphia area. Over the course of the next several months, he wore a hidden recording device, filling about 150 tapes, primarily with conversations between himself and Caramandi.

Through Pastorella's efforts, the FBI got a tip in 1985 that Rouse might be the victim of a major extortion attempt. To bolster his credibility with Caramandi and his associates, Pastorella allegedly went into debt with the mobsters, since federal authorities believed it to be commonplace among business contractors to borrow heavily from the mob when they got into trouble. Operation 'Hip Boot' had begun.

Pastorella recorded a conversation with the 'Crow' in Bogart's Restaurant in Center City on May 7, 1986. The bulk of the conversation concerned Caramandi's mixed feelings about being involved in organized crime. An excerpt follows:

THE 'MOBSTER'S LAMENT' TAPE*

NICK
CARAMANDI: I used to go up to Newark a lot, go to a club in Newark and, uh, it was in the downtown part of...

JOHN
PASTORELLA: I was never in downtown Newark.

CARAMANDI: No, I mean, it's just a club, just one of those... like, you know....Fucking guy there used to sell...He's dead now, the guy got killed. He lived in the Newark area. This guy had a motel, phew, he musta had three hundred units two blocks long right on the main highway, big restaurant, his, his, uh, farm, not his farm, his, this ain't his house. Now he had a man-made lake as big as the lakes...His own fish, he had horses, he had a lotta fucking ground. He had a house. It was, uh, it was copied from the Spanish mansion. I'm telling you, it was fucking gorgeous, grounds keepers, horse keepers, maid... *Marrone!* I called this guy for a year. He was, uh, around for about a year. We were pretty close, used to come to Annin Street. Remember you used to come when you came to Annin Street?

PASTORELLA: ...Yeah.

CARAMANDI: And we used to go upstairs and...we used to make the special food and everything...They found him with thirteen bullets in his head, twenty-dollar bills stick up his ass and he was

---

* Recorded in Book E, TAB#77 of the RICO TRIAL 10/88

worth about sixty, seventy million dollars this guy. Self-made man...He told me one day, "Nick, I have eight million on the street, and uh, I pulled it in, I took it in sharking it."...We used to cell together...So anyway, he was with this group, you understand, he was a member with this group, the Philly group. What a fucking man. He was sixty-seven, used to fuck two-three times a day...He got two and a half years trying to run over an FBI agent. An FBI agent tried to hand him a subpoena. You know, this guy, this guy for five years, the FBI was looking for him to give him a subpoena. He ducked the subpoena...He went to Europe...he loved to travel....Uh, couldn't find him, so they told this one guy, they gave him contempt in Jersey; you know, contempt is automatic. Give me a tag number and we'll let you go. The guy wouldn't do it. He did six years...uh, I don't know what the fuck happened to him. Boy, this guy, you know a good guy now but this, this guy, he's a motherfucker. What the fuck. There's money in the act. Phew!

PASTORELLA: He crossed somebody.

CARAMANDI: That's true, somebody fucked his head up cause he didn't need it. He was a beautiful guy.

PASTORELLA: That's a shame.

CARAMANDI: And the funny part of it is, I'm beefing with one of these guys, he's dead too, they shot him ten times. So we're down in Newark, so say this fucking guy's giving us a hard time, so, uh, Mickey Diamond, you remember Mickey?

PASTORELLA: Yeah.

CARAMANDI: He says that motherfucker... you know Nicky, I'm gonna pop him...It's a good thing I didn't do it 'cause this guy was dead two days later...And I was gonna do it [laugh]. This guy wanted to kill me anyway. He just had a hot nut for me for a year...you'll never see this what happened in this city.

PASTORELLA: You could write a book, I bet.

CARAMANDI: Oh geez.

PASTORELLA: I remember when I met you, the first time I met ya, you weren't really this involved.

CARAMANDI: Please, no I wasn't, I was around Nicky [Scarfo]. I was around a bad guy. This happened and...see I was getting in, getting the power, understand what I mean? Well...he was gonna put me in anyway and, uh, all of a sudden, this happens, understand?...But these other guys, I knew these other guys too. They always liked me. I never had no problem with this, this guy, nobody knows him like I know him really...We go back a long time.

PASTORELLA: This one?

CARAMANDI: Yeah.

PASTORELLA: If you, if you had to do it all over again, would you do it?

CARAMANDI: No siree brother! Not what I go through. They are paranoid? You know paranoid?

PASTORELLA: Yeah, I know.

CARAMANDI: You know the meaning of paranoid? Phew, these guys are jealous, vicious, try to put you in fucking traps!

PASTORELLA: And that's really not your nature.

CARAMANDI Nah, I used to do good, you understand? This is all fucking problems, problems...that I know.

PASTORELLA: Too late now.

CARAMANDI: Too late is right, uh, it has its good things.

PASTORELLA: ...On the outside it looks better than from the inside.

CARAMANDI: Umm. Inside.

PASTORELLA: That's what I meant.

CARAMANDI: Fucking loser with junk. You know how much

money I coulda made? I can't get near it. I coulda made millions and millions...So when I came out [of jail], they said don't do nothing, we got plans for you. I knew all these fucking guys when I got out, I know all of them...Coca-Cola, tons of it. These guys, fifty—sixty keys ain't nothin' for them to move, nothing. I had some good men, you know, some good guys. That's the way that things work out. I'm worst off now than I ever was. I lost my hustle, like the hustle of, uh, the street.

PASTORELLA: You lost your independence.

CARAMANDI: Yeah.

PASTORELLA: That's what happened.

CARAMANDI: See, you can get in a fuckin' plane and go, I can't. If I do, I gotta go say I'm going here.

PASTORELLA: There are little deals here and there that you can't you know, you don't have the time...'cause you're too busy.

CARAMANDI: For two years, I hadda take a bath once a week.

PASTORELLA: I can see, uh, day to day bullshit going on and sometimes petty ass makes you sick and you know it takes all your time, and you got no time for nothing else. Right?

CARAMANDI: Yesterday...I was supposed to meet you for something, they say wait. This is ten-thirty in the morning. Meet this guy at two o'clock, he's gotta go somewhere. I went where we hadda go, it was nonsense...

PASTORELLA: Bullshit, right? What can I tell ya?

CARAMANDI: I was always independent. I used to do my own fucking thing even. These guys hadda bug me 'cause I don't socialize as much as I should, but I can't, I just can't...

PASTORELLA: Have the time.

CARAMANDI: I always...did my own fucking thing.

How ruthless was the 'Crow'? Two vivid examples suffice. Caramandi warned Pastorella (during a bail hearing) that if Pastorella "ever crossed him, he would put three bullets in Pastorella's daughter's head."

On April 25, 1986, Caramandi told Pastorella that James Dougherty, an official of the Carpenter's Union, who was putting pressure on Pastorella to hire union carpenters for his projects "has got to get hurt. I'll break his legs. We got to break this guy!"

THE 'CROW' MEETS THE COUNCILMAN AND BOBBY

In the Summer of 1985, Caramandi met Beloff in the swank Versailles Room of the old Bellevue-Stratford Hotel on South Broad Street, where he hung out in the late afternoons. He bought the Councilman a drink and struck up a conversation about the local construction business. Beloff boasted that he controlled the territory and the jobs between Girard and Oregon Avenues and Broad Street to the Delaware River, which roughly paralleled the borders of his District.

Caramandi said he first met Beloff 15 years earlier after being introduced through a now deceased Mafia intermediary, Dominick DeVito.

"Beloff told me to get in touch with him and he would give out jobs to me," related Caramandi. "He boasted how he was 'with the *La Cosa Nostra*, not as a 'member', but had gotten an O.K. from Nicky Scarfo to do business with me and other members of the mob.

"A week later, I went to my new *capo*, Tommy Del Giorno, to get his approval and he said that he would go to 'Bobby' Simone (the Mafia lawyer) to get the O.K. for me to do business with Beloff and Rego. Simone was not an actual member of the Mafia, but 'like' a member."

Beloff went to get clearance from Simone to do business with the mob. He got it.

When Rego introduced himself to Caramandi in late 1985, he said: "Remember me?"

When the Crow answered: "No," Rego retorted, "I used to be with 'Lil Harry'.

"I told Rego," Caramandi replied, "that he would have to listen to me since he knew I was a member of the Mafia. He also knew that bodily harm would come to him if he didn't cooperate. He was afraid of me. He was on a hit list to be killed in 1982. So when I told him: 'You from Saint Mike's Street [St. Michael's Place?] and he answered: 'Yeh,' I knew he was under my direct control from then on.

"I told him that I wanted to get involved in construction work with the Rouse Co. It meant something for everybody and whatever we do, we'll cut it up. If the deal works, we'll give you a piece of it." This comment marks the first faint hint of the unfolding extortion scam — which was then in its incubation stage.

THE 'MESSENGER' GIVES DEVOE AN ULTIMATUM

One of the first tapes recorded by Pastorella for the Feds took place on November 14, 1985, in which Nicky Caramandi tells him that a developer, Harry DeVoe, wanted to buy a narrow stretch of the colonial cobblestone street in the Olde City section, so he could join two adjacent buildings that he was rehabbing into a high-priced apartment condo complex with a second-floor covered walkway. (Caramandi felt DeVoe could be squeezed for $600,000 in order to obtain title from the City to the small portion of the street that he needed to complete his project.)

On December 3rd, Pastorella taped a three-way conversation between himself, Caramandi, and DeVoe, in which 'Nicky Crow' played hard-ball and told the developer: "You can't have it [Oriana Street]. Do you want it? It's not extortion." [But it *was* extortion — plain and simple.]

Eleven days later, Pastorella and Caramandi reminded DeVoe that "a city guy wants a rent-free apartment for two years." (This was the first hint that someone high up in City Hall, namely Beloff, was seeking a payoff in return for getting city approval to turn the street over to DeVoe). DeVoe stalled at first on the request, but Beloff was not to be denied.

Beloff rubbed his fingers together during a conversation with 'Nicky Crow' in the Versailles Room of a local hotel and boasted: "He [DeVoe] won't get nothing unless he does business with me."

Caramandi sent the message to DeVoe through an intermediary, Tony 'Blinds' D'Antonio. DeVoe didn't respond within a week, so an exasperated Councilman Beloff told the 'Crow': "If he won't do business, we'll put a vending street there [on Oriana Street] for hot dogs, and we'll foul up the building codes."

Because Harry DeVoe owed Pastorella $200,000 for some legitimate contracting work on another rehabbed Philadelphia apartment building, Caramandi boasted that he would "shoot DeVoe if he didn't pay up."

DeVoe faced a difficult ethical dilemma. He knew that to obtain his long-cherished goal — the closing of Oriana Street — there was only one course of action: he would have to acquiesce to the high-handed demands of these unsavory people.

Philadelphia: corrupt and contented with its municipal government...

-Lincoln Steffens[*]

7 THE FREEBEE APARTMENT

HARRY DEVOE COUGHS UP A FREEBEE APARTMENT

HARRY DeVoe, a graduate of the University of Virginia Law School, was a self-employed real estate developer and the owner of several apartments in the redeveloped sections of Olde Philadelphia down near Penn's Landing. Among other buildings he owned was the Smythe Stores condominiums at 107 Arch Street which he had transformed from abandoned stores and lofts into luxury apartments.

Because DeVoe wanted to close off an alley (Oriana Street) between two of his buildings to make a private courtyard, he approached Councilman Beloff to get an ordinance passed in City Council to transfer the little-used, narrow street to his ownership. DeVoe's original development plan was not to close the street but to join the two buildings with a second-floor connecting corridor, thus leaving the street passable. He admitted giving $50 each to ten City Licenses and Inspection staffers at a 1984 Christmas party to "keep them happy," but that didn't solve his problem.

He first met the Councilman at a $250-a-plate fund-raising party for Beloff's 1987 re-election campaign at the Bellevue-Stratford Hotel on October 6, 1985. Leland told him: "If you have any problems, come and see me." Before Beloff would

---

[*] Author of *The Shame of the Cities* (1904), a seminal muckraking exposé of the times.

consent to introduce the necessary legislation to help DeVoe solve his problem on Oriana Street, Bobby Rego quietly informed DeVoe that there would have to be a payoff to get the zoning change approved. The developer noted at the party "that both Bobby and Lee rolled their eyes, which meant that a big deal was in the works."

The extortion went down as follows: Rego told DeVoe that he understood there were some "nice apartments at the Smythe Stores and we might have need for one of them from time to time." DeVoe realized he was facing a dilemma. If he didn't come across with the free apartment, he wouldn't get the necessary variance to close off Oriana Street.

On December 3, 1985, Pastorella repeated the demand for a free apartment to DeVoe and on the next day, an irritated Caramandi reminded Pastorella (as recorded on a government tape): "Make sure you get the fucking apartment!"

Pastorella brought up the subject of whose name should be on the lease: "I don't see any reason why he [Beloff] shouldn't use his own name [on the lease]."

But Caramandi rejected this arrangement, saying: "No, he ain't gonna use his fucking name. What the fuck?...ya know, you can't put this guy [Beloff] in the shithouse."

Caramandi then told Pastorella that DeVoe should be reminded that his needed legislation would be enacted the "same minute that he [DeVoe] gives you the key" to the apartment.

Later that day, Pastorella delivered the message to DeVoe: "As soon as they get the key, you'll get the street. They'll sign it over that day. That's what you want."

"If I didn't go along," DeVoe explained later, "I would be turning a potential friend into an enemy."

Later, Councilman Beloff and Deborah Scullin came to De-Voe's office near the Smythe Stores complex where Beloff introduced the attractive blonde as his girlfriend. DeVoe got the keys to three empty apartments and together the couple picked #4H as their love nest.[*]

For 17 years, during and between his three marriages, Beloff

---

[*]Scullin told Beloff that she needed an address in town, so he filled her request and told her she "would not have to pay any rent since a friend of his owned the building and no rent would have to be paid."

kept Deborah Scullin on a string as his special mistress. He provided her with the amenities that any rich man gives to maintain a back street girl: money, clothes, a job, and a new ritzy apartment.

DeVoe then went back to his rental office to prepare a two-year lease for Scullin with her name on it. She appeared to be quite nervous, but a smiling Beloff calmed her, saying "Don't worry, honey, it's all taken care of." The apartment would normally rent for $945 a month or $22,680 for the two-year length of the lease.

There was no discussion of the rent and none was ever paid, according to DeVoe. Beloff thanked DeVoe, saying: "Anything else I can do for you in the future, I will do it." Beloff and Scullin left.

On January 27, 1986, Caramandi gave Pastorella another instruction for DeVoe from Beloff and Rego, demanding a receipt from the developer to make it appear that the apartment's rent had been paid.

An eager DeVoe complied with the request and wrote out a phony receipt to Deborah Scullin on his DeVoe Ltd. stationery for one year's rent despite the fact that he had not received any.

Scullin moved into Apartment #4H in mid-December, and a month later when DeVoe testified at a routine City Council hearing into the proposed zoning change to close Oriana Street, Beloff came up to him, patted him on the back and said, "Everything's fine." The bill passed unanimously, since Beloff as the District Councilman involved had given it his official blessing. When this proposal was raised in Council, no other Councilpersons, out of official courtesy, would oppose it.

DEBBIE MOVES IN AND GETS HERSELF A NICE JOB IN CITY HALL

Beloff came through for his kept woman in an even more generous fashion when he got her a job with the newly elected Common Pleas Judge Mary Rose Fante Cunningham. Deborah began working for the Judge as a secretary and receptionist for $19,500 a year in January, 1986. Beloff thereafter discovered she was seeing another man and became insanely jealous. He stormed into the Judge's office in May, 1986, while Deborah was out on an errand and demanded that she be fired immediately.

The Judge reportedly suddenly asked her to resign without giving a reason.

But the Judge, who was beholden to Beloff for her post, soon found herself in an embarrassing predicament because of another rash, unethical act that she had committed just before assuming office. On December 18, 1985, Judge Cunningham had accepted a bribe of three hundred dollars from Stephen Traitz, the Secretary-Treasurer of the local Roofers' Union. She was one of 16 local judges who accepted unreported gifts from this union in return for favorable sentencing of its members whenever they appeared in their courts. These judges, including Cunningham, were later to be indicted and recommended for dismissal from the bench in the Summer of 1987 by the Pennsylvania State Judicial Review Board.

Confronted by the FBI with the damning evidence of a taped recording of the bribe transaction, Judge Cunningham agreed to become a government mole and tape her fellow judges who were also in on the Roofers' scam. One of those whom she taped was another female Judge, Esther Sylvester, who was promptly indicted for accepting a similar bribe.

In May, 1986, after Scullin had lived in the apartment for over four months, Rego called DeVoe and told him to change the locks on Apartment #4H, saying Deborah had moved out.

The next day, an angry Beloff called DeVoe, shouting over the phone: "Why weren't those fucking locks changed? I want them changed!"

By late May, DeVoe had complied with the Councilman's request and given him the new set of keys. Beloff even had the apartment redecorated at his own expense and kept it until September.

After Scullin was fired, Judge Cunningham counseled her several times to cooperate with the FBI and Deborah consented to make a monitored, taped telephone call to Beloff protesting the lock change and her eviction.

The angry, taped phone conversation between Beloff and Scullin (on the morning of May 23, 1986) was presented as the prosecution's most emotional weapon in Beloff's later trials after numerous defense motions had been made to suppress it because of obscene language. In that now infamous tape of the call made by Scullin, with an FBI agent sitting next to her sending her notes, she shouted denunciations at her former lover as he sat subdued in his Council office listening to her non-stop invective. The phone call went as follows:

SCULLIN: (to the Councilman's secretary): "Hello, this is Deborah Scullin. Tell him I want to talk to him. I don't want to walk over to talk in person. (a pause while Beloff picks up the phone in his inner office) (Debbie is shouting now) "What are you trying to do to me, kid? Your henchmen are doing dirty work. You called the Judge to fire me, and Bobby Rego, that slimeball, tried to get me out of the apartment by Wednesday. I have everything in writing. Are you going to physically throw me out?"

BELOFF: (an inaudible low-keyed response)

SCULLIN: "You're making my life miserable by being vindictive. You can't do this to me, you fucking pussy. You don't call me up to fire me, you get your friends to do it, like your partner Bobby Rego. How do you expect me to get out of this apartment?"

BELOFF: "You go get some advice from your lawyer."

SCULLIN: "You got all the cops in your pocket. It's your dictatorship that got me fired from my job."

BELOFF: "Your job? I earned that post through 40-50 years in politics. It's MY job!"

SCULLIN: "What am I to do? Wait around for you to come once every three weeks? What's the deal? I'll call the [Philadelphia] Inquirer, The Daily News, and your wife. You don't dare move on this apartment Wednesday. You beat me up once and once is enough, pal. Men don't hurt women (highly excited now). How are you going to get me out, dear? I have the ownership in writing!"

BELOFF: (Getting angrier and louder) "Let him [her boyfriend] get you a job."

SCULLIN: "I got news for you, we are not talking about my job."

BELOFF: "I'm taking it — the job."

SCULLIN: "I've got news for you. You're not taking my job."

BELOFF: "I AM taking it. It's my job!"

SCULLIN: "You've been doing nothing but make my life miserable. You're trying to hurt me and you're not going to do it. Tell your friends not to threaten me. I know you don't give a fuck, pal. I don't have the money to move out. If anyone comes in Wednesday, I'll have the police here. I have a statement that the rent is paid through 1987. You're a slimeball hoodlum!"

BELOFF: "I don't care what the fuck you think...Every time I say something, you're going to make my fucking life miserable."

SCULLIN: "Big fucking deal. Just because I go out with another boyfriend. Nicky Scarfo owns this building."

BELOFF: "This time, you're barking up the wrong tree!"

During the replay of the tape in court on March 27, 1987, nine months later, Diane Beloff sat behind her husband, impassively, without shedding a tear, but she clearly did not like what she heard from the other woman in her husband's life.

"After all," Scullin said on the stand, "this man was a friend for many years, but some of his friends were out to hurt me and that made me angry...I was furious — I did intend to move out but not in two days. That was impossible. I did move five days later. Beloff paid the rent for one month...for me...but at a reduced rate. I had a new job and could afford to pay the rent after that."

Debbie Scullin was trying hard to sever the 17-year-long relationship to Beloff — and the FBI tape ended it forever.

HOW DIANE REACTED TO DEBORAH

Beloff's wife, Diane, admitted later that the toughest part "of finding out about her husband's girlfriend and the apartment was to read about it for the first time in the newspapers..."

She admitted vaguely knowing some details of the long-time liaison, but not all, so she confronted Lee with the headline news story of the taping of the Scullin-Beloff phone call.

"It's something that we resolved," said Diane frankly. "I don't think it was quite as big an issue as it was portrayed to be. She was an old girlfriend of Lee's and um, she was going through some problems in her life...I'm not going to comment on whether he did or didn't have an affair with her. I think that whether or not anything took place, it was certainly blown out of proportion....Lee's the kind of guy who's remained friends with all of his old girlfriends and all his old wives. And he's always a soft touch, he started carrying less money to the office because he'd get hit up all the time. You go to Lee with a hard luck story and he's going to help you out."

She felt that she and her husband were closer after the story broke in the media. "Up until now," she confessed, "there was never any major thing that we had to face together to force us to be totally honest.

"We had a family discussion about the problem," Diane said. "Obviously it is now something that has been resolved between him and me....It was not fun to read about it in the headlines, and yes, it has probably been the most personally difficult part because it is so embarrassing...and humiliating."

Diane was particularly incensed with the Federal prosecutors leaking the story of Beloff's private apartment with Scullin to the media before his attorneys were even informed of the indictment. She felt it was a deliberate ploy to "drive a wedge between my husband and myself so that I would possibly turn state's evidence."

THE BELLY DANCER SULTAN CASHES TWO CHECKS

James Tayoun, the owner of the Middle East Restaurant in Olde City, Philadelphia, famed for its Lebanese food and oriental belly dancers, was asked to cash two checks in June, 1986, by Bobby Rego. Tayoun, the former Councilman in the first district for eight years, who was to retake the seat in January, 1988, had engineered the election of Beloff as his successor in a special election in 1984 as his personally hand-picked peace candidate.

He often boasted that he had known Beloff for 20 years and that the Councilman had been supportive in Tayoun's two ill-fated attempts to oust the local Democratic Congressman, Thomas

Foglietta, in 1984 and 1986.

He told Rego he was willing to cash the checks as a "favor" even though they were made out to a dead man, John D'Arbo.

The two checks, written by Dr. Bennett to Mr. D'Arbo, were unendorsed on the back, and made out for $7,000 and $9,000. Rego forged D'Arbo's name on the back side of the checks. Tayoun had no trouble cashing them at his bank on June 13, 1986, and he gave the $16,000 in cash back to Rego. Tayoun did not question this obvious forgery. Rego was his friend.

MRS. SHEARER CASHES A CHECK

On June 6, 1986, Beloff walked into the Oregon Avenue branch of the Philadelphia National Bank in deep South Philadelphia, where he had a long-standing account. He asked the service manager, Patricia Shearer, to cash a $9,000 check from a real estate developer, Dr. John Bennett, payable to someone named John D'Arbo. The check was not endorsed to Beloff who asked that it be cashed (since D'Arbo was a dead man).

Beloff told the bank cashier that he did not want his name on the check. A second bank official, William Allan, overheard Beloff's request from his location at a nearby desk and became quite concerned. He instructed Shearer to put both Beloff's initials and her own on the back of the check — so she could trace it later to protect herself, which she did before cashing it.*

Beloff was accompanied by another man, whom Mrs. Shearer could not identify. It turned out to be Rego.

These check-cashing episodes — involving a dead man — were merely a down payment on a million dollar scam involving the biggest real estate developer in the region. The seeds had already been planted by Beloff, Rego, Scarfo and Caramandi. They only needed some watering.

---

*Bank officials repeatedly allowed Beloff to cash checks for other parties and occasionally permitted him to cash checks without endorsing them with his own signature. "It was an exception we made for Beloff in some cases," she said, "since it had been a policy going back to 1980 that he did not need to endorse the checks."

Philadelphia is one of the most corrupt cities in the United States today.

-ex-Mayor Frank Rizzo[*]

8

THE MILLION DOLLAR SCAM AT PENN'S LANDING

THE TARGET OF THE MAFIA'S MILLION DOLLAR SCAM

IT was rumored in late 1985 that Mayor Goode had promised to lease Penn's Landing to Rouse and Associates for $1 a year, for ninety-nine years, to build a mini-city along the Delaware River bank — modelled after Baltimore's Inner Harbor development and New York's Battery Park City. When an irate Beloff heard about it, he shouted to Pastorella in a meeting: "He's got to be crazy! No one gets nothin' without me! I got to O.K. it first!"

Caramandi reported this information to his Mafia *capo*, Tommy Del Giorno, telling him: "I got a million dollar deal cooking."

"Do you want me to tell Nicky?", the *capo* asked.

"That's up to you," said Caramandi.

Nothing happened for the next four months on this deal, until May, 1986, when Caramandi received a phone call from Rego to come to City Hall right away.

"It's important," said a confident Rego. "We got this guy [Rouse]. He's looking for a loan of sixteen million for the Penn's Landing Project, but it's up to Lee to O.K. it."

Rego and Caramandi met at the Hershey Hotel in Center City, a few blocks from City Hall, where the 'Crow' told Beloff's assistant that "he should go back and tell his friend [Rouse] that

---

[*] At a Republican clambake picnic on August 23, 1987.

the price will soon double if he will not play ball."

Caramandi then informed his *capo* and his associate, Joe Esposito, that the proposed scam "looked like a good shot to get one million dollars. If he don't listen this time, he will have a lot of problems, street problems, union problems."

Another week went by, and Rego informed Caramandi that Rouse had passed the word that Mayor Goode had promised him the money so he could get the loan to move ahead on the Penn's Landing project.

Caramandi then talked with his boss, Scarfo, about Beloff and the Rouse deal, and the Mafia chief warned him: "Watch that guy [Beloff]. He's a little erratic."

Having cut their teeth in the minor leagues successfully extorting money and favors from the mid-sized developers Bennett and DeVoe; Beloff, Rego and Caramandi were now ready to enter the major leagues.

Their target was Willard Rouse III, 46, a highly successful entrepreneur and a major real estate developer. The tall, lanky, brusque-mannered developer was a graduate of the University of Virginia. His uncle, James Rouse, was the acclaimed developer of the new towns of Reston, VA and Columbia, MD, and Willard made up his mind early on to outdo the efforts of his kin. In the thirty years he has resided in the Delaware Valley in a Philadelphia suburb, the younger Rouse, a 6'4" father of six, has put his name on several major projects including Philadelphia's Center City Gallerys, I and II, — two pioneer urban multi-story shopping centers as well as the sixty-story Number One Liberty Place, the first skyscraper to break the sacred height barrier of Billy Penn's Hat on the Pennsylvania founder's statue atop City Hall.

He was ripe for the plucking — or so the Mafia believed.

THE GROUND RULES ARE LAID

When Caramandi next accosted Beloff a month later, early June, outside the Councilman's office on the fourth floor of City Hall, a boastful Beloff said: "I got these guys by the balls now. One of Rouse's men took Bobby Rego out for drinks and he asked: 'What do we have to do?'"

Caramandi muscled in by asking Beloff to "introduce me to

Rouse's man, then tell him: 'This fellow can help you' and then walk out."

It was agreed at this time between them that the forthcoming million dollar scam would be split 50-50, with half going to Beloff and Rego and the other half to Caramandi and the Mafia.

On June 2nd, Rego met with Peter Balitsaris, a vice president of Rouse and Associates in charge of the Penn's Landing Project, giving him every indication that Beloff backed the Penn's Landing project and would introduce the necessary enabling legislation in the form of two Council bills. During the conversation, a meeting was scheduled for June 5th between Beloff and company president, Willard Rouse III, but it was cancelled.

At 5 PM on June 4th, Caramandi met with Balitsaris, in a restaurant in Center City. Caramandi, who called himself 'Nick', made it clear in his low, gravelly voice that "nobody could help him but me," and that "money would have to be paid first before the legislation was passed."

"What kind of money are we talking about?" Balitsaris asked.

"I put up one finger," Caramandi related, "and added six circular zeros with my hand. When he asked 'how many zeros?' I replied: 'All of them.'" Caramandi let it be known later that "he had set the price" and that if "Rouse didn't cooperate they would double the price to $2 million."

Balitsaris got the message and replied that he would have to report the price to his boss, Mr. Rouse. They made an appointment for 9 AM the next day, June 5th.

Balitsaris, a tall Tennessean who spoke in a Southern drawl, informed Mr. Rouse of the protection figure set by the Mafia to allow him to move ahead on the Penn's Landing project.

WHY ROUSE WENT TO THE FBI

Rouse had three choices when he was faced with the extortion scheme. After the charges were made public, he held a press conference and said: "Either you pay or you go directly to whoever has made this proposition and say 'Hell no,' or...you go to the authorities. We opted to go to the authorities...on June 4th," he said. His decision was made quickly and instinctively, which set in motion the chain of events which would make shocking headlines with more to come.

A friend of Rouse's, Joseph Egan, president of the Philadelphia Industrial Development Corp., said in retrospect: "If they [Beloff and Rego] had to pick one developer in this city to try this kind of thing with, he was the worst possible choice...since everyone who knows Bill Rouse knows that he deals straight from the hip...and that he would be at the FBI's door the next morning."

"To be perfectly candid, I was frightened and scared to death," Rouse said. "The idea of going to anyone other than the authorities was not a choice I thought I had."

On the night of June 4th, Rouse contacted the local FBI, expressing his fears to the Federal authorities of the consequences of the million dollar demand. "We were afraid of the person that [Rego] introduced one of my employees to," he said.

At the request of the FBI, Balitsaris called Rego on June 5th and told him that he "thinks they can work something out. Can you and I talk...directly?" he asked.

At Rego's suggestion, they agreed to meet at DiLullo's Centro Restaurant at 5 PM on June 11th. Wired with an FBI hidden body microphone, Balitsaris arrived first and promptly told Rego when he arrived: "I'm afraid of these people."

Rego answered: "Don't be. You can't be!"

But a wary Balitsaris said: "I tell you, if that guy [Caramandi] is a movie actor, he overdid it. He scared the shit out of me...I don't want to deal with him and these people."

Rego assured him blithely: "There's no problem I'm tellin' ya. It [the paying of a million dollars] has to be done... Nobody's unreasonable....Just want to make sure you understand the problem."

Balitsaris replied: "This discussion makes me nervous. Uh, it's illegal."

A surprised Rego blurted: "Huh?"

Balitsaris stuck to his point: "It's illegal. Seriously illegal." A somewhat stunned Rego asked: "What's illegal?"

Balitsaris replied: "Yeah. I know," and laughed.

A few moments later, Balitsaris crossed Locust Street for a meeting with Caramandi at Marabella's Restaurant.

Caramandi told Rouse's man: "All right, the door will be open for a million dollars. Ya know. I don't want it all at once.

Break it down over several months, even if Rouse has to hock his wife's jewelry. But don't come up with a *hot dog* (a small shakedown) since the bill is coming up tomorrow for the first reading."

He then urged Balitsaris to come up with some money by the next morning, June 12th — the day when Beloff would have to introduce the Penn's Landing bills so they could get approved before the Council's traditional summer break. At this stage in the negotiations, the FBI decided to play hardball and put in a professional pinchhitter for Balitsaris in the negotiations with Caramandi and his cohorts.

THE FBI SENDS IN AN UNDERCOVER MAN

On the next day, June 12th, James Vaules, an FBI agent posing as 'Jim Vance', another Rouse employee, delivered $10,000 cash (in government money) to Caramandi.

Caramandi then told Pastorella (on tape) that "this guy [Jim Vance] thinks he is going to get it [Penn's Landing]. We won't give it to him for nothin'. He will get this message tomorrow morning. I sent a guy in a few days ago and he got no answer. This is a $500 million job. The fuckin' ground is priceless!...Did you tell this guy [Rouse] what I told you: that you don't even have to go up there to Council? Whatever he wants will be done!"

Pastorella assured 'Nicky Crow' that: "We got him [Rouse] where we want him."

"How dumb can he be?" Caramandi retorted, "I can't get this fuckin' Joe, I got him by the balls....You tell the guy: 'They can't get nuttin' until my friend [Beloff] makes a deal.' He [Vance] says: The 'head of the corporation can't get the money,' but he's worth $15 million. I can't believe he blew this opportunity."

A suspicious Caramandi told Pastorella: "We ask for one million, but I think — Rouse's man — is a fuckin' cop. He [Vance] don't show up. I'm supposed to meet him Thursday morning. Maybe he's afraid of me....He knows the guy who can do it."

Pastorella assured the Crow that "the fuckin' guy [Vance] doesn't even know me. I'm going to see him this morning."

Caramandi replied: "If he says O.K., I'll send Vincent up

there. I'm going to kill this guy!"

Caramandi, who was still skeptical of Vance, since his was a new face in the deal, told Rouse's man when he next met him that the ten grand was "O.K. for openers, but that he wanted $90,000 more right away."

Vance agreed to this new demand, but only after he was notified that Beloff had introduced the bills.

Caramandi then walked up the four blocks to City Hall and told Rego that he had gotten the $10,000 and then went to his partner Charlie Iannece's house to split the money and check it to see if it was marked. He counted out $5,000 for Beloff and Rego, $2,500 for the 'shore' (Scarfo), and $1,250 each for himself and Iannece — on the latter's kitchen table.

He gave Rego the $5,000 later in the day at a Passyunk Avenue Restaurant in South Philadelphia. Still later that morning, Beloff quietly introduced Bills #990 and #991 in the Council's regular Thursday morning session.

FIRE IN THE HERSHEY HOTEL

Shortly thereafter a suspicious Caramandi met with Vance again, in the bar of the Hershey Hotel in Center City. A strange thing happened. The 'Crow', fearing that Vance might be wired, handed the latter a note with instructions to relay back to his boss, Willard Rouse, how, when, and where the next $90,000 partial payment on the $1,000,000 extortion was to be paid.

The mob's payment demands had escalated now with a time limit tied to the scheme. Caramandi grabbed the note back from Vance after the FBI agent had read it, pulled a cigarette lighter from his pocket and promptly burned it. The mobster then threw the still-burning note over his shoulder, without looking where it landed. It soon set a hotel lobby planter on fire, which was promptly put out with the help of an alert bartender.

THE ARROGANCE OF LEE BELOFF — THE BILLS ARE STALLED

Meanwhile, Beloff continued to exert his political muscle and even though the payoff was 'going down' he delayed indefinitely the passage of the pending legislative district. Sadly, not one of his colleagues on the Council challenged him on his brazen tactics despite the fact that the future of a billion dollar plan which had wider citywide interests was at stake. He believed that his hidden shakedown plot would be upheld by his colleagues since no Councilperson ever challenged fellow members in their own bailiwick. He was a prince in a political fiefdom where his word was law and his rule was absolute. Even the Mayor could not override his whims.

THE MAFIA BRASS MEETS ON THE BOARDWALK

On Monday, June 16, Caramandi drove down to the Scarf, Inc. headquarters to report progress in the scam, where he met Phil Leonetti, the underboss who took him to the boardwalk at Park Place for an open air meeting of the Mafia heads. In a foursome with Charlie Iannece and Leonetti, he reported to Nicky about the proposed 50-50 split of the take from Rouse, but Scarfo objected strenuously.

"That's too much money for Beloff. He only has two mouths to feed. I want to give Bobby Simone [the Mafia lawyer] ten percent. So we're gonna cut Beloff and Rego down to thirty-three percent. You tell 'em that."

Unknown to the four Mafiosi, an alert New Jersey police official, Anthony Gatto, who happened to be in the area at 1 PM on that day, observed this get-together at a distance. Although he was too far away to overhear any of the conversation, he had a method of silently recording the meeting. Spotting Scarfo and the three others in conversation by the railing, Gatto made a phone call and ordered that the stationary surveillance cameras that were coincidentally located high up in a nearby building be turned on. He directed the monitor to make a tape of the group.

After returning to his office, Gatto made a duplicate of the tape of the meeting and turned a copy over to the FBI. (Nine months later, on March 12, 1987, Gatto was asked in a Federal courtroom in Philadelphia to identify who was standing with Scarfo and Leonetti in the foursome. Pastorella and Caramandi were identified as the other two. Although the Judge ruled that this tape was not admissible at the time, he noted that it might become so later.)

Returning to Philadelphia, Caramandi met with Rego on June 18th at Bogarts' Restaurant and told him: "I'm not going to argue with the boss [Scarfo]. He says you're only going to get thirty-three percent, but that there is more than enough for all of us."

A few hours later, 'the Crow's' colleague, Charlie Iannece, called to say that Scarfo had a change of heart and now felt that "thirty-three percent was still too much of the cut for Beloff and Rego and that they should be told their cut was now to be only thirty percent." Rego took this information to Beloff and reported that Beloff reluctantly agreed to the new figure.

At a Sunday meeting back in Atlantic City, a greedy Scarfo had a further change of heart and stated that "thirty percent was still too much for Beloff and Rego. I think twenty-five percent should be enough," he told Caramandi. "If Rego gives you any beef, just let me and Iannece know, O.K.?"

Caramandi then met with 'Jim Vance' at 11:15 AM on that same Monday, June 18, at the Hershey Hotel. "Where's the $90,000?" demanded Caramandi. Vance told the 'Crow' he was having problems coming up with the promised $90,000 payment, because of Rouse. "He needs a sign. I'm just doing my job."

Vance asked the Mafia soldier: "How much power do you have?"

Caramandi retorted: "My connections go all the way to Atlantic City" (which the undercover FBI agent understood to be an oblique reference to Scarfo).

Soon after, the 'Crow' met with Rego and relayed the Rouse demand that he get some positive sign from Beloff. He suggested that Lee call Rouse and tell him that "the Council bill looks good."

Rego promptly called Beloff at his summer home in Margate and asked his boss: "Are you dressed?...Then go outside and call me."

Beloff went out to a payphone and returned the call (not knowing that it was taped). Rego answered and said: "Our friend is here."

Beloff replied, "He's [Caramandi] crazy. I'm worried about the phone being wired."

A SIGNAL IS AGREED UPON

After the brief call, Caramandi gave Rego orders: "When you see Beloff tonight with Vance and Rouse, I'll walk into the office and shake Lee's hand....That will be the signal, O.K.? There will be no other sign." (Rego agreed).

The next day, Caramandi received a phone call at 6:30 PM from his *capo*, Tommy Del Giorno, and was told to go immediately to Atlantic City to "make six more guys" (induct them into the Scarfo crime family).

The 'Crow' then called Rego and told him that he couldn't make the planned meeting with Rouse and Vance and that he would talk with them Wednesday morning someplace.

That place was the Hershey Hotel, and Caramandi met Vance at 10 AM and prepared to go across the street together to Marabella's Restaurant to meet with Beloff. "You'll see me shake Beloff's hand," he said, "and Beloff will scratch the left side of his chest twice to acknowledge that the deal is on."

Vance said that he would pay the next $90,000 after this hand-signal act of faith was observed, and after the bill in Council was approved.

THE SIGNAL IS GIVEN

When Vance and Caramandi arrived at Marabella's, a half-block from the Hershey Hotel, the 'Crow' went up to Beloff sitting at the bar and shook his hand twice — as the signal for him to return the O.K. sign to Vance.

But an uptight Beloff shouted at Caramandi, saying: "What do you want me to do, bark like a dog?" After everybody laughed, Beloff went into his agreed-upon act, and scratched his opposite shoulder twice, according to Caramandi and Vance.

At this meeting, Vance also gave Caramandi $1,000 in $100 bills as a sign of acquiescence by Rouse in the ballooning extortion scam.

Upon leaving the restaurant soon thereafter, a demanding Caramandi faced Vance and said: "Are you satisfied? How fast can you get me the $90,000?" Vance retorted that he would give him the part that was due in two and a half hours — at 4 PM.

The two negotiated a compromise where $45,000 would be made available the next day with the remaining $45,000 in cash to be paid on June 26th.

Caramandi agreed to this brief postponement of the payoff and then contacted Beloff to explain that his split had been cut again to a mere twenty-five percent of the melon. "I got this [information] from the 'Lil Guy' [Scarfo]," said Caramandi, "since there are more mouths to feed on our team."

A somewhat taken aback Beloff then asked: "Will he help me get re-elected?"

"Don't worry," answered the Crow, "we'll help you when the time comes."

But a shaken and worried Beloff queried: "How about [Mario] Giordano, Foglietta's man [who was planning to run against Beloff]?"

"Don't worry," replied a confident Caramandi. "We'll shoot him the night before he is elected."

After the meeting, the FBI trailed Caramandi to Beloff's office in City Hall. He met with Beloff in the fourth floor hallway outside his office — where they believed they couldn't be picked up by any 'bug'. But they did not take into account the undercover FBI agents monitoring them talking from a spot down the hall. The FBI also watched the two go back into Beloff's office and then leave the building together.

Beloff kept his promise and re-introduced the two bills on Thursday, June 19th, after which the U.S. Attorney Edward S. G. Dennis informed Mayor Goode about the secret Federal investigation of Beloff and Rego.

The 4 PM time rolled around and Vance reappeared without the $45,000. A suspicious Caramandi was beginning to have more fears that his adversary was "a cop." His suspicions were heightened when Vance made the strange comment: "Don't tell my boss I gave you $10,000 and another $1,000."

An hour later, Caramandi met with Beloff, Rego, and Bobby Simone, the lawyer, at Marabella's, where Caramandi told the conspirators: "He's a cop for sure. The whole thing is a mess. But don't worry, they don't have anything on you, only on me."

The 'Crow' explained to his partners, "They said nothing and seemed to feel that I was going to kill Vance pretty soon."

On the next morning, a still suspicious Caramandi went up to City Hall and told Rego outside Beloff's office to "kill the bill" because he had not received any of the promised extortion money.

"There's still plenty of time. He [Vance] will come back to you." Beloff nervously protested.

Just before the Thursday, June 26th, morning session of the Council, a surprised Craig Schelter, the Executive Director of the Philadelphia Industrial Development Corporation (who had been previously assured of the passage of the two bills) called Rego after learning that there was a problem to inquire what had changed the status of the bills, telling Beloff's assistant: "You can't do this!"

Rego answered curtly: "Watch!"

THE BILLS ARE PUT ON HOLD — INDEFINITELY

Rego gave a phony reason to Vance why he and Beloff waited until the last minute to delay the project. He claimed that the city officials' request for Beloff to introduce and support the measures "came so fast that they did not have time to evaluate them. We really didn't have the time. We were anesthetized and the anesthesia is wearing off."

He also rationalized that the delay would give him and the Councilman time to further 'evaluate' the proposal and the city's involvement in it. He even hinted that "another developer might step in if the deal with Rouse failed..."

"Believe me, if it's viable Thursday, it'll be viable Friday," Rego said. "We want to see what the bottom line is."

At the end of that Thursday session on June 26th, Beloff went up to Council President Joe Coleman on the marble dais in Council chambers and told him quietly that his bills would not be considered on that day for personal reasons — after having assured the Mayor the day before that he was still behind them.

Beloff gave another excuse for deliberately delaying final action on the two bills. Beloff argued that in an unrelated dispute with Goode, he accused the Mayor's Redevelopment Director, Robert Hazen, of holding up separate legislation designed to erect a wall behind Rego's home to keep out the traffic noises from the Delaware Expressway, I-95. That was the main reason Beloff offered for stalling any action on the bills during the Council session. Beloff called Mayor Goode and demanded that he fire Hazen, but Goode refused.

After the bills were put on hold at Beloff's request, Mayor

Goode and U.S. Attorney Edward Dennis briefed Council President Joe Coleman about the real reason for the delay. They clued him in privately about the extortion conspiracy aimed at Rouse.

THE SCAM COMES TO A SHARP HALT

Before any further action was taken in Council, the Federal officials lowered the boom on Beloff, Rego, and Caramandi. They were all arrested, June 27th, for attempting to extort $1 million from Rouse and Associates in return for labor peace on the Penn's Landing development. News of the scam and arrests flooded the local and national media for weeks.

Every time we set up a camera and turn the lights on a stage aimed at the mob, politicians appear immediately. I defy anyone to investigate organized crime apart from political corruption — the actors play on the same stage.

-Neil J. Welsh, ex-Assistant FBI Director
For Eastern Pennsylvania[*]

THE GOOD GUYS
MAKE A MOVE

FOR the first time in modern Philadelphia history, the U.S. Justice Department's investigation into the Penn's Landing Affair, with the help of the FBI, found a direct, documentable corrupt relationship between an elected public city official and a member of an organized crime family. The detailed government indictments of Beloff and Rego came as something of a surprise to many current and former federal law enforcement officials.

WHAT THE CHARGES MEANT

The former U.S. Attorney for Philadelphia, David Marston, said: "The implications are very sinister. There is nothing anywhere close to this...nothing at all...where organized crime has been shown to be capable of poisoning the government. That's about as bad as you can imagine for justice."

L. George Parry, a former federal prosecutor with the Organized Crime Strike Force and an ex-Assistant District Attorney in Philadelphia, pointed out that the allegations against Beloff and Rego were "more sinister than Abscam [where several East Coast Congressmen went to jail for taking money from a phony Arab sheik] because not only do you have an alleged extortion under

[*] *Inside Hoover's FBI* (1983) co-authored with former Philadelphia U.S. Attorney David Marston.

the color of official right, but you also have these ties to organized crime. The citizens have to wonder who their public servants are working for — the citizens of Philadelphia or people with a hidden agenda, who are working for organized crime. The implication is that any honest businessman who wants to consider investing in Philadelphia has got to think twice before committing their projects to this city and coming into the area."

Edwin Guthman, the Editor of *The Philadelphia Inquirer*, following the arrest of Councilman Lee Beloff on extortion charges, opined in his Op/Ed column of June 29th that "Over the last decade, I would bet Philadelphians have seen more of their public officials indicted, tried and convicted and sent to prison for a broad range of corrupt hustles than people in any other American city.

"But that is not so disturbing. Every major city has its share of felonious pols [politicians] and Philadelphia just has happened to have been the center of some very dedicated tough investigations of official corruption.

"What is disturbing is that despite the parade of Philadelphia pols to prison, the beat goes on.

"What the Scarfo family had tried to accomplish, in the words of federal prosecutor Ronald Cole of the Philadelphia Organized Crime Strike Force, was 'something I don't think we experienced during the [late] Angelo Bruno's regime. This appears to be part of Scarfo's agenda to get a hook into the political process and exploit it.'"

Guthman pointed out that he believed the charges against Beloff were not a "case of his orchestrating the alleged extortion scheme, but rather Beloff being used by organized crime."

A SOCIAL VISIT TO SEE A BABY

The FBI knew of an overt association between Beloff and Scarfo going back at least four years. Back in February 1982, agents from the New Jersey State Commission of Investigators followed Scarfo and 'Crazy Phil' Leonetti to Beloff's summer home in Longport, N.J., just a few miles south of Atlantic City. Beloff later described the visit (which the agents photographed outside his home) as "strictly social"...since Scarfo stopped by "just to say hello and see my baby daughter." But was that really all the Big Two of the Mafia came for?

REGO WAS 'SHOCKED' AT HIS FIRST ARREST

Rego was arrested inside Beloff's City Hall Council office in late June, 1986, by agent Couples of the FBI in front of his nineteen-year-old daughter, Robin, a summer office aide on leave from Brandeis University. Rego said, "At first I thought it was a joke. I thought someone from the Sheriff's Department had come up to play a game. We were waiting for a gorilla to come up with balloons, but when he put the handcuffs on me, citing my breaking the Hobbs Act, then *I knew it was no joke.*"

THE DAY AFTER

A day after the indictments and arrests, a defiant Beloff told the world from his ocean-view summer home in Longport, N.J., that his two ex-felon friends, former State Senator Henry 'Buddy' Cianfrani and former Congressman Michael 'Ozzie' Myers, had both told him to "keep his chin up...and hang tough."

"I'm going to do just that," the well-tanned, but rumpled Beloff stated. "There will be better and happier days ahead. As for the alleged one million extortion [of Rouse], I didn't know anything about it."

He claimed that he had received more than one hundred phone calls in the past 24 hours to hang in there all the way, which is just what he planned to do.

THE PENN'S LANDING BILLS PASS...AT LAST

On July 7th, a special session of Council passed the two bills (#990 and #991) previously blocked by Beloff and guaranteed that the city would support the developer's plan to build a $50 million retail and entertainment complex on the waterfront.

Beloff, still defiant, saying he "knew nothing about any alleged extortion plot," attended the Council session, but when it came time for him to vote, he hunched over his desk and grunted: "Present," when his name was called by the clerk. (His answer was an accepted parliamentary method to acknowledge that he was at the meeting, yet did not vote aye, nay, or abstain.) The bills were unanimously approved by a 13-0 vote.

Beloff told reporters that it was "not expeditious at this time for me to vote on the bills," and he reaffirmed his defiance of the indictments by declaring that he would not resign from the Council.

THE GOVERNMENT REVERSES ITSELF

Less than two weeks after the first extortion charges were dropped in the laps of Rego, Beloff and Caramandi, they were mysteriously withdrawn (on July 8th) by the federal prosecutor's office. The reason for this abrupt reversal was because the government needed more time to get its 'ducks in line' and to widen the scope of the investigation...to possibly include more persons.

The printed statement put out eleven days after the initial arrests was not an unusual step by the government. The charges were temporarily dismissed because the federal prosecutors knew they could not produce indictments to back up the charges within thirty days.*

Beloff tried to promote the sudden turnabout as a sign that the government had lost confidence in the case. He told a group of reporters: "There was never anything to this case as far as I'm concerned, *I never did anything wrong.*"

But he was mistaken. The prosecutors made it clear that they would not drop the case but would turn it over to a federal grand jury to investigate "both the extortionate scheme charged in the complaint and any other similar or related situations."

'THE CROW' CHANGES HIS TUNE

After he was arrested, Caramandi was allowed to make phone calls from jail to guys who owed him money. "Charlie Iannece owed me $70,000," said the 'Crow', "and I sneaked a call to him which the FBI didn't know about, and told him that if he didn't pay up I would inform the authorities. It was money from a drug deal that we engineered, and when I got it from him, I did not give it back." Although he got away with this subterfuge under the noses of his captors, something happened that would soon end his arrogance.

After being arrested in the Penn's Landing scam, the 'Crow' had a change of heart when asked by the Feds to turn government informer. It had been an essential part of his oath to the Mafia

---

* The Speedy Trial Act, passed by Congress in the 1970s, required any prosecutors to produce indictments within thirty days, or lose the case. That is why the prosecutors in the Beloff-Rego case sought and received a court order dismissing the charges "without prejudice," meaning that the charges could be filed again — at a more advantageous time.

brotherhood never to go against the Mafia, but when he was told in jail by an informant that he was going to be killed, Caramandi became convinced it was time to switch loyalties. 'Bobby' Simone allegedly said to Scarfo, "We are going to go with Beloff and sell Caramandi down the river."

"That meant that I was being put on the hit list," said Caramandi. "I'm not being a rat, but that's why...in November [1986] I went with the government. There was a time when all three of us, Beloff, Rego and I were in jail — that we were afraid Rego would talk. If he did, we would have killed him...so, I pleaded guilty to four murders. After all, the Mafia is not the Boy Scouts!"

'THE CROW' CONFESSES TO A MURDER

When he turned government witness, Caramandi admitted participation in the murder of Pasquale 'Pat the Cat' Spirito in 1983, in which 'Charlie' Iannece, Caramandi's mob partner, and Ronald DiCaprio had also been involved. They were leaving a wedding reception in South Philadelphia when they asked Spirito for a ride. The men asked Spirito to pull over at 11th and Miflin Streets where Iannece allegedly shot Spirito in the head. They got out of Spirito's car and were picked up by the escape driver, DiCaprio. The hit was made because Spirito failed to carry out a contract to kill another mobster-turned informant, Mario 'Sonny' Riccobene, who later testified at several trials in 1984 concerning mob killings. Mob leaders also suspected that Spirito was "stealing money from the organization," government officials said.

On June 17, 1986, in a taped conversation, before becoming an informant, Caramandi told Pastorella the nuances of a recent mob hit. It included this exchange (as played in a later open court hearing after a Grand Jury indictment had been handed down):

Pastorella: "How good are you? How do you keep score?"

Caramandi: "By putting two fucking bullets in a guy's head...close range. I can't shoot far. [He had threatened to rough up Harry DeVoe for disputing an alleged $220,000 bill submitted by Pastorella who had worked on the developer's project on Front Street.] We'll tear this place apart. He [DeVoe] went to them [the FBI, pointing to his own eye as a signal of who they were]."

Caramandi then made a gun motion with his hand and pulled the imaginary trigger with his finger and then shouted: "Bang!"

BELOFF SENDS UP A TRIAL BALLOON FOR RE-ELECTION TO COUNCIL

After the latest series of indictments, Beloff stubbornly refused to concede that he was politically dead. As one political observer put it: "He has not yet recognized that his problems are so deep and so broad that they have killed him politically. He still says he's going to remain on the Council, and he's going to run for re-election. But how can he?"

Beloff still denied all the charges and announced that he would actively seek re-election to the Council for a four-year term.

After his series of 1986 indictments, Beloff seemed somber, but kept protesting that he was innocent of all charges. He plead "not guilty" to all charges. As one of his South Philadelphia political colleagues, State Senator Vincent Fumo, put it: "I think he's beginning to realize that these guys [the Feds] are shooting real bullets. This is the first real cross he has had to bear in his life."

A seemingly chastened Beloff, dropping his usual arrogant front for the first time, stated that, "I don't have a whole lot to laugh about at this point. My whole life has been one of giving. I never took from anybody. I never had to. Now there's these charges, but I can't do anything about them at this point but to deny them."

In his three and a half years service on the City Council as Beloff's mouthpiece and alter ego, Rego boasted that one of his chief legislative triumphs was the introduction of a 'diaper' bill for the horse-drawn carriages which catered to tourists who came to visit the Independence Hall National Park. The bill, which passed unanimously, was sought by upper-class residents in the historic neighborhood who protested the horse manure deposited in the streets in front of their homes by these quaint carriages. (The diaper consisted of a large leather pouch that served as a receptacle for the horse droppings.)

Leaders of several civic groups complained that Beloff had failed to listen to their cries to introduce legislation to clean up other aspects of Center City life besides horse manure.

On October 23, 1986, four months after his original extortion indictment, Lee Beloff, acting as if he were oblivious to his precarious situation, hosted a cocktail party at a local Center City watering hole where the partygoers contributed $250 each to enjoy Lee's company for a few brief evening hours.

Five days later, on October 28th, the Feds reinstated the

original extortion charges and added a few more. The U.S. government also indicted Nicky Scarfo for the same scam. Furthermore, Beloff and his wife, Diane, were also indicted on separate counts of election fraud.

Ironically, money still flowed into Councilman Beloff's political re-election campaign coffers from his numerous deaf and blind supporters.

THE GUILLOTINE DROPS A SECOND TIME ON BELOFF AND REGO

On October 28th, 1986, two sets of federal indictments were handed down charging Beloff, Rego, and Caramandi with trying to extort one million dollars from Rouse, holding up Council bills needed by the developer, and extorting a free apartment for Deborah Scullin. This time, the Feds had their legal ammunition ready to use in court to back up the indictments.

Additional indictments were handed down against Beloff and three Committeepersons in the 39th Ward, including his wife Diane, accusing them of forging their names on absentee ballots in the November 1984 election.

These indictments, which the *Philadelphia Inquirer* categorized as "Mugging City Government," were the latest headline-making episodes in the Penn's Landing scam that had been simmering on the back-burner all summer long. Two days later, a chastened Beloff stepped down temporarily as Chairman of the Council's powerful Labor and Civil Service Committee until the situation cleared up.

A week later, Beloff and Rego appeared in court and pleaded "Not Guilty" to the charges. Beloff was released by a U.S. Magistrate after posting a $125,000 performance bond. Rego was released on a $100,000 bond, while Diane Beloff was released on a $25,000 recognizance bond until trial.

After the second series of indictments were handed down, a feisty Beloff declared in a press conference that his "spirits were good" and that he was "ready to fight." He was in a combative mood as he described his forthcoming confrontation with the law. "I'm looking forward to it...I love the combat!", he boasted. "I love the tension! I love the limelight! No denying that, but I just wish it wasn't this kind of limelight."

Once again, he rejected calls that he resign his seat on the Council or take a leave of absence, although he hinted that he might give up the chairmanship of the other Council committee he still chaired.

The basis of these new indictments were rooted in two rather recent pieces of federal legislation.

HOBBS AND RICO

In the late '60s and early '70s, the Congress of the United States put federal law enforcement agencies squarely into the business of investigating and prosecuting local corruption with the passage of two important statutes: the Hobbs Act and the RICO Act.

The Hobbs Act made it a federal crime for someone in public office, or exercising the authority of public office, to use their official status for extortion. Edward Dennis Jr., the US Attorney for Philadelphia, put it this way: "This really means the obtaining of something of value from a person by using that office in a wrongful way." Thus, the Hobbs Act made it a crime for a public official to accept money or anything of value, if the official knows it is being given because of his or her position.

Beloff and Rego were indicted on six counts of extortion under the Hobbs Act, which made it unlawful to receive property from another "through fear of economic harm" by threatening to withhold information.

The second statute, the Racketeering Influence and Corrupt Organization Act (RICO), allows federal prosecution or investigation and prosecution of state bribery and other offenses where it is done as a pattern of racketeering activity. In order for the U.S. government to use RICO, it must first show felony violation in at least three areas, for example, gambling, prostitution, and drug smuggling.

Clearly, these two acts provided the groundwork for building the indictments against Beloff, Rego, and Scarfo by the local District Attorney's office and/or the State Attorney General's office. But since the charges in the Rouse extortion case cut across state lines, the federal government was able to exercise its prerogatives and move in first with its indictments.

TWO MOBSTERS CROSS THE WIDE RIVER

By mid-November, 1986, word was leaked from the federal prosecutors that two Mafia members of the Scarfo family, Thomas Del Giorno and Nicholas Caramandi, had agreed to cooperate with the law enforcement officials in the upcoming trials and further investigations of the Scarfo organization. The nature of the agreements between the government and these two men, who agreed to testify against their former brethren, were not known at the time. But the fact that they were willing to speak out sent shock waves through the underworld and gave credence to the government's case against Beloff, Rego, and Scarfo.

Four months later, on March 27, 1987, Del Giorno pleaded guilty in a New Jersey Superior court to a series of racketeering, conspiracy, loansharking, and gambling charges that rocked the foundations of Philadelphia and gave the city a new nickname, "Sin City on the Delaware." It also became known for the first time officially that Del Giorno had been cooperating with the federal officials in the Penn's Landing million dollar extortion scam.

'THE CROW' GIVES HIMSELF A CHRISTMAS PRESENT

On December 23rd, a humbled Nicholas Caramandi threw in the towel before a trial and pleaded guilty in U.S. District Court to participating in two extortion conspiracies with Beloff and Rego. He also agreed to testify against both of his co-conspirators in return for protection from his former colleagues. The federal government had provided him with a new name and address that would hopefully remain unknown to the Mafia hit-squads that were after him. The government acknowledged that his "life would be in jeopardy" after his confession, and promised to relocate him until the trial in early 1987, assuring him a measure of safety.

BELOFF HIRES AN ATTORNEY WITH COWBOY BOOTS

By mid-December 1986, Beloff knew that if he was to stand any chance of beating the new indictments leveled against him he would need a top-flight, nationally respected, criminal defense attorney. Since his former attorney, 'Bobby' Simone, the silver-haired counselor for the local mob, had resigned because of a potential conflict (having been told he was an unindicted co-conspirator with Nicky Scarfo on the Rouse extortion scheme), Beloff needed a new lawyer.

He chose a former Philadelphian, Oscar Goodman, 47, a bearded, rather flamboyant Las Vegas attorney who wore hand-tooled black leather cowboy boots, his trademark, to court. He had built up a substantial reputation by defending a long list of well-known criminal clients around the country. His reputation was based on his courtroom strategy of attacking the government.

After being hired by the beleaguered councilman, Goodman warned his client not to discuss the case with reporters or anyone else. For the first time in his checkered career, Beloff consented to do what he was told.

THE UNEXPECTED END OF SCARFO'S FLORIDA VACATION

At 8:13 PM, on Thursday, January 8, 1987, a well-tanned Nicodemo Scarfo arrived at Atlantic City airport in a chartered plane from his swanky south Florida home in Ft. Lauderdale. He had no knowledge that eleven FBI agents were waiting to arrest him. As he stepped down from the plane onto the tarmac one agent moved forward, took him by the arm and led him to a waiting Oldsmobile, where he was first frisked and hand-cuffed before being driven to a local FBI office for processing. His unidentified female travelling companion stated to reporters that Scarfo had no warning of the arrest.

Scarfo was arrested on a warrant based on a "sealed indict-ment" returned by a Federal grand jury in Philadelphia. Although Beloff had once boasted that he and Scarfo had "lived in different worlds" since growing up in the same South Philadelphia neigh-borhood, this latest indictment brought them back together again.

The federal indictment used to arrest Scarfo also named Beloff, and marked the first time that an elected Philadelphia offi-cial had been charged in a criminal case, conspiring directly with the reputed head of the local organized crime family. Scarfo was stoic about his arrest and pleaded not guilty to the charges.

Besides listing the long series of violent acts approved by Scarfo in recent years, the indictments of Scarfo revealed that 'Lil Nicky' had approved the extortion plan involving Mr. Rouse. Joel Friedman, head of the U.S. Organized Strike Force in Phila-delphia, categorized it as a "classic illustration of infiltrating of the political process by organized crime."

Among the charges against the mob leader, one labeled him "killer" for ordering, approving or participating in the killing of at least six Mafia members since 1984.

After being held overnight in the Cape May County jail, Scarfo was taken to a hearing the next day in the Camden district court where Federal prosecutors succeeded in persuading the judge to keep him in jail as a "menace to society."

After two days of hearings in mid-January 1987, federal magistrate, Edwin Naythons, ruled that, the 57-year-old mob leader was 'unequivocably' the head of the organized crime family that controlled most of the rackets in Philadelphia and Atlantic City and that his "business as usual involves threats and crimes of violence."

SCARFO LOSES TWO BIDS FOR FREEDOM

The mob chief lost his first bid for freedom, because of the testimony of the former Mafia member, Thomas Del Giorno, who had admitted that he participated in five slayings and had plea bargained with the prosecutors, giving them information in return for a shorter sentence. He also accused Nicky Scarfo of ordering or approving at least 14 murders or attempted murders of mobsters who did not toe the line.

When the hearing took place, Scarfo's attorney, 'Bobby' Simone, suggested that Del Giorno and a second unidentified Federal informer concocted the allegations to avoid long-term prison sentences. But Simone's tactic did not work.

On February 2, 1987, Scarfo lost his second bid for freedom. On the weight of Del Giorno's testimony, Chief U.S. Judge John Fullam rejected Scarfo's request again. The government prosecutors brought Del Giorno in to testify, after the Judge had made it clear that he could not justify keeping the alleged mob boss behind bars on the testimony of law enforcement authorities alone. The Judge cited Scarfo's willingness to kill if released on bail — and therefore kept him incarcerated.

WHY THE FEDS WENT AFTER SCARFO

The long-range goal of the federal justice department in bringing Scarfo to trial and jailing him was to shatter the influence of the largest organized crime syndicate in the region. Some government officials predicted that if Scarfo could be convicted and sentenced to a long jail term in any of the cases brought against him, he would not only lose control of his mob but a severe dent could be put in its ability to operate.

"This [jailing of Scarfo] is one of the most significant blows to *La Cosa Nostra* in the area in recent years," said Carl P. Brown, Director of Intelligence for the Pennsylvania Crime Commission. "It takes the entire center out of the hierarchy of the mob in Philadelphia. If Scarfo and his chief lieutenants go away, who's left but the very old? Only the very young and they are too inexperienced to take control."

THE COUNCIL MOVES AT LONG LAST TO CLIP BELOFF'S WINGS

After six months of doing nothing but winking at Beloff's escapades, his brethren on the Council finally felt the heat of the citizenry for tolerating his presence in their midst. They did not have the courage to ask him to step down or take a leave of absence until his legal problems were resolved, but by mid-January 1987, Council President Joe Coleman, with the approval of a majority of his colleagues, agreed not to assign legislative bills to him, even if they impacted on his district.

This belated action came after a second set of Federal indictments had been handed down on January 9th recharging Beloff with extorting money from a series of developers, including Rouse. Beloff, meanwhile, refused to resign his Council seat or give up his $40,000 annual salary, which meant that he still retained the right to vote in the Council even while his forthcoming trial was underway.

At the same time, Oscar Goodman, the attorney for Beloff, and Joshua Briskin, the attorney for Rego, asked the judge to prevent the prosecutors from making any references during the trial to organized crime, the Mafia, or the Mob because their clients would suffer from the "devastating prejudicial effect" that this might have on the jury.

They were also deeply concerned that "there is a real and present danger that the government...will utilize the trial proceedings in an effort to link the defendants with some popular concept of organized crime and portray the defendants as racketeers or mobsters." The Judge thought it over but rejected their requests a short time later.

WHEN THE GOVERNMENT BECOMES A LAWBREAKER

A month later, a still arrogant Beloff took the floor of the Council, on the eve of his trial, to thank his supporters and the many members of the Council for walking tall and standing beside him during his ordeal. With that brief farewell, Beloff got up from his seat on March 19th, buttoned his sportcoat and left the ornate chamber. No one rose to applaud him or wish him well, except Francis X. Rafferty, a fellow blue-collar Councilman from South Philadelphia who shook his hand and told him: "Good Luck."

He still expected to attend the Council meetings from time-to-time to vote on bills and when eventually exonerated, come back to his empty seat. He told the press that "if I'm found guilty, then I'm going to have to say that the American jury system doesn't work. *I am not guilty*!! I have never in my entire life committed a crime, and I didn't do so in this case...."

Hold onto the second bottle [of skunk oil]....There is an attorney downtown that I don't like and I want to dump some in his office... as well as in Mayor Goode's office.

-City Councilman Leland Beloff*

10

THE SKUNK OIL SCAM

BELOFF AND THE SKUNK OIL SCAM

IN November 1986, while waiting for the next series of indictments to be handed down, Beloff found himself embroiled in a hilarious mini-scandal. Nick Marrandino had been hired by the owner of the Bala Theatre, Steve Fox, to put two leaky bottles of foul-smelling skunk oil in a rival movie house in Narberth as part of his effort to drive the owner, Matthew Wax, and his father out of business. Fox had been a major contributor to Beloff's political campaigns in 1984/85.

Marrandino, who spent had 37 days in prison in 1984 for theft and receiving stolen property, made an agreement with the FBI.†

Beloff instructed his gofer, Marrandino, to wait for Fox to call him and explain "what needed to be done." But before the call came through from Fox, Marrandino placed a call of his own to FBI Special Agent Larry Owens. He was then accompanied by Owens and another agent to a location on the edge of Philadelphia where he met a nervous Fox, who kept looking around to

---

* As related by a co-conspirator, Nicholas Marrandino, in a Federal District Court trial in Philadelphia on February 24, 1987.

† Between April 1984 and February 1986, the FBI paid Marrandino $18,000 for information to help the government build up a case against Beloff on a series of criminal counts, including absentee vote fraud in the Councilman's ward #39B.

see if his Mercedes was being followed while he drove Marrandino to the targeted theater.

Wearing yellow plastic gloves, Marrandino got out of the car and stood in line, followed by the FBI agents who did not enter the theatre. Fox gave him a $100 bill and a $5 bill to get into the moviehouse and left. Marrandino stayed in the theater briefly but did not spread the skunk oil.

He came out quickly, and handed the leaky bottles to Owens, who attempted to recap one of the bottles in the car. He didn't succeed, however, and "the bottle spilled," Marrandino said. "We had to drive all the way home with the windows down...to defumigate the car."

THE FOUL SMELLS FROM THE SKUNK OIL TRIAL

The 'skunk oil' caper surfaced again three months later at the trial of Stephen Fox, the owner of the Bala Theatre. In the nonjury trial in U.S. District Court before Judge Edmund Ludwig, Marrandino was the star witness against Fox. When he took the stand February 24, 1987, Marrandino told the Judge that Lee Beloff suggested he save the remaining bottle of skunk oil because he might want to put some of the smelly liquid in Mayor W. Wilson Goode's office to "harass him."

Marrandino had reported back to Beloff after failing to spread the remaining bottle. He told the court: "The Councilman was home. No one else was there. I showed the Councilman the skunk oil, the gloves, and the screwdriver. We then went to the basement and we contacted Fox."

He lied to Beloff, telling him that he had only used one of the two bottles that Fox had given him to dump in the theatre. "I told him that people had begun choking and coughing and leaving the theater and that I did not have time to dump the second bottle."

Under cross-examination, Marrandino said that Beloff told him to "hold onto the second bottle...since there was an attorney downtown he did not like and he wanted to dump some of it in his offices...as well as Mayor Goode's office."

Two weeks later, Judge Ludwig found Fox, the owner of 22 theaters, guilty and fined him $5,000. In an interview at the conclusion of the trial, Assistant U.S. Attorney William Carr, Jr. said that Beloff was an 'unindicted co-conspirator' in the case (which would foreshadow his own double reindictments for more serious Grand Jury criminal charges just two weeks later) but declined to say whether Beloff would be charged in the Fox skunk oil case.

In October 1986, Fox was indicted by a Federal Grand Jury for the skunk oil caper and threatening bodily harm to Matthew Wax in the attempt to ruin his legitimate place of business.

I want the developer, Willard Rouse, to come and see me! Damn it! *I am the council!* He's gotta come to me!

-City Councilman Leland Beloff[*]

11

THE UNITED STATES VERSUS BELOFF AND REGO

THE JUDGE

CHIEF U.S. District Judge, John Fullam, age 67, is a white-haired, senior judge who has been rated as highly intelligent, articulate and fair by most lawyers who have appeared before him. At times, though, he can be impatient, intolerant and sarcastic towards both prosecuting and defense attorneys who appear in his courtroom. Born on a small farm in Bucks County, Pennsylvania, he graduated from Harvard Law School with honors.

Appointed by former President Lyndon Johnson, he served 23 years on the bench, presiding over such famous cases as the dissolution of the Penn Central Railroad, the Abscam cases in which he sent several Councilmen and Congressmen to prison, and the case of the former Speaker of the Pennsylvania House of Representatives, Herb Fineman, who received a two-year prison sentence for obstruction of justice.

THE PROSECUTORS

The behind-the-scenes preparations of the indictments against Beloff, Rego, and Scarfo fell to the somewhat obscure U.S. Attorney for the Eastern District of Pennsylvania, Edward S. G.

---

[*] In an FBI taped conversation with G. Craig Schelter, the Executive Vice President of the Philadelphia Industrial Development Corporation, June 1986.

Dennis Jr. After graduating from the University of Pennsylvania Law School, Dennis became a law clerk to U.S. District Judge Leon Higginbotham, a prominent Black jurist. Dennis, who is also Black, worked his way up the career ladder as an Assistant U.S. Attorney and eventually came to Washington D.C. where he was appointed the Chief of the Narcotics and Dangerous Drugs section of the U.S. Justice Department. After two and a half years there, he was nominated for the position of U.S. Attorney in Philadelphia by the two U.S. Senators from Pennsylvania, Heinz and Specter, at the beginning of the first Reagan Administration.

Ronald Cole spent a decade with the Organized Crime Strike Force as a CPA/lawyer, successfully prosecuting such figures as former City Council Majority Leader Isadore Bellis for a series of extortion cases and former Wilmington Teamsters Union leader Frank Sheeran. He was chosen as the lead prosecutor in the Beloff-Rego trial and was assisted by Thomas Lee II, a tall, boyish-looking trial lawyer.

Cole, a Temple Law School graduate, described himself as a methodical prosecutor. Both he and Goodman, Beloff's defense attorney, grew up in Southwest Philadelphia.

THE TRIAL BEGINS FOR BELOFF AND REGO

On Monday, March 23, 1987, the Beloff trial got underway with an almost two-day-long, exhausting selection of a jury. Before the trial and jury selection got started, Beloff's attorney argued successfully before Judge Fullam that any jury would "be poisoned against both Beloff and Rego" if they were tried with Scarfo. So, the Judge postponed Scarfo's trial until April 30th.

A JURY IS PICKED AT LAST

The jury was finally selected. It had become a cross-section of the surrounding populace, consisting of eleven married and four single people between the ages of 24 and 63. They came from four surrounding counties (including Philadelphia). A nurse, a clerk, a bank officer, a retired machine shop foreman and a cook, among other professions, were represented.

Judge John Fullam told the jury: "I don't know whether to

congratulate you or sympathize with you in this important case."

He then admonished them to be careful and not talk about the case with their families or friends over the next two to three weeks at their homes since they were not to be sequestered in a motel under guard by the U.S. Marshals. "I don't want you to listen to the radio, watch TV news programs, or read the news-papers covering stories of this trial until it is over," he said sternly.

In the old days, such a warning by a judge to a jury was fairly easy to carry out since there were only the printed words of newspapers to contend with, but in these days of radio and TV news, with references to the Beloff trial being aired on news-radio stations every hour, how could a jury member returning home after a full day in court avoid TV and radio commentaries covering the trial?

The jury selection process usually ends up with a group that represents a cross-section of citizens. A sampling of those chosen by the Judge and lawyers included the following:

Tammy Leeds, a young blonde from Strasbourg, Lancaster County, said she didn't read any papers, nor did she watch TV, and had never heard of the Beloff case during the past months.

Tom O'Toole, an elderly Philadelphian whose son had lost a leg in a gang fight, and who had been a personal friend of the late head of the Roofers Union, John McCullough, and who said he only read *The Philadelphia Daily News*, was picked.

Joyce Morris, a Black divorcee from Mt. Airy (one of five Black women on the jury), had never heard of the case and stated that she did not watch TV news or read the papers regularly.

One of the alternate jurors, Martin Witt, from Levittown, Bucks County, was mostly worried about the safety of his family if he was picked because of the "Mafia connection of the defendants."

Another alternate, Susan Yamada, the only Asian-American on the panel, stated firmly that she did not read the papers nor listen to the radio, and only watched cable TV news.

THE DEFENSE PAINTS A PICTURE

In his opening remarks to the jury, Beloff's defense attorney, Goodman, stated that, "you can anticipate that the defendants [Beloff and Rego] will take the stand. The defendants are innocent unless proven guilty." He tried to impress upon the jury that Beloff lived in a rowhouse neighborhood and "performed his councilmantic duties admirably."

He painted the two government witnesses, Pastorella and Caramandi, as 'walking bugs' and criminals who were confessed drug dealers and murderers, but admitted that "Beloff is luckier than I am. His family is independently wealthy and owns nursing homes which pay him $200,000 a year, after taxes."

Goodman tried to put the government on the defensive immediately by trying to discredit its star witnesses, particularly Caramandi, whom he accused of "cheating all...including the *La Cosa Nostra* and Scarfo."

Rego's attorney, Joshua Briskin, chose not to give an opening statement to the jury.

DR. BENNETT TESTIFIES

When Dr. Bennett, the head of Historical Developers Inc., took the stand as the prosecution's first witness, he described how he was conned by Beloff and Rego into doing renovations for Beloff in his home at 2330 South 8th Street, to expand the kitchen, upstairs bedrooms and build a playroom and powder room in the basement.

"I know it's against the city building renovations," Bennett claimed that the confident Beloff had said, "but I can take care of it with the Department of Licenses and Inspections."

Bennett described the chain of events leading up to his role in the scam.

After making coffee in the Beloff's kitchen, Diane left Rego, the hatchet man, alone with Bennett. He told Bennett that the solution to his labor problems at the Charles Building site, to stop the Carpenters' Union from picketing, was to pay the union chief $100,000 (through Rego).

After Rego left, Diane and her husband came back, and she said to Beloff, "Can you help him, Lee?"

Since Beloff had boasted that he controlled fifteen to twenty judges, the question came down to which judge might hear Bennett's case against the Carpenters' Union. As it turned out, Bennett never paid any of the $100,000 extortion money to either Rego or the union.

Bennett advised Beloff not to go ahead with all of the proposed renovations in his home, since it would cost at least $35,000. "It's crazy to put that much money into it," he said.

Lee answered, "I have to stay in it since it was my father's home." Bennett politely declined to do the job.

A few days later, in late June 1985, Rego suggested to Bennett at a meeting in the Versailles Room of the Bellevue-Stratford Hotel that he retain 'Bobby' Simone as his attorney on union problems. But Bennett believed that Simone "was a lawyer with mob connections" and decided not to hire him.

Bennett testified that he showed Beloff three apartment buildings in October 1985 for his long-time girlfriend, Deborah Scullin, who needed an apartment. They were located at 2nd and Market, 1222 Locust, and 1213 Green Street (all in Center City).

After looking them over, alone, according to Bennett, Beloff commented that "the units were nice but were not valid for a clandestine affair and furthermore he didn't like the 'ethnic' types in the neighborhood." Bennett never got to supply any apartments for the Councilman. Beloff then put the screws to DeVoe for his 'freebee' apartment in the Smythe Stores complex.

On cross examination by Goodman, Dr. Bennett stated that he had given up his medical practice and hospital license in January 1984 when he went into the more lucrative construction business. "There were time constraints, emotional stresses and the prospects of more money," he said, plus the fact that his father had been in the contracting business for forty years.

"To tell the truth, I felt I was being extorted," Bennett stated, although he did admit that his three previous projects were written off as "a five year operational loss" and as a "tax shelter program to get federal tax credits" for his own benefit.[*]

Goodman used a subtle ploy during his cross-examination of witnesses, when he tried to portray Rego as a fixer, and the real extortionist, with Beloff playing the role of a middleman and an introducer. Rego would then carry out the dirty work for his boss.

---

[*] Bennett was lucky. He got a letter of immunity from the prosecution in return for telling the 'truth' in court.

CARAMANDI TAKES THE STAND

The star witness took the stand midway in the government's case against Beloff and Rego. This was Nicholas Caramandi. The stocky, dark-haired man, appeared in court dressed in blue pants and a black turtleneck shirt under a brown suede sports jacket. If he did not tell the truth to the judge and jury, his agreement with the Federal government would become null and void, and he would be prosecuted to the full extent of the law.

So he had nothing to lose by telling all, since he had most recently served a four-year sentence in Lewisburg, Pennsylvania, Federal prison for counterfeiting $1 million in phony bills, and mail fraud, plus a sixty-day local jail sentence for being involved in a $500 'flim-flam' deception in Mays Landing, New Jersey.

Caramandi explained to the judge and jury how the Mafia operated its underground construction industry extortions.

"We subbed it out," he said, "giving some of it to union subcontractors and some to non-union guys. When the people didn't pay us back for loans after the first time, there was no second or third opportunity....For instance, we collected payments on loans of $1,000 at $120 a week. My partner, Charlie Iannece, and 'Johnny Cupcakes' took care of the loansharking end of the business.

"There is a habit in our business of not mentioning names when we talk. We used code words like — 'this guy' or 'them' if a member of the Mafia, and the word 'other guy' if he was not a mob member. We knew that Rego could get some 'juice' [money and influence] out of City Hall, so we could refer to him in our conversations as 'City Hall.' Rego was looking for favors from us because he was going to do me favors later."

'TOMMY DEL' BACKS UP 'THE CROW'

Tommy Del Giorno pleaded guilty to one count of racketeering in his agreement with the U.S. and exposed himself to a possible twenty-year prison sentence for confessing to a series of conspiracies and participating in several Mafia murders over the years. He also admitted to loansharking, gambling, extortion, narcotics, and being a *capo* in the Mafia family, which he described as: "this thing of ours."

Del Giorno described how he hoodwinked the U.S. Army into giving him a General Discharge from the service. He "wanted to get out," he told the jury, "so I gave them a lot of trouble. I told the Doc I had a mental disorder and wanted out on the grounds of 'emotional instability...under stress!' I told the Doc to write it down just that way, and he did. I was pretending that I was crazy, being 'not all there'. He did his job. I got out."

The prosecution showed the court a silent TV picture of the famous meeting in Atlantic City of the four members of the Scarfo crime family.

The replay of the June 16, 1986, video tape on the TV monitors — showing the four Mafiosos (Scarfo, Leonetti, Caramandi and Del Giorno) conferring at the boardwalk railing — looking out towards the beach — got stuck. The exasperated Judge Fullam broke in to tell the Beloff-Rego jury to "disregard what has just been shown, but someday soon we'll get to it." After laughter from the audience, and a long pause, Caramandi identified the four figures in the half-hour meeting on the tape as his brethren in the mob.

Finally, Judge Fullam interrupted to inquire: "Will there be any further scenes of seagulls flying across the screen?" After that gibe, the Federal prosecutors turned off the video. The judge and jury had seen enough.

ROUSE TELLS WHY HE WENT TO THE FBI

Rouse took the stand midway in the trial, stating that he was the developer of a number of projects in Florida, New Jersey, Virginia, and Pennsylvania, worth $200 to $300 million.

The Penn's Landing project was to include retail and office buildings, and a parking area located around the Great Plaza on the waterfront where William Penn first set foot in the Commonwealth back in 1683. Rouse stated that the original cost estimate for Phase #1 was $140 million, but that no plans had yet been drawn. He was hoping to obtain a Federal Urban Development Action Grant (UDAG) of $10 million to help get his project off the ground.

The rest of the loans were to be underwritten by Fidelity Bank and the Chase Bank in New York. However, the loans were tied to the crucial UDAG grant from the Department of Housing and

Urban Development (HUD), which stipulated a series of cut-off dates, making legislation from the City Council a key to the success of the whole project.

The HUD cutoff date was early July 1986, and Beloff's delays "backed us up against that deadline," Rouse said when he described how he had gone to Beloff with this information to help speed up action on the bills. According to Rouse, Beloff claimed that "there were no obstacles" and "he would cooperate."

When Peter Balitsaris informed him on June 4th of the $1 million extortion scheme, Rouse said: "To be perfectly candid, I was scared to go to anyone but the authorities and was afraid of who my employees might introduce me to, so I went straight to the FBI."

A COUNCIL COLLEAGUE REFUSES TO CHALLENGE BELOFF

Council President, Joe Coleman, testified that in his seven years as head of the city's legislative body, no other Councilman had requested a 'hold' be put on legislation affecting his district. "I did not ask Mr. Beloff why he had requested a hold on the two [Rouse] bills in our pre-session caucus," he said, "but I went along with him. Later in the day I asked him why the delay? He just said he wanted them held over, without giving a reason."

Coleman knew the importance of the bills, but did not wish to antagonize Beloff about a project in his own district, and regarded the sovereignty of such elected officials as near absolute. So, Coleman did not challenge him further on the matter, even though Mayor Goode informed Coleman that the timing was getting crucial.

BELOFF'S WIFE TAKES THE STAND

The weakest witness for the defense was Diane Beloff, who took the stand dressed in a dark suit and no makeup. She was nervous and stammered as she floundered through her testimony. She kept sending wounded glances to the jury, repeatedly mentioning her children as she confessed to the overcharges of claims to the insurance company to compensate for the sewer pipe break.

BELOFF ENTERS THE RING TO DEFEND HIMSELF

When Beloff took the stand in his own defense, he vehemently denied all of the government accusations that he had conspired to extort money from the developers, Bennett, DeVoe, and Rouse. He also denied that he had gotten Bennett to perform at least $5,000 worth of free sewer pipe repair work in the basement of his South Philadelphia home.

Beloff claimed that he paid Bennett in cash, which he had kept under his mattress — but did not ask for a receipt. He claimed to have paid cash for the $945-a-month apartment for Scullin. Beloff also insisted that he had never discussed any type of criminal activity with Nicky Scarfo or Caramandi.

On cross-examination by Ronald Cole, Beloff professed ignorance that Scarfo was a crime boss.

"I did not know he was boss of anything," he said confidently. Beloff also denied sending any messages to Scarfo through either Rego or Simone. "If I wanted to talk with Mr. Scarfo," Beloff said, "I would do it myself."

Beloff told the jury he had a net worth of nearly $3 million and he produced recent tax forms showing his yearly income from the family nursing home business and his trust fund to be approximately $250,000, plus his $40,000 a year salary from the Council, and another $565 a month ($7,000 a year) in retirement benefits from the state from his years as a State Representative. He claimed that the latter two amounts of money went into a separate checking account to maintain several satellite council offices. He also said that he usually kept $5,000 to $6,000 in cash in the top drawer of his dresser.

Strangely, none of the prosecuting attorneys brought up the possibilities of poor quality nursing home care for the elderly patients which was the basis of the fortune of the richest City Councilman. Nor did they question the highly inflated costs of nursing home care imposed by Mrs. Emanuel Beloff, in order for Lee to have his $250,000-a-year 'play money.'

Beloff also tried to deflate one of the central issues in the government's case against him: the meaning of the silent gesture of his double hand rub of his shoulder in Marabella's bar as a signal of his approval of the $1 million extortion scheme against Rouse Inc.

Rather than agreeing with the government's assertion that he made the gesture voluntarily as a pre-arranged agreement between the FBI agent and the 'Crow', Beloff claimed that Caramandi had inexplicably grabbed Beloff's arm and pressed it twice against the Councilman's chest...After he leaned over to whisper something in his ear.

"What the hell are you doing?" an exasperated Beloff claimed to have queried.

"I'm just kiddin," Caramandi was supposed to have replied. Beloff told the jury that he had never agreed to give such a signal.

With his testimony, Beloff was injecting a new issue into his case, i.e., the credibility of the defendant vs. that of the key witness, Caramandi.

Beloff also claimed that he had a serious vision problem, and couldn't see Caramandi's signal across the bar at Marabella's.

Beloff admitted to becoming upset when Robert Hazen, the Redevelopment Authority's Executive Director, had questioned the "appropriateness" of spending city funds on a questionable project to build a noise abatement wall behind Rego's home. When he was told by the Chairman of the Democratic City Committee, Robert Brady, that the Mayor refused to fire Hazen at Beloff's request, the Councilman became infuriated and decided to retaliate by withdrawing approval of the Penn's Landing bills.

In the eyes of the jury, the credibility question came down to Beloff's word against that of the FBI, the two Philadelphia National Bank employees who testified about the D'Arbo checks, who cashed the dead man's check, and most importantly, the Mafia soldiers.

This was a calculated gamble that Beloff and his attorney, Goodman, were taking to impress the jury that his client, though far from perfect, was more truthful than his accusers. If truth became a relative, gray thing, and not something either black or white in the minds of the jurors, then Beloff felt that coming out slugging his opponents might help him win the war of words in the courtroom and obtain a possible acquittal.

REGO BACKS UP HIS BOSS

On the day following Beloff's testimony, Bobby Rego took the stand and wept softly several times as he recounted the "difficult memories" he still retained of the violent threats made by Caramandi against him and his family. He admitted that he mistakenly thought Caramandi had just wanted an introduction to Rouse so that he could get the concrete work on the Penn's Landing project.

As the final witness, he claimed he had become frightened when a tough-talking Caramandi told him on June 4, 1986, "Do you know who I am? I'm a killer...From now on, you are going to do what I'm telling you to do with this Rouse Project. If you don't, you are not going to be around. If you tell Mr. Beloff, you won't have any more kids or wife left." (Rego broke down and wept again).

Earlier in the trial, Tommy Del Giorno had taken the stand stating that Rego was on a "mob hit-list drawn up by Scarfo." Joshua Briskin, Rego's attorney, asked the mobster: "Is Mr. Rego still here?" to which Del Giorno responded curtly: "We'll see."

When this previous testimony was repeated in the courtroom, a tearful Rego took a deep breath and said haltingly: "I took that to mean I'm going to get killed."

Caramandi eventually told Rego that he had been ordered to make the hit in 1985-86. The 'Crow' sat outside Rego's home on many a night, but confessed that Scarfo had decided later against the hit.

After Rego's tearful testimony from the witness stand, one *Philadelphia Inquirer* reporter wrote: "I've seen better acting on the daytime TV soap operas."

Rego reiterated what Beloff said the day before, denying any participation in any scam or conspiracy against the three builders. He did admit that his half-brother wrote a couple of checks to Dr. Bennett, the developer, that bounced.

In explaining the $25,000 he extorted from Bennett, Rego claimed that it was done as a "favor requested by Bennett," in which Bennett asked Rego to "prepare a phony invoice" for flooring and to cash checks for less than $10,000 (which would be hard to trace), because Bennett needed the cash.

He claimed to have been with Beloff when Beloff took the check for $9,000 payable to John D'Arbo to the South Philadelphia bank to be cashed. But Rego claimed, after the checks were cashed: "The lady gave me the envelope, and I put it in my pocket and I brought it home." The cashier, Mrs. Shearer, did not remember Rego being there when she cashed the unendorsed check for the Councilman.

Rego was challenged by Assistant U.S. Attorney Thomas Lee to explain why he had prepared a phony invoice for a man he hardly knew, asking: "Is that the kind of help you give people as a legislative aide?" An angry Rego retorted: "Do you want to ask me, Mr. Lee, when I beat my wife last? He asked me to write an invoice out for him and I did."

Rego also confessed that he never reported any of Caramandi's so-called threats to himself and his family to the Philadelphia Police Department, the FBI, the DA, or to his boss, Beloff, because he "hoped that everything would work out for the best."

Although he did not sound nervous on the tapes played in court, he rationalized his outward bravado by stating: "I know how I felt deep inside."

When he was shown an enlarged photo of himself, smiling and relaxed with his arm around Caramandi standing outside the Democratic City Committee headquarters in Center City, he claimed that he was just "trying to calm" his tormentor.

When the "very volatile Caramandi kept shouting 'when, when, when?' [referring to the balance of the extortion money from Rouse]," Rego related, "I still tried to calm him down some more...When he said: 'Give me some money, I'm broke,' I took out $50 from my pocket. He took two $20 and left me $10, saying 'it was enough for you.'"

REGO AND ROUSE: WHO WAS TELLING THE TRUTH?

Rego also claimed that he asked nothing from Rouse in return for assuring passage of the two bills. But when Rouse mentioned he was in favor of an entrance and exit ramp to I-95 from the Penn's Landing project, Rego said that he met with community groups about questions of noise, traffic, safety, and pollution problems of the proposed development. "I felt the neighborhood groups' plans were cheaper and better than Mr. Rouse's plan on the ramp problem," he said.

He half-jokingly told Craig Schelter, the head of PIDC, that, "The Philadelphia Port Authority was giving Rouse the land and Maritime Museum and that Rouse was putting up zero dollars."

Rego finally agreed on behalf of Beloff to give Rouse every-thing he wanted in the deal — except the ramps. Rego also con-fessed that he met Caramandi — "a gentleman in the concrete business" one night at a local bar, early in 1986, and that he made a "passing remark about being interested in ground at the water-front."

After negotiating with Caramandi, who told Rego that Rouse was a "bigger crook than we are," Rego went to Beloff who said: "I'm not satisfied with Willard Rouse....He's a phony, I got a gut feeling that he's never going to build it [Penn's Landing]. The city gives him everything."

Rego also tried to rationalize the whole scam by telling the court that on June 3, 1986, he and Beloff believed there was a chance Rouse might just "go away from the Penn's Landing project," and that the (extortion) plan might unravel.

Two days later Balitsaris called to say that he did not want to meet with Caramandi. A somewhat frustrated Rego began to have doubts about the whole extortion scheme. "I didn't want to talk about the whole situation. It kept getting worse and worse. I didn't know what to tell the guy [Caramandi]. I wanted it [the scam] to just go away. How do you get $43 million for Willard Rouse in the bills for Penn's Landing when there is no money for schools and to fix potholes and erect street signs?"

THE JURY HEARS THE CLOSING ARGUMENTS

On April 3rd, the prosecuting attorney, Ronald Cole, on be-half of the government, portrayed Beloff and Rego as two men who had used their City Hall office to shake down three devel-opers and who willingly conspired with the mob to do so.

"You have witnessed some of the awesome and devastating results that can occur when two public officials join forces with the Mafia," he said. He told the jurors that the events were not mere coincidences, but were "orchestrated" extortion schemes.

Cole also pointed out to the jury that if "you believe in the testimony of the two defendants, then all of the government wit-nesses lied...but they had no motive to lie...why should they want to come in here and embarrass themselves?"

Rego's lawyer, Joshua Briskin, in his closing arguments, tried to undermine the credibility of Caramandi by saying sarcastically that "this Crow — a bird who is a flesh eater...was involved in four murders. Our government tells you that you don't have to believe them, but they bring them [Caramandi and Del Giorno] in here."

The rest of Briskin's summary was a repetition of his client's denials of all the charges filed against him, "We live in an era where it is fashionable to indict, arrest, and convict public figures." He proceeded to attack the testimony of FBI agent James Vaules Jr., ("Jim Vance"), describing him as a "professional witness. I'm not telling you that he's lying, but getting convictions was what he's paid to do."

A SOAP OPERA IN THE COURTROOM

Beloff's attorney, Oscar Goodman, put on a dramatic display in the final closing argument. On a large sheet of newsprint, he went over all of Caramandi's admitted crimes — from book making to drug dealing — to discredit him as a witness.

He accused the Feds of being "intellectually dishonest" in saying that Beloff had "withdrawn the bills," when in reality he "only held the Penn's Landing bills" for later action.

He made fun of the prosecution's electronic weapons, pointing to the vast array of TV monitors, videotape machines, earphones, loudspeakers and piles of tapes, saying: "Look at this courtroom! It looks like 'Star Wars'."

He assailed the government's use of two confessed gangsters as their prime witnesses against Beloff and Rego. "What the prosecution is asking you to do is to rely on speculation and conjecture, and our system of law does not permit that," he said.

Goodman stalked up to the jury box during his closing argument and demanded to know how an intelligent man like Beloff could have a thug like Caramandi shakedown an affluent developer like Willard Rouse III.

"Is he gonna send some goon?" Goodman boomed, and then stooping down in front of the jury box, mimicked the low, gravel-voiced Caramandi, with a mobster's accent: "Hey, mistuh Rouse! I wanna hundred thousand from you! I want a million from you! If you don't gimme the money...." (The audience laughed at this melodramatic act by the defense lawyer wearing the expensive hand-tooled cowboy boots.)

Then Goodman stopped, and implored the jury with a smile: "Come on!" Goodman had found a humorous and diverting way to undercut 'Nicky Crow's' testimony — which lay at the heart of the government's case.

After laughter in the courtroom subsided, Goodman implored the jury "to think about what separates us in our country from the Communists and Fascists, i.e., proof of guilt beyond a reasonable doubt. That is our system, so in the most important day in Lee Beloff's life, I ask you to return a verdict of Not Guilty on all counts."

After Goodman's tour-de-force, Prosecutor Cole's rebuttal made the point that "Caramandi and Del Giorno were our witnesses by necessity, but theirs by choice."...(referring to their induction into the mob).

THE JURY GOES INTO SECLUSION

The jury filed out of the courtroom at 2:36 PM on Friday afternoon, but after two hours, they sent a note to the Judge at 4:40 PM asking to be sent home for the weekend since they had not been able to reach a verdict.

The Judge agreed, saying: "It's apparent that it's not convenient or even possible for you to continue into the evening," letting them go, but warning them not to read or listen to news accounts of the case. The deliberations would resume at 9:30 AM on Monday.

THE JURY SPEAKS AT LONG LAST

When the tired jury came back into the courtroom with a verdict on the eleventh day of the trial at 3:15 PM on Monday, April 6th, most courtroom observers felt that they would render a guilty verdict on all counts. But they were wrong.

After deliberating for less than eight hours the jury sent a handwritten note to the Judge that they were hopelessly deadlocked on the main counts of extortion and conspiracy. "Due to diverse opinions of several jury members, we are unable to come to a unanimous decision."

They acquitted Beloff and Rego, however, of three minor counts of the fourteen charges. Many courtroom spectators gasped when the jury said it had not been able to reach a decision on the main charges, but that it did agree to acquit the duo of demanding $100,000 from Center City developer Bennett in return for helping him with union shakedown problems at his Historical Developers Inc. construction sites in Beloff's district. Furthermore, the jury also found Rego not guilty of extorting free repairs performed by Bennett in the basement of Beloff's South Philadelphia rowhouse.

After the dramatic and unexpected announcement by the jury, a spectator in the audience shouted, "Sweet Jesus! Thank you, Jesus!", while Beloff embraced his wife, Diane, and Rego wiped away tears.

The Judge then announced a mistrial at 3:20 PM and swiftly dismissed the jury. He stated there would be a second trial in the near future, and the courtroom soon emptied.*

---

* One in twenty juries in America ends up deadlocked.

We're sending out our usual priority requests for constituents. It's usually tree and pothole and caterpillar season: 'Get the trees sprayed and potholes filled and streets paved.' Usually, they're the things that come across in the summer.

-'Bobby' Rego[*]

12 THE 'CLEANSING' OF CITY COUNCIL

A PHYRRIC VICTORY PARTY

AFTER the deadlocked verdict, Beloff, Rego, their families, lawyers, and friends retired to the nearby posh DiLullo's Restaurant to celebrate.

An exhausted Beloff commented to a reporter that, "Given the history of political corruption trials in the city, I'd say I feel great. They [the government] used everything they had and couldn't get a conviction. I think it is clear that we will prevail in the second trial. I don't think there is any doubt about that . . . I'd like to do it tomorrow and get it done."

Oscar Goodman summed up the mood of the post-trial party to honor his client. Although the hung jury verdict had not been a clean sweep for acquittal, he felt that would come later at the next trial.

"It feels like a victory," the Las Vegas lawyer exulted. "Any place else in the country, I think my client [Beloff] would have a complete acquittal. I think in Philadelphia, there's a presumption that a politician has to be treated harsher than an average citizen. If it was an average citizen on trial, we'd be having a party to end all parties."

[*] Administrative Assistant to Councilman Leland Beloff, June 30, 1986, (on the day after the arrest of his boss and himself on multiple charges of extortion.)

WHY THE JURY COULD NOT REACH A CLEARCUT DECISION; THE WEAKNESSES OF THE PROSECUTION

The federal government would most probably have won a victory in the first Beloff-Rego trial had they not made two crucial mistakes: (1) not requesting a sequestered jury in some hotel to keep them from being 'tainted', and (2) keeping one juror in particular off the panel. These two errors proved fatal for the government's attempt to win a clear-cut conviction in the case.

In trying to assess the deeper impact of the hung jury in the first Beloff-Rego trial, a *Philadelphia Inquirer* reporter interviewed G. Thomas Munsterman, the director of the Center for Jury Studies for State Courts located in Arlington, Virginia. Munsterman stated: "It's not quite an acquittal, but it's damn close. Maybe the reason the jury hung is due to the fact that the evidence wasn't quite clear enough." Because of the complex evidence presented in the case and the big number of counts, Munsterman felt that the indecision of the jury could have signified a message from the jurors aimed at the prosecutors, saying: "Try it again, but this time do it right."

And that is what both the prosecutors and the judge decided to do — go for a second trial.

The hung jury's non-decision stymied a quick resolution of the government's case and would cost many more thousands of taxpayers' dollars to retry the case in federal court at a later date.

After the deadlocked jury was discussed, several jurors agreed to answer questions from the media.

Several jurors said that the failure of the prosecution to come up with a 'smoking gun' during the trial caused them to question the lack of more solid documentary evidence to buttress the testimony of the confessed killers, mobsters, and the developers like Bennett and DeVoe, who took the stand to accuse Beloff and Rego of participating in the main shakedown scheme against Rouse and Company.

One juror seemed to accept the far-fetched theory, put forth by Rego's attorney, Joshua Briskin, who accused Caramandi of cooking up the $1 million extortion plot of Rouse and Co. virtually on his own. "I think he [Caramandi] was a crook," said one woman juror afterwards. "I think the alleged Rouse plot was a set up!"

Two other jurors were unconvinced that Beloff had hand-signalled his role as a partner in the extortion plot at a meeting at Marabella's Restaurant on June 25, 1986. "To me, that signal didn't mean too much," one doubting juror said. "It was just stupid. It could have really meant anything."

Several jurors felt that the government's use of the two mobsters as their star witnesses "did the prosecution more harm than good." "You had to discount those guys," said one juror, who believed that both Beloff and Rego were guilty on some counts. "But there is no way that someone can get twelve people to believe those [Caramandi and Del Giorno] people."

The failure of Cole and Lee to use more photographic blow-ups of key evidence for emphasis, i.e., a copy of the $9,000 check written by the developer John Bennett to the dead man, John D'Arbo, and cashed by Beloff, could have helped the government's case. Furthermore, one lawyer-observer said that the original $9,000 check should have been passed to the individual jurors for examination but never was.

The inability of the two assistant federal prosecutors to counteract the defenses' denunciation of the prosecution's two star Mafia-tainted witnesses, Caramandi and Del Giorno, whom Oscar Goodman labeled as "human vermin," effectively shifted the emphasis in the closing arguments to the credibility of the two prosecution witnesses and not the credibility of Beloff and Rego.

ONE JUROR HOLDS OUT FOR ACQUITTAL

A majority of the jury had agreed on a guilty verdict on most of the nine extortion counts by late Friday afternoon, but a mistrial became impossible to avoid when one woman on the panel, Mary Anne Mongelluzzo, insisted that she would never be able to vote to convict either of the defendants.

One juror confessed: "It was more or less one person holding out for acquittal and she was extremely stubborn."

"She wasn't convinced of guilt beyond a reasonable doubt," commented another fellow juror. "It became a stalemate by Monday when we realized that to stay and fight would not have been too smart."

Another juror said that the problem with the stubborn holdout-thinking of Mongelluzzo for acquittal was that she was unable to concede that the two men MAY have been guilty. "It was more or less trying to convince her that they could be guilty. You couldn't really get her to look at the other side at all."

With so many Italian-Americans listed as witnesses, plus one defendant (Rego) and one conspirator (Scarfo), the prosecution had tried to be very careful about picking any jurors of Italian extraction. The makeup of the final twelve member jury included two suburban Italian-American residents: Joe Lembo, born in Italy, but presently living in Springfield, Delaware County, and Mary Anne Mongelluzzo, born in South Philadelphia, but now living in Upper Darby, Delaware County.

When questioned by the various defense and prosecution attorneys during the pre-trial jury selection period, Mrs. Mongelluzzo stated that she had come from South Philadelphia but had left it to move to the suburbs and that her roots would not cause any biases during the trial testimony.

When the prosecutors next asked her if she was related in any way to the late Philadelphia Traffic Court magistrate, Lewis Mongelluzzo, she answered that "she wasn't sure, but believed that he was a distant relative."

She was later apprised of the fact that her father-in-law, Joseph Mongelluzzo, was a nephew of the magistrate who had been involved in a local traffic court scandal.

MARY ANNE HAS SOME SERIOUS DOUBTS

A week after the trial was over, Mary Anne Mongelluzzo consented to a lengthy interview in which she made the following points of why she had voted for acquittal on all counts.

"I was being labeled by the press as the holdout," the strong-willed administrative secretary, who took copious shorthand notes during the trial, declared. "I'm proud of my Italian descent, and I have refused to be associated with the so-called mob."

She admitted during the selection processes to being proud of her roots in South Philadelphia, the home of many Italian-Americans in the city and where most of the residents feel a closeness as part of a large, extended family neighborhood.

She related how the jury deliberated in the case, beginning

after lunch on Friday afternoon, April 3rd 1987. The male foreman who was selected as the first person to take control of our deliberations was wishy-washy.

"I asked him when he would become more assertive to get his act together, but we never did get organized properly. I asked for a list of priorities so that we could make some decisions in the two-hour time period before we agreed to adjourn for the weekend, but we never arrived at any," she said.

"Two or three jurors said they were willing to stay into Friday evening, but the rest wanted to go home or to their local bank to cash their jury duty paychecks. Then one elderly gentleman popped up and said: 'I'm for finding them guilty on all counts, and no one will change my mind!" So, after two hours, the jury went home for the weekend without reaching any decision.

On Monday, the jury tried to unravel the complexities of the week-long trial. "There were just too many counts thrown at us by the prosecutors," she related. "They seemed to assume that the jury was stupid. They insulted our intelligence when they asked us over and over again to put on the stupid headphones and listen to the government's boring wiretap tapes. They only served to mess up our hair."

"I felt like the biggest fool on earth during that trial, which was like a Broadway play being reenacted in front of us. I did not like the way the FBI used the same tactics as the mob that they were after. I couldn't believe some of the things I heard from the two confessed murderers, Caramandi and Del Giorno. We were told that the government witnesses were telling the truth to escape long prison sentences, but I couldn't believe what they said and I started to believe I was losing my mind.

"I asked my fellow jurors: 'Do any of you know why these gentlemen [the two mobsters who confessed to numerous murders] were given immunity to prosecution?' Nobody answered my question."

Finally, she confessed that the main reason she voted for acquittal was that there "was just too much reasonable doubt in my mind about the case. I can believe in the characterizations portrayed by Mario Puzo in his *Godfather* books and movies, where his Mafia characters showed 'honor and loyalty' to the organization. But these guys [Caramandi, Del Giorno, and Scarfo] were nothing but gangsters who would stab you in the back.

They were all out for themselves and would sell out their own mother for $10."

There were several other extenuating factors which may have indirectly influenced Mary Anne's thinking that led to her holdout posture during her stint on the Beloff-Rego jury. Consider the following fact:

Her mother owned and operated a small dress shop on South 9th Street in the heart of South Philadelphia, just across the street from the residence of the late 'Frankie Flowers' D'Alfonso, who was allegedly rubbed out by Nicky Scarfo and his henchmen for being disloyal to the Mafia.

BELOFF'S CAMPAIGN FOR RE-ELECTION

During the spring primary campaign of 1987, Beloff declared that he had $103,051 in his political campaign bank account, far more than any other of the 17 council members running for re-election. This large figure showed that he had quite a bit of clout with the PACs (Political Action Committees) and developers in the high-rise Center City area who had to come to him for approval of their building projects.

Despite the first set of charges against Beloff, the political campaign money continued to flow in steadily. More than $74,000 came in to his office after the first June 27th 1986 indictment bombshell — $40,000 of which came from Beloff's wealthy mother, Jean.

One $250 check came from the largest union in the city, the Philadelphia Federation of Teachers' Committee on Public Education. The union justified its contribution with the spurious argument that since the schools were publicly funded, the union had to "establish personal relationships with the people who will be making the decision."

By early February, Beloff had received almost twice as much in campaign contributions as any of the other incumbent Council candidates or challengers seeking re-election.

Beloff boasted that "a lot of the money came in while the indictments were raining down on my head."

When it came time to endorse incumbent Councilmen in the 1987 spring primary, Beloff's colleagues on Council unanimously backed him for re-election. The endorsers included two former state officials who had themselves been convicted on political corruption charges, another who had been indicted twice and never convicted, and a fourth, ex-councilman Jimmy Tayoun, who was running against Beloff for his seat on the Council. (Tayoun chose to support the convicted Beloff instead of himself, because he only had one ward leader's vote out of 10 — his own.)

Tayoun was disappointed, since he had anointed Beloff as his 'peace candidate' successor three years before when he had resigned his Council seat to run unsuccessfully for Congress. When it came time for the ward leaders in the first district to endorse a party candidate, three went for the former Congressman and ex-City Democrat Party Chairman, Joe Smith, and one for Tayoun. The other six votes were a clear majority for Beloff.

A week before the Primary, a still confident and optimistic Rego felt his boss could obtain the support of a majority of the Democratic voters in his re-election bid.

In a personal interview, Rego said confidently, "If you throw out the fiction of the recent trial of Lee and myself, don't you agree that we have done a better job as Councilman than either of our two opponents, Jim Tayoun or Joe Smith? That's why we are going to win the Primary and the General Election in the Fall."

But Rego was overly optimistic.

BELOFF IS BURIED UNDER A VOTERS' LANDSLIDE

Beloff became the chief issue in the three-way race and even though his second trial had not started, the voters had been educated before they went to the polls about what sort of legislator they had to misrepresent them in City Hall. They had been embarrassed long enough.

Early in the campaign, Beloff had met with Tayoun and former felon, ex-State Senator, Henry 'Buddy' Cianfrani, to engineer a deal whereby Tayoun would agree to get out of the race and support Beloff for re-election if Beloff were not convicted. If Beloff was convicted before the Primary, then he would fulfill a promise to leave the race and support Tayoun. But the backroom deal unravelled when Beloff failed to be exonerated before the election.

When the votes were tallied in the First District after the

spring primary on May 19th, it revealed what the people thought about Beloff. His former colleague and nemesis, Jim Tayoun, slaughtered him by 3-1 (15,600 to 5,100 votes) and even former City Chairman Joe Smith, a weak campaigner, finished second with 9,700 votes, a 2-1 plurality, over Beloff — leaving the incumbent bringing up a distant and ignominious third place.

When the votes were tallied after the General Election in November, Tayoun won by the narrowest margin of any city candidate — 259 votes. His opponent, Connie McHugh, an ex-Democrat turned Republican, almost upset the veteran ex-Councilman. She was aided immensely by none other than Lee Beloff who helped to carry his half of the largest ward in the city, the 39th, for her and against his old comrade-in-arms, Jimmy Tayoun, by quietly 'passing the word' to 'cut' his fellow Democrat.

THE SHADOW OVER COUNCILMAN BELOFF

In the outer office of the Philadelphia First District Councilman, located to the City Council's ornate gilded chambers, a visitor's eye immediately focuses on a huge, almost life-sized oil painting of the Councilman's distinguished father, the late Common Pleas Judge Emanuel Beloff. Try as he might, Leland was never able to live up to the image of his father.

As one fellow South Philadelphian put it: "Part of his [Leland's] problem goes back to a personal problem he's had for a long, long time. Throughout his life he's tried to live in his father's footsteps. He idolized his father and always has, and I think Leland wanted to be another Judge Beloff, who had an excellent reputation in the community. But I think that out of his desire to be like his father, he's tried too hard and he's lost what that means — he thinks being like his father means being a *Tough Macho Politician*. That's a very immature image of what his father was like, but I think that emotionally and intellectually, Leland never got past that point . . . I think Leland's image of his father got warped somewhere along the line."

...Here, because you are of a certain religion or nationality or race or associate with a certain group...that is not enough to convict you. This, ladies and gentlemen, is the Italian Inquisition!

-Robert 'Bobby' Simone[*]

13

'LIL NICKY' IN THE HALLS OF JUSTICE: THE U.S. vs. NICODEMO SCARFO

IT was now the Mafia boss's turn to face his accusers in the million-dollar Penn's Landing scam. The government was now ready with Grand Jury indictments to bring him into court. They had some choice witnesses who volunteered information to help send Nicky Scarfo to prison for a long time.

TOMMY DEL GIORNO SWITCHES SIDES

During the summers of 1985 and 1986, while Tom Del Giorno was relaxing in his Ocean City, New Jersey, condominium, the mobster let down his hair about life in the Mafia. Unknown to him, two New Jersey police detectives were listening to his remarks in his bugged, beach-front pad.

Del Giorno's characterization of his associates, including Scarfo, was classic. "They're all pussies," he said. "Four Irish guys from Northeast Philly could run the Philadelphia-South Jersey mob better."

After his arrest for racketeering, extortion, and loansharking, Del Giorno was allowed to listen to some of the 800 tapes that

---

[*] Scarfo's defense attorney in his opening statement to the trial jury, April 28, 1987.

had been recorded by the New Jersey State Police. What he heard convinced him that he could be better served by accepting a deal offered by the authorities.

By defecting soon after his indictment on October 31, 1986, Del Giorno "convinced us [about] what we already knew but couldn't prove in some cases [about the Mafia]," said one crime investigator. "He filled in holes in our information by his defection and confessions."

His finger-pointing at the conspirators in the Mafia murders, drug rackets and the Rouse scam not only backed up Caramandi's earlier confessions but helped to lead to indictments of his former colleagues in crime. The most important of these was his former boss, Nicodemo Scarfo.

'Lil Nicky' Haunted by the Ghost of 'Chickenman's' Son

On April 10, 1987, Scarfo and six Mafia associates were arraigned on federal charges for murdering Salvatore Testa, 28, the son of the late head of the Philadelphia mob, Philip 'Chickenman' Testa, on September 14, 1984.

The seven were ordered to jail without bail. Scarfo was already there. The charges were the most sweeping ever made against top crime figures in the area and marked a new thrust by the federal government to put the local Mafia out of business for good.

The US Attorney Edward Dennis called it a "historic occasion!"

The day before, Scarfo and Nicholas 'Nick the Blade' Virgilio had been charged in a New Jersey indictment with the murder of former Somers Point Municipal Judge Edwin H. Helfant in February, 1978. The indictment also accused Scarfo and Virgilio of being part of a racketeering conspiracy that resulted in eight other organized crime killings and two murder attempts.

Within hours of the Testa indictments in Philadelphia, the six remaining men were rounded up, arrested and held in jail based largely on statements made by the former Mafia captain, Thomas Del Giorno. He confessed to participating in these crimes before becoming a government witness.

One more associate, 'Charley White' Iannece 52, who was the father of one of the seven indicted mobsters (Vincent), was also charged in Testa's slaying, but had gone into hiding in January when he was indicted in the Rouse scam.

He was still in hiding and the Feds had no idea where he was or when he would surface.

SCARFO STAYS IN JAIL

In denying Scarfo bail before his trial from the time of his arrest in January, the government contended that he was a dangerous man who should not be allowed to walk the streets. Prosecutor Ronald Cole insisted that the mob chief should remain in jail since he allegedly had ordered, approved or participated in fourteen murders or attempted murders dating back to 1978.

Furthermore, Cole asserted that Scarfo had no legitimate source of income "even though he had purchased a home in Florida worth at least $400,000 and a large boat."

The Judge agreed to keep Scarfo in jail.

THE FEUD BETWEEN THE US ATTORNEY AND THE DA OVER PROSECUTING SCARFO

Ever since the days in the 1930s, when the New York City District Attorney Thomas E. Dewey rode his successful prosecution of the late Charles 'Lucky' Luciano to the governorship of New York, dozens of subsequent big city DAs have tried the same avenue to political fame.

In Philadelphia, the new Republican DA, Ronald Castille, asked U.S. Attorney General Edwin Meese III, in April, 1987, to force the U.S. Attorney Edward Dennis Jr. to cooperate with the city's law enforcement officials to immediately prosecute Nicky Scarfo and his associates in connection with a series of Mafia murders. Relations between them deteriorated to the point that Castille sent a letter to the Attorney General stating that Dennis had blocked his attempts to begin the arrests.

A month before, Dennis had quietly informed Castille that it was clearly impossible for the two offices to continue cooperating in the investigation of Scarfo and his associates since there were so many disagreements over what charges should be brought and when.

Dennis tried to reach an agreement with Castille that the latter would only prosecute two or three cases, i.e., the September, 1984, slaying of Salvatore Testa, and the July, 1985, slaying of Frank 'Frankie Flowers' D'Alfonso, with the Feds developing the remaining cases into one major racketeering case. He felt that if Castille moved too soon, it would prejudice the extortion case against Beloff, Rego, and Scarfo.

Castille wrote Attorney General Meese saying that Dennis had threatened to sever all relationships with his office, a threat which the DA contended was "not in the best interests of law enforcement."

Meese, who at the time was up to his neck in the Irangate controversy, chose not to fan the flames of the local feud between two Republican appointees. He opted for the Dennis go-slow policy.

THE FEDS CHANGE THEIR TACTICS

After its disappointment over the outcome of the trial against the two Philadelphia politicians, the prosecution team set out to revamp the way the case was presented and to figure a way to make its star witnesses Caramandi and Del Giorno more convincing to the next juries — in both the retrial of Beloff and Rego, as well as the upcoming trial of Nicky Scarfo.

So, Dennis picked a new prosecutor to present the bulk of the government's case against the head of the Mafia: himself — Philadelphia's first Black US Attorney.

"I had forgotten what it felt like to be in the fish bowl," he reminisced later. (He hadn't tried a case in over four years and felt a bit rusty.)

The Scarfo trial would once again prove a crucial test of the credibility of the two mobsters-turned-federal-informants, Nicholas Caramandi and Thomas Del Giorno. They had failed to convince all of the jury of their truthfulness in the prior Beloff-Rego trial, but would be given a second chance to testify against their old boss and to implicate him in the extortion scam in front of a new jury.

Unlike the jury of the Beloff-Rego trial, the Scarfo panel would be sequestered in a hotel room for the duration of the trial and their names would be kept secret. The hoped-for conviction would be very important to the government to overcome the negative after-effects of the dead locked jury in the prior Rouse extortion trial.

THE TRIAL BEGINS . . . A JURY IS PICKED

The show trial of Nicodemo Scarfo began on April 29, 1987, in the same courtroom, high up on the 15th floor of the Federal Courthouse, where Beloff and Rego had been tried a month earlier. It took place before the same judge, Chief District Court Judge Fullam. The dapper, diminutive Scarfo was ushered into the courtroom daily in handcuffs, which were removed by security guards before he sat down at the defense table next to his lawyer, 'Bobby' Simone.

Scarfo even hired an outside sociologist, James Burgund, from Massachusetts, to help his defense team in the jury selection — hoping to choose jurors who "were independent, flexible people" who might have the fortitude to acquit Scarfo.

THE JUDGE TAKES EXTRA SECURITY PRECAUTIONS

The identities of the twelve selected and sequestered jurors of nine women and three men would be kept secret by orders of the judge so that they would not be subjected to any outside influences during the case. This change of procedure was initiated because of the unfortunate aftermath of the hung jury in the first Beloff-Rego trial.

This decision by Judge Fullam to keep the jurors' names anonymous marked the first time in modern Philadelphia federal district court history that such a step had been taken. There was a precedent for this procedure — the recent trial of the reputed New York organized crime boss, John Gotti.

Judge Fullam assured the jury of the virtues of not giving out their names to the public.

"In my twenty-seven years as a Judge, I've never heard of a case where a defense tried to hurt a juror's family, but we've seen the *Godfather* movies...and know about that possibility. I assure you, your anonymity protects you, and from the defense's standpoint, he [Scarfo] does not want to be put in a position where a 'scurrilous' person on the jury is out to 'get him.'"

THE U.S. ATTORNEY SPEAKS TO THE JURY

When Edward Dennis took over center stage in his opening address, he acknowledged that the government's case relied strongly on the testimony of Caramandi and Del Giorno, but said they both should be believed because they began cooperating with the government for a very good reason: they feared for their own lives.

He contended that Caramandi's testimony implicating Scarfo in the extortion scheme would be corroborated by the tapes made by contractor John Pastorella after he went undercover for the FBI. Dennis contended that these 150 tapes would help contradict what was expected to be Scarfo's chief line of defense — that Caramandi planned and tried to carry out the $1 million extortion scheme with Beloff and Rego on his own.

"The Pastorella tapes," said Dennis, "showed that he's part of a larger [mob] organization . . . that there is more to Nicholas Caramandi than just a flim-flam artist."

Dennis outlined the sequence of events leading up to the shakedown of Rouse and Company for $1 million, highlighting significant excerpts of the dialogue on the tapes linking Scarfo to the scam.

He confessed that the information on the Pastorella tapes was not good enough to bring Scarfo to trial. But after the October 1986 indictments of Beloff, Rego, and Caramandi, a gold mine of new facts became available when Caramandi turned federal witness.

"The central issue in this case," said Dennis in the windup of his opening, "is Nicholas Caramandi's credibility. His testimony based on his twenty-five years of a life of crime...makes this case not just one of Caramandi vs. Scarfo."

The question of 'Nicky Crow's' credibility would permeate the next week of trial testimony and the cross-examinations of various witnesses.

'BOBBY' SIMONE TAKES OVER THE DEFENSE OF SCARFO

'Bobby' Simone, 53, has long been known as a mob lawyer. In the trial of Beloff and Rego his name surfaced time and again as one who would eventually get ten percent of mob proceeds in the plot to extort $1 million from Mr. Rouse. Because he was an unindicted co-conspirator in the case, he had to withdraw as Beloff's lawyer, but he had no qualms about being the defense attorney for Scarfo.*

The government prosecutors argued unsuccessfully in March that Simone not be allowed to represent Scarfo. Simone, with his premature gray hair and boyish smile, admitted that Del Giorno was "mad at me," for declining to represent Caramandi after his arrest in June, 1986, because he had already agreed to represent Beloff in the same case.

Simone had successfully skirted any indictments against himself in the series of mob-related cases, although the government continued to offer "no comment" answers to queries about possible future indictments of him.

North Philadelphia born, Simone, a fellow Italian-American, had been Nicky Scarfo's lawyer for years and had never failed to point out in court representations for his client that there is "a conspiracy against Italian-Americans by the judicial system." When asked why he was willing to represent a man [Scarfo] with such an unsavory reputation, he explained that as a criminal lawyer, it is his job to represent and defend people who get into trouble.

Simone, had also defended 'Crazy Phil' Leonetti when he got into scrapes with the law, and even defended Caramandi in a counterfeit case earlier.

'BOBBY' THROWS DOWN THE GAUNTLET

In his opening remarks to the jury, defense attorney Simone assailed the federal trial of his client by bringing in both religion and ethnicity to show the court's bias in the case.

"Here, because you are of a certain religion or nationality or race or associate with a certain group...that is not enough to convict you. This, ladies and gentlemen, is the Italian Inquisition."

These words, coming from an Italian-American lawyer about an Italian-American client, were obviously made to arouse sympathy from the jury against the overriding power of Big Brother — the U.S. government.

---

* Both Caramandi and Del Giorno had characterized Simone as a courier to and from Scarfo about the alleged plot.

He warned the jury: "If you pay attention, as I know you will, if you do your sworn duty, and I know you will, there won't be any doubt that Mr. Scarfo is not guilty of the charges in this indictment."

"The real question," Simone said, "is are you people going to be independent enough to judge this case the way it's supposed to be judged: fairly and squarely?"

Simone pointed out to the jury that in the tapes and videos the government would present as circumstantial evidence "you will not hear Nicodemo Scarfo say anything that incriminates him in this case."

THE GOVERNMENT PRESENTS ITS CASE AGAINST THE MOB CHIEFTAIN

There was already one significant difference between the two trials, even though the Scarfo trial had yet to hear its first witnesses. In the Beloff trial, it was the word of the Mafia vs. a City Councilman and his assistant. In the Scarfo trial, it would be the Mafia vs. the Mafia.

The prosecutors also used a number of new and different trial tactics which were not used in the Beloff-Rego trial. For example, they showed a previously unused videotape showing Beloff and Rego entering La Cucina Restaurant in Center City on December 19, 1985, on the same afternoon that Scarfo threw a private Christmas party there.*

Among other innovations at this trial were several enlarged (12" x 18") color photos of a gathering of the extended Scarfo crime family, which the government showed to the jury. It depicted a happy crew of fifteen mobsters and some of their children, in August, 1986, on a beach in front of Scarfo's swanky winter home, Casablanca South in Ft. Lauderdale, Florida, located next to a Hilton Hotel. This picture proved Caramandi's authenticity and credibility as a spokesman for the inner workings of the mob.

Instead of playing all of the fifteen-minute-long, silent videotape of Scarfo and three of his Mafia henchmen on the boardwalk

---

* Dennis felt the tape was an important piece of evidence, since it provided additional proof of the closeness of Beloff and Rego to the mob boss.

in Atlantic City during the early afternoon of June 16, 1986, the government only played one minute of the meeting this time to prevent an overkill of boredom on the judge, jury and courtroom observers.

Since the Beloff-Rego case, Dennis had implemented some of the suggestions aimed at improving the prosecution's case, like getting a photo enlargement of the $9,000 check written to the dead man, D'Arbo.

THE WITNESSES FOR THE PROSECUTION

Pastorella, Rouse, Balitsaris, Vaules, Gatto, Schelter and others again took the stand to repeat their testimony offered at the first Beloff-Rego trial on the background facts leading up to the Penn's Landing scam.

But the key prosecution witnesses were yet to come.

FBI agent, Jim Vaules, alias 'Jim Vance' added a note of black humor to his testimony in addition to what he had said when he testified at the earlier Beloff-Rego trial. In describing his confrontation with Caramandi in the lobby of the Hershey Hotel, in June, 1986, where the suspicious mobster set a house-plant on fire by burning the note of the Mafia demands to Rouse, Vance said, "Please don't be a firebug," when 'the Crow' set a second note on fire while the hotel people were putting out the first smouldering fire.

After Vance's 'fire prevention warning,' a nervous Caramandi deliberately set a third note on fire to remove any trace of his written demand for $1 million.

On one of the tapes recorded by John Pastorella, 'Nicky Crow' tells his partner in crime that: "We [Scarfo and I] go back a long time. I would not go through it [the Rouse extortion plot] again. They [the Mafia] are paranoid. They try to put you in traps. I'm worse off now since I've lost my hustle of the streets."

He had been caught in a double trap — one run by Scarfo with Beloff and Rego's help as messengers and co-conspirators, and the other by the long arm of the Federal government, which already had wind of the developing scam. Dennis told the jury that Caramandi was both "cannon fodder for the [Scarfo extortion] deal" and "insulation for Beloff and Rego, and not the other way around."

On another tape Joe Esposito, a New Jersey businessman operating on the fringes of the mob, was asked by the 'Crow' if he knew Willard Rouse.

"Yeah," said Esposito. "I've known him for twenty years. He's the biggest crook I've ever seen." This information had convinced the 'Crow' that Rouse could be taken to the cleaners.

Agent Vaules testified that Caramandi asked him if he knew who he represented. Vaules replied: "I assume — the man in Atlantic City...I understood it was Nicky Scarfo." Caramandi nodded in assent to this guess.

Midway in the proceedings a trial-watcher offered an opinion of the testimony. This courtroom observer opined confidently: "Nicky Scarfo's gonna walk. They got nothin' on him. He's too slick. If the government don't put their best foot forward they ain't gonna catch nobody. Those tape replays are boring, just a rehash of the Beloff trial — that's all."

CARAMANDI MAKES A COMEBACK IN HIGH FASHION

When Caramandi reappeared as a star government witness in the middle of the Scarfo trial on April 30th to incriminate his former employer, he was sporting a newly permed hair style, dark sunglasses, a yellow sports coat, a white shirt, and brown print tie. The dramatic difference, obviously masterminded by the Federal prosecutors, was to present a new non-mobster-type image to counteract the one which had hurt the government's case against Beloff and Rego a month earlier, where he wore a tough-looking black turtle neck and suede sports jacket.

'Nicky Crow's' new look marked one of several changes made by the government to show more respect to the Judge and jury.

As Nicholas Caramandi was ushered onto the witness stand he came face-to-face with an impassive Nicky Scarfo. He told the jury that he began to cooperate with the law enforcement authorities for one reason.

"I knew I was going to get killed," he said in his gravelly voice. This was his excuse and rationalization for breaking the Mafia's Code of Silence.

He also reconfirmed the bottom line of the Rouse scam, when he reiterated his earlier testimony that he let Peter Balitsaris,

Rouse's V.P., know that a million dollars was the price to get the two enabling bills for the Penn's Landing development through the Council.

"The door will be open for a million dollars," he told Balitsaris on a tape, "and ya know, I don't want it all at once."

TIMES CHANGE

To show his reverence for the head of the mob, 'the Crow,' a devoted Mafia soldier, presented a pre-Christmas gift to his boss on December 2, 1985. It was a poster-size blownup photo of the late, heavy weight boxer, 'Rocky' Marciano knocking out 'Jersey Joe' Walcott in the 13th round of their title fight. Caramandi told the jury he was proud of the fact that Nicky Scarfo chose to hang this photo of the Italian-American boxer beating the former champ on the wall of his outer office at Scarf, Inc. in Atlantic City.

Caramandi later told the jury that while he was in prison for the Rouse scam, a fellow prisoner informed him that the word was out that Scarfo and 'Bobby' Simone were going with Beloff and then used a hand signal to convey a message that he (Nicky Crow) was going to be shot to death.

Caramandi described Scarfo as a cold-blooded murderer who "kills for nothing. This guy's a killer," he said, facing his former boss and looking him in the eye from his seat on the witness stand. "He loves to kill! He *loves* to kill!"

Caramandi made this accusation after he received a 'message' from a friend that his two little girls were going to be killed. Then, glaring angrily at Scarfo sitting hunched over in his chair, the 'Crow' growled: "He's gotta remember that he's got kids too!"

A hush fell over the courtroom after this outburst. Scarfo blinked and rubbed his fingers together.

In the three hours on the witness stand, Caramandi described the role of Scarfo in approving the extortion of Rouse and making the decision about how the $1 million was to be divided. He even said that Bobby Simone was to get ten percent of the take from Rouse.

When asked by Dennis how he first learned of Rouse's grandiose waterfront project, Caramandi replied: "From two associates of mine, Leland Beloff and Bobby Rego." He told the jury that he first discussed the proposed scam with Scarfo during a social gathering of the mobsters in a Center City restaurant in the Spring of 1985 and again on the boardwalk in Atlantic City in June, 1986 (which was videotaped).

Caramandi also implicated Scarfo in two slayings. He told the jury that Scarfo ordered the 1984 killing of mob figure Salvatore Testa and that he himself had helped dispose of the body.

The 'Crow' also contended that Scarfo ordered the killing of Salvatore 'Chuckie' Merlino, a former mob underboss in 1986. "He thought there was a treason attempt that Chuckie might have wanted to overthrow Scarfo," he said. "He didn't like Chuckie's conduct and eventually took his position away. Scarfo demoted him to a soldier and in this business that is a disgrace."

'TOMMY DEL' BACKS UP 'THE CROW'

When Tom Del Giorno took the stand, he corroborated Caramandi's testimony. Del Giorno was — and still is — the highest ranking member of the Philadelphia-South Jersey organized crime family to agree to cooperate with the government in helping to bring his former family members to justice. As a top insider, he broke the sacred code of silence in November, 1986, after his life was threatened, disregarding the Mafia law of *Omerta*, that states: a 'made' mob member would rather die than betray his crime family.

Since agreeing to cooperate, he, his wife and two children have been under the protective custody of the New Jersey State Police and the FBI. He gives a rare inside view of the workings of the mob and the bloody internal turmoil that pervaded the Mafia following the murder of Angelo Bruno in March, 1980.

Del Giorno admitted on cross-examination that he "robbed P2P from others, but never sold any drugs. I did flim-flams with Nicky Caramandi, but I never categorized myself as a shake down artist."

In response to a question to test his credibility, he further said: "Do you recall beating your wife with an ironing board?"

He answered, "No, I threw a plastic flower pot at her and I told her I had a gun for her former boyfriend. And my four-year-old son told the TV repairman that my father would shoot him if he did not come and fix the TV set."

He also confessed to owning two machine guns.

A Surprise Courtroom Appearance by Lee and Bobby

On Monday, May 4th, at 12:15 PM, both Councilman Beloff and his aide, Bobby Rego, were subpoenaed on short notice by Simone to testify for the defense. Their attorney had recommended that they take the Fifth Amendment — since their criminal case was still pending.

Beloff, who should have been serving his constituents in City Hall, came into court wearing blue jeans, white sneakers, and a gray windbreaker. He had presumably been out jogging somewhere. He apologized to the court for the way he was dressed, since he had not expected to be there.

He then said that "I will not testify under the Fifth Amendment rights." He was excused. When his sidekick, Rego, took the stand — wearing dark blue sweatpants with white stripes, a blue sweatshirt and a tan rain jacket, he spoke one sentence: "On the advice of counsel, I was told not to testify."

When Judge Fullam asked him: "Is that because your testimony might incriminate you?" he replied sheepishly, "I don't know, your honor."

Scarfo Opts Out as a Witness

Unlike the Beloff trial, where both Beloff and Rego took the stand, Scarfo did not take the stand in his own defense but relied on his defense attorneys' attempts to discredit the government's case and the testimony of its star witnesses — Caramandi and Del Giorno. This time the two mobsters were better prepared and stood their ground during the vicious cross-examination.

The Prosecutor Closes His Case

Dennis dramatically opened his trial summation for the jury repeating the Mafia oath: "May I burn like the saints in hell if I betray my friends." He then outlined the Crow's life of crime, beginning as a ninth grade dropout from a South Philadelphia school, and then playing on people's greed to accomplish his various flim-flams. Dennis tried to impress the jury that Caramandi was a credible witness and had not lied.

Prosecutor Dennis defended the government's case of the

extortion conspiracy between Beloff, Rego and Scarfo to milk $1 million from Willard Rouse III.

He pointed out that Scarfo not only sanctioned the extortion scheme but had supplied the various formulas through which the proceeds were to be divided.

In the windup of his hour and a half long summation, Dennis portrayed Scarfo as a "shrewd, dangerous criminal who keeps his soldiers in mortal fear. These are violent and greedy men who would stop at nothing, living on dirty bucks that maintain them in their limousines, their homes in Florida, and their perpetual suntans. He rules his empire with an iron fist."

With his voice rising to a crescendo, Dennis implored the jury to, "take the cover off this bag of spiders. The evidence compels it! Justice demands it!"

When Miles Feinstein followed with the defense summation he picked up the 'spider web' analogy offered by Dennis and said poetically: "Oh what a web we weave — when we first begin to deceive."

He used this line to point out how Caramandi and Del Giorno contradicted each other with inconsistencies in their testimonies, to imply that they alone were the spiders and not his client, Scarfo. But he got bogged down in a repetitive, boring denunciation of the two mobsters that appeared to put the jury to sleep.

Then it was 'Bobby' Simone's turn to try to persuade the jury to his cause.

THE DEFENSE RESTS

In his brief rebuttal, Simone asked rhetorically: "Why are they [the government] picking on 'Nicky' Scarfo and the Italians? It is obvious. The government is a bunch of sheepherders using electronic gadgets to put on their staff to herd their sheep. You the jury must decide this case based on the government's theory in this case, i.e., 'The end justifies the means to get Mr. Scarfo off the street.' Your job is not to clean up the mob, as the government contends, but to decide the guilt or innocence of one man.

"When we convict people based on guilt by association [as he flashed the color photo of the Crow, Scarfo and others at Casablanca South in Florida], we are taking the first step away from democracy. What is the next step? They lack a frame and this whole case is a frameup....The case boils down to one thing: *'Do you have the guts to do the right thing despite all the pressures and prejudices that have crept into this case?'"*

Simone cited as analogy the government's clampdown treatment of Blacks in the 1960's and of the anti-war protestors in the 1970's and then made an apparent reference to the nationwide crackdown of the mob, saying: "Now we come to the '80s. So, I don't think I have to explain to you why they are picking on Mr. Scarfo. I think it is obvious!"

Miles Feinstein, the co-defense counsel, followed Simone and pounded away at the credibility of Caramandi contending that he had admitted lying on numerous occasions.

"To corroborate Caramandi as a murderer, drug dealer, conman, extortionist, liar, perjurer and plea bargainer," he said sarcastically, "the prosecution offered you Del Giorno, a murderer, dealer, con-man, extortionist, liar, perjurer and plea bargainer.

"What you have here are two men trying to save their skins from the death penalty and other charges. They knew a way out and that way out was to involve Nicky Scarfo. Both men would do anything to stay out of jail," he said.

And again picking up Dennis' portrayal of Scarfo as a 'spider', Feinstein said of the two key government witnesses: "The real web [is that of] Caramandi and Del Giorno and their lies."

When Simone and Feinstein completed their closing remarks to the jury, Dennis had one last turn.

Dennis rejected Simone's suggestion that the government was wrongfully prosecuting Scarfo when he made a short rebuttal to the jury, stating: "I don't want the Lee Beloffs or the Robert Regos or the Nicky Scarfos telling me what good government is."

THE VERDICT AND ITS AFTERMATH

When the jury returned after six hours of deliberations, Scarfo sat stoically as he was told by the foreman that he had been found guilty on both counts of conspiracy and extortion. For these crimes, he faced up to a maximum of forty years in prison, but more importantly, it meant "the beginning of the end" of his bloody six-year reign over the area Mafia, according to U.S. Attorney Dennis.

The verdict meant that the jury believed the stories of both Caramandi and Del Giorno — beyond a shadow of a doubt. They were the only two witnesses to implicate Scarfo directly in the $1 million extortion scheme.

Dennis said that "there was a lot riding on the outcome of the trial since it was now going to put a lot of pressure to cooperate on many people who may have thought that Del Giorno and Caramandi would not be believed."*

Dennis pointed out that the "key was really Nicky Caramandi. I had to get to know him, let him talk a lot, let him reminisce a lot, take him back to his old neighborhood, so the jury could understand him. I wanted him to tell his story in his own words and not feel inhibited." His tale, told during eleven hours in the witness box, paid off for the government.

An acquittal of Scarfo would not have boded well for Dennis or the government in its preparations for the second Beloff-Rego trial and other Scarfo trials slated down the road. It marked a high-risk gamble on Dennis' part, going back into the courtroom after years of masterminding government prosecutions from his office and allowing his assistants to handle the court proceedings. A 'not guilty' verdict could have dealt a crushing blow to the government's frontal attack on the Mafia.

"It was a gutsy move on his part," observed a criminal defense lawyer. "Dennis took a risk and it paid off. If he'd lost, it could have put the government in a desperate position . . . It certainly would have raised serious doubts if he could get any conviction with these witnesses. Today, they [the Feds] must be in Fat City."

At the conclusion of the Scarfo trial, Dennis — who had just won the most important case of his career announced that the same prosecution team that won this case, including Assistant U.S. Attorney Lee, and FBI agents Michael Leyden and Robert Brown who had assisted him in preparation, would be kept together to conduct the Beloff-Rego retrial within a month.

'SCARFACE AL' SURVEYS THE ASHES

In the offices of Scarf, Inc. in Atlantic City, one of Nicky Scarfo's most prized possessions hangs on the wall. It is a por-

---

* He was alluding to other mobsters still awaiting trial or facing indictments. He also pushed to have the jurors' names and addresses kept secret so they would not fear retribution.

trait of the late Al Capone, the ruthless gangster who ruled Chicago during the 1920's Prohibition era. Capone was his patron saint and under his watchful eye, many Scarfo plots were hatched.

With Scarfo in jail for a long time to come, chances were good that few new underworld projects would be planned there in the near future. Even before his next criminal trials were held, Scarfo appeared to be doomed as an active Mafia Don.

But the legacy of Capone failed to help Scarfo in the clutch. He was a semi-tragic figure, who when he was ushered into court on the last day of his trial, quickly looked over the rows of packed observer seats and commented to his U.S. Marshal-guard: "Well, it looks like they're all here."

In the 1987 film, *Wall Street*, Michael Douglas, the villainous inside-trading stockbroker who thrived on buying and selling companies based on information supplied to him from within the secret walls of corporations ripe for takeover, tells the board of directors of one such company that: "I create nothing. I own!" He then counsels a young stockbroker with this admonition: "Money never sleeps, pal!"

This callous attitude reflects the operational life-style of Nicky Scarfo in his years as head of the Mafia. He made his money in the underworld by creating nothing, but owning a large share of the 'elbow' (extortion money) that trickled up to him as a payoff for giving his consent to various scams, loansharking and murders.

On October 17, 1988, the U.S. Supreme Court turned down Scarfo's appeal of May 6, 1987, to overturn his conviction in the one million dollar extortion case, without a word of comment.

This decision backed up the earlier rejection of his appeal in June, 1988, by the Third U.S. Circuit Court of Appeals, which had rejected the arguments of Scarfo's attorney, Robert Simone, that Judge Fullam had prejudiced Scarfo's rights by impaneling an anonymous jury and letting prosecutors use evidence of Scarfo's alleged role in mob killings. This decision also meant that he would have to serve at least seven years, or half of his 14-year sentence. But 'Nicky' Scarfo could not envision an early parole, since there were more and bigger trials slated for him in the near future.

...Turn away from mischief before sorrow befalls you again and again. Beware the dangers of folly and mischief, since mischief is blown back in the face of the fool. Nowhere can the fool hide from mischief forever.

-from the Hindu DHAMAPADA, 500 B.C.

14 THE SECOND TIME AROUND FOR BELOFF AND REGO

THE SPARRING BEFORE ROUND TWO

IT was agreed by both sides and the Judge in the retrial of Beloff and Rego to sequester the jury to keep them from being influenced at night by local newspaper, radio and TV coverage.

At the request of Beloff's attorney, the retrial was postponed by Judge Fullam from April 27 until after the Primary election, so as not to interfere with Beloff's chances of winning the spring primary nomination for the District One Council seat, and because his attorney was tied up in a Las Vegas trial that was expected to last a month.

On June 17th, the attorneys for Beloff and Rego once again asked the Judge to postpone the second trial, citing newspaper accounts reporting that Rego had been linked to a drug operation. "The latest onslaught of prejudicial publicity," said Rego's defense attorney, Joshua Briskin, "is so devastating, that the defendants can't receive a trial from a fair and impartial jury."[*]

---

[*] Court sources had leaked a story to the press on June 16th that Rego was "a significant member of a large drug operation to manufacture and distribute huge quantities of methamphetamine during the early 1980's, including the procurement of P2P." In an affidavit filed in Federal court in December, 1986, a government informant stated that an agent of the Drug Enforcement Administration had reported that a "clandestine methamphetamine laboratory" had been in operation at 116 North Second Street from 1982 until late in 1985. This building housed 10 companies owned and operated by Rego.

The Judge refused to grant another delay in the scheduled second trial. In Round Two of the struggle between the USA vs. BELOFF AND REGO, neither the prosecution, Edward Dennis and Thomas Lee, or the defense, Joshua Briskin for Rego and Oscar Goodman for Beloff, divulged details of their new strategies and tactics or hinted at any courtroom surprises.

ROUND TWO BEGINS

On Monday, June 23, 1987, the opening day of the retrial, after the jury selection of seven men and five women had been made, Oscar Goodman made his first play. He contended that the Councilman could not have flashed a hand signal to Caramandi signifying that he was in on the $1,000,000 extortion scam "because he was not wearing glasses."

"It would be impossible for Leland Beloff to see that far across the bar without his glasses on," said Goodman in his opening statement to the jury. He stated that Beloff's eye doctor would be called as a new witness to back up this assertion. The defense attorney contended that the fateful meeting in the bar of the Marabella Restaurant on June 25, 1986 had been orchestrated by Caramandi.

"All of this is a feigned situation in order to make the story fit," said Goodman to the jury, imploring them to listen very closely to the testimonies of Agent Vaules and Caramandi when they took the stand. Goodman tried to impress the jury with the fact that his client was a wealthy man, a dedicated public servant and had no need to extort money since he received $6,000 each week from the profits of the nursing homes that his mother, Jean, was operating on behalf of the family.

"So, why should he be interested in extorting $1 million?" the bearded, cowboy booted, Goodman asked. "He had more than enough money to keep him happy."

"The evidence is going to show that Beloff...had an annual income of about $250,000 as a result of family investments and...he wasn't about to jeopardize his office for $945 a month rent.[*] He admitted that Beloff knew Scarfo but that there was no evidence "of one bit of illegal conduct between Mr. Beloff and

---

[*] Referring to the Scullin Apartment.

Mr. Scarfo — except out of the mouths of Mr. Caramandi and Mr. Del Giorno."

In the prosecution's opening statement, Thomas Lee, told the jury that the government would prove beyond a shadow of a doubt that both Beloff and Rego had indeed participated in a series of extortion schemes in return for Beloff's support of bills that the developers needed to operate.

One by one the witnesses who testified at the first trial retold their stories to the jury, including FBI agent, James Vaules, Jr. Vaules testified that Beloff twice flashed his O.K. hand signal to him in Marabella's Restaurant "with his own free will" and had not been forced to do it by Caramandi as the Councilman so testified at his first trial. Vaules insisted that Caramandi "did not touch Mr. Beloff" and that after giving the key hand signal the second time, "I smiled and he nodded," signifying his concurrence and role in the million-dollar extortion plot.

THE TALL BLONDE IN A WHITE SUIT REAPPEARS

On June 25th, Deborah Scullin, Beloff's ex-girlfriend, appeared again as a government witness and testified that Beloff had told her that the apartment was being provided free. "My understanding was that Mr. Beloff did not have to pay any rent, nor did I," she said. Scullin did admit once again to becoming extremely angry with her former lover, after she was fired from the job that the Councilman had obtained for her with a local judge, and then was also told that she had to leave the apartment immediately.

It was then that she decided to contact the FBI and agreed to record the telephone conversation with Beloff on May 23, 1986, because Rego had threatened her. "I went to the FBI because I was afraid of Bobby Rego," she lamented. "I didn't want to hurt Lee Beloff."

The government prosecutors then replayed the tape as she sat nervously on the witness stand listening to a playback of her quarreling with Beloff over the phone. Wearing large, white-rimmed sunglasses, Scullin left the stand and disappeared into the elevator, talking to no one in the media. (She refused all interviews, with a curt remark: "I do not talk to the press." And she kept her pledge.)

The owner of the apartment, developer Harry DeVoe, who had provided the freebee love nest as a favor to Beloff, testified again stating that he had provided the condo for Scullin as a pay-off for Beloff's promise to push the zoning variance bill DeVoe required to close Oriana Street next to his Smythe Stores apartments.

THE GHOST OF THE TRIAL: "JOHN D'ARBO" WHO WAS HE?

Midway in the retrial, the jury was apprised of the existence of three checks totalling $25,000 and made out to a dead man, John D'Arbo. These checks, all drafted on June 6, 1986, on direct orders from Bobby Rego, were cashed as part of a shake-down of developer John Bennett.

Rego had stated previously that he did not know who John D'Arbo was. There was a mystery surrounding the exact identity of a man who was *not* listed in any directory, did not have a voting record or own a house in the city. No one involved in the first trial seemed to know whether this man ever existed at all or was just a figment of the dual imagination of Beloff and Rego. His name surfaced at the heart of one of the key extortion charges in the trial and was given added significance when City Comptroller, Joe Vignola, testified that he gave Rego a $1,200 check made out to John D'Arbo of 439 Tasker Street in Philadelphia back in April, 1984. It was "for printing and other campaign-related work" during the 1984 primary election campaign of Frank Lucchino, who was then seeking the Democratic nomination as State Auditor General. Rego told Vignola to put D'Arbo's name on the check.

Two years later, Bennett made out three checks to the same man at Rego's direction. Rego told Bennett that D'Arbo was the name of a deceased tile contractor. Rego later testified that putting D'Arbo's name on the three checks was Bennett's idea. Someone was lying.

No one named D'Arbo had ever lived at 439 Tasker Street. Rego had owned that property in 1984 according to city deeds presented by the prosecution. A local bank official took the stand to say that on April 9, 1984, Rego's wife, Gloria, deposited the $1,200 D'Arbo check in the couple's personal account.

In the first trial, Rego had stated that he had never known

anyone named John D'Arbo. In the second trial, he admitted for the first time that he and his friends had made the name up as youngsters many years ago. "It was a fun thing," Rego boasted. When one of his teachers would ask who had spoken out-of-turn in class, he and his classmates would reply in unison: "D'Arbo did it!" "We got lunchroom and hall passes for him [D'Arbo]," Rego said. "It was a prank kind of thing that high school kids do." He claimed he told Bennett of this prank and that the real estate developer had suggested drafting the checks in D'Arbo's name in June, 1986.

During a heated exchange with U.S. Attorney Dennis on this matter, Rego denied lying about D'Arbo.

"Are you lying to this jury?" Dennis asked pointedly.

"You know I am not lying!" answered Rego evenly. "I didn't lie and you know it, Mr. Dennis, because there is no individual named John D'Arbo!"

When Dennis then asked Rego why he did not explain those circumstances during the earlier trial, a confused Rego retorted: "Nobody asked me the particulars."

So, the mysterious John D'Arbo, used as a fictitious cover-up for phony checks, had been concocted in a classroom a generation earlier to fool a teacher. Now, years later, Rego was trying to use the same ploy for writing and cashing questionable checks.

'NICKY CROW' CLEANS UP HIS ACT

When Nicholas Caramandi took the stand on the fifth day of the second trial, he was dressed conservatively, unlike the first Beloff-Rego trial where he had looked like the stereotype of a mobster. He repeated the accusations made in the first trial about Beloff and Rego finally agreeing to a 25 percent cut of the $1,000,000 in the extortion plot aimed at Rouse and Co.

Under cross-examination, he asserted that Beloff was "with" Scarfo and "if there's any wrongdoing, he [Beloff] would report my behavior to Scarfo....Everything I did with Beloff and Rego was above board. *It had to be!*"

Caramandi spent five hours on the witness stand explaining that he tried to shield both Beloff and Rego by carrying the extortion demand directly to Rouse as the middleman in the deal.

He backed up FBI agent Vaules in the latter's previous assertion that Beloff had voluntarily given the hand signal at Marabella's to show that he had approved the scam plan. He claimed that he never touched Beloff's hand or tried to move it across his chest as Beloff had testified in the first trial. Caramandi denounced his former boss, Scarfo, calling him a "disgrace to the Mafia. When you are no good to him anymore, he just does away with you."

Caramandi and his superior, Del Giorno, who testified a day later, said that they both kept Scarfo apprised of updates in the illegal operation, including relaying the boss's orders to cut the Beloff-Rego share from 50 percent to 25 percent of the million dollar scam.

But Beloff denied all of these accusations when he took the stand on the sixth day, insisting that he had paid $5,000 in cash to the developer John Bennett for repair work from some petty cash that he conveniently kept under the mattress and that he had paid cash for the $945 a month apartment for his girlfriend, Scullin's use.

BELOFF AND REGO TRY TO SAVE THEIR NECKS

Beloff's broken-record replay of his denials included his insistence that the real reason he held up the Council's approval of the proposed Rouse development at Penn's Landing was not because he hadn't received the $1,000,000 that he and the Mafia were trying to squeeze out of the biggest developer in town. It was because of the dispute with Mayor Goode over obtaining the approval for a wall to be built near Rego's home as a sound barrier to deaden traffic noise from the nearby I-95 Expressway.

"I figured, let him [the Mayor] sweat," said an angry Beloff.

He also contradicted himself on the cashing of the $9,000 check to D'Arbo by saying in the second trial that he cashed the check as a favor to Rego, whereas in the first trial he stated that Rego accompanied him to the bank and handed the check to the cashier who gave him the cash.

Throughout his two partial days of testimony, Beloff and his attorney tried to convince the jury that he, and not Caramandi, was the only one telling the truth.

When Rego took the stand following Beloff's testimony he altered his previous statements made at the earlier trial by telling the jury that Caramandi had "guided" Beloff's hand to his chest at

Marabella's Restaurant as a gesture of approval to go ahead with the million-dollar Rouse extortion deal. He asserted that his recollection of what happened at that fateful June, 1986, meeting had changed.

"That's how I recall things at this time," said Rego confidently, after having admitted at the first trial that his back was turned when the gesture was allegedly made.

Furthermore, as in the first trial, Rego denied all of the counts lodged against him and his boss — giving almost identical testimony to his statements offered at the April trial, denouncing Caramandi as a murderer.

An added witness who had not appeared at the first trial, Dr. Frederic Kremer, was called to the stand by the defense in an effort to refute the testimony offered by the FBI agent on the hand signal agreement. Kremer told the jury that his patient, Beloff, had vision problems that would have prevented him from seeing someone smiling back at him from that distance across the circular bar.

THE JURY DELIBERATES THE FATE OF BELOFF AND REGO

In the closing arguments, the attorneys for Beloff and Rego tried to portray their clients as hard-working public figures who had been unjustly accused of wrongdoing. The prosecutors portrayed them as corrupt politicians who used Beloff's council office to shake down developers for all they could get.

Both sides were cognizant that the trial was ending on the eve of the Fourth of July celebration, and they relied heavily on this fact by mixing metaphors of American history, patriotism and the 200th anniversary of the writing of the Constitution in their closing speeches.

In his hour-and-a-half closing summation, Dennis said that Beloff had tried to "charm his way out" of the charges, and that Rego, the former carpet supplier, had tried "to throw a rug over" the allegations.

Dennis pointed out that Caramandi "was the one out front. He was supposed to be the insulation" to shield Beloff and Rego from their part in the scam.

In a more dramatic and effective closing than was presented in the first trial, Dennis sarcastically referred to Beloff as "the

Baron of South Philadelphia," (a title which Rego had given his boss in the earlier trial). "They are not noble men," Dennis concluded. "Baron Beloff has set himself up as a petty tyrant. He was going to use his councilmantic power to hammer developers into feudal obedience!"

In his 45-minute closing Goodman tried to portray his client as "an honest official who just happened to be a perfect target for ambitious prosecutors." (It had been rumored that Dennis was hoping to be nominated to a Federal judgeship if he was successful with this case.)

"Lee Beloff is wealthy; he's powerful. He's a politician. He has a girlfriend and he's a friend of Nicky Scarfo, the reputed head of the mob," Goodman told the jury. "He's the ideal target upon which careers may be built."

Finally, on July 1st, after a week-long trial, the second Beloff-Rego case went to the jury for a decision. As the jury deliberated, Beloff and Rego nervously and pensively paced up and down in the 14th floor hall outside the courtroom, chatting with the family members and friends and smoking cigarettes to calm their frazzled nerves.

While waiting for the jury to come back in, Rego nervously tried to entertain reporters, spectators and friends in the hallway by telling lame jokes and impersonating the defense attorneys. Nearby, a courtroom artist on contract with the local TV Channel #29 who drew pictures of the key players in the courtroom for each night's news program in lieu of the forbidden cameras in the courtroom, hawked some of his sketches by spreading them on the floor in hopes of getting an order or two. He found no takers.

The jury spent three hours on a Wednesday afternoon deliberating and then recessed for the night. At 7:05 p.m., a relieved Beloff, once again sensing a second hung jury with the court hopefully refusing to retry the case a third time, exulted: "I feel good. Tired but good," as he kissed his widowed mother, Jean, on the cheek outside of the courtroom.

A DECISION IS REACHED AT LAST

Finally, on Thursday, July 3rd, at 10:46 a.m., after a short morning period of deliberation, the jury signalled the Judge that they had a verdict. The jury foreman read out the word 'guilty' 11 times while Beloff looked downward. The courtroom was

silent. He sat stunned, staring ahead for several minutes showing no emotion, before moving over to his wife, Diane, sitting
behind him and patting her gently on the head. Rego closed his
eyes for a moment and sat expressionless as Judge Fullam
thanked the jury and set August 5th for sentencing.

Beloff, convicted on six counts of extortion and attempted
extortion, faced up to a maximum prison sentence of 120 years
and Rego, convicted of five counts, could be sentenced up to 100
years.

Several jurors who spoke to reporters after the verdict agreed
that the prosecution's case was thoroughly convincing and that
they felt they had an accurate grasp of the complex issues and
evidence.

"I asked God to be on my side," said one juror, "I mean
down on my knees. This is a big thing, saying two people are
guilty."

Although the jurors admitted that both 'Nicky Crow' and
'Tommy Del' — the two star witnesses — had been offered in
the words of one of them "sweet deals" by the government, they
all agreed that these two men were telling the truth and that both
Beloff and Rego lied.

Some of the factors that helped to convince the second jury of
guilt on all counts were:

1.) The de-emphasizing and submerging of the mob figures'
testimony into an ocean of less controversial evidence. As one
juror said: "They were bad men and I don't think we would have
gone on their testimony alone. But even before they testified, the
prosecution had enough."

2.) The lack of the defendants' personal credibility coupled
with the undisputed fact of Beloff's longtime friendship with
mob-boss Scarfo.

3.) The clearing up of the John D'Arbo mystery which had
been left hanging in the first trial. One juror put it well when he
said: "I think it was a name that Rego thought up to hide a lot of
his transactions."

4.) The make-up of the second jury included more older
people and more suburban residents, who according to experts'
profiles were more likely to convict, plus the fact that they were
sequestered.

Defense attorney Goodman, however, took exception to these
factors and felt that "media saturation" in both newspapers, radio

and TV hurt his client and that a jury in another city might have reached a different verdict.

Beloff stubbornly refused to resign after his conviction, preferring to wait until the last minute until final sentencing before giving up his $40,000 a year part-time post. Council President Joseph Coleman said that he intended to ask Beloff to resign immediately for the good of the Council. The Mayor stated that he believed the conviction would send a message to both civil servants and elected officials that corruption is *passe* in the city and "that corrupt behavior will not be tolerated."

U.S. Attorney Dennis commented that "if you are engaged in criminal acts habitually, it's going to catch up with you."

Judge Fullam said he found it difficult to comprehend how the earlier trial could have ended in a hung jury. "If they had listened to the same testimony, there's no way they could have reached a different decision."

THE PARTY IS OVER FOR BELOFF AND REGO

It was a long year between the first indictments handed down against Beloff and Rego, in June, 1986, when photos depicted their swaggering arrogance and protestations of innocence to their depressed state at the end of their second trials when they were convicted by a jury of their peers.

As *The Philadelphia Inquirer* editorialized on the day after the verdict: "Beloff and Rego stand convicted today because they tried to extort $1 million from the wrong man [Willard Rouse].

"It was a classic case of overreaching....His [Beloff's] conviction — like the Abscam convictions [of three councilmen six years earlier] won't forever end official corruption in Philadelphia. But his downfall [and Rego's too], his public humiliation, and his likely stretch in a federal penitentiary should fill other political crooks-in-waiting with a salutary degree of dread."

But Beloff and Rego were not ready to throw in the towel before sentencing. Through their respective attorneys, they requested a grant for a new trial based on various exceptions to the second trial verdict, including what Attorney Goodman called "a climate that made it impossible to get a fair trial and that's not just sour grapes."

But on July 27th, Judge Fullam turned them down with a stinging ten-page opinion, stating that the evidence against them was "overwhelming" and that the testimony of both defendants was "singularly implausible, to the point of being...incriminating."

The Judge particularly pointed out that both Beloff and Rego "frequently took advantage of the policy [of having Council members introduce legislation] in order to line their own pockets and those of their associates, and they did so by working closely with the local branch of organized crime."

Fullam's ruling cleared the way for his sentencing them a week later.

Beloff, Rego, and the public had just a short time to wait until the long-awaited fines and prison terms.

A LESSON FROM A GREAT JUDGE

A half-century ago, in 1937, a great U.S. Supreme Court Justice, Louis Brandeis, observed:

"Our government is the potent, the omnipresent teacher. For good or ill, it teaches the whole people by its example. Crime is contagious. If the government becomes the lawbreaker, it breeds contempt for law, it invites every man to become a law unto himself, it invites anarchy."

In the summary of the 730-page IRAN-CONTRA REPORT issued by the joint Congressional Committee on Irangate, dated November 18, 1987, it was the conclusion of the majority who signed the report that: *"The Iran-Contra affair resulted from a failure to heed* THIS *message* [of Justice Brandeis]."

Likewise, Councilman Beloff and his sidekick Rego did not heed this dictum when they agreed to break the law and become co-conspirators with the Mafia in a criminal shakedown.

[Beloff] engaged in corruption of the worst kind. Not only did he sell his office, but he enlisted the aid of organized crime, and in effect, made City Council, one branch of the local Mafia.

-Chief U.S. District Judge John Fullam[*]

15
THE SENTENCING OF NICKY, LEE, AND BOBBY

BELOFF QUITS THE COUNCIL

ALTHOUGH Beloff could have and probably should have resigned from the Council a year earlier, both Beloff and Rego finally handed in their letters of resignation on August 4, 1987, just a day before they were to be sentenced in Federal District Court for their convictions in the Penn's Landing extortion plot.[†]

In a letter to Judge Fullam, sent on the same day, Dennis recommended "substantial sentences of incarceration" for all three defendants, including Scarfo...whom Dennis called "the premier gangster of the region."

In his note to the Judge, Dennis buttressed his arguments by noting that on a tape (secretly recorded by an FBI informant), Pennsylvania State Representative Joe Howlett, a longshoreman friend of Beloff's who took his seat in the state legislature when Beloff ascended to the Council, could be heard recounting how

[*] In passing a ten-year prison sentence on Councilman Beloff, August 5, 1987.

[†] Under existing state law, he would have been stripped of his office automatically on sentencing — so he beat the deadline by one day. The date was significant since it was exactly one year earlier that Beloff and Rego met developer Dr. John Bennett. In a Center City bar after federal prosecutors had suddenly dropped the initial scam charges against them, Rego arrogantly announced, "We are back in business." "We have got this thing beat," Beloff boasted to Bennett. "They have nothing on us!"

Beloff once bragged to "another member of City Council that she would have plenty of money if she would vote with him" on a key legislative item. Howlett described Beloff as "having pulled out a wad of $50 bills that might have totalled $50,000 cash."

In his letter of resignation to Council President Joe Coleman, Beloff wrote that "his time in Council was the most rewarding and enjoyable of my adult life" and thanked Coleman for his support and "wise council." He also said, "I am sorry for any problems that I may have caused the Council and the City of Philadelphia."

But if he really was 'sorry,' he would have resigned a year before and *not* embarrassed his colleagues during those trying 365 days in which not one of them had the courage to stand up and demand that he resign. Although the Council had no legal grounds to oust Beloff because of its archaic rules, it did have ethical grounds to oust him, but no one picked up the torch of righteousness. They let it sputter out and die, leaving it to the judicial system to do the dirty work for them.

THE DEFENDANTS ATTEND A PRE-SENTENCING BASH

Beloff and Rego decided to spend their last night before sentencing drinking and enjoying life at one of their favorite watering places, the DiLullo Centro Restaurant, where much of the plotting in the Rouse scam occurred. They met with Beloff's wife, Diane, his lawyer, Oscar Goodman, and Scarfo's prominent criminal attorney and defense lawyer, 'Bobby' Simone. There were no tears on the night of August 4th, nor did they dwell on what sentence could be expected on the morrow from Judge Fullam.

The two defendants came dressed informally, with Beloff wearing a kelly green polo shirt and Rego a black sports shirt. The group was subdued and dignified.

THE PRELIMINARIES TO THE GRAND CLIMAX

At 9:30 AM, Wednesday, August 5th, Diane Beloff, who was near tears, got on a Courthouse elevator to the 15th floor with her husband, who was wearing a dark blue suit and red tie. Before they reached the already packed courtroom, the Beloffs passed a hundred curious onlookers who had been denied entrance and were standing in the hall. Rego stayed outside for a few minutes conferring with their lawyers and friends.

At 10:15 AM, Judge Fullam entered and everyone stood out of respect. He acknowledged that he had received 279 letters sent by various constituents testifying to the good characters of both Beloff and Rego and how they had helped them with neighborhood problems.

At this moment, 'Bobby' Simone, Scarfo's lawyer, sensing what was coming, tried to lighten the tense atmosphere by joking to the court: "We'll take credit for all those letters of commendation."

Judge Fullam, who had long been noted for his biting sarcasm, broke in, saying: "Unless Mr. Scarfo can claim to have fixed a lot of potholes, I don't think it would be appropriate."

The courtroom erupted in laughter.

Simone then asked the Judge to go easy on his client and consider leniency, since he was already facing a whole raft of other charges in future trials, and that "Scarfo was not a career criminal."

Oscar Goodman, defense attorney, then followed with a similar plea for leniency on behalf of his client Beloff, producing letters from two of the Councilman's doctors regarding his alleged health problems and pointing out that his father, Emanuel, was a model jurist.

"He stands before you," Goodman said, "and feels that he disgraced his family and his name and is now humbled. He has not displayed arrogance. He [Beloff] still hopes for a future as a human being to return to his family and children. He *loves* his family.

"There is no such thing as prison being a country club [in an obvious reference to the Allenwood, PA Federal Prison farm, where white collar criminals were usually sent]. It is a shocking experience when someone like Mr. Beloff is institutionalized and incarcerated. There will be resentment from his fellow inmates because he does have money. So I ask for compassion on the part of the court."

Joshua Briskin pleaded on behalf of Bobby Rego that his client had a "substantially negative net worth and was not a member of any organized crime family." He told the Judge that Rego had several job offers in the "trash removal and carpet businesses and that he will never again enter public employment."

Finally, he pointed out that Rego's life was in jeopardy since Thomas Del Giorno had mentioned during his appearance on the witness stand that: "It's [Rego's dealings with the mob] not over yet."

Then, just before Beloff's sentencing, Oscar Goodman introduced Harvard Law Professor Alan Dershowitz, who told the court that his review of the case had persuaded him that the one issue the Judge was wrong in was denying bail to Mr. Beloff.

Fullam interrupted and quipped: "That would not be unprecedented," and the audience laughed.

[*Time* Magazine had labelled Dershowitz as "the top American lawyer of 'last resort' — a sort of judicial St. Jude, who had successfully helped Claus von Bulow win a new trial for the attempted murder of his comatose wife, Sunny as well as Anatoly Shcharansky, the noted Russian 'refusenik.' Dershowitz had boasted that "When you've tried everything else and you've lost, then you come to me. Usually it comes at the desperate time of the season, which is the one I'm best at, the cold, cold winter."]

Dershowitz continued: "I listened to the entire tape of Miss Deborah Scullin with the FBI official at her side when she called Mr. Beloff. I feel that Miss Scullin should have testified and the defense should have had the right to question her on each point of the colorful-language phone conversation."

Dershowitz also told the Judge that he might seek a mistrial on appeal, based on the fact that Deborah Scullin's taped phone call to Beloff was an abridgment of Beloff's rights, since he had not been told in advance that what he said over the phone was being recorded by the government for use as possible evidence in the courts.

Fullam muttered: "It is a colorful issue but I don't quite see it [as an appeal item]."

The Judge was itching to get on with the sentencing now that the preliminaries were drawing to a close.

STIFF SENTENCES ARE IMPOSED BY THE JUDGE

While these last-minute motions were being made, Beloff sat impassively, with his eyes and mouth downturned in a frozen expression, waiting for the expected legal guillotine of a long prison term to fall on his neck. His wife came over to him for a moment, hugged him and whispered into his ear. She then went back to her seat in the second row reserved for family and friends.

When the three defendants approached the bench for sentences, Beloff grasped his hands tightly in front of him and slowly let out a long breath of air as he stood and waited for the dreaded judicial edict sealing his fate.

Fullam's remarks before sentencing pointed out that the attempted extortion of Rouse did not involve threats and violence so it "was not the very worst extortion in the world."

But it was a flagrant act all the same, Fullam said, "because of the corruption of a whole segment of the municipal government of Philadelphia, and because of the amount involved and because, in effect, it deprived the community of worthwhile development, or at least postponed its implementation for a long time."

The Judge came down hard on all three convicted felons. He excoriated Beloff for attempting "to make the City Council one branch of the local Mafia," as well as "selling his office," before he passed sentences.

None of the three showed much reaction as the Judge first sentenced Rego to eight years in prison, then Beloff to ten years and finally Scarfo to fourteen years behind bars — for his role as the kingpin in the extortion plot.

In addition to the prison sentences, Fullam fined Beloff and Scarfo $150,000 each. He also ordered Beloff, whose net worth was disclosed as $1.8 million, to pay another $7,500 in restitution for the extortion of contractors DeVoe and Bennett.

Fullam made it clear that he did not want the restitution to go to the developers directly, but to the government, because: "They [DeVoe and Bennett] were at least as crooked or more crooked than the people they were trying to bribe, so they deserve to lose the money."

He permitted Beloff and Rego to remain free on bail pending appeal but ordered Scarfo kept in custody at the local Detention Center, since he was being held for later trials on murder and racketeering charges.

Neither Beloff nor Rego admitted guilt in the wake of their convictions as they were surrounded by reporters as they left the courtroom.

In an ugly scene outside the courtroom after the sentencing, an angry Beloff cursed and threatened news photographers after his wife, Diane, was accidentally bumped by one of them. There was a spate of shoving and scuffling as reporters thrust microphones in front of his face as Beloff struggled to reach a white Lincoln sedan awaiting him in a No-Parking zone at curbside in front of the Federal courthouse. A political associate was finally successful in pulling the ex-Councilman and his wife into the car, which then roared up Market Street towards City Hall.

Later in the day U.S. Attorney Dennis issued a short statement, noting that: "Hopefully, it [the sentencing] sends a very strong message that if you're involved with public corruption, you can't get away with it forever."

Don't play with me, because you are playing with a bad person.

-Councilman Leland Beloff[*]

16

LAST GASPS BEFORE THE PRISON GATES SLAMMED SHUT

POST-MORTEMS OF THE THREE TRIALS

IN the aftermath of the three extortion trials, the public got to know about the intertwining of politics and organized crime, through the testimony of the ex-mobsters turned government witnesses about Nicky Scarfo, and his family. As one observer put it: "Once the toothpaste is out of the tube, you can't put it back in." The mob's long-time legal and public relations ploy — that the Mafia doesn't exist except in fiction — had been smashed forever especially along the Philadelphia-Atlantic City axis.

Furthermore, the City Council was going ultimately to be forced to reassess its rules and procedures concerning the granting to each district councilperson a dictatorial say over his or her bailiwick. The banks had already tightened up their check-cashing procedures. No longer could any dead men cash checks.

After his sentencing, Beloff was confronted with several family problems, one of which was how to explain a ten-year term in prison to his seven-year-old daughter, Lauren, and his two-year-old son, Emanuel II. The sentencing also had an obvious impact on his wife, Diane, since she had been indicted with him to be tried later for vote fraud.

At the end of September, a month and a half after their sentencing by Judge Fullam, Beloff and Rego, out on bail, made a

---

[*] On an FBI tape, conversing over the phone with his ladyfriend, Deborah Scullin, 1986.

trip to *The Philadelphia Inquirer* and tried to get into the paper's news morgue (for purposes of their appeals) to check on two stories that had been written during their first trial. They were stopped by a guard and asked to show some identification. They had none that would have permitted them through the barrier until Rego pulled out an Honorary Philadelphia Deputy Sheriff's card — which finally allowed them access to the newspaper's files.

Beloff so dreaded the ten-year jail sentence handed down by Judge Fullam that he not only filed an appeal to negate the original sentence on a technicality, but filed a motion three months later seeking a reduction in his sentence.

One of his attorneys, Nathan Z. Dershowitz, stated on October 31st that he feared the government prosecutors might try to treat the Beloff case under a new amendment (which had just been passed to limit latitude in reducing sentences), instead of the 'old rule' which was in effect when the sentence was issued in early August.

The court took both appeals under scrutiny — over the ensuing four months before the decision would be rendered in March 1988.

BELOFF, SCARFO, AND REGO REQUEST NEW TRIALS

Eight months after they were convicted in Federal court on extortion charges, Lee Beloff, Nicky Scarfo and Bobby Rego appealed through their lawyers to the Third U.S. Circuit Court of Appeals to grant them new trials based on a variety of arguments. Appearing before a three-judge panel on March 7, 1988, Alan Dershowitz, one of the lawyers, argued that his client had been unfairly convicted for his part in the $1,000,000 Penn's Landing extortion scheme and should be granted a new trial.

He focused his attack mainly on the taped conversation between Beloff and his onetime mistress, Deborah Scullin, arguing that it "only had marginal relevance and had prejudiced the jury against his client."

Dershowitz also argued that the trial Judge, John Fullam, erred in allowing the government prosecutors to play the tape in court — which led to extensive publicity, a "media blitz" that prevented a fair trial from taking place.

Unaware that he was being taped by an FBI agent sitting next to Scullin at the other end of the phone line, an angry Beloff had shouted: "Don't play with me, because you're playing with a bad person." The defense lawyer stressed that the use of this implicating tape was improper and amounted to "character assassination by Scullin and the FBI," which suggested that Beloff "had lived a life of crime, violence and political corruption."

"The error in this case was harmful and prejudicial," Dershowitz said.

During the appeal in the federal courthouse, Beloff and his wife, Diane, sat quietly in the back of the 19th floor courtroom, as the three-judge panel listened intently to the arguments by both the defense and the prosecution.

U.S. Attorney Thomas Lee, counter-argued that the appeals court uphold the convictions, based on the fact that the tape in question was "undeniably relevant" and was an essential part of the government's case.

The Scarfo appeal as argued by 'Bobby' Simone and his associate, was based on the complaint that the use of an anonymous, sequestered jury was "improper and unnecessarily heightened the atmosphere of prejudice and fear...There was no possible way the jury could have dispassionately viewed the evidence as proving or not proving an attempted extortion." Simone also criticized the mention of Mario Puzo's book and movie, *The Godfather*, to the jury and the court as the basis of the decision to invoke anonymity.

Lee contended that evidence about other crimes was necessary to counter the defense arguments that the two key mobsters-turned-informants, Nicholas Caramandi and Thomas Del Giorno, who testified that Scarfo had sanctioned the extortion scheme, had acted on their own.

Lee concluded that "it was absolutely essential for the government to be able to establish that Scarfo, as head of the area *La Cosa Nostra* crime family, had to approve that kind of scheme."

The three-judge panel, consisting of Circuit Judges Joseph Weis, Jr., Ruggero J. Aldisert and Morton Greenberg, did not indicate when they might announce their decision on the appeal. Court observers and attorneys opined that it might take months.

Meanwhile, both Beloff and Rego remained free on bail, while Scarfo remained in prison, where he was currently facing a first degree murder trial with eight other Mafia cohorts in the murder of the former Mafia soldier, Sal Testa.

On March 21st, the Appeals Court rendered its unanimous decision to uphold the jury's decision and the judge's actions in the trial of Beloff and Rego. Its four-page opinion rejected all three defense contentions that Judge Fullam had erred in allowing the damning Scullin tape to be played in court.

"As the district judge [Fullam] wrote," said Weiss, "a public official on trial for extorting a free apartment for his girl-friend...cannot reasonably expect to prevent the jury from hearing evidence tending to show that he was having an affair." He also stated that the appeals panel did not consider US Attorney Dennis' closing argument to be prejudicial or that Beloff and Rego had been hurt by pre-trial publicity.

The panel did not render a decision on Scarfo's appeal in the same case in which he was found guilty of conspiring with Beloff and Rego, but it seemed likely that a similar rejection would be forthcoming.

On April 5th, Judge Fullam ordered the two felons to present themselves for transport to prison on April 25th. On that day, Beloff was sent to the Loretto Federal Prison camp — a minimum security facility located near Altoona, Pennsylvania, and Rego was sent to the nearby Lewisburg Federal Penitentiary. Loretto (which housed 540 prisoners) was a former Franciscan Seminary and had handball courts for the inmates. The doors were not locked at night, since the white collar criminals assigned there were interned with few restrictions.

The camp included a factory which made wire cables. Even though this was a relatively 'soft' restraining place, it still marked quite a comedown from the playboy, high-style living pattern to which Beloff was accustomed.

His days as a once rising Philadelphia politician had ended...forever.

There is no week nor day nor hour, when tyranny may not enter
upon this country, if the people lose their roughness and spirit of
defiance — Tyranny may always enter — there is no charm, no bar
against it — the only bar against it is a large resolute breed of men.

-Walt Whitman*

17

VOTE FRAUD IN THE
NURSING HOMES

FOR most of her marriage to Beloff, Diane Segal Beloff spent
her summers at their Longport, New Jersey, beach vacation
home and in Acapulco, Mexico, and various Caribbean resorts
during some of the winter months. After giving birth to her two
children, a daughter in 1979 and a son in 1982, she became a
Democratic Committeewoman in Beloff's South Philadelphia
Ward #39B — one of the largest in the city.

But in October, 1986, her house of cards came tumbling
down when she was accused — along with her husband and two
other Ward committeepersons, Margaret Coyle and Charles Pollan — of illegally using the names of senile patients ensconced in
a Philadelphia nursing home controlled by the Beloff family to
cast absentee ballots in the 1984 general election.†

The case came to light in November, 1986, when another
Committeeman, Nicholas Marrandino, agreed to wear a 'wire'
for the FBI and allowed them to strap a microphone beneath his
clothes during the 1984 election in which he recorded Beloff
instructing another man to forge voters' absentee ballots. Beloff
also personally forged signatures in the presence of the informant

* "Notes for Lectures on Democracy and 'Adhesiveness'", 1876
(Walt Whitman's Workshop, 1926).
† Pollan was further accused of rigging his 1985 election as the Judge
of Elections in his division by fraudulently placing 'Xs' on a number of absentee ballots allegedly signed by nursing home patients.

and told him to use different colored pens, and pens with different types of ballpoints to sign the ballots.

Marrandino, who was paid $20,000 by the FBI over a two-year period in exchange for cooperation, taped the boastful Pollan, who bragged about how he had allowed votes to be cast by dead people.

"I haven't had a voter die in my division in 10 years," Pollan told the wired Marrandino. "I've had people who moved out 20 years ago who are still voting in my division."

When Marrandino jokingly asked the fat Pollan if he hosted birthday parties for voters who turned 112, Pollan replied: "I don't think I got anybody that's a hundred...although maybe, because they might have died, like at 80, and now they're about 100 on my voters lists...yeah."

When Marrandino asked Pollan a more philosophical question: "Have you been corrupt since you've been a committeeman or has the job corrupted you?" Pollan answered: "When I first ran for committeeman I wasn't corrupt, because then I lost. So I found you don't win by being honest...The next time I ran, I won."

When he ran for re-election as Judge of Elections in 1985, he lost by three votes. "So I had to maneuver the numbers to make sure I won...Nobody else knows what to do in there, so I'd have to do the job [of running the polls] anyway."

After the indictments of the four committee-people, Coyle, age 55, a field auditor in the State Auditor General's office, pleaded guilty to conspiring with Lee Beloff on November 5, 1986, after she heard the tapes in which she boasted about her ability to secure large numbers of falsely signed absentee ballots. She also agreed to testify against Beloff.

She admitted that Beloff had ordered her and Pollan to go to the Walt Whitman Convalescent Center in South Philadelphia to get the signatures of patients who could not go out and vote.[*]

Nine months later, Pollan, 40, pleaded guilty to 27 counts of election fraud, in exchange for the government's agreement to drop 20 other counts of fraud against him. On the FBI tape,

---

[*] Coyle, in exchange for her guilty plea, was also told by the court that she would not be charged with fixing traffic tickets in return for her cooperation.

Pollan was heard telling Beloff what he was doing and the Ward Leader-Councilman retorted: "Be sure to make the signatures look different, Charlie."

On Thanksgiving eve, 1987, U.S. District Judge Thomas O'Neill, Jr. sentenced Pollan to three years in prison for his vote-rigging crime. Assistant U.S. Attorney William B. Carr contended that such a substantial term was necessary to deter others who might wish to consider similar types of election fraud in the future.

"The systematic tampering of the election process is one of the most serious crimes I will ever prosecute," Carr said. "Mr. Pollan was the guardian of that right to vote...and he did nothing but abuse it."

LEE AND DIANE GO ON TRIAL FOR VOTE FRAUD

With the knowledge that their co-defendant, Pollan, had already pleaded guilty to similar charges, Beloff and his wife refused to do the same and opted for a trial in Judge O'Neill's Federal court. Lee's attorney, 'Bobby' Simone, taking a respite from defending Scarfo in a series of trials, asked the Judge to postpone the trial because of the undue publicity surrounding his client, and that of an alleged shooting incident involving the key government witness, Nicholas Marrandino. Shots had been fired at the Marrandino car a few days earlier and two bullets had been recovered from the passenger side of the car, which were promptly turned over to the FBI for ballistics' tests.

Simone felt these facts would make it more difficult to select an impartial jury. But O'Neill refused the request and attempted to get the trial underway. However, Diane found herself on the horns of a family dilemma. Former U.S. Attorney Peter Vaira advised his client, Diane, to put all the blame on her husband for getting her to commit vote fraud, then beg the court for mercy. Diane mulled it over.

A few days later, Diane made a key decision. She fired her lawyer and told the judge that she would defend herself.

"I just wanted to put out the truth," she confessed, pointing out that she did not want to dump on her husband by doing what Vaira suggested.

By September 8th, the Judge was at an impasse attempting to

find an impartial jury, so he postponed the trial indefinitely.

Seven months later, on April 22, 1988, Lee Beloff, on the verge of being put behind bars on the Penn's Landing case, decided to put his house in order, and plead guilty to the multiple vote fraud charges.

The Judge sentenced him to three years in prison (the same as he gave Pollan) but ordered that Beloff serve them concurrently with his 10-year extortion sentence. Diane attended the pleading, but announced that she was still undecided whether or not she, too, would change her plea from innocent to guilty. She was waiting to see what kind of sentence the Judge would hand down to Margaret Coyle, who also pled guilty to the same charges.

As they left the courthouse, a still arrogant Beloff told the press, "All in all, I'd rather be at the Four Seasons [a posh, upper-class local hotel]. Diane should never have been here in the first place," he said protectively about his wife at his side. "It's unheard of." But he was wrong. She was there because she freely conspired to fix votes illegally.

Beloff's parting shot to the media was a plaintive defense of his twenty years in various elective offices. "I'd like to think that I served my constituents well," he boasted.

The alleged $150,000 that Beloff paid to Professor Alan Dershowitz of the Harvard Law School to try to win an appeal on his ten-year prison conviction had failed to bear fruit. All the money in the world could not buy the convicted Councilman his freedom after the criminal justice system had rendered its verdict on his combined illegal extortion and vote fraud activities.

BOBBY REGO PLEADS GUILTY TO FEDERAL DRUG CHARGES

Although he knew that Scarfo and his cohorts had been acquitted of similar charges in the importing of P2P and manufacturing and distributing methamphetamine, Rego found himself facing similar charges in February, 1988 — a few months later. After he began serving his eight-year prison sentence in the Rouse extortion case, Rego had a decision to make.

Should he face another long and expensive federal trial or declare guilt and hope that Judge Fullam would impose a sentence to run concurrently with his present one? After his two co-conspirators in the drug ring, Robert Wrubel, age 52, and James

Burks, age 63, decided to plead guilty to participating in the drug conspiracy between 1980-84, Rego realized that his chances of being acquitted had been severely diminished, since they would most probably testify for the government against him.

So, on July 5th, 1988, the day his trial before Judge Fullam was to start, he appeared in court in a jogging suit and pled guilty. Rego knew that he could face a stiff sentence of up to 25 years when he was scheduled to appear in court on September 13th, but hoped the Judge would be lenient and give him a reduced sentence for his illegal business which allegedly netted millions of dollars.

DIANE BELOFF GETS TWO YEARS PROBATION

After a long series of plea-bargaining sessions with the Federal prosecutors in her 1984 vote-fraud indictment, Diane Beloff was granted two years probation on July 25, 1988, by U.S. District Judge Thomas O'Neill Jr. He took into consideration the fact that she pleaded guilty to the charges of forging the signatures of three women on absentee ballot envelopes — for which her incarcerated husband had also pled guilty.

The Judge was also touched by the prospective emotional turmoil of a trial on her two children, aged six and nine. After failing to persuade the prosecutor, William B. Carr Jr. to drop the charges against her, Mrs. Beloff decided to throw herself on the mercy of the court. The kindly Judge was persuaded by her tears and took pity on her with his probationary sentence. Robert Simone, who had become her attorney, said: "Lee Beloff seems to feel that he's responsible for the actions of his wife in this case."

Charles Pollan continued to serve his three-year prison sentence for the same crime. Margaret Coyle, who also pled guilty in the fall of 1986 and who had agreed to cooperate had not yet been sentenced.

AN IRONIC FOOTNOTE

Willard Rouse, III, the original whistle blower on the $1 million Penn's Landing extortion scam, announced a change of plans. On January 17, 1989, Rouse held a surprise press conference, a month after stating that he was ready to move ahead with his $90 million first phase plans.

Rouse stated that despite a $10 million Urban Development Action Grant from Washington and a $19 million city and state grant and loan to underwrite the centerpiece project, his company would lose at least $20 million if they proceeded. He announced that he was withdrawing from the project.

A high-ranking Philadelphia Common Pleas Court Judge offered his sardonic commentary on this latest turn of events: "I wonder if Lee [Beloff] isn't feeling sorry for himself now, sitting behind prison bars. Maybe he is silently asking himself the question: 'Did I do all this — that got me here — for nothing?'"

Men I find to be a sort of being very badly constructed. They are more easily provoked than reconciled, more disposed to do mischief...than to make reparation...and having more pride and even pleasure in killing, than in begetting one another.

-Ben Franklin[*]

18

THE 'SPEED' CONSPIRACY

A FTER the government's courtroom victory in the late spring of 1987 where Scarfo was found guilty of co-conspiring to extort $1 million from Willard Rouse — the Mafia honcho next faced a second in a series of a half-dozen federal and state trials. This time it was for alleged drug conspiracy.

THE CHARGES

In June, 1987, five Mafia mobsters, headed by Nicky Scarfo, were among twenty-eight indicted by a Federal Grand Jury in a landmark case in which the federal prosecutors charged the current leadership of the Philadelphia organized crime family with trying to control a lucrative branch of the drug business.

Scarfo, and four of his associates, 'Crazy Phil' Leonetti, his nephew and underboss of the Mafia family operations in Atlantic City and Philadelphia; Salvatore 'Chuckie' Merlino, of Margate, N.J.; Francis 'Faffy' Iannarella; and Charles 'Charley White' Iannece were slated for trial in the U.S. District Court on November 30th, 1987, on charges of trying to corner the market

[*] In a letter sent in 1782 to a friend in England, Dr. Joseph Priestley, the discoverer of oxygen and carbon dioxide. (From Ronald Bosco's "Benjamin Franklin: A Reassessment" in the Pennsylvania "Magazine of History and Biography," Historical Society of Pennsylvania, Fall 1987)

on the lucrative street drug methamphetamine —'speed.'

The two bosses and three soldiers were also indicted for allegedly engaging in the crime of attempting to exert a monopolistic control over the importation of phenyl-2-propanone, (P2P), the key ingredient used to manufacture speed.

The last government charge against the five Mafia members was based on the Continuous Criminal Enterprise statute (CCE), which was aimed at those who gave and supervised orders even if they never touched the drugs themselves. This act specified that those involved must include at least five people to be part of a conspiracy or a group involved in three or more similar crimes. (The charges seemed to fit all five Mafia members from the evidence presented in the indictments.)

THE HEART OF THE CASE

The indictment further stated that the crime family essentially took over three separate illegal drug operations headed by John Renzulli, Angelo DiTullio and Michael Forte, (see chart) all of South Philadelphia addresses, and consolidated them under one monopolistic conglomerate headed by Scarfo, the 'Speed King.'

The Scarfo-led drug empire began extorting 'street taxes' from these three groups of drug wholesalers in return for allowing them to continue to engage in further criminal drug-related activities. Scarfo and Company allegedly dictated orders to Renzulli, DiTullio and Forte through soldiers like Caramandi, concerning distribution and sales of the P2P.

Scarfo and his cohorts were not interested in the drug pushers at the end of the line who sold to the customers, just in the middlemen because they were fewer in number and easier to control.

In early September, the federal grand jury revised its original 46-count June indictment by adding ten new charges, including charging three of the defendants with attempted tax evasion. These new charges were not aimed at the five Mafia members, but at those on the fringes, like John Renzulli, whose P2P drug operations had been taken over by the mob.

WHO WAS RUNNING THE MOB WHILE NICKY WAS IN JAIL

Unlike legitimate business operations, where public announcements are made whenever there is a change in top management, this has never been the case in the secret Mafia management when a top boss dies, disappears from the scene, or goes to prison.

By early October, 1987, with Scarfo behind bars for the past ten months, a question arose as to who was conducting the daily mob business operations. Reliable sources claimed that Albert 'Reds' Pontani, age 50, a noted Trenton, New Jersey, mob figure whose activities allegedly included gambling, loansharking and narcotics, had quietly emerged as the caretaker boss of the Scarfo family.

Whether he had accrued enough power, influence and desire to succeed as the boss of the remnants of the severely depleted Scarfo organization was open to speculation, according to both federal and state authorities. But it was evident that the younger generation of Scarfo family members, like Nicky Scarfo, Jr., were too inexperienced and immature to conduct the complicated and dangerous Mafia operations.

Underground gossip had spread the word that if and when Scarfo was removed or stepped down from his position of *capo di tutti capi*, that either Pontani or Pasquale 'Patty Specks' Martirano, 58, a Newark-based crime boss, were in line to become his successor. "Trying to speculate who will succeed Scarfo is like trying to handicap the 1988 Presidential Primaries," predicted one mob observer.

Martirano, who has connections from within the Scarfo organization, had the stability and maturity to assume command if Scarfo gave up his mantle. However, others felt that with the Scarfo crowd so decimated by murders and imprisonments, the remnants of his once-powerful mob would eventually be absorbed by the only New York-based mob leader still out of jail, John Gotti, and his underlings.

Gotti, who allegedly headed the Gambino crime family, had close connections with Pontani, and the New Yorker seemed to have the power to anoint a figurehead replacement to run the business along the Philadelphia-Atlantic City axis.

But a stubborn Scarfo still tried to retain some semblance of mob control from behind prison walls through the young men, including his own son, and the children of the mob defendants in the various crime trials still underway.

'CHARLEY WHITE' SURFACES IN THE POCONOS

One of the five Mafia chiefs and soldiers who were indicted in June as a co-conspirator in the Scarfo-led P2P drug-importing organization was Charles 'Charley White' Iannece. He had become a fugitive from justice in November, 1986, shortly after his mob partner, 'Nicky Crow' Caramandi, became a government witness. While Scarfo and three others were languishing in jail over the hot summer, Iannece was enjoying a vacation, living in a duplex in the affluent Lake Harmony area of the lower Pocono Mountains in Northeastern Pennsylvania.

The FBI received information in September that Iannece might be hiding in the Poconos, just a two-hour drive from his home and family still residing in South Philadelphia. Several Pennsylvania state troopers living in the area were asked to be on the lookout for the graying curly-haired Iannece. When State Trooper Thomas Ansel called in the license plate number of a suspicious car parked in the driveway of a lakeside duplex, a check showed that it was registered to a South Philly bar. This information piqued the interest of FBI agents.

On October 29th, FBI agent Charles 'Bud' Warner pulled his car up beside Iannece as he was going out for one of his occasional afternoon strolls through the nearby woods with his three-month-old German shepherd.

Warner, a 17-year veteran of the FBI, possessed an arrest warrant for Iannece from the Federal District Court for "aiding and abetting conspiracy."

As he got out of his auto in front of the A-frame at #1331 Timberline Drive, Warner pulled out his gun and told Iannece that he was under arrest.

"Warner, don't shoot," said a somewhat startled Iannece.

"I told him to lie down, and spread-eagle his legs," related Warner, "and then I handcuffed him and when he stood up I read him his Miranda rights."

Warner got a search warrant and Iannece agreed to let him search the $440 a month condo. Entering the unlocked door a few hours after leaving Iannece at a nearby police barracks, Warner and Paul Hendrickson, another FBI agent, plus two policemen, found a .22 caliber pistol and a .32 caliber automatic in the bedroom in addition to a false ID card made out to Thomas John Pica. The law enforcement officers also found $900 in cash, a Pennsylvania Voters Registration Card and a Driver's License made out to Donald Marvin Cassalaro at phony addresses in Philadelphia.

"We later turned many of the objects over to Iannece's wife, Rosemary," said Warner at a later pre-trial hearing in early 1988. 'Charley White' gave his dog to the local police department and the food in the refrigerator to the Catholic Church in Lake Harmony.

Warner had been looking for three fugitive mobsters, Ralph Staino Jr., Nick Milano, and Iannece, since early January and after a short surveillance, he and his partner had managed to bag Iannece. Although the captured mobster declined to sign the #302 form after Warner read him his rights, the FBI agent noted at the bottom of the document that Iannece had read them but chose not to sign, although he stated that he understood his rights.

PRE-TRIAL SKIRMISHES

In the preliminary jockeying that took place before the onset of the drug trial in mid-November, 1987, District Judge Thomas N. O'Neill Jr. ruled that the Scarfo jury be sequestered in a hotel, but that they not remain anonymous, despite the contention of the government prosecutors that jurors might become fearful if their identities became known.

Robert Simone, Scarfo's attorney, had opposed the government's request, claiming that there was no evidence that either Scarfo or any of his co-defendants had ever attempted to intimidate a juror in any previous cases.

"The government wants an anonymous jury in this case," Simone wrote, "for the sole purpose of a chilling effect on the jurors in order to deny the defendants a fair trial and an impartial jury."

The five mob defendants came into court each day of the jury selection process and the trial itself dressed like minor business executives, wearing conservative suits and ties. They were all obviously well-coached by their defense attorneys and by Scarfo, who instructed them to keep cool to avoid antagonizing the jury.

WOULD A JURY EVER BE SELECTED?

As the tedious and time-consuming selection of a jury moved into its third day, an exasperated Judge O'Neill began to lose his patience. He asked the two federal prosecutors, Barry Gross and Michael Levy of the U.S. Organized Crime Strike Force, if they would be willing to withdraw their request to sequester the jury for the entire trial — which was expected to last for at least two and a half weeks — since it might spill over into the Yuletide season.

"There's no way I'm going to sequester this jury for Christmas," said the Judge. The government prosecutors declined his request — no matter how long the trial might last.

Several prospective jurors had been dismissed from the panel of selectees because they feared the wrath of the Mafia if they found Scarfo guilty. On December 3rd, the jury selection of twelve members plus three alternatives was halted temporarily, and one juror was replaced by an alternate after members of the jury panel expressed deep and very serious concerns that their identities had become public. One prospective juror had already been dismissed after saying he would probably vote to acquit Scarfo out of fear. Another was also dismissed after explaining that she was aware of the alleged crimes, and confessed: "My emotional reaction is one of fear."

A tape of a ninety-minute private hearing on the same day showed that most jurors selected were confused, and unaware that their names would be a matter of public record. Many did not realize that they would be sequestered in a hotel and that the trial itself would be public.

Finally, after a week's jockeying in the selection process, a jury was picked and the actual trial was ready to begin.

A New Jersey State Policeman: "Is there anybody else close to you that you haven't lied to or cheated?"

Thomas 'Tommy Del' Del Giorno: (after pausing): "Yes, my mother."

-A 1986 interrogation[*]

19 THE SPEED TRIAL: FROM START TO FINISH

WHAT ARE P2P AND METH?

KEVIN Whaley, of the U.S. Drug Enforcement Administration, testified that Phenyl 2 Propanone (P2P), which is also known as oil or phenyl acetone, had a street price of $20,000 a gallon in 1985 in the USA. It could be purchased in raw form in either Belgium or West Germany for a mere $135 a gallon. To convert the P2P into methamphetamine, Whaley pointed out to the court, it would have to be 'cooked' for 24 hours by mixing the oil with various chemicals like aluminum chloride, to make a sludge with a strong pungent odor.

The resulting 8-10 pints of 'speed' made from each gallon of P2P is in the form of a white powder like cocaine and commanded a street price in 1988 in Philadelphia of $10,000 a pound. By cutting the resulting product and thinning it out, up to 24 pounds could be gleaned from each gallon, bringing in a gross revenue of $240,000. This explains the lure of this drug to the underworld. Big profits could be made by those engaged in a methamphetamine operation.

Dr. Steven Weinstein, a psychologist who is the director of the Drug and Alcohol Outreach Program at Jefferson Hospital in Philadelphia, stated in a local newspaper that: "Speed is a dan-

[*] Of the ex-Mafia member in a jail cell, 1986, as related from the witness stand during the 1987 Rouse extortion trial.

gerous drug that has no legal or prescription use. Methamphetamines speed up the entire human system — movement,
thinking, hurried heartbeats — whether taken by snorting it in the
powder form or injecting it into the veins to get a high. It leads to
serious psychological changes leading to psychotic behavior and
paranoia that often sends the user inside the emergency room.
Some 'Speed' patients get the runs and may stay awake for three
or four days straight before they totally collapse in utter
exhaustion. Many can become violent.

"Speed is made from P2P via a smelly cooking process to
convert the raw chemical into the compound for which there is no
known continuous medical treatment other than to quiet and calm
the patient down as well as keeping him or her away from the
drug. It is another of the addictive 'party drugs' that are in the
cocaine class to give one a kick."

Another statement about the power of 'Speed' was made by
Dr. Eric Fine, a psychiatrist who heads the city- and state-funded
Alcohol and Mental Health Association (AMHA) Laboratory and
Clinic at 1200 Walnut Street, Philadelphia. He confirmed that
importation, distribution and sale of methamphetamines is now
big business. Methamphetamines and the like are a dangerous
group of drugs to our society. "Their use brings out dangerous
psychotic traits when abused, often releasing antagonistic paranoia in the patient."

THE OPENING STATEMENTS SET THE PARAMETERS OF THE TRIAL

When the trial got underway on Friday, December 4th, the
five defense attorneys urged the jury to put aside the reputations
of the defendants as mobsters and to reject the expected forthcoming testimony of Thomas Del Giorno, Nicholas Caramandi
and of Steven 'Steakie' Vento, a drug dealer now serving a term
in prison...all of whom were to be prosecution witnesses.

"The bottom line here, Ladies and Gentlemen," said Robert
Simone in his opening statement on behalf of his client, 'Nicky'
Scarfo, "is that this case is not so much about *La Cosa Nostra*,
drugs, and money; it's about credibility, believability and reasonable doubt."

He then pointed out, "You're going to hear that these particular people, Caramandi and Del Giorno, were up to their necks in

drugs, they were up to their necks in murders, and they were up to their necks in perjury...and in every single crime that's in the law books."

Simone said that the government "made deals with the two ex-hoods that enabled them to avoid prosecution....The government has made deals with several devils, and these devils will tell you that they can keep all of the money they ever earned from any source...because they did what the government asked: 'They blamed it on Nicky!'"

To counter the Simone ploy, prosecutor Barry Gross said that the evidence put forth would show that Scarfo, as head of the crime family, had approved all of the criminal undertakings of his subordinates, including involvement with the methamphetamine drug trade.

"You will hear how all decisions to be made, as well as all the money to be split, had to go up the ladder to be approved," said Gross. "All the money had to be split, one half to the soldiers, the other half up the ladder...all the way up to the boss."

He acknowledged that both Del Giorno and Caramandi had been involved in "some horrible crimes," but they were precisely the type of people who would become involved in organized crime.

"These defendants," he said, pointing to Scarfo and the others, "did not select them because they were nice guys. They selected them exactly because of the type of people they are."

But defense attorney Oscar Goodman countered this argument, calling the two mobsters who testified for the government "miscreants" who have "engaged in every crime known to man and breached every commandment known to God."

The courtroom was now ready for the first witness for the prosecution.

'NICKY CROW' AND 'TOMMY DEL' MAKE A RETURN APPEARANCE IN COURT

For the fourth time in the past eight months, the two mobsters-turned-informants, Caramandi and Del Giorno, were ushered into the courtroom as the key witnesses for the government in its case against the Scarfo five.

Once again, the two repeated essentially the same testimony

as they had in the first two Beloff-Rego trials and the Scarfo-Rouse extortion trials, detailing their links to and roles in the Mafia. Del Giorno told the jury: "You weren't supposed to do arson, counterfeiting, drugs, pimping and something about guns." But he stated that the rule on drugs was never strictly enforced.

He did admit, on cross-examination, however, that Scarfo was not personally involved in the plans to get money from the drug operations and was given details of the import-distribution plan on only a few occasions, but insisted that he had given the O.K. or clearance to move ahead on the 'street tax' scheme involving the drug operations and had supervised it.

Del Giorno claimed that Scarfo not only approved of the plan but got a fair share of the profits. He stated that out of $376,000 from one shipment, Caramandi and Iannece split $100,000 and he and 'Faffy' Iannarella each kept $92,000 and the remaining $92,000 was split between Scarfo and Leonetti, his underboss. He also said that $1.3 million from another shipment was split along the same lines.

THE PATTERN AND GROWTH OF THE DRUG CONSPIRACY

Based mainly on the testimonies of both Thomas Del Giorno and Nick Caramandi, the outlines of the multi-million dollar drug operation began to become clear to the jury and the court. The operation began in the summer of 1985, when Salvatore 'Chuckie' Merlino (then second in command under Scarfo before his abrupt demotion to soldier months later) told Del Giorno to instruct both Iannece and Caramandi to demand street tax money from Angelo DiTullio for each gallon of P2P imported from West Germany and Belgium. A similar tax was taken from John Renzulli who operated a separate organization. He was instructed to purchase the P2P from DiTullio, then manufacture speed from the P2P.

HOW THE P2P WAS SHIPPED AND PROCESSED IN THE USA

The three main government informants described in vivid terms the camouflage methods of importing the P2P into this country. They used a large air compressor to ship seventy-five gallons from Belgium in the early summer of 1985, several barbecue grills to ship thirty gallons of P2P in September, 1985, and some radiators filled with one hundred fifty gallons of the chemical in March, 1986.

The shipments were sent to companies that acted as fronts for the mob. The South Philadelphia Decorators Company, the Therapeutica Company, and the Rapid Equipment and Supply Company in South Philadelphia all received shipments.

After each of these shipments reached their respective destinations, the shakedown split would take place, with Scarfo and Leonetti getting at least a third, and Del Giorno and Caramandi splitting the rest (although 'Nicky Crow' claimed he had to kickback half of his to the boss).

According to the June, 1987, Federal indictments, over 650 gallons of P2P were imported from Belgium and West Germany between August, 1984, and October, 1986, with most of it being smuggled in to various locations in Philadelphia. In that two and a half year period, some 375 pounds of methamphetamine were manufactured in at least seven area locations, ranging from private homes in South Philadelphia and in the suburban towns around Camden, to a farmhouse in Bucks County, Pennsylvania, and a Mystic Island home on the Jersey shore.

The Scarfo-approved shakedown, however, appeared to be leveled at the importers of the P2P chemical and not at the distributors of the speed or the myriad of street pushers.

When Caramandi followed Del Giorno on the stand, his testimony was essentially the same, with a few minor discrepancies and some added information as to how much money Scarfo received in extortion money from the P2P drug operation. Where Del Giorno testified that Scarfo and Leonetti received less than $200,000 from two shipments, Caramandi had received more than twice that amount — $500,000 in 1985 and 1986, but had been disappointed because he was expecting much more, about $1 million from a one-hundred-gallon shipment.

'Nicky Crow' confirmed that both 'Tommy' and 'Faffy' made that statement about Scarfo's slice-of-the-pie, and that 'Faffy' also said Scarfo was a greedy guy.

THE PLOT TO KILL STEVE VENTO JR. IS HATCHED

Caramandi also recounted a botched plan to kill Steven Vento Jr., the son of Steven 'Steakie' Vento Sr., age 46, who was doing an eighteen-year term on drug charges in the federal Lewisburg, Pennsylvania, Penitentiary for drug trafficking. Vento had been a partner with Angelo 'Chickie' DiTullio in the P2P importation end of the business and DiTullio became suspicious that reputed mob soldier Ralph 'Junior' Staino had been involved in the theft of half of the hundred gallon shipment. The elder Vento became angry when this information was passed on to him about the alleged theft by a man who had been in hiding from the law and was an indicted co-conspirator in the case.

When the father passed on the information to his son, the younger Vento then began "shooting his mouth off that he wasn't going to pay us," said Caramandi. This arrogance against the Mafia started a debate within the Scarfo hierarchy about whether or not Vento Jr. should be eliminated.

After an April, 1986, meeting with Scarfo, Del Giorno informed Caramandi that a high-level decision had been made to kill the younger Vento — and that they would be involved in the hit.

When Vento Sr. took the stand as the seventh and last government witness, (and one of the key informants) he confirmed Caramandi's story about the assassination attempt on his son. He was heard on tape during an April 10, 1986, conversation with an associate, Joseph 'Mousey' Massamino to take a message to Charley Iannece.

"Tell 'em I said: 'Go fuck himself and everybody connected with him. And tell him if I don't have $10,000 from him Tuesday morning, I'm gonna do what I have to do!'"

"What is that fat motherfucker trying to tell me?" said Vento. "He's [Iannece] a tough guy but I'm in jail now!"

Then he asked plaintively: "What am I supposed to do if they go near my kid?"

Massamino answered him bluntly: "You've been fucked! That's the bottom line!"

An irate Vento shouted back into the phone: "Who the fuck is that 'lil motherfucker! When did he [Charley White] become a real tough guy?"

Vento was adamant that he was not going to pay the hated street tax to Scarfo and his cohorts and then have the nerve to belittle the messengers — like Iannece — that Scarfo had sent to collect the payoffs.

Massamino sounded surprised that Vento would be crazy enough to send such a threatening message to the mob — from behind prison walls.

"You serious?" he asked Vento.

"I'm as serious as a motherfuckin' cancer," he retorted. "You tell him [Iannece] that's the way it is, O.K.? Would you send that message? Tell him that's what I want! Because that's for his protection....I'm sure he'll know what I'm talking about...because that's the same message I got."

On May 26, 1986, Steve Vento Jr. was shot twice in the head and wounded as he sat in a car with his girlfriend near his South Philly home. It was not fatal and somehow he recovered. Caramandi then met with Scarfo and advised him that he was against making another effort to kill Vento.

Scarfo agreed and said: "I'll take care of it."

No further attempts were made on the life of 'Steakie' Vento's son. The murder contract was called off. On May 28, 1986, Vento told DiTullio in a taped phone call to relay to Caramandi how he felt about the shooting, "You tell him, all three of them [Scarfo, Caramandi and Iannece] are held responsible, you hear me?" shouted Vento. "And tell them if they don't find out who did this, they're held responsible!"

Despite his defiance of the mob, Vento is still alive and well in the Lewisburg pen and has continued to declare his independence. "I don't give nothing to nobody!" he boasted.

THE DEFENSE RESTS

The five defense attorneys decided (in caucus during mid-trial proceedings) not to call any of their clients or any character witnesses to the stand since "they didn't need to subject the five Mafia figures to any cross-examination by the government," said Simone. Instead they relied on the minds of the jury to reject the credibility of the two government-protected mobsters and that of Steve Vento — the imprisoned drug dealer.

On Wednesday, December 9th, after the jury left the courtroom for the day, Simone argued with the Judge that the drug charges against his client be thrown out. "He *may* be the boss of a *La Cosa Nostra* family, but he is *not* a drug kingpin. Mr. Scarfo was not the organizer, supervisor or manager of this drug operation." The Judge rejected his plea.

Later, Simone commented in a post-trial interview that: "I didn't concede it [that Nicky was the mob boss], but I said even if you believe it, it's not the issue!" This point would soon become a crucial element and key issue in the series of Scarfo murder trials in both Pennsylvania and New Jersey courts.

THE GOVERNMENT SUMS UP ITS CASE

Just before noon on Thursday, December 10th, federal prosecutor Mike Levy took the podium in a one hour and ten minute closing argument to the jury. He stressed that this case *is* about the Mafia and drugs and *not* one about your friends and neighbors....Caramandi, Del Giorno and Vento are not like members of your club or your friends and neighbors. The government has to take witnesses where it finds them and when you get into the sewer of a drug deal there are no swans swimming around. The issue is not whether Caramandi, Del Giorno and Vento are nice. They are not. *The only issue is whether they are telling the truth."*

Levy then went on to retrace the various shakedowns, the importation of P2P, its distribution and conversion into methamphetamines. He related the shakedown by Del Giorno, and Caramandi of the various P2P importers and distributors, pointing out the inconsistencies of Del Giorno telling the jury that the mob got $100,000 for each gallon of P2P brought into the country while Caramandi said it was only $75,000.

The prosecutor explained to the jury that any inconsistencies "which the defense will stress are coming from 'professional witnesses prepped by us,' is unimportant."

Levy recounted month-by-month, the various events of who did what to whom in the drug processing operations in which Scarfo and Leonetti got at least $1,000,000 in August ,1986, from a total shipment purchase of $1,500,000.

Levy told the jury that both Caramandi and Del Giorno faced twenty years and a $250,000 fine, approved by both the U.S. government and the State of New Jersey, if they were found to have lied. He said their plea agreements would be nullified and they could both face the electric chair for their murder confessions.

Near the end of his closing arguments, Levy flashed several miniaturized copies of Scarfo's five most recent IRS Form #1040 income tax returns on a small screen, showing that he only declared $15,000 of his 1982 return and with no tax filed in 1983, when he was in jail. For 1984, he declared an income of $50,830 with $45,000 coming from commissions and fees and $5,830 for his services as a consultant.

In 1985, he declared an income to the IRS of $41,000 (with $30,000 coming from commissions and $11,000 from miscellaneous). He paid a tax of $14,765 that year.

Finally, in 1986, he declared $45,000 gross income on his #1040 with $32,000 stemming from commissions and fees and $13,000 from miscellaneous.

For some unexplained reason, the government did *not* note whether he had been audited for these alleged phony returns with unexplained sources of his so-called commissions and fees.

But the government did point out to the jury how Scarfo made it a continuing habit of giving cash gifts to people and getting checks back as 'gifts' to cover up his illegal operations. He made payments of $49,200 on his winter home at Casablanca South in Ft. Lauderdale, Florida, where he had set up a Casablanca South Leasing Company for laundering his cash flow.

He also purchased a recent vintage Rolls Royce through Caramandi for $17,500 — with the latter giving him $6,000 for Scarfo's used Lincoln on the trade-in.

According to the government, the cost of these items alone came to $152,000, and did not include the cost of airline tickets, food, clothing, entertainment, etc. With only $86,000 reported to the IRS in 1985-86, there was an excess of at least $66,000 in cash needed to purchase the above items that had not been reported to Uncle Sam. Where did it come from? Nicky didn't say.

Levy's last words to the jury showed the parallel between the Mafia and General Motors, where those down below had to get the O.K. up the chain of command from their vice presidents and supervisors. "The man at the top of the Mafia is Nicky Scarfo and he gave the orders to those down below...like the president of General Motors does," he said.

'TIGER LIL' MAKES A DRAMATIC COURTROOM APPEARANCE

While the prosecutors and defense attorneys were making their summaries to the jury, a character from the past came into the courtroom and sat in the family section with two young men.

Wearing black tights and a white sweater, Lillian Reis, the ex-head of the chorus line of the defunct Latin Casino Nightclub in the early Sixties, appeared to be deeply concerned with the outcome of the trial. After all, her husband, Ralph Staino Jr., a fugitive from justice, was one of the indicted co-conspirators in the P2P drug case. When asked during a courtroom break if she knew where Junior was hiding, she answered with a shrug: "I have *no* idea where he is."

THE DEFENSE EXCORIATES THOMAS DEL GIORNO AND 'NICKY CROW'

When it came time for the defense to sum up its criticism of the government's case against their clients, 'Bobby' Simone pointed out in his opening words to the jury: "Isn't it ironic that after the testimony of Del Giorno and Caramandi you are the ones *locked up* and *they are free* to do almost everything they want. This case is about the *believability* and the *credibility* of Tom Del Giorno and Nick Caramandi and not about the *La Cosa Nostra*."

He pleaded with the jury to make an independent decision, and not to follow the whims of the biased press, since Mr. Scarfo had been convicted in the press already.

Simone then raked over the credibility of the "two lying government witnesses" with the government "paying out $210,000 a year" (including the cost of guards) to "keep Del Giorno and his family happy," and $121,000 to protect Caramandi. "So, it costs the government $331,000 a year to keep these witnesses in whiskey and not in prison," he sneered.

In his one-hour summation, Simone stressed that the prosecution had not presented "one bit of evidence, pictures or tapes" tying any of the five defendants to any drug dealers. "The source of their evidence is so polluted, so corrupt, it almost makes me sick," he said.

Simone wound up his plea by reminding the jury of the warning by Scarfo to both men at the *La Cosa Nostra* Mafia making ceremony when he said, "Don't deal in drugs!"

"Yet they did it," Simone reminded the jury, "so do you believe in their reliability now? Do you have the guts to do right? ....The government wants you to look the other way and compromise. Are you strong enough to resist the press and the public outcry for Scarfo's scalp?"

Then he concluded with a famous quote from the late criminal lawyer, Clarence Darrow, who said: "*I would rather be dead than live in an America in which even the lowliest of citizens can be convicted on the evidence of informers.*"

The other defense attorneys, led by Oscar Goodman, pushed the 'reasonable doubt' argument, imploring the jury to acquit their clients.

Goodman challenged the jury with a charge that "the buck stops here with you! That's what makes this country different! I don't concede that Phil Leonetti is a member of any secret organization — except out of the mouths of the sewer."

"No matter how much the government wants my client," he shouted, "They are not going to get him with *you* as the jury!"

He was the last of the defense attorneys to sum up the case, not for his client, but *against* Del Giorno and Caramandi. As Simone put it earlier: "Would you buy a used car from either of those guys or even a pedigreed French poodle?"

A LAST GASP FROM THE GOVERNMENT

In his brief rebuttal, Prosecutor Barry Gross agreed that both Caramandi and Del Giorno are "horrible and despicable people," but said, "we didn't choose these men...They were chosen by the defendants to become part of their thing, *La Cosa Nostra*, the Mafia."

This Catch 22 dilemma would soon present a problem for the jury when they retired to deliberate and agonize over their findings of guilt or innocence.

THE JURY RENDERS A SHOCKING VERDICT

At 11:15 AM on Saturday, December 12th, the jury came back into the courtroom after deliberating for seven hours over two days. When Judge O'Neill Jr. asked the designated jury Forelady Dr. Leona Laskin, 61, a retired anesthesiologist from Center City, Philadelphia, if the jury had reached a decision, she answered in a strong and clear voice: "We have, your honor."

As the clerk read each count of the multiple indictments on the drug charges, beginning with the five leveled against Mafia boss

Scarfo, an air of anticipation pervaded the electric-charged court-room. Several wives and family members of the accused fin-gered rosaries and held up their hands with fingers crossed in good luck signs for their relatives sitting beyond the fence. One young boy, a son of 'Faffy' Iannarella, wept softly into his hands as he sat on the bench — alone — waiting to hear the verdict against his father.

When — with a smile on her face — Dr. Laskin read the ver-dict of "Not Guilty" on the first several counts against Scarfo, the family members and friends of the accused in the back benches burst into hoots and applause. After Judge Thomas O'Neill twice threatened to clear the courtroom unless the observers quieted down, silence ensued until Dr. Laskin read the final, incredible "Not Guilty" verdict on the twenty charges leveled against the five Mafia mobsters.

Unrestrained bedlam broke out in the fourteenth floor court-room and the Judge was unable to restrain the applause and obscenities that were hurled in his chambers as he dismissed the jury.

After denouncing the three key government witnesses, Cara-mandi, Del Giorno and Vento as liars, a jubilant Scarfo left his place from behind the defense table and walked quickly over to the jury box and grabbed the hand of one female juror to thank her. In a moment, a blue-coated U.S. Marshal grabbed him by the shoulder and ushered him away from the jury box. The highly emotional courtroom scene continued with Scarfo shout-ing: "This is the beginning of the end of the lies!"

"I just wanted to shake their hands," said Scarfo. "Thank God!" called out one red-haired woman, as family members and supporters burst into spontaneous applause at the unanimous verdict of acquittal on all counts of the indictments against the five defendants for conspiring to control the importation and sale of the P2P chemical.

AFTERSHOCKS SHAKE THE COURTROOM

"Silence!" ordered Judge O'Neill, but no one seemed to pay attention to him as the jury was quickly ushered out a side door.

At this moment, the Mafia *capo*, Francis 'Faffy' Iannarella, cupped his hands over his mouth and started shouting obscenities towards the government law enforcement officials — which Assistant U.S. Attorney Barry Gross interpreted as "offensive to us and the FBI."

Losing his cool momentarily, the six-foot-three-inch Gross shouted back to the defendants to: "Shut the fuck up...You assholes!"

The spectators gasped at this outburst and at Scarfo's immediate retort: "No, you shut the fuck up! Fuck you, you shit! It's the end of the lies!"

As Scarfo and the other four defendants were led away by the Marshals through a door at the front of the courtroom, he turned to the FBI men and prosecutors standing behind the government table and shouted one last threat of defiance: "Who lied?"

He answered the question himself: "Caramandi and Del Giorno!! Both are fucking liars, the lying scum, and tell them — the FBI — to stay away from our women!"

Scarfo's attorney, Bobby Simone, explained later that his client was referring to an FBI agent who had been "running around trying to interview wives" of some Scarfo associates to obtain information.

Gross later apologized for his emotional remarks, even though he and his partner, U.S. Assistant Attorney, Mike Levy, both stated that they accepted the jury's verdict even though they were disappointed in the outcome.

On the following page is a chart showing the structure of the 'speed' operation.

The Scarfo P2P (Speed) Operation

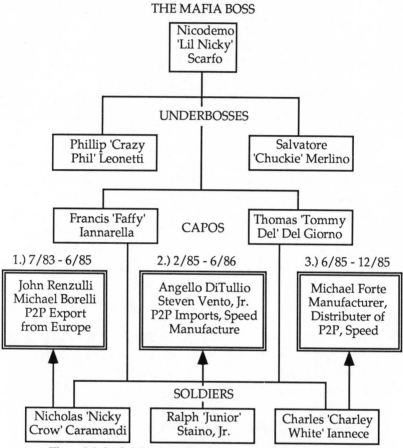

THE MAFIA BOSS

Nicodemo
'Lil Nicky'
Scarfo

UNDERBOSSES

Phillip 'Crazy
Phil' Leonetti

Salvatore
'Chuckie' Merlino

Francis 'Faffy'
Iannarella

CAPOS

Thomas 'Tommy
Del' Del Giorno

1.) 7/83 - 6/85

John Renzulli
Michael Borelli
P2P Export
from Europe

2.) 2/85 - 6/86

Angello DiTullio
Steven Vento, Jr.
P2P Imports, Speed
Manufacture

3.) 6/85 - 12/85

Michael Forte
Manufacturer,
Distributer of
P2P, Speed

SOLDIERS

Nicholas 'Nicky
Crow' Caramandi

Ralph 'Junior'
Staino, Jr.

Charles 'Charley
White' Iannece

These Mafia Soldiers received orders from Iannarella and
Del Giorno to collect 'street tax' of about $2,000/gallon of P2P
from the import, manufacture and distribution organizations.

1.) John Renzulli was the head of the organization.
2.) DiTullio and Vento were partners.
3.) Forte received his material from DiTullio and Vento.

Consolidation of these three Methamphetamine organizations into one
by the Mafia took place June 24, 1986.

Source: 11 indictments by the U.S. Attorney for the U.S District Court,
Eastern District of Pennsylvania, June 1987, based on violations of 10
sections of Title #21, 2 of Title #26 and 1 of Title #18 of the U.S. Code.

Francis 'Faffy' Iannarella
- Capo

Phil 'Crazy Phil' Leonetti
-underboss (Scarfo's Nephew)

Nicodemo 'Lil Nicky' Scarfo Sr.
-boss of the Crime Family

Salvatore 'Wayne' Grande
- Soldier

Salvatore Scafidi - Soldier

Joe Grande - Soldier

Aerial View of Penn's Landing on the Delaware River in Philadelphia where the founder of Pennsylvania first landed in 1683. This was the site of the million dollar extortion scam by the Mafia against Rouse and Co., to insure that the firm would be 'protected' on the $730 million development project.
-photo courtesy Rouse and Co.

Leland Beloff wearing autographed trunks during his short-lived boxing career.

Beloff on the set in Hollywood, where he made a film with his friend, the late comedian, Ernie Kovacs. —photo courtesy *Philadelphia Magazine*

Nicodemo Scarfo (2nd from left) talking to fellow mobsters including Thomas Del Giorno (wearing striped T-shirt) in front of his home on North Georgia Avenue, Atlantic City, New Jersey.

Phil 'Chickenman' Testa, boss of the Philadelphia Mafia for one year (1980–81) walking on a local street with his successor, Nicodemo 'Lil Nicky' Scarfo.

(L to R) Nicholas Caramandi, Charles Iannece and an unidentified mobster with their dates at an Atlantic City hotel casino, 1986

Thomas Del Giorno sitting in a hotel room overlooking the Atlantic City Convention Center with a friend.
— photo courtesy the FBI and U.S. Organized Crime Strike Force

(R to L) Tom Del Giorno, Charles Iannece, Nicholas Caramandi, Frances Iannarella seated between the two lower ropes at ringside at an Atlantic City boxing match in 1985. (These photos helped to prove the credibility of the two mob 'turncoats' to buttress their court testimony.)

Willard Rouse, III, a Partner in Rouse and Associates and the man who first 'blew the whistle' on Nicky Scarfo's million dollar extortion scheme regarding the development at Penn's Landing.

Ex-Councilman Leland Beloff leaving the Federal Courthouse in Philadelphia with his wife, Diane, on July 2, 1987, telling reporters that he was "stunned."
-photo courtesy *The Philadelphia Inquirer*

carfo Acquitted in Drug Trial

One of Scarfo's few court victories was the December 12, 1987 jury acquittal for his alleged involvement in the P2P methamphetamine 'Speed' conspiracy

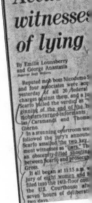

Inside La Cuchina Restaurant, 121 South Street, Philadelphia, with columns reminiscent of the ancient Roman Forum.   The Scarfo mob often met there in small groups to conduct business. Beloff often ate there since it was located in his district. La Cuchina was owned by Sam 'the Barber' La Russa, who made his home available to Scarfo for a Mafia initiation.

Charles 'Joey' Grant, Assistant District Attorney of Philadelphia who won the landmark conviction of Scarfo and his cohorts for first-degree murder in the 'Frankie Flowers' trial.

The Sweet Shop in South Philadelphia where Sal Testa was murdered by Sal 'Wayne' Grande on September 14, 1984.

Edward S. G. Dennis, Jr., former U.S. Attorney for the Eastern District of Philadelphia and presently the Chief of the Criminal Division of the U.S. Justice Dept. in Washington. He successfully prosecuted both Scarfo and Beloff on the extortion indictment.
— photo courtesy U.S. Justice Dept.

Nicky Scarfo's palatial winter home, Casablanca South, located in
the Coral Ridge section of Fort Lauderdale, Florida. Built in 1979, it
contains 4 bedrooms, 5 bathrooms, a pool, whirlpool, patio and a boat
slip on a lagoon, where his 40' cabin cruiser, *Casablanca, The Usual
Suspects,* was docked.
   -FBI photo

'Captain' Nicodemo Scarfo, with hand on the railing of his cruiser,
Casablanca, The Usual Suspects, taking his guests on a cruise in Fort
Lauderdale, Florida, 1985.
   -FBI photo

Aerial view of the Coral Ridge section of Fort Lauderdale where Scarfo's home is located (see inset)

Nicky Scarfo standing inside the foyer of Casablanca South by the side of his prized wrought-iron flamingo fountain

(L to R) Phil Leonetti, Nicky Scarfo, Sal Scafidi and Joe Grande on an Atlantic Ocean beach at Fort Lauderdale — during palmier days

Phil Leonetti, Nicky Scarfo, Nicholas Caramandi and Joe Grande enjoying a Florida vacation together when 'Nicky Crow' was still a loyal part of the mob.

The verdict at the end of the dramatic, two-month-long RICO trial (November 19, 1988).

—photo courtesy
The Philadelphia Inquirer

Federal District Court Judge Franklin Van Antwerpen, who presided over the 1988 RICO trial, wherein Scarfo and 17 of his cohorts were found guilty on 40 counts. (District Court Photo)

The Four Horsemen plus One. U.S. Organized Crime Force Prosecutors, Lou Pichini, Arnold Gordon, David Fritchey, and Albert Wicks, with Joe Peters of the Pennsylvania State Attorney General's Office, who conducted the RICO case against Scarfo and his crime family.
(USOCSF photo)

Exterior of the Spanish style architecture of the front of Scarfo's mansion, *Casablanca South*, Ft. Lauderdale, Fla.—purchased on an annual income of $30,000 a year (as reported to the IRS).

—photo courtesy the FBI

The use of methamphetamines brings out dangerous psychotic traits when abused, often releasing antagonistic paranoia in the patient. *I am frightened* when I see such 'speed' users coming to our methadone clinics who are suffering from abuses of amphetamines.

-Dr. Eric Fine[*]

20 SCARFO, THE 'SPEED KING', IS VICTORIOUS

THE DEFENSE INTERPRETS THE MEANING OF THE DECISION

THE defense attorneys all agreed that the jury's decision marked a repudiation of the testimony of Del Giorno and Caramandi. Simone said, "It's hard for me to believe that any jury would accept their testimony. The momentum has switched." Then using a football-game analogy, he said, "We are going into the second half of future trials with our side having the momentum. There is no question that Nicky Scarfo is now cleared of being a 'drug overlord.'"

Oscar Goodman, the swashbuckling, cowboy lawyer from Las Vegas, speaking on behalf of his client, 'Crazy Phil' Leonetti, chimed in, saying, "The jury did the right thing. Caramandi and Del Giorno were the backbone of their [the government's] case and it is now like a shattered spine....This case was a giant win for us!! Since it was more serious than the other ones because people get shaky when the drug distribution business becomes an issue. I'm happy that this case marks the beginning of the end for these two bums. Let the government put them out on the street and see how they make out. The government has nothing else but the mouths of these two liars....The government

---

[*] A psychiatrist, who heads the Philadelphia AMHA (Alcohol and Mental Health Assoc.) Laboratory and Clinic, in a statement made after Scarfo's acquittal in December, 1987.

should not have brought this case in the first place. They had nothing but rats as their chief witnesses."

When some sympathetic onlookers shouted almost in unison to Goodman and Simone, "You are the best lawyers in the world," an expansive Goodman responded, "You're darn right, we are!"

THE AFTERMATH FOR A DEFEATED GOVERNMENT STAFF

Both Levy and Gross felt that the verdict would not hurt further pending prosecutions of Scarfo. Gross said, "I think this decision has no ramifications beyond this case." Two other juries accepted the testimony of Del Giorno and Caramandi and rendered guilty verdicts, based largely on the testimony of the first two Philadelphia area mobsters to break the Mafia's once sanctified 'Code of Silence.'

The legal battle of the five Mafia figures who had just gained a 'Phyrric Victory' was far from over. Scarfo and his four henchmen were taken back to prison in handcuffs to await their next trial, scheduled for January 25, 1988 in Philadelphia's Common Pleas Court. The five, plus four others, were slated to be tried for the 1984 murder of mob figure, Salvatore Testa, the son of the slain former mob boss, Philip 'Chickenman' Testa.

In April, 1988, all four except Iannece, plus four others, were scheduled to face a second murder trial for the 1985 killing of Frank 'Frankie Flowers' D'Alfonso and again on September 6, 1988 in New Jersey, where all five, plus seven accomplices, were scheduled to stand trial for the 1978 murder of former Somers Point Municipal Judge Edwin Helfant — who had once ruled against them.

In those upcoming cases, Caramandi and Del Giorno would be called as key witnesses once again, but the government hinted that it would rely on other testimony than just that of the two ex-Mafiosos. These new trials would be a further test of the sanctity of U.S. law vs. Mafia law.

The Mafia did suffer a psychological and costly scare despite the acquittal. If any of the five defendants were ever freed from jail following their subsequent trials for murder of fellow Mafia members, the escalating legal costs and time required for their defense, might give them and their associates some pause before getting involved in any new drug operations. The fear of new arrests following their initial branding by the government for allegedly being in the drug importation and distribution racket, could only lead to a dampening of their enthusiasm to try to tangle with the Feds again sometime in the distant future. The government hinted that it might be getting ready to bring new RICO charges soon.

From now on, the defendants could never be sure if another 'Tommy Del' or 'Nicky Crow' was somewhere out there taping them for future courtroom evidence.

TWO JURIES — BUT DIFFERENT VERDICTS

Four days after the twelve member jury found Nicodemo Scarfo and four Mafia underlings "Not Guilty" of running a monopolistic $1,500,000 drug importing and distribution racket in the Delaware Valley, a similar jury in Palermo, Sicily, found another group of Mafiosos guilty of heroin trafficking.

In the Sicilian case, the largest Mafia trial ever held in the world, 338 out of 452 defendants accused of running a vast criminal empire exporting heroin to New York were found guilty by a jury of four women and two men. That jury sentenced nineteen members of the Sicilian Mafia to the maximum penalty — life in prison.

One of those convicted, Mitchell Greco, 63, was nicknamed 'the Pope' because of his place atop the Mafia hierarchy in Sicily. He was also found guilty of ordering seventy-eight homicides, including the assassination of several important government officials, including one for which he will soon stand trial.

Ironically, the most important evidence in both cases came from Mafia informers. Tommaso Buscetta and Salvatore Contorno testified in Italy. Nicholas Caramandi and Thomas Del Giorno spilled their guts in the United States.

Buscetta was also a key prosecution witness in the so-called 'Pizza Connection' trial held in New York, in early 1987. Eighteen of nineteen New York Mafia family figures were convicted in March for being part of an international Mafia ring struggling for the control of the heroin trade that sold more than $1.6 billion of the drug using pizza shops as fronts.

Tommaso Buscetta was the first Mafia boss to break the Sicilian Mafia Code of Silence just as Del Giorno and Caramandi had here. Buscetta described a hierarchical organization with its precise chain of command decision-making process similar to the one described in this book. He alleged that Greco was the chief of a twelve-member ruling commission on the island, which ordered major crimes to be committed and tried to mediate clashes between rival clans. His view of the Mafia became known as "The Buscetta Theorem," and it was the keystone of the prosecution and the vehicle to press homicide as well as drug charges against members of the commission — the court holding them collectively responsible for the crimes listed.

The Sicilian prosecutor, Giuseppe Ayala, told reporters after the verdict was announced on the evening of December 16th that: "Their testimony was accepted when other facts confirmed it." In the Philadelphia case, the testimony of 'Nicky Crow' and 'Tommy Del' was *not* accepted, since not enough other facts were presented by the prosecution to back up the assertions of collusion in the drug racket.

What was unique about the Sicilian case, as deduced from the testimony, was that it marked the first time that the Mafia had been prosecuted as a single, unified organization with its own leadership. The 'maxi-trial' as it soon became known, was viewed throughout Italy and Sicily as a demonstration of the state's willingness to strike at the heart of a major criminal organization that had grown steadily more powerful and murderous as it expanded its illegal tentacles inside the lucrative global drug trade.

Edward Dennis Jr., the U.S. Attorney in the Eastern District of Pennsylvania, had been attempting to accomplish the same ends here with his series of criminal prosecutions against Scarfo and his flock of Mafia mobsters, but came up a loser on the 'speed' charges.

What a stark contrast with the bold headline about the Mafia trial in Sicily's largest newspaper, *Giornale di Sicilia*, which read: "Maxi Condemnation," and *The Philadelphia Inquirer* on Sunday which ran a front page banner headline: "Scarfo Found 'Not Guilty'."

Unfortunately, the Mafia is still very much alive in both countries after these public trials. Proof of the true nature of the mob in Sicily was evidenced four hours after the sentencing of Greco and his henchmen, when Antonio Giulla, one of the Mafia defendants declared innocent, was murdered in cold blood as soon as he was released from custody.

In America, Del Giorno and Caramandi are still *in communicado*, with new names and new addresses, protected by the Feds at a cost to the taxpayers of over $250,000 a year — so they can testify again, hopefully with better supportive evidence — at future trials of Scarfo and Company.

Whereas the Scarfo trial took just a little over a week to come to a conclusion, the Greco-led Mafia trial in Sicily took almost two years, beginning on February 10, 1986, with the major defendants being incarcerated in the courtroom inside thirty grilled cages lining the back of the room.

In contrast, Scarfo, along with 'Crazy Phil' Leonetti, 'Chuckie' Merlino, 'Faffy' Iannarella, and 'Charley White' Iannece were ushered into the courtroom in handcuffs, which were removed while they sat at the defendants' tables and reapplied by the U.S. Marshals when they were taken back to Holmesburg Prison to await trial for the murder of Salvatore Testa in January.

The mass trial technique, in both America and Sicily, has marked a new approach by law enforcement officials to prosecuting the Mafia, but without parallel successes.

SOME OVERSIGHTS BY THE FEDS

The five defense attorneys were obviously jubilant at winning the case for their clients, according to post-mortem interviews outside the courtroom. Oscar Goodman felt particularly happy since he had gone down to defeat earlier in the year, not once but twice trying to defend Councilman Lee Beloff.

So, in the flush of victory, Goodman boasted about "how the jury forelady announced the verdict. She seemed to have such a feeling of pride in her voice."

Yet, several long-time court observers, including reporters, who had covered the three previous trials that year, could not quite understand how this jury could come up with a unanimous Not Guilty verdict, while the other juries found the defendants, including Scarfo himself, Guilty on all charges, using the same key witnesses.

An analysis of some reasons why this jury rendered its decision the way it did includes:

THE NON-ANONYMITY OF THE JURY

Although the jury had been sequestered for over a week at a nearby hotel with all meals and expenses paid for as "guests of the U.S. Treasury," in the words of Judge O'Neill, they were not selected from an anonymous panel of one hundred. The co-prosecutor, Michael Levy, had requested the court that they remain anonymous for their own protection, but Judge O'Neill overruled his request.

So, the reporters and defendants knew not only the names, but the street and hometown addresses of each and every one of the eight women and four male jurors, of which ten were White and two were Black.

Several members of the panel of prospective jurors who were rounded up from all over the Delaware Valley were respectively excused from service on the grounds that they feared the mob, or feared for their own safety, or the security of their families if they rendered a Guilty verdict. After all, many already knew that Scarfo and his cohorts were soon to stand trial for the killing of a New Jersey judge in Cape May, who had ruled against them, a case in which Scarfo had been fingered for driving the getaway car.

One lawyer close to the case felt that "this jury was intimidated and felt afraid to render a 'guilty' verdict. Some may even have been threatened through underground means before they rendered their verdict."

OVERSIGHTS BY THE PROSECUTORS IN PRESENTING THE GOVERNMENT'S CASE

When asked why the U.S. government had not included an extortion charge against the five Mafia figures in light of 'Bobby' Simone's closing statement that he felt that the "government had a probable extortion case against his client" but didn't list it, Assistant U.S. Attorney Michael Levy said: "We didn't want to complicate the jury's thinking with the possible inconsistencies of extortion since we felt we had enough of a case to win without it."

Unfortunately, they did not, in light of the final decision, but Levy did not rule out a future trial on the extortion of drug dealers by the Scarfo-led Mafia. Maybe it was because the extortion in this case was 'bad guys' vs. 'bad guys' while in the Rouse case, it was 'bad guys' vs. 'good guys' and that the jury might not care who was conned in the mobsters' sting operation in the 'Speed' Conspiracy trial. Yet extortion seemed to fit under the broader federal RICO investigation then underway.

Levy left it open, however, whether his office might bring in an extortion case against the Mafia Five in the near future. The prosecutors could have used more graphics in presenting their earlier case, i.e., blowups of Scarfo's federal income tax returns.

One of the mysteries that pervaded the trial was why the government brought the case to trial to begin with.

Gross explained, "If we had not felt that there was sufficient evidence to convict in our list of June charges...we wouldn't have brought the case into court the way we did."

THE CONDUCT OF THE TRIAL

One of the problems in the conduct of the trial was the lack of control in the courtroom, when the onlookers, families and friends of the accused almost got out of hand on several occasions.

When Levy was asked why he did not bring in any witnesses to speak on the deleterious impact of methamphetamines on drug users, he said he feared that, "the Judge might not have let us use them if we had asked him to let them testify on the effects of controlled substances on individuals since that information was not directly tied to the charges on the docket."

Nowhere during the trial did any prosecutor, defense lawyer, judge or witness bring up the nature of 'Speed'.

But two local authorities, Dr. Steve Weinstein and Dr. Eric Fine, had information which might have swayed the jury into looking at the evidence brought forth by the prosecution in a different light than that presented by two confessed killers and 'Steakie' Vento Sr., who admitted on the stand that he still carried on a drug dealing operation from inside prison walls.

If both the Judge and the prosecutors in the recent trial of THE UNITED STATES vs. NICODEMO SCARFO, *et al*, had taken some or all of Weinstein and Fine's facts into consideration before or during the recent trial, some on that jury might have had second thoughts about acquitting the defendants.

POSTSCRIPT TO THE SECOND TRIAL

While 'Bobby' Rego was out on bail pending an appeal from the eight-year jail sentence for his part in the $1 million Rouse conspiracy extortion plot, he was indicted on another charge involving the manufacturing of methamphetamine on February 10, 1988. He was charged twice by a Federal Grand Jury with obtaining the key chemical P2P between July, 1980, and July, 1983, from Mario 'Sonny' Riccobene, the half-brother of a convicted mob figure, Harry Riccobene.

According to the indictment, Rego and his cohorts rented the top floor of a four-story building in Olde Philadelphia and commenced their operations in 1981 under the front name of the Philadelphia Flooring Co. If convicted on these latest 'speed' charges, Rego could face up to 40 years in prison and would have to pay a maximum fine of $500,000 since this crime was considered far more detrimental to society than the extortion of $1 million from a real estate developer.

Joshua Briskin, Rego's attorney, made a stinging comment after the latest series of charges were leveled against his client, saying that he "was a little surprised by the indictment. The government seems to want more than a pound of flesh. They want eight pounds of flesh on this one."

SIXTEEN WHO GOT CAUGHT FOR 'SPEEDING'

In March, 1988, twelve additional defendants (of the twenty-eight indicted back in June, 1987) were convicted before another jury on the same charges, although the jury could not reach a verdict on the guilt of one of the defendants.

Then on April 21st, 1988, four more Mafia members were convicted in the same Federal court after a two-and-a-half week long trial before Federal Judge Thomas O'Neill for their roles in a major methamphetamine distribution conspiracy. Guilty verdicts were rendered against Angelo DiTullio, 48, Joseph Kelly, 31, from Pennsauken, New Jersey, Edmund Gifford, 42, and John Romolini, 44.

Their drug scam operated with the approval of Nicky Scarfo, who beat the same rap. Relatives of some of the four defendants gasped and started to weep as the lengthy verdict sheets were read to the court. They were hoping for acquittal based on the earlier case, but such a verdict was not forthcoming.

They were each later sentenced to long prison terms and hefty fines.

The mob world is a world of lies.

-Thomas Del Giorno

21

THE MAN WHO GOT 'TOO BIG FOR HIS BRITCHES'

THE STALKING OF SALVATORE TESTA

AFTER the shotgun death of Angelo Bruno, the former Philadelphia/New Jersey Mafia chieftain, in a car parked in front of his South Philadelphia home in March, 1980, the man who succeeded him was Phil 'Chickenman' Testa, a Center City restauranteur. He had a son, Salvatore, who sought membership in the Mafia and his father obliged.

The younger Testa had been initiated into the Mafia by his father and "relished being a tough guy and a gangster," according to a Pennsylvania Crime Commission report. Sal continued in his father's footsteps after his father's demise in early 1981.

When Scarfo succeeded his former patron, Phil Testa, it seemed that he would return the favor and let the younger Testa have some perks as a second-generation mobster. Sal Testa was admitted to the inner circle, was a frequent guest at Scarfo's home and was often seen in the company of the new boss. When Scarfo emerged from the Federal Penitentiary in Texas in January (after serving a two-year sentence), Testa was one of the small cadre of intimates who flew down to greet him. When the plane landed in Philadelphia, Sal Testa walked down the exit ramp with Scarfo, carrying the mob boss's suitcase.

Meanwhile, the Mafia under Scarfo flourished and young Sal Testa soon grew wealthy and powerful, working as a loyal underling. He owned fancy cars and kept a yacht moored in Ventnor, an upper middle-class suburb located just south of Atlantic City. He was a key inner-circle combatant in Scarfo's war

against Harry Riccobene for control of the Atlantic City-Philadelphia Mafia axis.

THE CANCELLED WEDDING

Sal Testa proposed to Maria Merlino, the daughter of Salvatore Merlino, the then Mafia underboss in early 1984 in what was
supposed to be a "marriage of convenience." A noon wedding
was planned for April 28, 1984, at the Epiphany of Our Lord
Church in South Philadelphia, just two blocks from the Merlino
family home. A cascade of wrapped gifts began arriving for the
couple.

Then, on March 13, someone called the church to say that the
wedding had been cancelled.

Two weeks later on March 28th, Sgt. James Ghe, a young
Black Philadelphia cop who had been recruited to serve in the organized crime unit early in 1984, saw Testa standing on the steps
of his house at 2117 Porter Street "laughing and smirking" while
Maria ran in and out in an "upset" state carrying gift-wrapped
packages and clothing to a waiting U-Haul van. She left in a red
Camaro for her father's house.

After the van left Testa's house, Sgt. Ghe stopped the truck
and the driver told him that the wrapped gifts were from the cancelled wedding, so he let it proceed on its way to the next destination, her father's house. The men then drove the truck to her
father's house and carried everything inside. An area police officer noticed that Maria was quite upset as she helped to load the
van.

The many bruised feelings and wounded egos caused by this
abrupt broken engagement between two powerful figures in the
Scarfo crime family of what was to be a 'royal' match created a
rift between Sal Testa and Sal Merlino. Merlino became enraged
and began fanning rumors that Testa was trying to take too much
power from Scarfo. After March 13th, Testa was no longer seen
at the side of Scarfo when he came to town.

According to Frederick T. Martens,[*] when Sal Testa started
getting 'uppity', Scarfo put a tail on him, and ultimately put out a
'contract' because the Mafia boss felt "he was getting too big for

[*] Executive Director of the Pennsylvania Crime Commission

his britches and was threatening Nicky's power base."

In early 1984, *The Wall Street Journal* ran a front page story on the rise of Sal Testa in the Scarfo organization and implied that he "was the heir apparent to Nicky Scarfo or whatever you want to call it."[*] This headline story irked Scarfo and he became more convinced than ever that Testa had to go.

At 8 p.m. on April 13, 1984, Officer Lawrence Trush of the Philadelphia Highway Patrol was covering a "Show and Tell" bash at the C/R Club attached to the famed Palumbo's Restaurant in South Philadelphia when he observed a half-dozen mob members, including Nicky Scarfo, Sal Testa, Sal Merlino, Philip Leonetti, Nicholas Caramandi and Thomas Del Giorno enter the facility.

At this local benefit for handicapped children, Caramandi and several other Mafia soldiers noticed a change in Testa's once arrogant posture. Testa did not sit at the head table with Scarfo, and other *capos* were cold-shouldering him.

"He could not understand why he was being demoted in the eyes of the rest of us," said Caramandi later. "It was a direct insult to him because he was supposed to sit with the boss. No reason was given to him and appearing to be quite upset, he left the meeting early. We have a rule in the *La Cosa Nostra*, that 'no one leaves until the boss leaves.' But he left anyway."

At 3 a.m., still on duty, Trush had witnessed an agitated Testa, accompanied by Frank Narducci and one other mob member leaving the club. "He was visibly upset at something," said Trush, who saw Testa slam the waiting car door shut with a loud bang.

At 3:45 a.m. Scarfo and the rest of his close Mafia members left and headed for the nearby Society Hill Towers. Finally, at 5 a.m., on April 14th, a Cadillac Seville left the C/R Club driven by Nicodemo Scarfo, Jr., and headed off into the dawn.[†]

A further slur was suffered by Testa at the end of April when Nicky Scarfo, Phil Leonetti, Faffy Iannarella and Chuckie Merlino flew off to Puerto Rico without telling Sal where they were

---

[*] According to Thomas Del Giorno when he testified later at the Testa murder trial

[†] This limo had been labeled "The Atlantic City Express" by law enforcement officials since it was the chief mode of transportation used by the boss to shuttle him between the two cities.

going or why. This affront conveyed an unwritten message to Testa from the mob chieftain that he was a marked man.

After the contract was put out on the life of young Testa by Scarfo, there followed a series of 17 bungled attempts by Mafia soldiers in this family to do away with the son of the former mob boss:

(1) Shots Ring Out Above the Fruits and Vegetables

The first attempt to wipe out Testa took place in July, 1982, at a well-known Philadelphia landmark. While he was sitting in the front of a store near the famous Italian Market in South Philadelphia, eight shots were aimed at Sal Testa, critically wounding him. The shooting was later linked to the continuing battle between Scarfo and Testa, and the counter-forces of Harry 'The Hunchback' Riccobene. But Testa recovered from this attack.

(2) A Near Fatal Auto Ride Through the Streets of South Philly

A little more than a year later, in December, 1983, Sal Testa and two bodyguards were riding in a car in South Philadelphia and they were cut off at an intersection by another vehicle. Four men in the other car from the Riccobene faction opened fire point blank on Testa and his associates, but amazingly no one was hit.

When queried by Pennsylvania Crime Commission officials, Testa and his two companions refused to provide police with any details about the incident. After that second shooting and the cancelled wedding to Merlino's daughter, Testa fell completely out of grace with both Scarfo and the then-mob-underboss, Salvatore Merlino.

Testa Tests His Wings

Testa had by now carved out for himself a lucrative piece of the methamphetamine trade in the Philadelphia area and appeared to be developing his own dedicated following among what local police describe as a group of "Young Turks" within the Scarfo-led parent organization.

Adding to his problems of having too much bravado in challenging Scarfo was the growing personal animosity between

Testa and Merlino. Furthermore, rumors ran rampant within the Mafia community that Testa wanted to succeed Sal Merlino as underboss and run the Philadelphia branch of the Scarfo family.

Testa had spread his wings to other independent illegal enterprises which tried to bypass Scarfo and deny the boss his share of the profits.

Sal Testa and Thomas Del Giorno had a joint sports-betting business which had a bankroll of $75,000. When Scarfo asked them how much they had in the business, Del Giorno lied to the boss and said: "Only $35,000."

Shortly after this query by Scarfo, he told Del Giorno one day in April, 1984, during an auto ride with Merlino, that he had decided to do away with Testa. "Don't cowboy it," (which meant in Mafia jargon: 'Don't hit him on the street') "I want you to use 'Charley' [Iannece] and 'The Crow' [Caramandi] as the 'shooters' with 'Faffy' Iannarella as the supervisor," he continued.

'BROWNY' BECOMES THE NEW MISSION OF THE MOB

The conspirators assigned the new code name, 'Browny' to Testa, so that in case they were picked up on a police or FBI wiretap, the listeners wouldn't know who they were talking about.

A few days later, Del Giorno told Caramandi and others at the Mafia clubhouse located at 1214 Moore Street that 'Faffy' 'buried' him. This expression implied that Testa was as good as dead. Then pointing his finger towards the ground, Del Giorno said: "Sally's [Testa] gotta go! Nicky's 'bugged' with him... and he doesn't like the way he is acting...dealing drugs and committing treason to the family."

When Caramandi and his partner Iannece, were asked by Iannarella and Del Giorno if they had any ideas on how to do the killing, they first suggested a neighborhood restaurant. But that suggestion was immediately rejected as no good by the two *capos* as being too close to police surveillance cameras and neighbors in the nearby residences.

'Chucky' Merlino, the underboss, who had been the first to convince Scarfo to do away with Testa, originally wanted Caramandi and Iannece to do the shooting with 'Faffy' Iannarella and

'Tommy Del' Giorno supervising. After several meetings were held to discuss the plot at the Annin Street Café on South 11th Street, 'The Crow' and 'Charley White' felt that it was no good to have two supervisors, so they agreed to pick 'Tommy'. But 'Faffy' didn't like the idea since he was frozen out of the conspiracy and his feelings were hurt. The next day, Iannarella told the others that he didn't want to be involved in the killing.

Knowing they had to be careful, the two designated shooters, Caramandi and Iannece, put several guns in different places — the clubhouse, their homes and autos — so they would be available at any time.

"We were worried about being raided," related Caramandi, "so we didn't have any guns on our persons."

(3) TENNIS ANYONE?

In the second round of the projected Testa contract hit spots, a well-known Philadelphia sports duplex was chosen as the first target location. Sal Testa liked to play tennis and he held a membership in the indoor club at Pier #30 on the Delaware River at the foot of Washington Avenue. He liked to play on the first court inside the door so he could keep one eye peeled on who was entering the recreation facility. Caramandi and Iannece checked out the courts, but discovered that they were too busy with players going in and out. So the idea was abandoned with Iannarella's consent.

(4) SAL'S GIRLFRIEND'S HOUSE BECOMES A LIKELY LOCATION

'Faffy', who came back in the conspiracy after at first wanting out, next suggested the house of Testa's girlfriend, at 13th and Ritner, as a good murder locale. After the two would-be killers checked it out, they found that there was no place to park their getaway car and the area was too congested. So once again, a potential death site was abandoned.

(5) THE BEAUTY SHOP HITSPOT

After the 'Big Four' leaders of the Scarfo crime family returned from a Caribbean vacation, Caramandi and Iannece were told by the boss that they had selected The Headsup Beauty Shop at 18th and Shunk Streets in South Philadelphia — owned by Testa — as the next most likely spot for the fatal hit.

'Chuckie' Merlino took Caramandi and Iannece aside at the beauty parlor and said: "Guess what just happened? Salvie just took us into one of his apartments and we could have shot him right there." Merlino was especially obsessed and becoming fanatical about getting rid of Testa fast since he had broken off the marriage plans with his daughter. The beauty shop plan fizzled since there was no back door for an escape by the hit men and Sal failed to show up after a ten-day casing of the place by Caramandi and Iannece.

(6) 'FAFFY'S' HOUSE

By May, 1984, discussion took place about the possibilities of using others to do the killing. Iannarella and Del Giorno came to the club one day and announced that they had seen Testa, who wished to come to 'Faffy's' house to drop off a gift for Faffy's wife who was pregnant.

Merlino, who was still a *capo*, now designated Salvatore 'Tory' Scafidi to be the new trigger man. Del Giorno ordered Tory to proceed to Faffy's house and pretend that he was fixing the home, with one gun hidden upstairs and one downstairs to be used when Testa arrived with the gift. But his plan fizzled when Testa gave the gift to Faffy a few days later when Scafidi wasn't present.

During the spring and summer of 1984, 'The Crow' allowed some of the mobsters in on the Testa conspiracy to use his basement as a pistol-shooting gallery to practice firing their stolen .22 and .38 caliber pistols into a couple of used telephone books tacked onto the cement wall. Three years later, the local police retrieved bullet fragments and spent .22 and .38 caliber casings from the floor of Caramandi's house located at #1225 Pier Street and at a neighbor's basement at 115 Watkins Street.

(7) THE SWEET SHOP ON PASSYUNK

By early June, it was agreed that Joe Pungitore would take Testa to a sweet shop at 1600 Passyunk Avenue, some two blocks from the Mafia clubhouse where Sal Scafidi would be lying in wait to shoot him. Although this plan was temporarily shelved because a better opportunity suddenly surfaced, it was put on the back burner for later use if other plans were aborted.

(8) THE FUNERAL PARLOR BLUES

When Joe Pungitore's aunt died in June, Scarfo decided that the upstairs bar of the Carto funeral parlor where the bereaved congregated before and after the ceremonies would be "a good place to do it." He designated Sal Scafidi as the shooter and assigned Iannece and Caramandi to dispose of the body. Before the wake occurred, however, something happened that necessitated finding another hit man since Sal was arrested and imprisoned for another crime.

When Del Giorno broke this news to Scarfo, he became upset: "You can't depend on these kids," he fumed, "they're always running around." Scarfo, Leonetti, and Merlino came to a meeting with Caramandi and Iannece to decide who should pull the trigger. A disturbed Scarfo said, "We will still go ahead and do it, with or without Scafidi. Are you agreed?"

They all nodded their heads to affirm the boss's decision.

At the white stucco funeral parlor, a wary Testa stayed outside. Scarfo sidled over to Iannece and Caramandi and whispered: "Are you ready?" They nodded assent, each having a gun hidden on his person.

When the group went upstairs to the bar, Caramandi sat next to Testa when he came in and signalled to Merlino across the bar implying: "Do you want me to do it now?"

Word soon came back to Caramandi, the newly assigned hit man, that there were too many cops outside, so when the funeral was over, Scarfo called it off, but not before Testa shook Merlino's hand as a traditional good-bye gesture. At this moment, 'Chuckie' kissed Sal on the lips...which then made Testa more aware of the impending hit, since this gesture in the Mafia code was a sign of 'the kiss of death'.

Testa was visibly shaken, Del Giorno remembered. "We were all shocked, since it made our hit job harder from then on." Four of the mobsters went to Frankie Ford's place and agreed that Merlino was wrong to have kissed Sal. "He was nuts," said Del Giorno.

After a summer of failed attempts to do away with Testa, Del Giorno and the other *capos* decided that the only way to succeed in their mission was to use Joseph Pungitore, "since he was the closest guy to Salvie."

(9) THE KNOCKOUT DROPS AT 'TOMMY DEL'S' CONDO

As July approached, a new plan was hatched whereby Caramandi was to obtain some knockout drops and Joe Pungitore was assigned to bring Testa down to Del Giorno's condo at Ocean City, New Jersey, where the drug would be administered. Caramandi would wait in 'Tommy Del's' cellar and then come up and shoot Testa in the kitchen after he arrived. Del Giorno and Iannarella were already waiting when Caramandi brought the pills and capsules to the condo. They were placed in a cup and glass to give to Testa when he arrived. (Caramandi stated that he had obtained the drops from a friend, Ray Calvin, in Ft. Lauderdale, Florida.)

After dropping off the lethal, sleep-inducing drugs, 'The Crow' accompanied 'Tory' and 'Charley White' to a pizza shop on the boardwalk, so that Testa wouldn't see them at the condo when he arrived. The plan was to take Testa from the kitchen after the knockout drops had taken effect and shoot him elsewhere. However, this plan was aborted when 'Joe Punge' reported back to 'Tommy Del' by phone that he couldn't get Testa to come there.

Two weeks later, a druggist came up from Florida with stronger knockout drops (10 mg. of Valium) which were guaranteed to put a person to sleep in 30 seconds. The conspirators hoped that the tasteless, odorless drops would do the trick this time. The new plan was for Joe Pungitore to give Testa the drops over the following weekend in a drink and then Iannece and Caramandi were assigned once again to drive the unconscious man to some secluded spot where they would shoot him.

Caramandi told Pungitore: "Give him the whole bottle. He won't taste it anyway. You only have to use it once and it will put him in a coma."

But like the other aborted plans, this one failed when 'Joey Punge' was unable to lure Testa to the rendezvous so he could put the drops into a drink.

(10) THE PHONE BOOTH AT 18TH AND RITNER

With the failure of the knockout drops ploy, the frustrated conspirators next agreed that 'Joey Punge' would bring Testa up from the shore to an outdoor phone booth located in the heart of South Philly, at 18th and Ritner Streets. The plan was for Pungitore to get out of the car and for Caramandi and Iannece to get in and shoot Testa.

But once again, a scared Testa failed to show up and that outdoor spot was cancelled as an execution site.

(11) THE ATLANTIC CITY EXPRESSWAY EXIT RAMP

Following the demise of the phone booth kill site, 'Tommy Del' and 'Faffy' next suggested that the killing of Testa be conducted on a curved exit ramp, #12 A, at Tilden Road on the Atlantic City Expressway some ten miles west of 'America's Playground.' But after Caramandi and Iannece drove down to check it out, they came back with a negative report. "It was too big and open, with too many cars and no exit for us, so we abandoned that idea."

(12) SAL'S BOAT

August had come and still no agreeable spot had been picked by the mob to erase the now jittery Testa from the Mafia family. Caramandi and Iannece went down to Atlantic City to talk with 'Crazy Phil' Leonetti at the Scarfo Inc. offices. Leonetti said: "Salvie's getting on my nerves. I'd like to kill him myself. I can't stand to look at him anymore. He comes in here everyday and he knows something's up."

Then Leonetti suggested: "How about Salvie's boat?"

So, a new plan was hatched to lure Testa to his boat docked in Ventnor with the ploy of taking several of the mob members along for a ride. But Caramandi, who didn't like boats, objected, and pressed 'Charley White' to do the job with a neighbor to go along as a cover. But that plan fizzled also.

(13) WHY NOT DO IT AT WAYNE'S HOUSE?

Following the latest missed opportunity to bump off Testa, Del Giorno and Iannarella suggested that he be shot at Salvatore 'Wayne' Grande's house, where 'Wayne' would be the designated killer. Caramandi and White were assigned to remove the body.

Scarfo agreed, and 'Wayne' asked the boss if he could bring his brother, Joe, along. Scarfo approved this addition and Del Giorno gave 'Wayne' a .22 caliber pistol, which he put in a drawer along with some cigarettes. The plan was for Sal to ask for a smoke and when 'Wayne' went to the drawer to retrieve the pack, he would grab the gun instead and shoot Testa.

Pungitore brought Testa to the house as agreed upon, but the gun was not in place, so this latest in the black comedy of Mafia errors went down the drain, when Testa asked for and got the cigarette.

An irate Merlino accosted 'Wayne' Grande the next day and accused the Mafia soldier of 'dogging it'.

(14) THE SMELL OF FISH LEADS TO A NEW HIT SPOT

Frank's Sea Food Restaurant, located at 7th and Kater Streets, was next selected by Del Giorno in late August as a substitute for the previously aborted sites. This time, Caramandi was once again designated as the hit man, but the new plan never worked out. None of the co-conspirators could get Testa to come.

(15) TAVELLA'S SWEET SHOP — THE FIRST TIME AROUND

In late August, a new scheme evolved to lure Testa to Gary Tavella's Sweet Shop on Passyunk Avenue. The initial plan was for Joe Pungitore to escort Sal to the store but there were questions about whether he should be shot in front of or inside the store.

Scafidi was told to hide inside the store and when Pungitiore finally arrived with Testa shortly after lunch one day, Sal asked: "Where Tory?"

'Joey Punge' answered,"I don't know...." Testa then became suspicious and immediately left the place. As Testa suspected,

Scafidi was waiting inside the store with a gun in hand ready to do the killing.

(16) THE CASINO ON THE BOARDWALK

As the summer wore on, Merlino became increasingly angry about the succession of bungled attempts to eliminate Testa. He told Del Giorno to "tell 'Joey Punge' to go down to the shore and don't come back until Salvie's dead." He became so impatient, that he suggested the shooting take place inside one of the Atlantic City casinos.

"I thought that was a little silly," commented Del Giorno. "They have cameras. They have police. They have *everything* there."

So this wild plan died before any of the subordinates could go down to the Boardwalk to check it out. "It just wouldn't fly," Del Giorno testified.

(17) 'TOMMY DEL'S' HOUSE

After these sixteen earlier plans backfired, Joe Grande and Joe Pungitore appeared at Del Giorno's house and announced that they were going to try to bring Testa there that evening. But after 'Tommy Del' noticed two or three unmarked police cars trailing 'Nicky Crow's' car as he came to park in front of his *capo's* house, 'Tommy Del' promptly hopped into his car and drove to the cleaners to pick up some clothes, noting that he was being followed by one police car. When he returned to his home, he told the waiting Caramandi to call off the contract because the scene was "too hot." 'The Crow' obeyed the order.

(18) BACK TO THE SWEET SHOP

On September 12th, the two *capos*, Del Giorno and Iannarella, told Joe Pungitore to take Testa to the shore and tell him that there was a dispute over $10,000 that had to be resolved involving 'Wayne' Grande. 'Joey Punge' was also ordered to tell Sal who was still a *capo* to "straighten out this hassle." But then plans changed once again and Joe Grande came to the club two days later and told Iannece and Caramandi that 'Wayne' Grande should go and hide in Tavella's Sweet Shop where Joe Pungitore would take Testa.

'Joey Punge' arrived as planned on September 14th with the target in tow and took him inside. As Sal asked for a cigarette, Wayne took the .38 caliber gun, now hidden under the couch, and shot Sal in the back of the head.

His brother, Joe, said, "Shoot him again; his eyes are open," which Wayne did. Then they put the body behind the couch.

One hour later, Joe Grande stood outside the pizza shop across the street on Passyunk Avenue, held up his hand and kissed it. "It's over, it's over," he repeated to the waiting Mafia undertakers Caramandi and Iannece. "Sal Testa is dead!"

'The Crow' then went to a phone at 10th and Wolf to call 'Chuckie' Merlino and Del Giorno to tell them that Testa was finally no longer among the living.

Caramandi told them, "We're going over to New Jersey to locate a spot to dump the body, where there is less heat from the cops."

While the two Mafia soldiers were over in New Jersey seeking a place to put the body, Del Giorno made several calls to the rest of the conspirators and they agreed to meet at 8 p.m. at the La Cucina Restaurant where Del Giorno got final confirmation that Testa was really dead. When he arrived, Scarfo breathed a sigh of relief, saying: "I'm glad it's over." Everyone was congratulating 'Wayne' Grande on the successful hit at long last.

Del Giorno was concerned, however, when he was told that the store was a mess. There was blood all over the place, with some still showing on the neck of Charles Iannece when he arrived at the La Cucina Restaurant that night after helping to dispose of the body. He told 'Charley White' to wash his neck.

He also told the two Grande brothers to go back in and clean up the mess, which they did. The next day, Del Giorno took the gun and threw it in the Delaware River.

When you are around rats, you got to become a rat.

22

-'Nicky Crow' Caramandi[*]

THE BODY NEAR A LOVERS' LANE SANDPIT

THE SEARCH FOR A BODY DUMPSITE

BEFORE Sal Testa could be moved from the sweet shop, a proper site had to be selected to dispose of his body. With Sal Scafidi driving, Caramandi and Iannece crossed the Delaware River and drove down the freeway towards Atlantic City. They got off on the Sicklersville Road and drove some three miles to a sandtrap on a gravel road. After reviewing the site, they agreed to dump Testa's body there that evening.

On the way back to Philadelphia, the three hoods conversed about the need to buy a blanket in which to wrap the blood-spattered body and agreed to purchase it in New Jersey. They drove off the Freeway on to the Blackhorse Pike and proceeded into a mini-shopping mall in Audubon, New Jersey where they parked the car.

THE BLANKET

Caramandi went into a Penney's department store where he looked for two king-sized blue blankets. Finding only one left on the shelf, he purchased it for $60 in cash from Rita M. Markwartz, an elderly white-haired clerk. In her 15 years with the J. C. Penney Company's mall department store, she remem-

[*] Testifying against his former family members on trial for the killing of Salvatore Testa, April 14, 1988.

bered it was the *only* blanket of that type she ever sold.

"I thought that blanket was ugly because of the color. It wasn't attractive. It had a yellow tinge to it. It wasn't a true blue color."

She vividly remembered returning change of $15.48 from the $60 offered to her as payment for the $44.52 blanket and that it was a middle-aged white man who purchased it, but she didn't feel that she could recognize the man who bought it.

"There were no words spoken," she said, "he took the change and the blanket and left quickly."

THE ALTERNATIVE 'HEARSE'

Before the body could be moved, Iannece went up the street to a local hardware store and bought some rope to tie the body in the blanket which 'The Crow' had purchased.

At 8:30 p.m. while it was still light, Caramandi drove a friend's car, owned by 'Big Mike' Venuti to a public park near the sweet shop, where he parked it until darkness.

When it was time to remove the dead body of Sal Testa from the sweet shop, Iannece came out of the store and winked at Caramandi that it was time to remove the body.

'Charley White' signalled to the other conspirators that it was time to bring the car up to park behind the truck to block the view of any observers as the blanket-wrapped body was carried out of the sweet shop and stuffed into the van.

After the van started moving, Caramandi got into 'Big Mike's' car and followed him in case the Testa 'hearse' was stopped by the cops. If they were stopped, Caramandi would crash his car into the police car so the undertakers could get away.

When they arrived at the roadside burial spot, after crossing the Ben Franklin Bridge and proceeding to the sandpit off the Sicklersville Road, 'The Crow' got out of the car and asked his mob partner, "What took you so long?"

Iannece answered: "It was dark in the store and we couldn't find the body behind the couch with no lights, and it was hard to lift his heavy body."

Instead of dumping the body in the sandpit they dumped it on the side of the road nearby and quickly left the scene.

Upon arriving back in Philadelphia, the conspirators agreed to meet at La Cucina Ristorante at 117 South Street, near the river, to evaluate their actions. At the post-murder get-together at the restaurant, Del Giorno ordered Iannece to wash the blood off his neck and for others to clean the blood out of the van. A relieved Joe Grande confessed to the rest that: "We were lucky. A cop came by the sweet shop just a half minute before we killed Testa, but he couldn't have heard the shots inside because of the noise of a nearby jackhammer being operated by a street repairman."

FINDING THE BODY

After receiving an anonymous phone call at 9:45 p.m., New Jersey Police officer Albert Orr, drove to the sandpit next to the wooded road in Gloucester County, where he found the body of Sal Testa, wrapped in the bloody blue blanket.

The time was 10:23 p.m. on September 14th. He called in Karen Roseman, a criminologist and a crime scene examiner, who arrived on the scene at 11 p.m. She stayed until 3:30 a.m. working in a steady rain, searching for clues. Meanwhile, the medical examiner took the body with its feet still tied, to the Camden morgue at midnight.

IDENTIFICATION OF THE CORPSE

The next morning, an autopsy was performed on Sal Testa's body, beginning at 10 a.m. (11 hours after the body was found). The corpse was dressed in a white T-shirt, covered with blood and a Temple University sweatshirt, with its sleeves cut off.

At 5 a.m. the next day, Paul Scully, an investigator of the Prosecutor's office in Camden, took the fingerprints from the dead body across the Delaware River to the Philadelphia Police Department Roundhouse headquarters where positive identification was soon made.

On September 18th, another Camden County police investigator, Joseph Alesandrin, journeyed to the Daffy Duck Marina in Ventnor to look for Sal Testa's boat, *Alfie*. They checked the rope on his boat and found that it did *not* match that found on the trussed-up body of the late mobster. So the rope had come from some place else.

THE FUNERAL

At 6 a.m. Saturday, September 15, 1984, Maria Testa Muzio, the sister of Sal Testa and his only surviving family member, received a call from the police that they had the body of her brother and suggested that she make funeral arrangements, which she did. Just a few years earlier, she had had to bury her father, Phil 'Chickenman' Testa, and her mother.

She had known Scarfo all of her life, as well as the other defendants, particularly Joe Pungitore, Sal's best friend for the last nine years of his life.

She was disappointed that none of them showed up for Sal's funeral or the viewing held at the Pennsylvania Burial Co. Caramandi noted that "none of these guys went to Sal Testa's funeral, did they? Only in the movies do they show up at a wake for one of their own." 'The Crow' didn't show up either.

On the day after the funeral held at St. Paul's Church, Joe Pungitore finally showed up at the family residence. "He was cold and not attentive like before," noted a grieving Maria. Although flowers were sent, it was "done in a cold way, with the cards being signed not the way I expected them to be," said Muzio. She felt the absence of these men who were supposedly his friends was a slap in her face.

A LEADERSHIP SHAKEUP IN THE SCARFO FAMILY

Over the next several years after the killing, there was a series of changes in the Mafia hierarchy. Thomas Del Giorno, Francis Iannarella and Joe Pungitore were made acting *capos*. Sal Merlino was demoted in mid-1986 from underboss, and Scarfo's nephew, Phil Leonetti, ascended to the number two spot. Although the police still did not know *who* was responsible for the killing of Sal Testa, the law kept a regular surveillance of the mob's comings and goings from 1984-1986 at their favorite haunts in South Philadelphia and Atlantic City. Those Mafia hangouts included restaurants, taverns, clubs, card games and boxing matches.

By mid-1986, Scarfo, Pungitore and Del Giorno had an equity of $300,000 in an escalating sports-betting operation. When 'Tommy Del' suggested that they split it up and get out, Scarfo retorted: "No, let it [the profits] go to $500 grand." Scarfo's greed won out. The operation continued to flourish.

Meanwhile, Del Giorno got several more messages from FBI Agent Jimmy Maher and N.J. State Trooper Ed Johnson that Scarfo had put out a contract on him.

In July, 1986, Del Giorno was visited by some New Jersey State Troopers who told him that they had some information that he was going to be killed.

"I told them to get a tape," he said. The troopers let him listen to a tape where 'Faffy' Iannarella and 'Wayne' Grande were heard talking against Del Giorno.

After ten minutes, 'Tommy Del' said, "Turn it off. I don't want to hear it anymore. Then I went to Atlantic City and told Scarfo what the New Jersey Police had told me."

Scarfo said: "You don't believe them, do you?"

Del Giorno answered: "Nah, Nah!" But he told the court two years later: "We both lied."

Nothing works against the success of a conspiracy so much as the wish to make it wholly secure and certain to succeed. Such an attempt requires many men, much time and very favorable conditions. And all these in turn heighten the risk of being discovered. *You see, therefore, how dangerous conspiracies are.*

-Francesco Guicciardini[*]

23 THE GHOSTS OF PAST MAFIA MURDERS HAUNT 'LIL NICKY'

I T took law enforcement agencies two-and-a-half years to put together what they hoped would be an airtight case against Scarfo and his cohorts. That essential information was based largely on the voluntary 'singing' of the two ex-Scarfo gang members, Del Giorno and Caramandi, who had already played a prominent role in the trial and conviction of Scarfo, Beloff, and Rego in the Rouse extortion case.

HOW THE GOVERNMENT FOUND OUT WHO KILLED TESTA, ET AL

After the killing of Sal Testa, Nicholas Caramandi went into business with John Pastorella, an illicit operator who was a Mafia associate, but not a blood member. Caramandi did not know at the time that Pastorella was an FBI informant. As the result of some damning tapes supplied by Pastorella to the government of his conversations with Caramandi, the latter was arrested in October, 1986, at the mob's clubhouse on Moore Street in South Philadelphia and imprisoned.

While chatting in Holmesburg Prison a short time later with Raymond 'Long John' Martorano, who was serving a life sentence as a co-conspirator in the murder of John McCullough, the head of the local Roofer's Union, Caramandi became convinced that he was slated to be killed by the Mafia.

[*] In his *Ricordi Politici* (1528-1530) from *Out of Control*, by Leslie Cockburn, Atlantic Books, 1987.

His decision to move into the witness protection program was reconfirmed a few days later while he was discussing his dilemma with his lawyer, Robert Madden, in the Philadelphia Detention Center's Library at Holmesburg. A. Charles Peruto, a noted local criminal lawyer, entered the room and said to Caramandi, "I hear you've got a problem."

'The Crow' asked: "What problem?"

Peruto retorted brusquely: "Nothing. Nothing." He then turned on his heels and left.

A deeply disturbed Caramandi asked his lawyer to ask 'Chuck' Peruto about the nature of the problem. Caramandi then walked out into the prison yard to regain his composure and asked 'Long John' Martorano if he knew Peruto well enough to find out what he meant by the word 'problem.'

"Yeh, I know him," Martorano answered, "but it will take about a week or ten days to find out what he meant."

A week later, the two prisoners met again in the yard and 'Long John' pointed his finger into the ground. "You know what that means, don't you?" he asked. "You were sold down the river."

"Yes," said a shaken Caramandi, "it means that I'm going to be killed."

"At first I didn't believe it," reminisced Caramandi. "But then I realized that a guy like Scarfo could turn on his best friend of 25 years, and I know he would kill me in a second. The buck comes first with him. He'd turn on guys who didn't say 'Hello' to him 25 years ago...when he was a plain bartender."

So, late in 1986, Caramandi went to the FBI and spilled the beans on all of his Mafia activities, including the plot to kill Sal Testa.

CARAMANDI'S CONFESSION PAYS OFF FOR UNCLE SAM

On April 10, 1987, the federal government announced that Scarfo and six of his associates were ordered held without bail after they were arraigned in Philadelphia on Federal and State charges of murdering Sal Testa. The seven were among ten people for whom warrants were issued in connection with Testa's death. One day before, Scarfo and eleven of his associates in New Jersey were also the subject of the most sweeping charges ever made in recent times against mob figures in the area.

On April 9th, Scarfo and Nicholas 'Nick the Blade' Virgilio were charged in a New Jersey indictment in the murder of former Somers Point, New Jersey, Municipal Judge Edwin Helfant in February, 1978. Ten of his associates were also charged at that time with being a part of a racketeering conspiracy resulting in eight other organized crime killings.

On April 10th, U.S. Attorney Edward S. G. Dennis called the day a "historic occasion" and Philadelphia District Attorney Ron Castille simultaneously announced that "this is just a first of what we think is going to bring an end to organized crime as we presently know it...in the Philadelphia-South Jersey area."

Prior to these shocking front-page murder-conspiracy indictments, a behind-the-scenes dispute arose which threatened to disrupt relations between the U.S. Attorney and the local District Attorney as to jurisdiction in the case. It was settled quietly in Washington with an agreement at the U.S. Justice Department to share the testimony of ex-mobster Thomas Del Giorno.

SCARFO FACES YET ANOTHER TRIAL: THIS TIME FOR MURDER

On May 14, 1987, Scarfo and seven other associates were formally charged with murder, conspiracy, and weapons charges related to the September, 1984, slaying of Salvatore Testa. Municipal Judge Alan Silberstein ordered three of the eight, some of whom were already behind bars, held without bail.

A ninth defendant, Vincent Iannece, 24, who was accused by Nicholas Caramandi of helping the murders by blocking traffic at an intersection while the killing took place, was not held for trial. Young Iannece also allegedly cleaned the blood-splattered truck in which Testa's body was carried to the dump site in New Jersey. His father, Charles Iannece, who drove the truck, remained a fugitive after being charged as an accessory to the murder.

Caramandi said he could not be sure that the son of 'Charley White' Iannece knew of the murder plot, so all charges were dismissed against him. Scarfo, 'Chuckie' Merlino, and 'Wayne' Grande, the alleged triggerman, were kept in jail. Joseph Pungitore (who had lured Testa into the sweet shop where the murder took place), Salvatore Scafidi (who had been designated to be the original triggerman, but was in jail the day Testa was killed), and Frank Iannarella (the alleged supervisor of the murder plot) were each released on $750,000 bail. Lesser bail of $500,000 each was set for Joseph Grande who had signalled Caramandi that the murder had been committed, and Phil Leonetti, the right arm of Uncle Nicky, who was allegedly in on the plot and had complained to others that it was "taking too long" to execute Testa.

Two weeks later, Common Pleas Court Judge Charles Durham rejected the petitions of Scarfo and two others that they be permitted bail pending the trial tentatively scheduled for early 1988.

Most observers and law enforcement officials believed that a murder conviction in the Sal Testa case would effectively end Scarfo's control over his organized crime family that he had ruled since 1981.

A NEW MAJOR INDICTMENT IS ISSUED AGAINST SCARFO AND COMPANY

A federal grand jury handed down a new series of multiple criminal charges against Scarfo and eighteen associates less than a month before he was scheduled to stand trial in the Testa killing. On January 11, 1988, they were confronted with an eighty-eight page indictment accusing them of murder, extortion, drug dealing, racketeering, loansharking and gambling.

The indictment, which was announced by U. S. Attorney Edward S. G. Dennis, Jr., represented the most sweeping assault to date by law enforcement officials to undermine the grip once held by organized crime in the South Jersey-Philadelphia area. It included nine murders and four attempted murders and illegal methods to "maintain and extend the power" of the organized crime family.

This latest assault against Scarfo represented a much broader approach, using a racketeering indictment to prove that the Philadelphia Mafia had been operating as a criminal enterprise.

The five earlier charges against Scarfo had been more limited in their scope. This latest, broadly sweeping series of indictments appeared to be an attempt by the government to make up for the recent acquittal of Scarfo and four of his cohorts in the P2P 'Speed' distribution trial.

The new indictments covered a series of crimes committed over an eleven and a half year period — running from April, 1976 through October, 1987. Once again, the chief weapon was the RICO Act of Congress, which had been used successfully before in prosecuting the hierarchy of organized crime in Boston, New York, Kansas City, and Philadelphia.

Philadelphia District Attorney Ronald Castille, who participated in the indictment announcement along with Dennis and sixteen other federal, state, and local law enforcement officials, commented that "these charges mark the end of the Philadelphia Mafia as we know it."

Pennsylvania Attorney General Leroy Zimmerman said, "Never before has the leadership of organized crime in the Philadelphia area been confronted with such a comprehensive type of indictment. Law enforcement ganged up on them this time."

'Bobby' Simone, Scarfo's chief defense counsel and a spokesman for the Mafia, said that the indictment was not unexpected.

"This was what they have been talking about for some time. Actually, we are glad to get on with it, because now the defendants know where they stand."

THE DRAMA UNFOLDS IN COURTROOM #253

On a bitterly cold February 8, 1988, the first pre-trial motions took place in the spacious Philadelphia City Hall courtroom assigned to Common Pleas Court Judge Albert Sabo — located just around the corner from the Mayor's office. Seated quietly with their defense attorneys were the nine Mafia members accused of conspiring to murder Sal Testa.

Besides Scarfo, 58, and Phil Leonetti, 34, were Joseph Pungitore, 31, the alleged shooter 'Wayne' Grande, 34, 'Chuckie' Merlino, 47, 'Charley White' Iannece, 52, Joseph Grande, 27, Salvatore Scafidi, 25 and Francis Iannarella, 39.

What you have here is unlike any other organized crime family in that some of these deaths came to pass for relatively insignificant reasons, not for business reasons....Things like showing disrespect for a Mafia member or slapping another mob member's daughter would have been overlooked by organized crime in other areas, except here, where this crazy fool [Scarfo] is running the operation.

-Col. Clinton Pagano[*]

24 COMMONWEALTH OF PENNSYLVANIA VS. 'NICKY' SCARFO, ET AL

THE PROSECUTOR HURLS AN OPENING SALVO

IN the pre-trial skirmishing over the first attempt by the Commonwealth of Pennsylvania — or any other state — to prosecute a mob boss and his crime family for first-degree murder, Assistant D. A. Barbara Christie called the slaying of Salvatore Testa, "an organized crime killing." Pointing to several of Testa's alleged friends who had been indicted in his murder, Ms. Christie told a packed courtroom that "if these were Salvatore Testa's closest friends, the man didn't need enemies."

This was the signal that the prosecution intended to pursue a hardline approach in the murder trial.

Barbara Christie started out in the District Attorney's office two decades before as a 16-year-old intern under former Deputy District Attorney, Richard Sprague. After she completed her law courses at nearby Villanova University, she came back to the D.A.'s office and rose to head the important Homicide Unit.

The feisty Christie had built up a reputation as a relentless prosecutor and was tough in her courtroom pursuits.

[*] Commander of the New Jersey State Police, at a news conference in Trenton, April 9, 1987.

Judge Albert Sabo rejected motions by the defense to delay
the start of the trial and to discuss the murder indictments.
'Bobby' Simone asked the Judge to limit the testimony of the two
key government witnesses, Thomas Del Giorno and Nicholas
Caramandi, to only the specific charges in the case and not to allow them to expand on the inner workings of organized crime in
the Scarfo family.

Christie, however, said she would contend that the Testa
killing was an "organized crime killing" and that "the evidence of
organized crime would be relevant and admissible" along with
wiretap evidence the government had obtained.

The defense let it be known that they would try every tactic to
restrain and shackle the prosecution's attempts to make its case
airtight.

Barbara Christie, with her glasses perched on top of her head
and her sleeves rolled up for action, sat alone at the prosecution's
table. Allied against her to her right was a group of ten top defense lawyers, including Oscar Goodman and 'Bobby' Simone
who were defending Leonetti and Scarfo, the two top Mafia
leaders.

"It was orchestrated that way for the jury's sympathy," commented one veteran courtroom reporter. "It's David against Go-
liath. The lone female representative of law and order vs. the
mob's big gun lawyers. The dramatic impact of her standing up
to their objections and attempts in the pre-trial motions to limit her
questions of Caramandi and Del Giorno are all part of the drama.
The jury should get the message before the trial is over."

A LEAK OUT OF THE JUDGE'S CHAMBERS

During the pre-trial motions, Assistant District Attorney
Christie sought the naming of an anonymous jury out of concern
for the safety of the jurors. Defense attorneys opposed this move
and Judge Sabo ordered both sides not to comment on this sensitive issue after it had been discussed privately in his chambers.
He was irate when a court reporter for *The Philadelphia Daily
News*, Joe Daughen, reported that the issue had been brought up
behind closed doors.

A lawyer for the Philadelphia Newspapers (PNI), the publishers of the *News* and the *Inquirer*, argued in open court the

next day, asking for media access to all private hearings before the Judge. Judge Sabo told the papers' attorney that he would consider her petition, but that he had a "difficult problem" balancing the right of the defendants to a fair trial with other issues such as public access.

Defense attorneys argued that Daughen be subpoenaed to testify about the sources for his leaked story. But their plea was dropped when the defense was informed that Daughen would invoke the Fifth Amendment and the Pennsylvania Shield Law if called to testify about his sources.

BOTH SIDES JOCKEY FOR A PRE-TRIAL ADVANTAGE

For two weeks, the defense lawyers stalled the picking of a jury with largely irrelevant pre-trial motions regarding the playing of certain wiretaps during the forthcoming trial.

One of them spent a whole day cross-examining an FBI agent about hundreds of hours of tapes made by the chief government witness, Thomas Del Giorno, which were to be used as evidence. The tapes were mainly discussions of mundane family problems with the wives of several of the defendants, that had nothing to do with evidence pointing to the murder of Testa. Finally, the defense lawyers told the Judge that they would take "the first 12 jurors out of the box, no questions asked," and at the same time asked Sabo to excuse himself from the case (since they had lost faith in his impartiality). They also asked him to delay the trial because of extensive pre-trial publicity.

"He hasn't made a decision on anything," said one irate defense lawyer. "He is passing the buck."

Prosecutor Christie pleaded with the Judge to keep the jury anonymous from the defense team and the public so as to assuage any fear that they might have of deciding the fate of men reputed to be involved in organized crime. An additional reason for her request was to prevent any of the defense team from getting to the jury. When it was learned that a week earlier Simone had told one man on the first jury panel that he already had his address, Christie felt this was purposeful intimidation.

A COMPROMISE IS REACHED ON THE SELECTION OF THE TESTA JURY

After Judge Sabo discovered that 30 out of the first 36 jury panelists called into his courtroom had heard about Scarfo and the Testa murder from the media, he ordered that an out-of-town jury be brought to Philadelphia to hear the case. This move angered the defense and surprised the prosecution, but the Judge stuck to his guns that there was no other way to insure a fair trial.

His decision was immediately appealed to the State Supreme Court and a few days later, Chief Justice Robert N. C. Nix, Jr. and Judge James McDermott ruled on February 22nd that Philadelphia residents should be called to serve on the jury, with their names, but not their addresses being made public. This obvious compromise seemed to satisfy both sides and Robert Simone, speaking for the defense, commented: "This is the City of Brotherly Love and we have a lot of brothers on trial. The Philadelphians are the fairest people in the world."

As a result of the ruling, Sabo agreed to call another panel of 100 potential jurors whose names and addresses had not already been entered into the court records to appear three days later on February 25th for possible selection.

But Sabo said in court that he could not guarantee that the addresses of the jurors would remain secret.

"You're saying to me [referring to the Supreme Court justices' order], not to give the defense attorneys the addresses. Do you think for one minute, that's possible? To say: 'Give 'em the names and they won't find out the addresses?' That's an impossibility!" The two highest court justices also recommended that Sabo be responsible for checking the backgrounds of the jurors, so that even the prosecution would not have the addresses of the jurors.

After three days in court questioning the first 90 jury panelists, over half of whom were excused for hardship reasons since the Judge had announced that the jury would be sequestered for two to three months, only one juror was selected. Assistant D. A. Christie was asked if she thought a jury could be picked by Easter. Her reply: "Which year? Who knows?"

A week later, a second panel had been weeded out with most prospective jurors being excused for one or more reasons of personal family or job hardships by either the Judge or the lawyers involved. Many were excused because of their knowledge of the case gleaned from either hearing about it on radio or TV or reading about it in the papers. At the end of two weeks, only three jurors out of the 15 required had been selected.

On Wednesday, March 2nd, when Barbara Christie became ill, the Judge closed down the jury selection process until she was feeling better — five days later.

THE ESTIMATED HIGH COST OF THE TESTA MURDER TRIAL

Even before the final jury had been picked and sequestered for the duration of the expected two-to-three-month long trial, a cost analysis showed that the preliminaries had cost the taxpayers $100,000. There was a daily cost of $3,500, including $2,000 for extra Sheriff's Department security guards, to secure the courtroom, with its electronic airport-type passageways to prevent the smuggling of weapons into the courtroom, $1,000 for court officers and $500 for the D. A.'s office. This expense was expected to double once the final jury panel was selected and locked up in a nearby hotel for the duration. During the jury selection process, 16 sheriff's deputies and five court officers plus the Judge and two Assistant D. A.'s were in the courtroom at all times.

With each juror being paid $9 for the first three days and $25 thereafter, according to Common Pleas Court President Edward Bradley, plus free meals and lodging and overtime for guards to make sure that no one from either the defense, the prosecution or their families got to them, the final cost to the city was expected to rise to at least $1 million.

This figure would make the cost of this trial the third highest, next to the $1.4 million spent on the 1980 MOVE murder trial of the Philadelphia policeman, James Ramp, in the shootout at the MOVE house in Powelton Village, and the Martorano-Daidone trial for the murder of the Roofers' Union chief, John McCullough. The MOVE trial, without a jury, lasted 67 days and was preceded by 265 days of pre-trial action.

SCARFO'S SISTER, SCARFO'S SUCCESSOR — THEIR CRIMES AND FATES

On Leap Year Day (February 29th) two of Nicky Scarfo's closest associates, his sister, Nancy Scarfo Leonetti, 57, and his alleged mob-boss successor, Albert 'Reds' Pontani, both came up losers in two neighboring New Jersey courtrooms, with their freedom severely restricted.

His sister, who is also the mother of Nick's nephew and underboss, 'Crazy Phil' Leonetti, pleaded guilty in Newark, New Jersey, to one count of embezzlement of union funds, for which she was sentenced to five years probation.

The U.S. District Judge John Bissell also imposed a ten-year suspended prison sentence and an $8,000 fine — a light sentence considering the crime.

She had been charged with embezzlement and conspiracy in a thirteen-count indictment back on September 23, 1987 accusing her of having been paid $220,000 as an administrator of health, welfare and pension funds of local #158 of the Skilled Trades and Bulk Plant Workers over a five and a half year period while doing little or no work. This Teamster-affiliated union is based in Philadelphia — Nancy Leonetti lived in Atlantic City, New Jersey.

Meanwhile, Albert 'Reds' Pontani, 60, the alleged caretaker-boss of the Atlantic City-Philadelphia axis mob, was arrested and held without bail in the state capitol of Trenton on a combination of federal drug, conspiracy, loansharking and extortion charges. He was denied bail when a U.S. Magistrate declared him to be a "danger to the community" and posed a potential risk of flight if he were set free.

Pontani, whose once flaming red hair had now turned white, appeared in court wearing a blue sportcoat and a white, open-collared shirt. His legitimate business was trucking, which served as a front for his mob-related activities. He was arrested on February 18th at the Condado Beach casino hotel in San Juan, Puerto Rico, after being indicted along with six others by a federal Grand Jury in Newark. One of the charges concerned his continuing criminal enterprise and conspiracy to distribute cocaine and P2P, as well as supervising a narcotics distribution enterprise with Dan Marino, 56, of Cherry Hill, New Jersey. If convicted, he could face a life sentence in jail.

Pontani, who had been initiated into the Mafia by Scarfo himself, according to a 1983 report to the U.S. Senate's organized crime investigation, was believed to have shared a supervisory role on the remnants of the Scarfo mob, with Pasquale 'Patty Specks' Martirano of Newark, New Jersey, another Scarfo associate until, *if* and when Nicky ever got out of prison.

This latest clampdown on the attempts by Pontani to breath new life into the disarrayed remnants of the Mafia sent a further signal to the remnants of the mob that the law enforcement officials were not going to take the governmental heel off the prostrate Mafia.

NICKY'S PALS CANCEL A FUND RAISER

While awaiting the second attempt to select a jury for the upcoming trial, some friends of Nicky Scarfo and his fellow defendants attempted to arrange what one enterprising reporter called "the biggest mob social of 1988" to help pay the legal fees of the accused nine Mafia members. A date of March 1st had been pencilled in to hold a bash at $100 a head at the Enchante night spot in nearby Cherry Hill, New Jersey, just across the river from Philadelphia.

The program was to feature a Frank Sinatra imitator named Sonny Averone, but the singer cancelled his appearance a week before the event because of the "notoriety and publicity" surrounding the affair. A chance for the patrons to bid on Scarfo's 1973 Rolls Royce to help raise money to pay the nine lawyers also was lost.

'Bobby' Simone, who would have been the chief beneficiary of the fund raising social, sadly commented: "I thought I was going to get some money, but I guess that won't happen now." The subterfuge used by the organizers of the social was to announce a benefit for one Anthony 'Spike' DiGregoria, a former associate of the late pre-Scarfo Mafia boss, Angelo Bruno. (DiGregoria just happened to be the caretaker of Scarfo's Ft. Lauderdale, Florida, winter home, Casablanca South.)

Some observers wondered why Nicky Scarfo needed the money to pay his lawyer, Simone, since Caramandi had testified that in 1986, Scarfo had netted at least $280,000 from his drug-dealing shakedown operations.

With an expensive Florida home to maintain, leased at $3,500 a month, plus the upkeep of his leased yacht, the $17,500 cost of his 1973 Rolls Royce, and furniture worth $71,000 which he paid for with a check of $11,000 and the rest in cash to the furniture dealer in South Philadelphia, it's not difficult to see why he could have needed extra money to pay his lawyer.

I feel I can't serve on the [Testa murder] jury because I'm going to get married in a couple of months and I need the time to get ready for my wedding.

-Ms. Candace Herron Jury Panelist #43.

In that case, you can go off quietly into the sunset.

-Robert 'Bobby' Simone[*]

25

THE SAL TESTA
MURDER CASE

THE city's most notorious organized-crime murder case was about to begin after a month and a half long ordeal to impanel a sequestered jury of which each member said they were willing to be locked up for two months and were willing to recommend capital punishment if a guilty verdict was rendered.

The Sal Testa murder trial marked a *first* in recent Mafia trials in the United States. Whereas other celebrated trials in New York and elsewhere featured mob bosses on trial for conspiracies, racketeering, drug running, etc., in this trial, the law was putting a Mafia boss on trial for conspiracy to murder one of their own.

Although the mob maintained their code of silence for two years after the murder, the confessions of *two* members who participated in the plot "opened the darkened window of mob violence to underworld operations" according to Barbara Christie.

On the first day of the actual trial, April 5th, 1988, after the final alternate jurors had been selected, each of the nine defendants stood and pleaded 'Not Guilty' to each of the three counts of criminal conspiracy, possession of weapons and murder.

Following a statement to the jury by Judge Sabo, on "their

[*] Speaking for the defense on why they agreed to excuse a juror from jury service.

selection to perform a solemn duty of citizenship," the feisty, diminutive Assistant Prosecutor Barbara Christie took over.

THE PROSECUTION STATES ITS CASE

In her opening remarks to the jury, Ms. Christie stressed the point that the nine defendants — Nicodemo Scarfo, Francis Iannarella, Joseph Pungitore, Joseph Grande, Salvatore Grande, Charles Iannece, Philip Leonetti, Salvatore Merlino and Salvatore Scafidi — had "ordered, planned and carried out the murder of Salvatore Testa.... He was a marked man, stalked and sentenced to death over many months in 1984 by the defendants — members of a nationwide, clandestine organization [i.e., the Mafia, *La Cosa Nostra*, the mob, the outfit]; a disciplined, close-knit hierarchy of bosses, *consiglieres*, *capos*, soldiers in a regime with strict rules."

In painting the framework for the trial, Christie noted the "rewards of the megaprofits — never reported — which were channeled up the 'elbow'* to the boss."

Christie, 41, the city's top homicide prosecutor, exuded the combination of a tough but delicate presence in the courtroom. Early in the pre-trial hearings, Scarfo's attorneys asked Judge Sabo to make someone sit at the prosecution table with the diminutive Christie, so that the jurors would not think of her as one fearless but frail woman standing against a tide of organized crime buttressed by ten male defense attorneys. Sabo refused the request and Christie went on alone.

THE DEFENSE LAYS OUT ITS CASE

In his opening remarks, Robert Simone countered that his client, Nicodemo Scarfo, was charged with just one thing — *homicide.* "We cannot get tied up in a trial of the Mafia, a trial of *La Cosa Nostra*, or a trial of organized crime. We don't want you to think about the mob or the outfit, we only want you to think about the events of September 14, 1984."

He conceded that there had been no arrests in the Testa killing until Caramandi and Del Giorno decided to talk: "They say they

---

* *Elbow* is a term which can be easily defined as the pressure put on the soldiers to send money up the hierarchy to the boss and *capos.*

participated in the murder of Salvatore Testa. But that wasn't enough. They said nine other people participated. Does it make sense that 11 people are needed to kill one person?" he asked.

"You will never hear testimony from people more *corrupt* and disgusting," he concluded. One by one, the other eight defense attorneys reiterated the questionable reputation of the two main defense witnesses as "walking, talking reasonable doubts."

THE CHIEF DEFENDANT

Sitting behind Simone, Scarfo, who had spent the last year in jail, was beginning to show the ravages of his seemingly endless battle with the government to obtain his freedom. He was pale, no longer having his Florida tan. His once black hair was beginning to show some gray about the temples. The stylish suits worn by the ex-bartender no longer appeared to fit quite as well. Scarfo's head and neck twitched nervously during the trial, interrupting his usual placid appearance.

SHORT FUSES AND TEMPERS

During the first full day of the trial, various defense attorneys tried in vain to debunk Christie's contention that their clients had formed an organized crime unit. Rather, according to Simone, they were "just a close band of buddies who were constantly under the watchful eyes of the police."

As the proceedings heated up at the end of the next day, April 6th, electric fuses blew twice, knocking out power to the lights, microphones and TV sets used to play police-made videos.

Tempers also shortened, when, following a shouting match, Judge Albert Sabo cited Joseph Santaguida, attorney for the defendant Salvatore Grande, for contempt of court. He fined him $500 for a 'snide remark' about a particular piece of evidence offered by the prosecution. Santaguida had also told the judge to "pay attention," and complained that Christie kept getting two chances to ask questions after the defense team objected that those questions shouldn't have been answered in the first place.

"I saw that after that remark to the judge to "Pay Attention!" that he *was* paying attention," Santaguida said with an unprecedented grin, "and I'll take it [the $500 fine] on the chin for the team," Santaguida said.

'THE CROW' TAKES THE STAND

On April 11th, a neatly dressed Nicholas Caramandi, dressed in a brown suit, white shirt, brown and white tie with coiffured hair, took the witness stand, as the first of the two star government witnesses. He retold for the jury his life in crime, his relations with the boss, Nicodemo Scarfo, and with the other defendants. He told how the money from their criminal activities was split up — how the 'elbow' from the boss ensured that the boss got his share.

'The Crow' emphasized that if one doesn't 'touch base' with his superiors and keep them informed of his actions for the mob, he is soon in serious trouble. The penalty for violating this unwritten rule of the Mafia is *Death*.

With the jury riveted on his testimony, Caramandi confessed to a series of crimes, including his participation in seven murders. He described how as a 'flim-flam' artist, he sold cheap prescription drugs, stolen spark plugs, and black and white TV sets as color sets. "I told the customers that I had the products in my truck [which had two doors]. We would go in one side after taking their money, and then out the back and disappear. The customers were crooks who thought they were getting a bargain, but their greed got to them and they lost. My business was greed. Everyone has greed in him. You can't rob honest people."

Christie rapidly went over Caramandi's criminal background and, step-by-step, the plot to kill Testa with all the failed attempts before the final death blow on September 14. The jury seemed to pay close attention to her face and his answers as she retraced the threads of the plot.

Robert Simone acknowledged that the Commonwealth's witness, Caramandi, had been well-prepared and compared his performance to that of "an actor who had rehearsed his role many times."

Caramandi related from the witness stand that "I had nightmares over the killing of Sal Testa. I had good relations with him. I really liked the guy."

Simone, who had once defended Caramandi, sarcastically noted during the cross examination of his former client: "You told a fairy tale to another jury and they didn't believe you, did they?" (referring to the P2P methamphetamine case).

"Yes," retorted 'the Crow' angrily, "but the Beloff-Rego jury believed me."

The nine defense lawyers tried a constant repetitive drum beating tactic that this witness was not to be believed because of his shady past — getting him to admit over and over that he was a thief and a crook. By debunking him, they forced him to change his demeanor on the witness stand. He started to fidget, pulling on his collar as Simone and others bore in with cutting questions, pointing out to the jury minor cases of Caramandi's contradicting himself on points of fact.

One of the defense lawyers, Stephen LaCheen, tried to trip Caramandi up on his testimony about the color of the blanket that he bought to wrap Testa's body in. When shown the blood-stained blue blanket, 'the Crow' said: "I stated that the blanket was dark green when I bought it at the Penney's store. If you said it was purple, it is purple... but I agree now, that it is a light blue color..."

Midway during the cross-examination of his testimony, 'the Crow', with his voice rising, chillingly asserted that "I know this guy Nicky Scarfo and believe me, he would turn on anyone in a second. The buck comes first with him. He would order that anybody should be killed if he was in the mood. Although I am outside prison now, I'm constantly with federal agents day and night. I'm really behind 'invisible bars'."

'OPEN THE DOOR OSCAR'

When Oscar Goodman, the suave Las Vegas defense lawyer representing Philip Leonetti, proceeded to cross-examine Caramandi, he went over to a flip chart and outlined all the dozens of crimes committed by 'the Crow' since childhood in order to undermine his credibility as a government witness. After listing the 300 burglaries, several robberies, flim-flams, three murders, several extortions from which he grossed $5 million, drug running, and other crimes like welfare fraud, counterfeiting $1,000 bills and car theft — all confessed to by Caramandi — a seemingly satisfied Goodman pointed out to the jury that the witness had sustained a "varied career committing just about every crime in the book, right?"

Caramandi admitted that these myriad crimes gave him the necessary credentials to make new friends with Mafia members (like those sitting at the defense table).

Caramandi agreed with Goodman's assertion, saying that he "hoped to get a break... and go into a new life with a new name and social security number... but that depends on Mr. Scarfo and his friends."

Goodman gambled that his listing of 'the Crow's' many crimes would impress upon the jury not to trust any other testimony of this witness for the prosecution. Assistant D.A. Christie, however, jumped at this opportunity to explore some of Caramandi's past crimes — including the Rouse extortion case in which Scarfo had been found guilty. Most of the defense lawyers wanted to keep a strict limit on Caramandi's testimony — to that of the alleged killing of Testa, but now the cat was out of the bag for the government to probe other Mafia crimes in which 'the Crow' and the nine defendants had been involved.

One of the defense lawyers quipped to the media that Goodman should now be called: "Open the door Oscar," since he had been the one who had made it possible to widen the case from just the murder of Sal Testa to other crimes committed by the mob. Many other defense lawyers feared that his ploy marked a turning point against their chance of getting their clients off the hook, since the prosecution could now bring in evidence extending beyond the Testa murder.

MIDWAY IN THE TRIAL

Scarfo didn't like the way Caramandi was answering questions during his cross-examination by various defense attorneys. Eventually, a long hollering match ensued on one mid-April afternoon between the defense attorneys and Judge Sabo over the extent of the testimony offered by Nicholas Caramandi. The three-ring courtroom circus was punctuated by the frequently shouted opinions offered by Christie objecting to the defense objections.

An irate and harassed Judge Sabo took the ten defense attorneys to task when he said: "I tried to give you a little advice, but you didn't listen to me. If you listened to me in the first place, you wouldn't be in this mess."

The normally soft-spoken Sabo shouted a few minutes later: "I'm still trying to get out of this mess!"

"You put yourself in it, Judge," shouted back the sarcastic Robert Mozenter, who represented Charles Iannece.

"Don't tell me I put you in this mess! I tried to keep you out of it!" shot back the exasperated Judge, threatening to cite Mozenter for contempt and fine him as he had done previously to Santaguida.

As court adjourned for the day on April 14th, a shackled and despondent Nicodemo Scarfo shouted to the whole courtroom as he was being led back to jail by the guards: *This is a kangaroo court* !"

MAFIA HUMOR?

There were some rare moments of black humor to relieve the tension of the long trial. Once, under cross-examination by Bobby Simone, Caramandi was asked how he could secretly call two people while he was in the custody of the FBI to get his share of the $350,000 that he and his partner 'Charley White' were to split as the profit of a P2P drug deal. The FBI was supposedly constantly monitoring his every move.

'The Crow' answered: "Well, they don't follow you into the bathroom or when you make a phone call to your mother. I told the FBI I had to make a personal call and they let me. There is nothing wrong in trying to get back money that is owed to me, is there?"

Later on, Simone asked Caramandi if he had any qualms about being a 'crash blocker' with his willingness to hit a police car in the rear so that Iannece could get away with the Testa body in the van.

"At the time, I did not care if I injured or killed a policeman," said 'the Crow'.

Simone zeroed in: "Have you ever told the members of the jury you were sorry for that thought of maybe killing a cop?"

"No," said Caramandi, "I haven't had the opportunity yet."

There was much tittering in the courtroom after this remark.

AN UNEXPECTED DELAY

On Wednesday, April 20th, Judge Sabo suddenly recessed the trial for four days because of the unavailability of the next witness, Thomas Del Giorno. The move infuriated defense attorneys, particularly Oscar Goodman, who had been away from his Las Vegas home base for several weeks.

"This is a sham and a joke," he fumed.

Sabo explained after he adjourned the court that the "Commonwealth doesn't have witnesses standing by. The D.A. lets me know when she's going to be late. What can I do? I can't force her to come out and sit there."

The reason for Del Giorno's absence was the arrest of his son four days earlier for murder. Having tried to raise bail for his incarcerated son Robert, Thomas Del Giorno was "in no great shape to take the witness stand" said a court employee during a recess in the trial.

The sequestered jurors soon heard about the arrest — which had caused the senior Del Giorno to go to Maryland under police escort to aid his beleaguered son. Defense attorneys started chipping away at 'Tommy Del's' credibility upon his return. They hurled a series of rapid fire questions at Del Giorno on April 27th, after the trial resumed, which were aimed at rattling the relatively unflappable Del Giorno.

Robert Mozenter shouted inquiries at the witness about where he got the $9,000 needed for his son's bail, by repeating the key question: "Who'd you call? Who'd you call?"

"Whose ten grand is that," demanded the arrogant Mozenter, "mine or yours?"

Del Giorno shot back: "Look, my son's arrest has nothing to do with the killing of Sal Testa. The money was my own, reaped through illegal activities conducted during my years with the mob." (Mozenter was trying to imply that the bail he paid might be Federal money from the witness protection program made available to Del Giorno.)

Meanwhile, another defense attorney, Steven LaCheen, presented a six-page petition to the Judge calling for a mistrial, on behalf of all the defendants and his own client, Joe Pungitore. His so-called *Catalog of Horrors* charged prosecutor Christie with being late nearly every court session, ignoring the Judge's directives on questioning witnesses, withholding evidence from the defense, and wrongfully introducing evidence from other crimes committed by the mob.

But the Judge rejected the petition and the trial continued.

THE SUPREME PENALTY FOR LYING

Both Caramandi and Del Giorno told the jury and the court that they realized the maximum penalty for not telling the truth could be the electric chair if they violated their signed agreements with the government on entering the witness protection program.

The cocky Del Giorno boasted how he and a group of New Jersey State Troopers had stopped at a cocktail lounge on their way to his confinement after his last arrest. The troopers allowed him to approach a hooker and he had a quick sexual liaison with her for money. "The troopers were later suspended for this action," he told the jury, "and one of them stole my funds."

The nine defendants barely acknowledged Caramandi's and Del Giorno's existence while they were on the stand. However, at the end of Caramandi's first day on the witness stand, Salvatore 'Wayne' Grande, the alleged Testa hit man, made a 'negative' gesture. He cupped his hands together, then let them unfold close to his face. His index finger and little finger on the right hand pointed directly at 'the Crow' — a common Italian gesture for casting bad luck.

DELAYS AND FRUSTRATIONS

On April 20th, an irate, frustrated Oscar Goodman hollered out during a long recess: "Do you know who is holding up this trial? The princess [Barbara Christie], that's who! This is a waste of the taxpayer's money. If this happened in Nevada [his home state], she would be disciplined. If her delays had occurred in Nevada, she would be canned by now and the Judge would have dismissed the case... and the jury would have applauded. Imagine what [Federal] Judge Fullam [who presided over the Rouse extortion trials] would have done if he were presiding here. This building [City Hall] then would be redesignated as 'The Barbara Christie Memorial Courthouse' and Ms. Christie would be fired. This [delay] is all Judge Sabo's fault."

Neither the judge nor Christie responded to this sarcastic remark.

THE TIRE TRACKS, A TELEPHONE BOOTH AND TESTA'S FUNERAL

The van used to transport Testa's body to the dump site in New Jersey was finally confiscated by the FBI in early 1987. It was placed on a flatbed truck and shipped to the FBI Serology Unit Lab in Washington, DC. David Attenberger, a Special Agent with the FBI serving as a documentary examiner for the U.S. Justice Department Laboratories in Washington, testified at the trial as an expert on handwriting and tire tread. He concluded that the plaster cast impression of the tire markings made at the dump site of Sal Testa's body matched the right rear tire size of the van, but that there was a significant change in the tread wear over the two-and-a-half-year period between the murder and the retrieval of the van. The cast did show that the design and size of the tire was the same.

But impressions made of the tire tracks of the van used to transport Testa's body to the dump site could not be definitely matched to those on the van since the tires had been marred by thousands of miles travelled in the interim.

The defense also made a major issue about the absence of the outdoor phone booth in 1984 at the site near the killing which Caramandi claimed he used at the time of the Testa murder to relay a message. The defense produced a phone company employee who testified that the phone did not exist at that spot until 1987. But the outdoor phone could have been located at an adjacent spot in 1984. The Commonwealth rebutted with a phone company sales representative who testified that a phone could have been there in 1984.

When Maria Testa Muzio took the stand in the most heartrending performance offered by any trial witness, she noted the stark contrast between the attitude of the Mafia members at her father's and brother's funerals — both of whom had been killed by the mob.

"When my father [Phil Testa] was killed," Muzio testified, "Scarfo, Merlino and Leonetti paid their respects at both the viewing and the funeral. They were very attentive, friendly and warm. They were like members of the family."

But the reverse happened at her brother, Sal's funeral. None of them showed up.

When the defense declined to put any of the defendants on the stand to testify, or to bring in any character witnesses, a local CBS-TV reporter commented with tongue in cheek, "the best character witnesses for the defendants would be two nuns and two cement contractors."

The defense did produce several peripheral witnesses, like Louis Palladino, 75, a caretaker at the Girard Park in South Philadelphia, who claimed that he saw Sal Testa at 5:30 p.m. on the day of the alleged killing hours after both Caramandi and Del Giorno claimed that he had been shot, and Brian Pflanc, who testified that his hardware store did not sell the rope that had been used to tie up the body of Testa in the blue blanket.

But these witnesses did not discredit the main thrust of the government's case or the credibility of its two main witnesses.

THE DEFENSE RESTS

When it came time to give the closing arguments to the jury on May 4th, Oscar Goodman starred for the defense. Speaking in a dramatic cadence, Goodman reiterated the main theme of the defense in the trial, i.e., that the government had bought perjured testimony from their two key witnesses. He implied that his client, Leonetti, and others, were portrayed as being akin to the Salem witches. "He is being tried, not because of the charges against him, but because of what the country, the TV and the press think he is...."

"I want you, the jury, to come back and shout to the rafters, those words so eloquently spoken by Phil Leonetti, "Not Guilty! Not Guilty! Absolutely Not Guilty!"

The other defense lawyers, especially Mozenter, echoed Goodman's assertion that Caramandi and Del Giorno were liars, and that there was "no murder gun, no bullets, no fingerprints or photos of the dead body or the alleged kiss of Testa by Merlino," as reasons for the jury to bring back an acquittal. There remained, in Mozenter's opinion, a 'shadow of doubt' about the guilt of the nine men.

There was much repetition in the nine separate closings —

averaging 30 minutes each, since each defense attorney felt psychologically bound to satisfy his particular client and earn his full retainer. Before the defense completed its closing arguments, Ms. Christie became ill, so the Judge recessed the trial for a long four-day weekend. An exasperated 'Bobby' Simone commented to the press: "I'm not falling for that bullshit. She's a women, so she gets sick....I'm not going to close until she goes on and I know the judge will back me up since I think it's fair that one defense counsel makes a closing at the same time she does." Simone stressed the point in his closing argument that "we spent more time selecting a jury than in the trial, since we wanted an *intelligent* and *independent* jury."

He walked over and tapped his client, Scarfo, on the shoulder, and then turned to the jury, boasting: "See I'm not afraid!" He then asked a rhetorical question: "Why did Nicodemo Scarfo drive to Philadelphia from Atlantic City on the day of the murder to meet at a restaurant with some Mexican friends?"

He answered the question: "If he knew of Sal Testa's murder, he would have stayed in Atlantic City or Florida!" Simone sarcastically referred to the high cost to the government for the support of both the Del Giorno and Caramandi families which he claimed had reached $240,000 to date for the expense of each family in the witness protection program.

"What is the Commonwealth trying to do with this 'reward' money?" he retorted. "Buy a conviction?"

As he wound down his 52-minute plea, Simone gestured with his fist and pounded on the rail in front of the jury box and shouted: "What this trial boils down to is a cry of *'Bring me the head of Nicodemo Scarfo!'*"

At the end of his closing statement, Simone said, "The press has caused the hysteria surrounding the Testa case as they did at the turn of the century in New Orleans when the biggest lynching in the USA took place."[*]

"In Philadelphia," Simone ranted, "it was the press that created a storm over the MOVE incident and now it is doing the same thing in this case."

---

[*] In that city, an angry populace stormed the local jail where several Italian-Americans had been incarcerated after a police captain had been killed. When the local press ranted that their acquittal in court was a "miscarriage of justice," a vigilante mob stormed the jail and strung up 17 prisoners.

CHRISTIE'S LAST STAND

When it came to the prosecution's turn after Ms. Christie recovered from her brief illness, she pleaded with the jury "not to compromise" in their decision but to issue a verdict based "not on the defendants' rule of law, but *our* rule of law." She asked the jury to "lift the veil of blood secrecy" and to break the Mafia's "code of silence."

Christie admitted that her two chief witnesses were not pure but that "the Commonwealth doesn't have the luxury of having witnesses like Winston Churchill or the Rev. Martin Luther King, Jr." She pointed out to the jury that the *La Cosa Nostra* "uses people like Caramandi and Del Giorno and then sheds them like a snake sheds its skin."

While the nine defendants sat silent and pensive in their seats, Christie went on to excoriate the mob for operating by its underworld rules in defiance of the rule of law.

"I ask you to consider," she said, "the dilemma of Caramandi and Del Giorno. They had no choice but to tell the truth or go back to the mob and take a chance on losing their lives."

As she wound up her 78-minute dramatic closing for the prosecution, Ms. Christie walked over to the defense table, and standing behind each of the nine defendants, she summed up the role of each in the Testa murder conspiracy. Then with dramatic intensity and in a strong voice, she called upon the jury to find each one guilty of "Murder in the first degree!"

Before the Judge charged the jury, defense lawyer Joe Santaguida pleaded with Sabo one more time for a mistrial since the prosecutor had mentioned other crimes during the trial.

Once again the Judge denied this request.

THE JURY SPEAKS

Just before rendering its long-awaited decision, after six hours of deliberation on May 10th, the jury asked the judge for the court reporter to read back the FBI evidence of the examination of the tire tracks of the death van. The time was 10:15 a.m.

With the clock in the City Hall Tower ringing at precisely 12 noon, they retired to the jury room to deliberate for the last time.

They returned at 12:20 p.m. looking somber. The courtroom was deadly still and family members of the defendants started nervously fingering their rosaries and crossing their fingers in a good luck sign. There were six more minutes of suspense until Barbara Christie could be found. She had gone back to her office across the street thinking the jury would be out for a longer period of time.

When she returned, the clock on the wall showed 12:26 p.m. The jury forelady, Ollie Minze, dressed in a bright yellow dress and wearing dark glasses, stood up to answer the 27 charge questions posed by the court brief. When she answered, "Not Guilty" to the first count against Joseph Grande, the courtroom burst into spontaneous applause and cheers. After she read the same verdict for each of the 27 counts against the nine defendants, the friends of the accused broke out singing "God Bless America" — despite strong objections by Judge Sabo who tried in vain to maintain the proper decorum in his courtroom.

Barbara Christie sat motionless in her chair while the exultant clamor descended around her. She then slipped quietly out a side door and refused to comment to the media. But several jurors did feel free to speak up.

One said: "We're not saying these people are innocent, but give us proof, give us more. One of them probably did it, damn it, and that's what's so bad."

"Ah, believe me," another said, "We were frustrated. Nothing was substantiated."

One confessed that the jury disregarded all evidence about the Mafia and organized crime before beginning deliberations, but did not explain why. "We had to say 'That [the Mafia] is not part of this trial, no matter how much it was brought in'," said the anonymous juror. The jury eliminated the organized crime factor after about "thirty minutes of heated deliberations." There were no dissenters on this point.

Although the jury believed some of Caramandi's and Del Giorno's testimony, most felt that there wasn't enough solid evidence, leaving reasonable doubts about the guilt of the accused.

Some felt that the killer of Testa was among the nine defendants but they couldn't agree on which one, or even whether Nicky Scarfo was boss of the Mafia.

After six weeks of dramatic courtroom drama, the jury went home convinced they had rendered a just verdict regarding the Testa murder trial.

What fools these mortals be.

-Puck *

26

THE ORGY AT THE FOUR SEASONS' HOTEL

A RAUCOUS group of 70 — lawyers, relatives and friends of the nine men acquitted in the killing of Sal Testa — retreated to the nearby Four Seasons' Hotel to celebrate the victory in the courtroom. While the nine were handcuffed and led back to prison to await future murder and racketeering trials, the happy followers sipped $50 a glass of Louis XIII cognac and $100 a bottle of Tattinger champagne— supplied by a smiling Nicky Scarfo, Jr.

"God Bless the jury! God bless the jury!" shouted the revellers. Some parodied characters in *The Godfather* film while others danced on expensive sofas in the hotel lounge. Oscar Goodman, who had promised to swim naked in a city fountain if he won an acquittal for his client, reneged. He tried to come downstairs to the lobby in his robe, as a compromise on his verbal promise to splash with the mermaids in the fountain at Logan Circle, but was turned back by security guards.

Goodman did take a bath, however, in champagne, courtesy of some of the defendants' relatives. The swirling crowd, some well-dressed, others in jeans and T-shirts, messed up the lobby of the city's poshest hotel. Nervous security guards and hotel staff stood helplessly watching the mob splashing drinks over the luxurious furnishings. The hotel later billed Scarfo, Jr. for extensive damages.

The man of the hour was Robert Simone, the leader of the ten-member defense team.

---

* In William Shakespeare's *A Midsummer Night's Dream*

"Bobby! Bobby!" came the cheer as he happily sipped champagne and mingled with the exuberant crowd.

"Thank God for the jury system!!," shouted Mark Scarfo, 17, the youngest son of the mob leader.

Everyone was happy, but the nine Mafia members who were escorted back to jail, still not free men.

WAS JUSTICE SERVED AT THE TESTA TRIAL?

"Justice has been served," shouted an exultant brother of Joe and Sal Grande. But was it? To many observers the sequestered jury of eight women and four men were frightened at the prospects of retribution by the long arm of the *La Cosa Nostra* if they had rendered guilty verdicts, since it would be relatively easy for anyone to seek out their residences in the local phone book.

WHAT WENT WRONG AT THE SCARFO-TESTA TRIAL

In the first Mafia murder trial of the late Roofers' Union head, John McCullough, held in Philadelphia, Christie had the paid killer, Robert Boyle, and the gun as evidence to convince the jury of the guilt of the two Mafia defendants: Raymond 'Long John' Martorano and Albert Daidone.

In the Testa trial, she had neither, just the words of two ex-mobsters, neither of whom were witnesses to the actual killing, although they each confessed that they had a key role in the conspiracy to kill Testa. The alleged hit man in the Testa case, the accused defendant, Salvatore 'Wayne' Grande and all the other defendants, did not take the stand, and Christie could not question him. So the evidence presented was mainly circumstantial and hearsay.

But the jury chose not to believe 'Tommy Del' or 'the Crow's' stories, and was encouraged to mistrust their testimony by the repetitious denunciations of their credibility by the nine defense lawyers.

The Testa trial reputedly cost the Commonwealth at least $1 million, including $110-a-night motel rooms, which included several weekend side trips to restaurants both in and out of town for each of the twelve jurors — and four alternates.

True, the trial cost the mob members plenty in expensive

defense lawyers' fees. The likes of 'Bobby' Simone and Oscar Goodman did not come cheaply. But after all, the Mafia has garnered millions from its ongoing illicit businesses and underworld scams and can afford to hire above-average defense attorneys.

The Testa jury seemed to be sending a message to both the state and federal government to stop using Thomas Del Giorno and Nicholas Caramandi as witnesses.

But would the government give up? The next trial would answer that question.

There were a number of reasons for the acquittal of the Scarfo conspirators in the killing of Sal Testa. In the judgment of Philadelphia District Attorney Ron Castille, a major reason was the fearfulness of the jurors. If they came up with a guilty verdict, the Scarfo clan would have been able to seek retribution against them because of their lack of anonymity. This fear was a real one since the jury had heard testimony about the violent methods used by the Mafia in vengeance against its enemies. And the jury would have been enemies if they had come up with a guilty verdict.

Furthermore, Barbara Christie did not have access to many of the key tapes held by the FBI and the Federal Organized Crime Strike Force that they were keeping for a later trial against Scarfo. Those omissions hurt her case, as did the court's rulings which limited or excluded much of the tape and photographic evidence she sought to present to the jury. These rulings were made either in the Judge's chambers or at the sidebar with the defense attorneys complaining about the admission of this dramatic evidence. But the Judge took a narrow view of her requests and prevented their use.

Finally, one former Assistant District Attorney who worked on background research for the case observed that the main reason the prosecution lost the trial was the back-room infighting between the Feds and the State over which trial would go to court first: the Sal Testa murder case, or the Federal RICO case, which also included the Testa killing as one of the key indictments.

But behind the scenes, Del Giorno and Caramandi had benefited from the experience of being cross-examined by the defense and they would be better prepared the next time around. And there would be another time in court.

THE SCARFO EXTORTION ATTEMPT VERDICT IS UPHELD BY THE APPEALS COURT

On June 29, 1988, a three judge Federal Appeals Court for the Third Circuit upheld the conviction and sentencing of Nicodemo Scarfo in the Rouse extortion plot. Speaking for the court, Circuit Judge Joseph F. Weiss Jr. wrote in the 29-page decision that Chief U.S. District Judge John Fullam was justified in conducting the *first* case in the Eastern District of Pennsylvania in which the jury was anonymous. This was also the *first* time that the Third Circuit, which handles appeals of federal cases from Pennsylvania, New Jersey and Delaware, addressed the propriety of anonymity.

"Jurors' fears of retaliation from criminal defendants are not hypothetical; such apprehension has been documented," said Weiss in justifying Fullam's decision to keep his jurors' identities secret to prevent them from worrying about retaliation.

Weiss and Circuit Judges Ruggero J. Aldisert and Morton Greenberg also decided that both Caramandi and Del Giorno's testimony about slayings allegedly ordered by Scarfo had been necessary to show that the informants' own fears of being killed had prompted them to cooperate with the government.

"That Scarfo had such tight control over an organization capable of executing those who incurred his displeasure was obviously an essential fact the jury needed to evaluate in considering the extent to which fear swayed the two witnesses."

Scarfo's latest appeal for freedom ended in a rejection by the law.

I'm a free man and have no worries — except 'Buddy Boy' [Warner, of the FBI] coming here.

-Ralph Staino, Jr.[*]

27 WHEN A DIARY BECOMES A 'SMOKING GUN'[†]

'JUNIOR' SURFACES AT LAST...AND IS CAUGHT BY THE FEDS ON THE BEACH

AFTER missing the late 1987 Philadelphia methamphetamine drug trial with four of his co-conspiratorial Mafia buddies, a suntanned Ralph 'Junior' Staino was finally arrested at a beachside villa at Puerta Plata in the Dominican Republic on January 13, 1988. Staino, 55, was using the alias of 'Joseph Esposito' on both his passport and driver's license. The dapper Staino, who had been a long-time Mafia associate, was brought back to the USA to face several Federal indictments and trials on multiple charges of importing a controlled substance (P2P), racketeering and murder.

The son of a South Philadelphia grocer, 'Junior' Staino is the husband of the notorious Lillian 'Tiger Lil' Reis, the former owner and head of the chorus line at the now defunct local Latin Casino nightclub.

They were both tried in the famous 1959 burglary of the Pottsville home of coal baron John Rich (once known as 'Ricci-

---

[*] Writing in his diary on August 7, 1987, from his haven in Santo Domingo where he was ducking a federal indictment for participating in a Mafia-led methamphetamine import and distribution conspiracy.

[†]See Chapter 18 The Speed Conspiracy for details of the Mafia's methamphetamine drug operation.

oni'). Police accused Lillian of masterminding the heist by getting Staino and other hoodlums to travel up to the Pennsylvania coal country to do the 'job.'

Over $500,000 in cash was taken from a basement safe. The bizarre trial led to the slayings of two hoods (the Blaney brothers) to silence them as witnesses to the alleged burglary. Rich insisted to his death that no more than $3,500 had been taken from his home.

As one of the six alleged participants in the heist, Staino, who is two years younger than his wife, served 28 months of a 4 to 9 year prison sentence for the Rich burglary. He was released on a technicality.

After two trials in the burglary case, further criminal charges were dropped.

The strikingly glamorous, dark-haired, ex-chorus girl, Reis, emerged with enough cash after the burglary and trial to buy a posh Center City night spot called the Celebrity Room.

Reis married Staino and went into quiet seclusion in a South Philadelphia 13th Street rowhouse, where she kept out of further trouble in the ensuing years after closing down the Celebrity Room for lack of business.

Charles B. Warner, nicknamed 'Buddy', a Special Agent for the FBI for 18 years, worked predominantly out of the Philadelphia office. In recent times he had been concentrating on gathering evidence to help indict and convict various members of the Nicky Scarfo-led branch of the Mafia.

At Staino's trial in July, 1988, one of the key items presented by the prosecution was the reading of Staino's 1987 diary to the jury which he kept in a blue 8" X 6" spiral notebook. It was written mainly at his seaside home at Puerta Plata in the Dominican Republic between July 18, 1987, and the date of his arrest by the Dominican Police on January 13, 1988. The Dominican Police turned the escapee over to a waiting Charles B. Warner, whom Staino had nicknamed 'Buddy Boy.'

Following are some telling and rare excerpts of Staino's state of mind as he awaited eventual capture and extradition to the United States:

HIGHLIGHTS FROM THE DIARY OF RALPH STAINO, JR.

6/18/87 Philadelphia — "Got a frantic phone call. 'Buddy Boy' is looking for me." (An arrest warrant had just been issued for Staino, Scarfo and four other mob members in the P2P import conspiracy. He flew to Hollywood, Florida where he applied for a faked passport in the name of Joe Esposito, a pseudonym with a false Social Security Number 169-29-5853, false ID cards, driver's license and birth and voter registration certificates).

6/21 Hollywood, Florida — "Being alone is not for me. It is just the beginning."

6/22 Hollywood, Florida — "Needed certain documents."

6/23 Hollywood, Florida — "Lonely, scared..."

6/25 Hollywood, Florida — "Passport issued."

6/25 Hollywood, Florida — "Had Wally drive me to airport."

6/25 In flight en route to Dominican Republic — "Left airport [Miami] nervous and scared. Off, off away. Arrived safely but 400 miles short of destination [Puerta Plata]. Tried to charter plane but could not, so took a cab. Beautiful country."

6/26 Puerta Plata - "A beautiful ocean front home."

6/28 Puerta Plata - "Umberto says [that a car is] a must. $16,000 [for a 1977 Nissan]. I could have got the same thing back home for $3,000."

6/29 Puerta Plata - "I miss you terribly Lillian...My life is over...I'm sure."

8/7 Puerta Plata - "Am free man, Have no worries except 'Buddy Boy' coming but he has failed so far."

8/10 Puerta Plata - "Several opportunities here to make money. Buy and sell property. Bad water problem. Spent $270 for new cistern."

9/11 Puerta Plata - "Off to Santiago."

9/21 Puerta Plata - "Instead of elation. Tears, tears, tears! I wish something would happen to 'Buddy Boy.'"

9/24 Puerta Plata - "Assured that Dominican Republic has no extradition with the U.S. and that family can come to visit me."

9/25 Puerta Plata - "Am really beat."

9/26 Puerta Plata - "Off to Umberto's. 'Buddy Boy' has not been near him."

9/27 Puerta Plata - "Met with attorney. Can buy a condo — with tennis, pool, villas, marina — for $110,000 — furnished."

10/14 Puerta Plata - "Encouraging news from Gary."

10/23 Puerta Plata - "Went to the opening of a nearby casino. No Vegas or A.C. Left a 'donation' of $1,000. Oh well, I'll get them another time. Lost $1,000 at blackjack. I'll get them tomorrow."

11/7 Puerta Plata - "I'm getting very bored being alone. I just miss everything about my family and also the States. There's no place like home....There was a knock on my door, scared. Thought the party was over but it was only a drunk. Was I happy to see him, so we had a drink together."

12/4 Puerta Plata - "Spoke to Gary. Have cash for attorney."

12/17 Puerta Plata - "It's been 6 months since my hasty departure from the USA. Could it be that long? Saw attorney and got guarantee to prevent my extradition to the U.S. Wants $25,000 — high — I hope I won't need his services."

1/5/88 Puerta Plata - "Another beautiful day. Somehow it's nice to know they're freezing back home. (Especially, 'Bud' Warner, Ha-ha.)."

'JUNIOR'S' CAPTURE

A few days later, 'Junior' Staino's freedom abruptly ended when the Dominican Police knocked on his door. After arresting him, they turned him over for extradition to a waiting 'Buddy Boy' Warner, standing in the driveway. When accosted by his nemesis on January 13, 1988, Staino at first declared to the Dominican Police that Warner was "insane, and crazy. I have never seen this man before and I am not Ralph Staino. I'm Joe Esposito." But Warner had seen him some 30 times before back home. Soon thereafter, a handcuffed Staino was flown home to jail to await his trial.

The local gendarmes went inside the house and retrieved the following documents which were turned over to the FBI agent: a list of 40 countries from a local Dominican newspaper which did not have extradition treaties with the U.S., his false identification papers and a photo of his Dominican girlfriend, L. Munoz (who was pregnant at the time). A list of Staino's net worth was found in code — S.D. (Santo Domingo) $1,470,000; Fla. apt. — $500,000; Uncle Sam (the $100,000 cash taken by Warner from Staino's S. 13th Street Philadelphia home in December, 1986, hidden inside a kitchen closet); and $305,000 miscellaneous: Total = $2,375,000.

'Bobby' Simone, Staino's defense attorney, was asked what he felt the impact of the diary might be on the jury after the prosecutor read excerpts from its contents during the closing arguments of the P2P trial.

"Bullshit!" he answered emphatically.

Although Staino never once wrote in his diary that he was guilty of any crime, nor did he mention the damning word — P2P, or any of his mob co-conspirators by name, his unwritten confessions, between the lines, appeared to be strong enough to implicate him in the plot and convince the jury of his guilt.

THE TWO MISSING NAMES

'Junior' also carried a list of the names of the Philadelphia Mafia on his person when he was arrested, but two names were missing — those of Nicholas Caramandi and Thomas Del Giorno — who had broken the sacred Code of Silence. The government stressed this omission both during the trial and in the rebuttal to show that Staino was still connected with the mob.

PRE-TRIAL WRANGLING, JULY, 1988

Knowing that the Staino diary kept by the accused while he was a fugitive from justice contained damning indirect evidence against his client, Simone tried to squelch its use in court on spurious grounds. He argued that the FBI, which has no jurisdiction in the Dominican Republic, might have played an illegal role during the search of Staino's seaside villa at the time of his arrest. But U.S. District Judge Thomas O'Neill ruled that not only the diary, but other documents in question seized from the home of Charles 'Charley White' Iannece and the $100,000 seized from the South Philadelphia rowhouse that Staino shared with his wife, Lillian Reis, could be admitted as evidence.

After these preliminaries were agreed to, jury selection began and a panel of predominantly young white women were selected. There was only one elderly, white-haired woman and no black females. Two black males and three young white males rounded out the jury. The defense was obviously trying to play on the emotions of the jury to gain sympathy for the distinguished-looking, lantern-jawed Staino.

'JUNIOR' IN THE DOCK

Staino was still a handsome man and well-tanned despite his six month stay in the Chester County prison. He was slightly balding and wore glasses. Graying at the temples, he wore a conservative gray suit in court with ankle-length black boots. He never turned to greet his wife, Lillian, daughter, Barbara, and teenage granddaughters who sat in the second family row of the courthouse every day. He seemed to be preoccupied and isolated mentally from his family even though they were physically seated only ten feet away. His wife came to court each day wearing wrap-around designer sun glasses, to mask her identity.

The only one Staino talked to regularly during the trial was his lawyer, and he would occasionally beckon to Simone to query him on a bit of evidence or a question that he wanted him to ask of the government witness on the stand.

HOW THE P2P SCAM GOT FOULED UP

According to the US Government's case against him, Staino sent two young emissaries, Joe Kelly and Edmund Woodward Gifford, to get 50 gallons of stolen P2P in West Germany in May, 1985, and arrange to have it shipped to Philadelphia under a phony label. Evidence at the week-long trial showed several direct connections between Staino and members of the mob — besides Caramandi and Del Giorno — who were involved in the conspiracy. Although he was not a member of the mob when he began to get the oil into the U.S., he later became a full-fledged member of the Mafia according to FBI informants.

The conspiracy began to unravel when Staino informed Caramandi and Del Giorno in mid-1985 that Angelo Vitullio, one of the conspirators, was not telling the whole truth about the number of gallons en route. But since more was consigned to come in, Junior passed the word that he wanted the new batch of oil to be stolen. In March, 1986, court testimony by the government showed that 100 gallons of P2P were stolen, as confirmed in several phone calls from Brussels by Kelly to Dominick Staino, 'Junior's' nephew, in the U.S. Meanwhile, Steve Vento, Sr. who was serving an 18-year prison term at the Lewisburg, Pennsylvania, federal penitentiary for importing P2P, was informed by a subordinate, Joe Massimino, that "the mob wants it all" (referring to the take on the oil).

When his son, Steve Vento, Jr., refused to pay the street tax to the Mafia on the shipment of P2P, he was shot in the head on May 28, 1986, on orders of Scarfo — but somehow survived.

Between June 13 and June 17, 1986, Vitullio visited Vento, Sr. in Lewisburg and informed his partner that much of the P2P had been stolen by Joe Kelly who was with the mob. On June 17th, Vitullio also told Caramandi that Joe Kelly did steal the oil from an apartment in West Germany under orders of 'Junior' and Dominick Staino. When both Caramandi and his partner, Charles Iannece, confronted Staino with this information, he denied the charges. 'The Crow' and 'Charley White' did not believe his story. (This was the same day that a Philadelphia policeman, Officer John Murphy, observed Caramandi gesturing wildly and dressing down Staino while they stood together on the sidewalk outside the mob's clubhouse at Camac and Moore Streets in South Philadelphia. Although he could not hear what was being said, it was obvious to the cop that 'the Crow' was accusing 'Junior' of something that had gone wrong.

When Caramandi and Iannece went to Staino's rowhouse two days later, they were informed that he had gone to Del Giorno's house. Arriving at that location, they confronted a shaken Staino who admitted he stole 50 gallons of oil. On June 20th, Del Giorno ordered Staino to meet him in Ocean City.

On June 22nd (as corroborated by an FBI wiretap), 'Junior' told Del Giorno that he actually stole 100 gallons of the stuff from Vitullio. He [Staino] also rationalized why he was stalling on sharing his portion of the P2P with the rest of the mob. 'Tommy Del' answered: "I really think the kids [Kelly and Gifford, two non-Mafia hoodlums] took it from us."

A somewhat confused Staino said, "OK, I'll check into it."

'Junior' soon realized that he needed a new agent to serve as the customs broker for the importation of the oil. Since the two previous firms used in the cover story, Livingston International and Stern, Inc., could no longer be used safely, he asked Charles

Iannece to approach the Rapid Supply Co. in Philadelphia, an importer of heavy equipment, in late June, 1986, to do the job.

After a series of international phone calls, the 50 gallons were smuggled in during August, 1986 and consigned to an agent named Romolino. The oil was then sold and the money distributed with Staino getting his share.

In mid-October, Staino informed Caramandi and Del Giorno that there was a problem in bringing in 32 radiators filled with 90 gallons of oil and that there would have to be a 30-day delay in the shipment.

On November 5th, it arrived, consigned to the Rapid Supply Co. Distribution was then made and the money flowed in.

After both Caramandi and Del Giorno began to cooperate with the FBI in November, the government began to close in on Staino. They got a warrant to search his home on December 11, 1986. Behind a sliding panel in a false wall in his kitchen cabinet, the FBI agents found $100,000 in cash after Staino denied that any money was there. His limp explanation was that the greenbacks came from some recently-cashed, legitimately-obtained CD's and from the $50,000 sale of real estate from some property given him by his late father. The government refused to give him back the $100,000, for obvious reasons.

THE COURTROOM BLOWUP

Midway in the trial, after Caramandi once again described the process of initiation into the Mafia under questioning by the prosecution, Simone asked the witness for the prosecution whether "initiated members carried some form of identification documenting their affiliation" with the mob. Smiling smugly, the cool Caramandi replied in his deep gravelly voice: "You know how its done...You been around these guys so long. You know what it is. They wanted to 'make' you, in fact."

A somewhat shaken Simone interjected: "By the way, I'm *not* a member of the Mafia."

But Caramandi shot back: "Pretty close."

When pressed again to acknowledge that Simone was *not* a member, during his cross-examination, Caramandi admitted: "Not that I know of," but then added a sarcastic afterthought: "You might know...Nicky might have *made* you!" Simone then tried to show the court that it would have been impossible for him to have been initiated into the mob, because Scarfo — who must preside over all induction ceremonies as boss — had been in jail since around the time that 'the Crow' had become a government witness.

Caramandi then turned to Judge O'Neill, who had interrupted the harangue by ordering them to stop the bickering, and said, "He sounds like a *made* member, your honor."

During a recess a short time later, Simone sarcastically commented to the media on Caramandi's accusation, "It's absurd. I got 'made' when Nicky was in prison, and now I am *boss* of the Mafia."

Caramandi previously told other juries about the close relationship that existed between Simone and Scarfo. "He's not just his lawyer, but a friend and adviser....He's been [in] on discussions where there were killings discussed."

'TOMMY DEL'S' REPRISE

Appearing once again in court for the prosecution following Caramandi's moment on the stand, 'Tommy Del' Del Giorno told the court how he and the other co-conspirators, including Staino, put up at least $10,000 each as front money for the P2P operation. He then claimed that 'the Crow' and 'Charley White' got $100,000 each from the shakedown as their return on their investment and then $50,000 as the 'elbow' to be given to Scarfo and Leonetti.

Del Giorno claimed that Scarfo determined what his cut of the pie was to be after he decided the total score, but confessed that he differed with the boss on what "I felt was the right amount and I told Nicky: 'Here's your end.' I lied to him and I'm sure, you [Simone] lied to him at times."

Simone immediately changed the subject.

'BOBBY'S' CLOSER

Simone's entire 40-minute-long closing argument was an attempt to knock holes in the conflicting testimony of the two star government witnesses, Caramandi and Del Giorno, to try and impress the jury with their motives for lying and staying out of jail — which allegedly had already cost the government upwards of $500,000. "These people, the government attorneys, are being conned by Caramandi and Del Giorno....The question is: 'Have they sold you a bill of goods?' I don't think they are going to con you," he asserted. "The judge will tell you that if a person has been convicted of a felony (as they have), that you should question their testimony.

"How can the government reconcile who is telling the truth, when 'the Crow' says he got $92,000 from the August, 1986 drug deal, but Del Giorno said 'the Crow' got $158,000?" He then ran off a list of several other contradictions in the testimony of the two men to cast doubt and bore holes in the authenticity of their statements.

"Association with somebody means nothing," Simone told the jury in his windup. "The misuse of the system by the government prosecutors in this case where they are telling you, 'We don't have to work hard to convince you since we have Caramandi and Del Giorno to testify. With this new federal RICO law, suspects are arrested, they go directly to jail with no bail... except for 'rats' like Del Giorno and Caramandi...and those two presented the only damaging evidence against my client Staino. Are you going to believe them?"

THE VERDICT

The twelve-member jury convicted Staino on three of the four counts lodged against him, including co-conspiracy, importing 47 gallons of the P2P liquid in August, 1986, and attempting to import 100 gallons in September, 1986, but acquitted him of importing 50 gallons in April, 1986. Associate Prosecutor, Michael Levy, of the U.S. Organized Crime Strike Force hailed the verdict as positive evidence that juries would accept testimony once again from the government's two controversial chief witnesses, Caramandi and Del Giorno, after two other juries had refused to believe them twice in the past year on similar P2P charges made against Scarfo and Co. as well as the charges against them for the Sal Testa murder.

With an increasing wave of public concern for harsher punishment of drug pushers in this country, the jury, in this case, appeared to be reacting to the change in the current political atmosphere.

As one of the US Attorneys put it after the decision, "He took his chances. If he had come home to be tried with Scarfo in December, he would have most probably been acquitted. But he chose to be a fugitive and he lost."

So, Staino was sent back to jail in handcuffs to await yet another major trial with Mafia boss 'Nicky' Scarfo and his friends on multiple federal racketeering charges.

Nicky Crow is just a cannibal whose lust for blood is great,
A dirty crum, a low-life scum, he's really Satan's mate.

He'll tell of stalking victims, with vigor and with zeal,
He'll fantasize, he'll tell lies, to keep himself from jail...

You can't believe this babbling crow, though he cackles like a hen,
For he is vile, so full of guile, this Judas among men.

-Ralph 'Junior' Staino, Jr.[*]

28

NICKY TRIES TO PREVENT HIS OWN WATERLOO

AN OMINOUS WARNING FROM THE NORTH

TWO weeks before the start of the Scarfo RICO trial in Philadelphia, a psychological blow was struck against the prosecution by a Federal court decision in Newark, New Jersey, just ninety miles to the North. A federal jury acquitted twenty reputed mobsters of the Lucchese crime family on August 25, 1988, after the longest federal criminal trial in the nation's history involving twenty criminal defendants.

The crime family, headed by Anthony 'Tumac' Acceturo of Hollywood, Florida, was involved in illegal gambling, loan-sharking, drug dealing and fraudulent credit card operations.

When the jury forewoman read off the first of seventy-seven mob verdicts, the courtroom broke out into pandemonium, the defendants and their attorneys hugged each other and gave a standing ovation to the jury which had deliberated for fourteen hours before giving their verdict: a stunning and a shocking de-

[*] Lines from an unpublished poem, "The Talking, Stalking Crow" — written about Nicholas 'Nicky Crow' Caramandi, during the RICO trial, October, 1988.

feat for the government. The jury forewoman even wept as the Assistant U.S. Attorney V. Grady O'Malley sat grimly as the Not Guilty verdicts were read one by one.

Some of the jurors seemed to feel the length of the racketeering trial against so many defendants had caused resentment in the minds of the non-sequestered jury. Many of the jurors blew kisses, waved and smiled broadly at the defendants and their families, before leaving in a waiting van outside the courthouse.

Observers felt that the testimony of the star cooperating witness against the defendants, Joseph Alonzo, who had been diagnosed as schizophrenic, an admitted drug addict, an alcoholic, and a convicted criminal who had shot one of the defendants — his own cousin — five times, obviously boomeranged against the government.

The message to the fellow prosecutors in Philadelphia from the Newark jury's verdict was that a predicted three-month-long trial of Scarfo and his family could also lead to an overkill effect on the about-to-be-picked jury. Would they take heed and try to tighten up their case so it would end before Thanksgiving?

A DEFENSE WINDFALL BLOWS UP FROM THE SOUTH

Coincidentally, with the bad psychological blow to the Scarfo prosecution from the massive government loss in the New Jersey trial, another surprise blow fell on August 29th which threatened to throw a dual pall over the case before the start of the jury selection. The chief government witness, Nicholas Caramandi, was accidentally spotted in his secret government hideout by the relatives of two Scarfo family defendants, Philip and Frank Narducci, Jr., at the beach, pool and bar of the fancy Bay Princess condominium complex in Ocean City, Maryland.

The friends and relatives of the Narducci brothers, who had been vacationing at Ocean City, first saw Caramandi by the condo pool with a man they assumed to be a federal agent. Later they witnessed the pair that night in the bar of the Ocean City "Sneakers," a plush restaurant located above the most popular health club in town.

The next morning, August 30th, as a dozen residents of the condo watched in shock, three carloads of the Narducci family members pulled into the parking lot of the Bay Princess and staged a demonstration, shouting for Caramandi, calling him a "liar and a murderer." When the taunting started, Caramandi appeared on the balcony of his room and shouted back: "So what!" Then he quickly retreated into his room. This raucous scene left many of the condo's residents uneasy. Some even talked of moving out when they were shocked to discover that 'Joe' as they had known him, was a mob informant who had been living under federal protective custody.

Several of the condo residents had assumed that 'Joe' (Caramandi) and the two men who had leased a room next door to 'the Crow' were gays, since they noted that the men never appeared with women in their company. When the news of this incident reached Philadelphia, the government quickly moved Caramandi from the condo where he had been residing for the past ten months to a new secret location under another assumed name.

More important to the defense, however, was the golden opportunity for the defendants' lawyers to use this "waste of the taxpayers' money" in an attempt to further undermine the credibility of Caramandi.

Smelling blood, Joe Santaguida, who represented Frank Narducci, Jr., remarked before the start of the trial: "If he comes off saying that 'he's been spending his time in jail or something like a jail,' as he has said, then I'll show the court that not many jails have pools and bars."

Defense lawyer Donald Marino, who represented Frank's brother, Phil Narducci, assailed the FBI for letting Caramandi, an admitted alcoholic, near the bar.

"The family was very upset," he said bitterly. "Here's this guy who says, 'Yes, I did kill people,' and now is being wined and dined at taxpayers' expense; he's a thief, a murderer and a liar."

The government was embarrassed by this unfortunate incident which erupted on the eve of jury selection for the forthcoming trial. Prosecutors were concerned about how much this revelation might hurt their case and the credibility of the government, and not just that of Caramandi.

THE FEDS LOWER THE RICO BOOM ON SCARFO'S CRIME FAMILY

The Federal indictments were handed down in January, 1988, against Scarfo and sixteen members of his crime family. Louis Pichini — lead prosecutor for the upcoming Scarfo-RICO trial for the U.S. Organized Crime Strike Force and fifteen-year veteran of chasing the mob — and four of his associates, under the supervision of Joel Friedman, another fifteen-year veteran civil servant, had been preparing their complex case for eight years. They had been quietly collecting and sorting evidence with the help of the FBI and local State Police officials.

Among the charges issued at the broad Federal RICO indictment against the seventeen defendants was a conspiracy to conduct racketeering acts which included participating in nine murders and four attempted murders. Each of them were accused of conspiring in one or more of these previously unsolved murders and/or attempted murders of thirteen Mafia members.

With so many illegal enterprises conducted by the Scarfo crime family, it was fairly simple for the government to come up with multiple RICO indictments against the sixteen followers of Nicodemo Scarfo.

THE PATTERN OF THE SCARFO MOB'S RACKETEERING: MURDER

The June 13, 1988, RICO indictment listed fourteen racketeering acts of murder or attempted murder leveled against Nicky Scarfo and his clan. In chronological order, they were:

1. The murder of Municipal Judge Edwin Helfant of Cape May, New Jersey, in Atlantic City on February 15, 1978.

2. The murder of Michael Cifelli on January 4, 1979, in Philadelphia.

3. The Vincent Falcone murder in his Margate, New Jersey, home on December 16, 1979.

4. The killing of John Calabrese in Philadelphia on October 6, 1981.

5. The murder of Frank Narducci, Sr., in Philadelphia on January 7, 1982.

6. The attempts to murder Harry Riccobene in Philadelphia on June 8, 1982, and on August 21, 1982 (both of which failed).

7. The attempted murder of Joseph Salerno, Sr., at his Wildwood Crest, New Jersey, Motel on August 10, 1982.

8. The murder of Pasquale Spirito in South Philadelphia on April 29, 1983.

9. The attempted murder of Frank Martines in Philadelphia on October 14, 1983.

10. The murder of Salvatore Tamburrino on November 8, 1983, in Philadelphia.

11. The killing of Robert Riccobene in Philadelphia on December 6, 1983.

12. The Salvatore Testa murder in an empty Philadelphia candy store on September 14, 1984.

13. The Frank D'Alfonso murder in Philadelphia on July 23, 1985.

14. The attempted murder of Steven Vento, Jr., in Philadelphia on May 27, 1986.

This Mob bloodbath, mainly centered around Mafia crime family members — with the exception of Judge Helfant — took place over a three-and-a-half year time span, with most of the murders and attempted murders occurring in the South Philadelphia neighborhoods where the Mafia members lived, worked and played.

THE MAFIA'S BUSINESS AS A RACKETEERING CONSPIRACY

Besides the murder charges, there were other criminal acts listed in the indictment against Scarfo and his clan. They included extortion, illegal lotteries and bookmaking (sports and numbers), loansharking or illegal extension of credit, and distribution of controlled substances (particularly methamphetamine).

These illegal businesses were all conducted under the umbrella of the Scarfo mob's supervision by member soldiers and *capos*, who had all been inducted into the Mafia through the secret ritual ceremony. These crimes of the Mafia businesses — known as "The Enterprise" — will be examined in depth in the next chapter.

THE ACCUSED

The eighteen members of the Scarfo crime family who were indicted and stood trial for their accused crimes under the RICO statutes were:

'Lil Nicky' Scarfo, age 59, the boss;

'Crazy Phil' Leonetti, age 35, Scarfo's nephew and underboss;

Francis 'Faffy' Iannarella, Jr., age 41, a *capo* ;

Joseph 'Chickie' Ciancaglini, age 53, a *capo* ;

Anthony 'Tony' Pungitore, age 35, a soldier;

Joseph 'Joe Punge' Pungitore (Anthony's brother), age 32, a soldier;

Ralph 'Junior' Staino, Jr., age 56;

Frank 'Windows' Narducci, Jr., age 35;

Phil Narducci, his brother, age 32;

Salvatore Scafidi, age 26;

'Charley White' Iannece, age 53, a soldier;

Nicholas 'Nick-the-Blade' Virgilio, age 61, a soldier;

Lawrence Merlino, age 42, a soldier; and his brother

Salvatore 'Chuckie' Merlino age 49; former underboss, now a soldier;

Eugene 'Gino' Milano, age 29, a soldier;

Nicholas 'Nicky Whip' Milano (Eugene's brother), age 31, a soldier;

Joseph Grande, age 28, a soldier; and his brother —

Salvatore Wayne Grande, age 35, a soldier.

Just before the trial, defendant Joe Ligambi pleaded guilty on all counts lodged against him, so he did not have to appear in court. He awaited sentencing pending the outcome of the trial.

THE JURY SELECTION GETS STICKY

The RICO trial of Scarfo and his cohorts marked the *first* time in Philadelphia's history (and only the second in America after the recent Lucchese family trial in Newark, New Jersey) that an *entire* alleged mob hierarchy had gone to trial together.

When a pool of 250 potential jurors from the Southeastern Pennsylvania region were assembled on Monday, September

10th, the question of whether the jurors should remain anonymous and be sequestered for their own protection from mob retribution again became paramount.

Federal District Judge Franklin Van Antwerpen ruled that both of these requests should be granted, even though it meant serious hardships on all potential jurors who passed muster — since he told them that they might be incarcerated in a hotel for up to three months under the watchful eye of Federal marshals.

After over two weeks of tedious jury selection, in which the pool had to be increased to 311 because of hardship cases, a reluctance to serve, a confessed knowledge of the case, or biases expressed by prospective jurors, a panel of eighteen (including six alternatives) was finally picked.

The twelve jurors would be cooped up in a hotel, and allowed only a few carefully monitored phone calls, and even fewer visits with their families, to protect them from hearing or reading any accounts of the trial by the media.

Some of the questions thrown at them by the judge, prosecutors and defense attorneys include: "Do you think it's glamorous to be in the mob? Is it O.K. for one mobster to kill another mobster? Do you think the government should bother to investigate illegal gambling operations?"

Only three of the jurors lived in Philadelphia. The rest came from adjacent areas in the lower Delaware Valley. During the process, both sides, with the help of a psychologist for the prosecution and a sociologist for the defense tried to root out those who they felt might get 'cabin fever' or be made otherwise uncomfortable by their long confinement, which the Judge warned them might last to Thanksgiving and possibly until Christmas.

During the jury selection process, Ralph 'Junior' Staino, Jr., one of the defendants, got bored and penned a long *Ballad of Nicodemo Scarfo and His Alleged Associates* to amuse himself and his fellow Mafia crime family members. It contained some black humor and doggerel written in a crude-rhyming series of quatrains. His stream of consciousness poetry, made available to the press by his defense attorney, Michael Pinsky, starts with the following verse:

Gather round me my friends
And listen to my story,
Our long awaited trial begins
With the selection of our jury.

Near the end of his fifty-six verse 'ballad', Junior lashed out at the two chief government witnesses: Del Giorno and Caramandi:

The two key witnesses in this case
Are liars as you all know
They're vermin and they're scum bags
'Tommy Del' and 'Nicky Crow.'

Stories they will make up
and vicious lies they'll tell
They'd rat on their own mothers
To avoid a prison cell.

And all our taxpaying dollars
Out the window they do go,
To cultivate these parasites
Tommy Del and Nicky Crow.

They wine them and they dine them
This fact they don't refute
And we in jail are denied bail
While they're with prostitutes.

They're kept in high-life places
Very few of us could afford
They're paying them a salary
Living in luxury like a lord.

They're coddled and they're cuddled
As they tuck them into bed,
As we in jail get mighty frail
With these thoughts in our head.

They're gutless and they're spineless
We can throw in they're wimps too,
Don't let them do this to us
Cause they'll do it to you.

Now if this story shocks you
You can help us strike a blow,
Help us rid this world of scoundrels
Like Tommy Del and the Crow.

THE TRIAL JUDGE FACES THE BIGGEST CASE OF HIS CAREER

The judge assigned to hear this important case in which the government pinned its hopes for the final dismantlement of the Scarfo family was new to the bench. Franklin S. Van A. Antwerpen, 46, had only been sworn in as a Federal District Judge in December, 1987, but was known to be "firm but fair" by courtroom observers. He had only presided over one other federal criminal trial before taking on the Scarfo-RICO case. So, defense lawyers and prosecutors wondered about the judge, who appeared to be amiable in the early courtroom skirmishes during jury selection, but had built a reputation as a strict law-and-order man, known for sending guilty parties to jail for a long time.

THE ROLE OF THE ORGANIZED CRIME STRIKE FORCE IN THE PROSECUTION

Unlike most of the previous federal prosecutors of the Mafia, which had been conducted by Assistant U.S. Attorneys, this one was assigned to Special Attorneys of the local Organized Crime Strike Force of the U.S. Department of Justice. The U.S. Organized Crime units, attached to the various Federal District Courts scattered around the country, differ from the more glamorous U.S. Attorney's offices, in that there is more stability to their field of operations. This state of affairs is due mainly to the fact that this branch of the Justice Department does not change every four years, with each new Presidential Administration, but continues to work directly under the supervision of the central office in Washington.

Despite the past successes of the OCSF, US Attorney General Dick Thornburgh announced on June 19, 1989 the merging of 14 Department of Justice strike force units around the country into their respective local US Attorneys offices. An era had come to an end.

Louis Pichini, the lead Philadelphia Strike Force Prosecutor, and his four associates: Arnold Gordon, Albert Wicks, David Fritchey, and Joseph Peters from the Pennsylvania State Attorney General office, were confronted by an adversarial team of eighteen high-priced criminal defense lawyers headed by Robert Simone.

One of the problems facing the defense was the proliferation of so many lawyers (six of the eighteen being court-appointed). Joe Santaguida, the lawyer representing Frank Narducci, Jr., was worried that with so many defense lawyers, everyone would try to get into the act to make his mark for his client — resulting in an overkill atmosphere in the courtroom.

THE SETTING FOR THE TRIAL

Ironically, the Federal RICO trial against Scarfo and his Mafia soldiers was conducted in a Federal courthouse, located just one block from the repository of the nation's most sacred symbol, the Liberty Bell, on which is inscribed the words, "Proclaim Liberty Throughout the Land." In this respect, the Scarfo crime family showed, by its actions over the years, that they welcomed the liberty and freedom to do their thing, their way, regardless of how it circumvented the law of the land.

To get into the fourteenth floor courtroom, a defendant's relative or courtroom reporter had to pass through not just one but two electronic gates similar to those found at airports, to check for hidden weapons. Sixteen Federal Marshals lined the walls of the courtroom, just in case any trouble occurred.

PROBLEMS IN AN OVER-PACKED COURTROOM

Before the anonymous, sequestered jury came into the courtroom for the first time on September 28th, after two weeks of an exhausting selection process, the prosecution complained to the judge that Phil Leonetti, the Mafia underboss, was sitting too close to the government lawyers and that he should be moved closer to the other defendants. The judge stood up, and after looking over the jammed courtroom in front of him, ruled: "Everybody [on the defense side] please move over six inches to the right. Fine, that's fantastic! It's a good thing I went to law school for seven years to learn how to make a decision like that."

The audience roared at this moment of pre-trial levity.

And it is still true, no matter how old you are — when you go out into the world, it is best to hold hands and stick together.

-Robert Fulghum*

29 NINE PLUS FOUR EQUALS THIRTEEN (MURDERS, THAT IS)

THE GOVERNMENT OPENS ITS CASE

ALBERT WICKS, a special U.S. Attorney, opened the RICO case for the United States of America. "The evidence will come to you in pieces via witnesses, photos, tapes, and letters. All will give you only part of the story. The government will present a picture of life in the *La Cosa Nostra* — the Mafia — from 1976-1987, a picture of mob violence, gambling, loan-sharking, internal strife; how the mob uses public officials, high and low; the mob boss who rules by fear and the soldiers who obey; power and the gangland murder of fellow members."

He then spent two hours outlining the various indictment counts against the seventeen defendants, including the nine murders and four attempted murders.

THE DEFENSE OPENS ITS CASE

One by one the various defense attorneys addressed the jury, asserting the lack of credibility of the two chief government witnesses, Thomas Del Giorno and Nicholas Caramandi. Joseph Santaguida, for one, called the latter a "shrewd bird," being a parody on his nickname, 'the Crow', and said their "testimony

---

* In his best-selling book of essays, *All I Need to Know I Learned in Kindergarten: Uncommon Thoughts on Common Things*, Villard, New York, 1988.

would be a shrewd test of the government's 'garbage theory' of piling garbage statements [by their two key witnesses] on top of more garbage."

Hope Lefeber, the lawyer for Salvatore 'Wayne' Grande, and the only woman on the defense team, pointed out to the jury that the prosecutors' photo evidence they were about to see would be a "case of guilt by association and the laws do not permit guilt by association. Ask yourself, what do they mean [when they show pictures of Caramandi and Del Giorno with other mob figures]? Nothing. So, please, keep an open mind, because under our system, there are no 'good' guys and no 'bad' guys."

Oscar Goodman, the defense showman, representing under-boss Phil Leonetti, dripped venom when he denounced 'the Crow' as an "arrogant, man-eating, shrewd bird," who would do anything to escape 8500 years in prison, the total that could be meted out to him for all of his confessed crimes.

"The government wants the head of Nicky Scarfo so bad," Goodman declaimed, "that they are willing to use Caramandi and Del Giorno as 'the spine and backbone' of their case...and that you will conclude that their kind of testimony [lies] will result in a perversion of the truth since they are immunized felons."

Robert Simone satirized the government's attempt to try all the defendants together. "This is a way of clearing up every un-solved murder in Philadelphia," he said, "putting it all on Scarfo." He warned the jurors that the government would try to frighten them into conviction of Scarfo and the other sixteen men.

"Are you going to be frightened to death?" he asked the jury. He then implored them to put aside their prejudices and listen carefully as the defense proved the two chief witnesses, Cara-mandi and Del Giorno, to be liars.

SOME VERY EXPENSIVE TECHNOLOGICAL COURTROOM AIDS

One of the innovations which upped the overall cost of con-ducting the RICO trial, was the introduction of sixty new, state-of-the-art battery-powered earphones for use by the judge, jury, prosecution and the defense. These large, electronic sophisticated marvels, with various dials to control volume and static from the government surveillance tapes, which were played as evidence against the defendants, each cost $500 for a total expenditure of

$30,000. They were made by a West German firm and gave the courtroom an appearance akin to the famous Nuremberg War Crimes trials after World War II, where Hitler's cohorts sat in the dock with earphones clapped around their heads.

Meanwhile, courtroom observers sitting on the back benches had to cope with listening to the garbled tapes via old-fashioned loudspeakers placed around the courtroom.

After donning their headsets, the jurors, lawyers and defendants would listen to the tape replays of defendants' conversations recorded on bugging devices, while reading the transcripts of these conversations from one of the fourteen large looseleaf notebooks arrayed in front of their seats. The government provided this backup help to provide clearer wording of some garbled conversations between the conspirators.

MURDER: THE ULTIMATE WEAPON OF THE MAFIA

After the completion of the defense openings, the prosecution commenced its case with a rundown of the last-resort weapon used by the Mafia to enforce its illegal business operations. That weapon was *murder*.

The Mafia originally established its operations in America as a kind of alternative extra-legal society, existing separate from, but side-by-side with, the mostly legitimate big business operations. The gang warfare that permeated Mafia families from the time they became part of the American scene were mainly internecine, with few outsiders being caught in the cross fire. When things did not go right within the Scarfo family, murder and the threat of murder became the ultimate weapon of discipline.

As testimony unfolded during the long trial on the stalking and killing of various targets, a pattern kept repeating itself. Those targeted for murder, mostly mob members who had strayed, were usually warned by a fellow mobster that "they had a problem" — which meant that they had aroused the wrath of either Mr. Scarfo, his underbosses 'Chuckie' Merlino or Phil Leonetti, or one of the *capos*. The members designated to be the executioners by Mr. Scarfo, who had to approve all killings in advance, would often postpone the final hit because of fears of police detection.

When the murder was finally committed, ski masks and

gloves were often used to camouflage the killers. Guns, minus fingerprints, were immediately discarded, often being dropped near the scene of the crime. Any extra bullets that fit those murder weapons were discarded down sewers or dumped in obscure places.

No weapons were ever found in the homes of 'made' mob members. The mob was always very careful to leave as few clues as possible.

THE ATTEMPTS TO WIPE OUT THE RICCOBENE MOB FACTION

Scarfo had ordered the murders of a long-time mob figure, Harry Riccobene, and seven of his associates, including Salvatore 'Sammy' Tamburrino, who was gunned down in his variety store located underneath his Southwest Philadelphia home on November 3, 1983. The Riccobene faction of the Philadelphia crime family had not been showing Scarfo enough respect, according to the government indictment. Harry 'the Hump' Riccobene had failed to share his profits with Scarfo, "because he felt that Nicky was too selfish, too vicious and too greedy," said Del Giorno candidly.

THE MURDER OF FRANK MONTE

The Scarfo-led blood bath began in April 1982 after Mafia *consigliere*, Frank Monte, a top advisor to Scarfo, made the mistake of going to Riccobene's half-brother, Mario 'Sonny' Riccobene, and in a case of incredible misjudgment, asking him to help set up Harry Riccobene's murder. The Riccobene faction of the area's Mafia families were informed about the request and became irate because they now had proof of Nicky Scarfo's murder plans. They responded by killing Monte — sending a bloody message back to Scarfo.

This killing set off a chain reaction within the Scarfo faction to get back at Riccobene to revenge the slaying of one of their own mobsters. Scarfo and/or some other top ranking lieutenants in his family then ordered the assassinations of several of Riccobene's associates.

THE MURDER OF JUDGE EDWIN HELFANT

The first RICO racketeering murder indictment accused Scarfo and Nicholas Virgilio of killing Municipal Judge Edwin Helfant of Cape May, New Jersey, for his failure to play ball with the mob. He had already allegedly been paid a bribe of $10,000 to influence another judge handling the case of Virgilio, who faced serious criminal charges. But the influence did not work and Virgilio had received a stiff sentence.

On February 15, 1978, Scarfo drove Nicholas 'Nick the Blade' Virgilio to the Flamingo Motel in Atlantic City where the Judge was sitting in a darkened lounge with his wife. With Scarfo sitting in a car outside, Virgilio, wearing a ski mask and carrying a snow shovel, shot Helfant to death, at point blank range. After leaving the Motel, he dropped the shovel, a .38 caliber pistol and one glove in a snowbank outside, where it was retrieved by local police.

A mysterious woman, Kathleen Residence, in a blonde wig and dark glasses, testified for the government that Virgilio had told her "maybe twenty times" that he wanted to kill Judge Helfant, beginning back in 1977. Dressed in rose colored slacks and a dusty pink blazer, she claimed to have worked with Virgilio in an Atlantic City restaurant back in 1977 and that he told her he would wear a ski mask and old clothing when he would accost and kill the Judge in Atlantic City's Flamingo Motel.

Unfortunately, when it came time for her to identify Virgilio, a thin, gaunt-faced man, she couldn't pick him out from the thirty-five lawyers and defendants sitting in front of her in the crowded courtroom.

"If she took off her glasses, she might be able to see," interjected Oscar Goodman for the defense.

To make matters worse for the prosecution, she then pointed to Scarfo as the man who "could possibly be Virgilio," whom she had not seen in twelve years. She acknowledged that she once threw a drink at Virgilio when he failed to keep a date with her, but admitted that she had no idea that he was the one who killed the Judge. She insisted that she was not lying and that she "didn't say anything bad" about Virgilio during her time on the stand.

Ms. Residence was an inept witness. She got the prosecution's case off to an embarrassing and rocky start.

THE MURDER OF MICHAEL CIFELLI

On January 4, 1979, Nicky Scarfo and Sal Merlino conspired with Sal Testa to kill Michael Cifelli, a.k.a. 'Mickey Coco', a drug dealer, in cold blood, with Merlino and Testa shooting their victim in a South Philadelphia bar as he was sipping beer. The murder had been ordered because Cifelli had sold drugs to the son of a Mafia member, Frank Monte. Wearing ski masks, Testa and Merlino had entered Firoe's Restaurant at 10th and Wolf Streets and opened fire point blank at Cifelli. He died instantly. They left the murder weapon behind, but Testa and Merlino were never connected to this crime until Del Giorno and Caramandi identified them as the alleged killers.

THE MURDER OF VINCE FALCONE

Vincent Falcone was a mob associate who ran a legitimate business as a Margate, New Jersey, cement contractor. It took the testimony of a former mob groupie, Joseph Salerno, Jr., (now in federal custody) to describe to the jury just "how vicious the mob could be," according to Prosecutor Louis Pichini.

Joe Salerno Jr., 44, a plumber, related how he at first enjoyed "the glow of association" with Nicodemo Scarfo. "If you went somewhere with him," he said, "the people would cater to him, look up to him. It was a good feeling to me. But other people were scared to death of him."

He had ultimately become a prisoner of the mob, when he had borrowed $10,000 from Leonetti in the late 70's to help prop up his financially troubled plumbing business. Then he found he could not afford the high $250 a week interest payments on the loan. He then moved into an apartment above Scarfo's after becoming separated from his wife.

He told the jury that he started getting nervous toward the end of 1979 when Scarfo asked him whether he had any guns. Salerno eventually gave a .32 caliber handgun to Scarfo which would later become a murder weapon. He also noted that Vince Falcone, who was an acquaintance, had stopped showing up at the offices of Scarf, Inc. The day before the killing, he had such a strong feeling that something bad was about to happen that he talked it over with his estranged wife.

"I think somebody's going to be killed," he told her. "I said it could be Vincent. I don't know...If anything happens to me, I want you to know who I was with."

His worst fears were confirmed the next day when Leonetti and Merlino picked up Falcone for a holiday get-together and took him to an apartment in Margate, New Jersey, where Scarfo was already waiting for them to arrive. (This murder scenario was previously described in Chapter 1).

Later that night, during a dinner at Scarfo's, after the Falcone shooting, Salerno, the mob associate, was informed of the motive for the murder of Falcone. Vincent Falcone had told 'Chuckie' Merlino that Phil Leonetti shouldn't be in the concrete business and that his Uncle Nicky was "crazy," according to either Merlino or Leonetti. Salerno could not remember which one said it.

When Salerno met Leonetti even later on that fateful evening for drinks at an Atlantic City Casino, the hit man, Leonetti, boasted, "If I could bring that guy back, I'd kill him again."

After this grisly incident, Salerno worried that he, too, might be soon marked for death and "killed on the spot, since he knew too much" after which he agreed to cooperate with the law enforcement authorities.

THE MURDER OF JOHN CALABRESE

Del Giorno described to the court how one drug dealer, John Calabrese, "resisted giving Scarfo any money." In 1981, under the dual supervision of Joe Ciancaglini and Francis Iannarella, Caramandi and Del Giorno were assigned as co-conspirators along with Pat Spirito to eliminate John Calabrese for disloyalty. It took five months in 1981 before they got their quarry. Ciancaglini escorted Calabrese down Christian Street in front of Cous' Little Italy Restaurant in the heart of South Philadelphia on October 6, 1981. 'Faffy' Iannarella and 'Tommy Del' Del Giorno, the manager and owner of the store at the time, sneaked up behind them and shot Calabrese in the back, according to Caramandi. Although they each had planned to wear ski masks to hide their faces, neither did so.

The police were able to retrieve two gloves which signalled

that two different men were in on the murder. By the time the final hit was made, Del Giorno confessed, "We were really too disgusted with the five months spent trying to kill him to care whether we were spotted or not. Down there [in South Philadelphia], if people did see us, they wouldn't say nothing because they would know we was with the mob."

Scarfo and Sal Merlino later complimented the two hit men on "doing a good job, and promised them that they would soon be 'made'", Caramandi told the jury. However, the two eager mob members-to-be were also told by the boss that they would have to wait until Frank Narducci, Sr. was murdered.

THE MURDER OF FRANK NARDUCCI, SR.

From the Fall of 1981 until January 7, 1982, under orders from Nicky Scarfo and Joe Ciancaglini, Joe Pungitore and Sal Testa stalked Frank Narducci, Sr. with intent to murder him. On a cold January 7th, he was gunned down — as he left his car at his home — by the two soldiers who fired ten bullets into Narducci's body. They later reported to Del Giorno that they had accomplished their goal, after which 'Tommy Del' was made an official member of the Scarfo family in a secret ceremony.

Ironically, Narducci's two sons, Phil and Frank, who were also defendants in the RICO trial, sat somberly in the courtroom just a few seats away from Joe 'Punge' Pungitore, the man who had been accused of killing their father. Philip Narducci sat next to Scarfo, who the government said ordered his father's murder.

Observers wondered how they must have felt deep down inside. Neither son gave any outward clue that he was bothered at being so close to the accused conspirators, the two men who had been allegedly responsible for that crime against their own family. They were visibly upset when they and the other defendants viewed the enlarged graphic photos of the dead body of Frank Narducci, Sr., but showed no enmity against their co-defendants who allegedly engineered the grisly assassination.

THE ATTEMPTED MURDER OF HARRY 'THE HUMP' RICCOBENE

The senior mobster to be targeted for death by Scarfo for showing lack of respect to the boss was Harry Riccobene, who had been a member of the Mafia since 1929. He had not been transferring a large enough cut of his illegal business operations 'upstairs' to Scarfo, and so two crews of mob members were assigned to knock him off. The first six under the supervision of the *capo*, Joe Ciancaglini, failed to do the job, so a second crew under Sal Testa was ordered to commit the act, since Riccobene had been so hard to track down.

On June 8, 1982, Sal Grande and Joe Pungitore found Riccobene making a call in a public phone booth, and they shot and wounded him. After Riccobene was released from the hospital, Pungitore and Joe Grande, wearing jogging suits, found their target sitting in an auto on Watts Street in South Philadelphia, and Grande fired several more shots. Pungitore, who was the getaway driver, wounded him again. When he recovered a second time, a fearful Riccobene, now seventy-eight, went into hiding from which he subsequently was arrested, accused and sent to jail for life for the attempted murder of another mobster.

THE ATTEMPTED MURDER OF JOE SALERNO, SR.

Scarfo next ordered the shooting of Joseph Salerno, Sr., a mob associate, because both he and his son had agreed to cooperate with the law and had testified against the mob boss in 1980, and also against underboss Phil Leonetti, and Lawrence 'Yogi' Merlino, in a murder trial in New Jersey in which all three were acquitted.

The elder Salerno testified that his assailant, dressed in a jogging suit and wearing a ski mask and goggles, appeared at the door of his motel office in Wildwood Crest, New Jersey, and fired two shots with his left hand. One bullet struck Salerno in the neck, but he recovered in the hospital, refusing, however, to identify his assailants. He did testify that after his release from the hospital he received a phone call from an anonymous person who said, "Now youse are *all* dead!"

THE MURDER OF PASQUALE 'PAT THE CAT' SPIRITO

Caramandi described from the stand how a suspicious Pat Spirito started "to drag his feet and failed to go to a funeral home" for a viewing of a mobster's relative when ordered to do so by higher-ups in the mob. Both Caramandi and his partner 'Charley White' Iannece went, since their *capo*, 'Chickie' Ciancaglini, had demanded their presence at the wake.

Upon arrival back in South Philadelphia, the two mobsters were confronted by a greatly agitated Ciancaglini after he met them. The underboss, Salvatore 'Chuckie' Merlino, "was also unhappy and upset," according to Caramandi.

He said to 'Nicky Crow', "Your gang stinks!" and then stormed out of the clubhouse room located at #921 Catherine Street in South Philly. They had not yet spoken to Ciancaglini about Merlino's negative reaction to the Spirito snub, so they went to see Thomas Del Giorno for advice in setting up an appointment with the *capo*, Ciancaglini.

This incident occurred early in 1983, before both Caramandi and Iannece became 'made' mob members. (They were still just 'associates' at the time, trying to make points with the mob hierarchy.)

"We wanted to tell our side of the story," said Caramandi, "and to protect ourselves." Meanwhile, Spirito started mouthing off and blamed them for the misunderstanding. "He then dug himself a hole and bad-mouthed both Nicky Scarfo and Phil Leonetti. The only good ones [on Spirito's account] were Caramandi and Iannece."

When Merlino heard about this backbiting, he issued orders to kill Spirito and assigned Caramandi and Iannece to do the job. "And take Joe De Caprio with you as your getaway driver."

The two hit men then enticed Spirito to get in a car to drive on a routine errand using the ploy of going out to get 'Sonny' Riccobene. Spirito fell for the set-up and was assigned to drive the car with Caramandi in the front passenger seat and Iannece in the back. When Caramandi saw the traffic backing up behind them in the rear view mirror, he signaled 'Charley White' Iannece in the back seat, who then shot Spirito twice in the back of the head. 'Pat the Cat' immediately slumped over the wheel, and with the car still in gear, he crashed into the car in front.

'The Crow' and 'Charley White' jumped out of the car and fled in De Caprio's waiting getaway auto. The next day, they reported to Ciancaglini that they had carried out the orders (since Scarfo was unavailable) and they also reported their deed to Del Giorno.

Prosecutor Pichini showed an enlarged, black and white police photo of the dead body of Spirito slumped over the wheel with the passenger seat pushed over into the windshield to allow Iannece to escape. It seemed to impress the jury, who looked intently at the photo as Caramandi described the killing from the witness stand.

THE ATTEMPTED MURDER OF FRANK MARTINES

On October 14, 1983, Frank Martines, an associate of Harry Riccobene, was traced by the mob to a South Philadelphia hangout* where an illegal card came was being played. When he came out the door, he was shot and wounded.

Joe Pungitore later told a mob associate that he was frustrated because "we didn't kill him." After Martines recovered from his bullet wounds, he refused to identify his assailants for the government, so the mob left him alone.

THE MURDER OF SALVATORE 'SAMMY' TAMBURRINO

Another victim of the gang was Salvatore 'Sammy' Tamburrino, a mob soldier in the Riccobene faction, who was killed inside his Southwest Philadelphia variety store. On the night of November 11, 1983, 'Faffy' Iannarella and co-conspirator Tom Del Giorno drove Phil Narducci and co-conspirator Nicholas Milano to the store. There, Narducci and Milano entered the store and shot Tamburrino to death. As they fled the scene, they threw their guns down, and were driven away in the getaway car by the other two mobsters.

No one had ever been apprehended for that murder until the Scarfo RICO trial five years later. The Feds kept their powder dry until they were ready to impose the power of the law on the entire mob, instead of trying to pick them off one at a time. Furthermore, the Scarfo family had been lucky with a string of acquittals in state murder trials in Pennsylvania and New Jersey for the murders of Judge Helfant, Sal Testa, and Vince Falcone.

* Ninth and Morris Streets' clubhouse

THE MURDER OF ROBERT RICCOBENE

Sal Testa had told Caramandi in the Fall of 1983 that "Nicky was upset because nobody's getting killed...seven, eight months or a year and nobody's getting killed." By that time, Mario Riccobene had already been marked for death because he had refused to help set up the murder of his father, mob figure Harry Riccobene, then feuding with Scarfo. So, Caramandi and seven other mob members stalked Robert Riccobene, Harry's half-brother, for nine months, trying without success to set him up for the kill at a Center City jewelry store, then at a funeral home, and even at Riccobene's own home. They tried eight different murder attempts and they all failed.

The mob first tried to kill Riccobene at his girlfriend's house in the swank suburb of Huntingdon Valley, but they found that the neighborhood was "not conducive to catching someone by surprise," so they abandoned it.

"It was a pretty wide street," Caramandi said, "Everybody had driveways where you can park three or four cars, plus garages."

The mob also had to abort an elaborate plan to 'bushwhack' Riccobene by blocking off a street where he lived and popping out of a Winnebago camper where they were hiding, but that plan failed, because of a fear of being detected.

Finally, on December 6, 1983, Joe Pungitore drove 'Faffy' Iannarella and Charles White to Riccobene's mother's residence in Southwest Philadelphia. After switching cars, Iannarella and White got out and lay in wait for their quarry with a twelve gauge shotgun loaded with buckshot. When their target came into view, 'Faffy' fired his gun and killed Riccobene. When his mother, who witnessed the murder, rushed over and tried to restrain him, Iannarella hit her on the head and climbed over a nearby fence to escape. "She started screaming and it was a mess," 'Faffy' said later, according to 'the Crow.'

This latest mob death marked the end of the internecine warfare between the Scarfo and the Riccobene faction, since both Mario and Harry Riccobene had been found guilty of conspiring to kill one of Scarfo's mobsters (Frank Monte), and began serving long prison terms. "That's enough. We proved our point," said Merlino, the underboss.

THE MURDER OF SAL TESTA

The full-length story of the stalking and murder of this mob soldier in September 1984 has already been told explained previously. Despite the overwhelming evidence presented by the Philadelphia District Attorney's office which prosecuted Scarfo and his associates, that jury found Scarfo and his co-conspirators innocent on all counts.

In the Salvatore Testa case, seventeen attempts were made on his life over a five-month period, before he was finally rubbed out in an empty South Philly sweet shop by one of the trial defendants, Salvatore 'Wayne' Grande. Caramandi explained that the reason it took so long to wipe out Testa was that the order to kill him, which came from both Merlino and Del Giorno, "was not an emergency, such that it had to be accomplished immediately." The many postponements of the killing were a literal repeat of the bungling by old Keystone Cops in the silent movies.

THE ATTEMPTED MURDER OF STEVE VENTO, JR.

On May 27, 1986, the mob attempted to kill young Steve Vento, Jr. because he refused to pay the dreaded street tax and for "mouthing off too much" about the Scarfo leadership. Del Giorno ordered Caramandi to "kill the kid," using Joe Pungitore and 'Faffy' Iannarella as his support group. Anthony Pungitore and Sal Scafidi were designated as the shooters, and they both fired into Vento's car, seriously wounding him, while his girlfriend was sitting beside him witnessing the act.

Scafidi later remarked, "I can not understand why the kid did not die." He was shot in the head but somehow miraculously survived.

"A PICTURE IS WORTH A THOUSAND WORDS"

Throughout the trial, the government kept introducing large blowups in both color and black and white of Scarfo-instigated murder victims, of Mafia clan get-togethers at Camac and Moore Streets in South Philadelphia, where a prominent sign on the wall inside read: "For Members Only." The blowups also showed vacation reunions at Scarfo's Casablanca South retreat on the beach at Fort Lauderdale, Florida. Many of the scenes showed Caramandi and Del Giorno cavorting with other mob members, which the prosecution hoped would enhance the credibility of their two witnesses. The defense did not dispute the authenticity of any of these damning photos. Nobody claimed that any of them had been doctored in any way by the government.

MURDERS WERE ONLY THE TIP OF THE MAFIA ICEBERG

Although the thirteen murders and attempted murders committed by the Scarfo crime family marked the more notorious Mafia crimes, since they made the big headlines, it was the illegal underground businesses conducted by the Mafia that made up the bulk of the RICO indictments.

The following chapter describes the criminal business affairs of Scarfo and Company.

The business of America is business.

-President Calvin Coolidge[*]

30   THE ENTERPRISE

I N his recent book, *The Last Days of the Sicilians*, Ralph Blumenthal, a veteran *New York Times* investigative reporter, contends that the way to look upon the mob's approach to business is to view it as an "economic phenomenon." He concludes that the mob's operations are "not a slam-bang crime story anymore. It's now a story about financial ledgers and how money moves, political corruption and that kind of thing."

His description applies to the business workings of the Scarfo crime family in recent years. The Scarfo organization's approach to business reflected this philosophy, with some major variations.

DIVIDING UP THE TERRITORY

The foundation of Scarfo's expanding business enterprise was cemented further on June 11, 1986, when Scarfo and his nephew, Phil Leonetti, made a one-day helicopter trip to New York to negotiate territories with representatives of the Columbo and Gambino crime families.

An FBI agent, James Kossler, related how a surveillance team in New York had spotted Scarfo meeting with several members of New York City organized crime families on that day. He identified the four Mafioso as: James Angelina, the then acting boss of the Columbo family, Joseph Gargone, a soldier in that family, Joseph 'Joe Butch' Corrao, a *capo* in the Gambino family and James 'Jimmy Brown' Failla, another *capo* in the Gambino

---

[*] In a speech before the American Society of Newspaper Editors, January 17, 1925.

family which was headed by the number one mob figure in that city, John Gotti.

On that day in the Big Apple, the surveillance officers followed Scarfo and several acquaintances to the meeting with Angelina in a coffee shop, and later with Corrao, Failla and Gargone at a restaurant in New York's Little Italy. Kossler admitted under cross-examination that he had no proof that Scarfo and the others were "doing anything wrong" at those get togethers, but that they "were probably discussing something illegal."

Simone made fun of the testimony of New York policewoman, Barbara Werbock, who had personally observed Scarfo and Leonetti in the West 53rd New York coffee shop. She identified secret surveillance photos of the two that had been taken that afternoon. On cross-examination, an acid-tongued Simone asked her but one question, "They didn't rob the coffee shop, did they?" When she said, "No," with a straight face, the courtroom burst into an uproar.

That evening Franco Russo, another New York City Detective, was assigned to follow the pair to Taramina's Restaurant on Mulberry Street in the heart of 'Little Italy.' At 9:25 p.m., they were observed meeting in a booth for thirty minutes, with Joe 'Butch' Corrao, an emissary from the reputed New York mob boss, John Gotti.

On cross-examination in the trial, a sarcastic Robert Simone taunted Russo by asking him: "Did you eat in the restaurant that night?" When Russo answered "Yes," Simone followed up by asking a question calculated to evoke a reaction from the courtroom, "How was it?"

"Very expensive," answered Russo.

More laughter erupted in the courtroom and the Judge had to warn the onlookers to restrain themselves.

FBI agent Kossler confirmed the government prosecutors' prime contention that the Scarfo-led, Philadelphia—Atlantic City crime family was one of twenty-six such groups located around the country. "It's a secret, nationwide Italian-criminal group — known as the *La Cosa Nostra* — that functions throughout the United States. *La Cosa Nostra's* purpose is to make money through crime."

The reasons the prosecution brought this evidence into court was to present for the *first* time in American jurisprudence, a broad picture of the existence of twenty-six intertwined Mafia crime families operating in other cities and states. This was a major prosecutorial point, which was hoped to have a positive impact on the minds of the jurors.

HOW THE MOB BUSINESS WORKED

The two-month-long trial served as an open book into how the local Mafia conducted its business affairs. "The Enterprise," the prosecutors' term for the Mob operation, was comprised of a tight-fisted organization that gave structure to an underground economy dealing in various business and untold millions of dollars of profits.

Indeed, the risks in any business venture are high, but they're mostly of the financial type. In the business of organized crime, the risks are graver. There is always death for those who cross the boss.

To enforce the rules of the criminal organization, strict discipline was utilized. All members were sworn to maintain the Code of Silence. Routine violence and threats of violence were used, murder and attempted murder being the ultimate weapon to keep subordinates in line.

UNDERCOVER BUSINESS OPERATIONS OF THE MOB

The 'made' members of the mob used every means to conceal from the law the very existence of the 'Enterprise' and the identities of its members and associates. They even solicited and successfully secured the corrupt assistance of public officials, like Beloff and Rego.

An analysis of the numerical and geographical spread of the Scarfo-led crime family, the ways in which it conducted its business, and the types of illegal businesses as outlined by various witnesses in the trial presents a clear picture of how the multi-million-dollar enterprise operated.

Thomas Del Giorno, a former *capo* in the local mob, testified during several trials that the current organization headed by Scarfo numbered "sixty to seventy 'made' members."

The organization had members in Atlantic City, Philadelphia, Trenton, Newark, and Northeastern Pennsylvania according to both Del Giorno and Caramandi. This tight-knit group was organized in a crude military bureaucracy.

In order to confound the Internal Revenue Service, law enforcement agencies, and state and local tax collectors, the pattern of mob operations looked like this:

- All transactions were conducted in cash; checks were usually forbidden, since they could be traced.

- There were no books, no audits or ledgers; only slips of paper or handwritten memos, and no annual reports.

- There were no news releases to the media on promotions, demotions, or the making of new members in the mob hierarchy.

- All orders were given orally and never in writing by the boss, underboss or *capos* to the soldiers.

- There were no membership cards. Members were addressed by nicknames such as 'Chickie,' 'Faffy,' and 'the Crow.'

MOB BANKS

The mob rarely used commercial banks to deposit its illegitimate income. Instead, it used shoe boxes, kitchen cabinets, closets, walls, dressers, and mattresses in the bedrooms of various members as well as secret hiding places inside the headquarters of Scarf Inc. on North Georgia Avenue in Atlantic City.

Most serious discussions on future operations took place "in bars, restaurants, or walking on the street," according to Del Giorno, "because we were less apt to be seen or overheard by the law in those places."

There are five major means of generating income within the local crime family. They include: drug dealing, numbers and sports betting, shakedowns and extortions, loansharking and the imposing of a street tax.

Although Mr. Scarfo reportedly counselled new members of the mob to stay away from drugs, many soldiers and associates dealt in the importation of P2P. The local organization usually stayed away from heroin and cocaine.

Del Giorno testified that he gave half of the $150,000 share in a one-year take from his P2P operation to Joe 'Chickie' Ciancaglini who would share it with the boss, Mr. Scarfo. He was instructed by the underboss, Sal Merlino, to keep $75,000 of another split of drug earnings after Ciancaglini was sent to prison.

Michael Madgin, a combination loanshark, drug dealer and bookie who could not be inducted into the mob because he was of Irish origin, related how he was forced to split his income on a 50-50 basis with the mob after the crime family discovered he was a big-time drug dealer. Joe Pungitore, a Scarfo soldier, on behalf of the underboss, Sal 'Chuckie' Merlino, told him to pay or else.

When Madgin asked 'Joe Punge', "What would happen if I don't pay this guy," the mob soldier replied, "Believe me, Mike, they're going to kill you, your wife, your kids. They did it to my friend, Sal [Testa]."

In 1983, a mob fivesome, supervised by Joe Pungitore, including Sal Merlino, Tom Del Giorno, 'Nicky' Scarfo and Sal Testa, ran a sports bookmaking business that had numerous employees, taking action on over thirty betting books. (In 1986, after Sal Merlino had been 'taken down', Phil Leonetti took his place.) It was not unusual for the business to accept over $200,000 in bets on a single day, with larger amounts being bet on big football weekends.

Norman Lit, a bookie, testified at the trial that an outside Mafia 'associate' like himself had really only two choices: pay a weekly tribute to the local crime organization or join the mob as a partner.[*]

Lit said that his operation averaged between $175,000 to $200,000 in bets on each Sunday's pro football games as well as the World Series and the Super Bowl.

Del Giorno testified that Scarfo even made an unusual decision by allowing the profit-in-the-pot of their jointly-owned illegal numbers and sports betting business to go over the $300,000 ceiling, before the customary 50-50 split up. Del Giorno evaluated this decision by the boss to be another clue that he was being "set up" to be killed, so that the head man could get all

---

[*] Lit could never become a 'made' Mafia member since he was Jewish.

of the pot — which is the way the 'estates' of the mob members were divided when a member disappeared from the scene. Del Giorno testified that he had made over $1 million, most of it illegally between 1982-1986.

Nicholas Caramandi testified that he and his partner, Charles 'Charley White' Iannece, brought in between $6,000 and $8,000 a week in the guise of a 'street tax', from sixty to eighty bookies, in the years 1982-1984.

Although this take dwindled to about $4,000 a week by 1986, "because many of the guys quit the racket," according to Caramandi, it still brought in substantial amounts to both of these soldiers even after they channeled a fifty percent split upstairs.

The mob also had been in violation of Pennsylvania law by conducting illegal numbers and sports book lotteries. At least four RICO counts were lodged against a half dozen members for participating in this branch of the enterprise.

Mafia operated bookmaking on illegal numbers took place six days a week during 52 weeks of the year, taking in thousands of dollars in bets every day, according to the FBI. With the inauguration of the legal 'Daily Number' game in the late 70s, under the aegis of the Pennsylvania State Lottery, the mob switched its winning number pick from a daily horse race to the 'night number' picked on TV. But unlike the legal state lottery which paid out $500 for every lucky $1 hit on a three-digit pick, the Mafia paid $600, which was tax free to boot.

EXTORTIONS AND SHAKEDOWNS

Extortions and shakedowns took on several forms, including 'flim-flams' like the selling of fake color television sets which in reality were just cheap black and white ones. Also, there was, for example, the bungled extortion of Willard Rouse III to 'protect' him from mob and union violence in his Penn's Landing development project.

The mob got money from legal businesses as well as the illegal gambling and drug enterprises. Most soldiers 'hit' from two to five 'targets' every day in making their collection rounds. The only ones who were left alone were favored bookies and drug pushers who were so designated by Scarfo himself.

Caramandi testified that, "If a target didn't pay, he would be dealt with severely. He would be killed. He had no choice when he was told that he had a 'problem' by a Mafia soldier." Del Giorno reiterated this threat, but boasted that, "We never really killed any of them."

Some of the shakedown victims who were 'taken to the cleaners' by the mob were: Hardy Burke, Sam Malone, Joe DeMedici, Sandy 'Springs' Simone, Michael Madgin, and John Leone. These men had their arms twisted regularly by mob soldiers who acted as the 'bomb squad' in the words of the late 'Pat-the-Cat' Spirito, who was one of the collectors for Scarfo.

Other soldiers who served on the 'bomb squad' were Charles Iannece, Nicholas Caramandi, who made the rounds for the 'weekly shakes' and the 'one shot hits' of drug dealers and bookies who were not regulars in their underground business ventures. Caramandi related to the jury how he and his partner, 'Charley White', would compile a weekly slip of the totals garnered in their 'shakes' operation, sending fifty percent to Scarfo to share with the other *capos* and the underboss.

In the selection process of picking shakedown victims, Ralph 'Junior' Staino told fellow Mafia soldier Nicholas Caramandi on a tape recording made by the FBI, "I wish you'd go get somebody today, like 'Slim' Craig, the drug dealer. He's good for $300 a week, after we 'hit' him for $10,000 up front first."

A little later on the tape, Charles Iannece was overheard saying, "Tell him [a reluctant shakedown victim] that we're coming up with everybody [meaning all of the local mobsters, if he didn't comply with the demands]."

By 1985, the shakedowns expanded beyond the 'bomb squad' Mafia members, and those associated with the mob, to include such non-Italian-American 'associates' as Sol Kane, who was an alleged Philadelphia drug dealer. He allegedly served with the mob in order to facilitate the conduct of his businesses. Most of those who were hit up, paid because they were scared, according to Caramandi. Prosecutor Pichini said, "They feared the strength of the mob behind the collectors." In many cases, shakedowns took the form of 'extras', or lump sum payments from single extortions — like the $25,000 made as a one-time payment by Gumise Rosetti, a local drug dealer. Other evidence showed that some shakedown crews collected as much as $75,000 a week, according to government investigators.

THE 'STREET TAX'

Closely allied to the shakedowns of all illegal businesses in
Scarfo's territory was the dreaded 'street tax' imposed on *all*
bookies and drug dealers, whether or not they were mob
members. The 'take,' which was usually split on a 50-50 basis
between the collectors and the leadership, amounted to several
million dollars a year.

One of the main causes for mob underlings to fall out of favor
with the boss was when information was passed up the ladder
that certain members were not paying the boss his 'fair share' of
the street tax.

Del Giorno testified, "We lived in a world of lies...to stay out
of jail, we lied to each other."

LOANSHARKING

Madgin ran a major loansharking operation that netted 150
percent interest annually on big 'bulk' loans to bookies and drug
dealers who could not obtain legitimate loans from banks. A
short ten-week loan brought in one-hundred percent interest while
a twenty-eight week loan netted seventy-five percent interest.

Madgin noted in his testimony that if any of his customers
died or left town, he had to make good on the 'lost principal' to
the mob bankers, Scarfo and Leonetti.

On August 9, 1985, an FBI tape recorded the conversation
after one young mob associate, Lou Turra, 15, was beaten up by
six Mafia family members for refusing to pay the street tax to the
mob:

An exultant Grande boasted: "All of South Philadelphia is
shaking."

Del Giorno added, "That's the way you do it... right in the
fucking street. That's the best thing we did. Right in the street in
front of everybody." The message got out into the neighborhood
fast.

Then Wayne Grande agreed, "Yeh, that's the way we should
to it all the time."

Del Giorno pontificated, "What he, the kid [Turra] said is
wrong."

Joe Grande retorted, "I hope the kid learns."

'Faffy' Iannarella chimed in, "That's why he got beat up."

WHAT HAPPENED IF A RELUCTANT MOB VICTIM REFUSED TO PAY

There were various strong-arm methods used to enforce the shakedowns, running from threats to beatings to murder. In one case, Caramandi told Ralph 'Junior' Staino (on a 1985 tape): "We gotta go do something [about closing down 'Tootsie's card game for non-payment of the shakedown]. Just show your face."

'Charley White' interrupted to say, "Tootsie's game is going to get busted up. We tried to break the door down. We got to find them now."

A short while later, the muscleman, 'Junior' Staino, told another bookie (on tape), "I want you to bring that money. I told you to have it in an hour. That's the message I gave you. If you don't have that fucking money, I will personally put your other fucking crooked eye out. Just have that fucking money soon."

After he hung up the phone, enjoying the verbal threat he had just made to a shakedown target, he said to himself out loud, "Ooh, I loved it!"

Two shakedown crews used their strong-arm Mafia muscle on Frank Trachtenberg, a Philadelphia mob associate and drug trafficker. The crews successfully extracted $30,000 from Trachtenberg. During the course of this double Mafia shakedown, one mobster sliced open Trachtenberg's forehead with a razor when he balked at revealing the names of other drug traffickers with whom he did business.

There was one exception made by Scarfo to the mob rule of 'pay up or else'. That exception was would-be politician Stanley Branche, the former Tri-State head of the area NAACP. Norman Lit told the court that Branche allegedly netted $1,000 a week from one Philadelphia drug dealer. Branche, who announced his candidacy for US Representative in Philadelphia's First Congressional District in 1985, then risked the mob's wrath and retribution by refusing to turn over thousands of dollars in 'elbow' money.

Subsequent tapes showed that only his candidacy saved him from a mob hit. Lit was taped by the government saying, "if the guy gets elected, you understand it wouldn't hurt."

"You're exactly right," Joseph Ciancaglini the son of John 'Chickie' Ciancaglini answered.

And so the only prominent Black mob associate was let off the hook, temporarily, until he was caught on a different hook when the Feds indicted him in June, 1988, on extortion charges.

During a recess interview outside the courtroom, Branche called Lit "a liar and he'll be a liar in my case, when it comes up in court." Branche was convicted in Federal court in January, 1989, for selling 'speed'.

LACK OF DISCIPLINE AMONG YOUNG MAFIA SOLDIERS

A vivid example of the distrust of the younger Mafia soldiers in the Scarfo family, by their elder supervisors, to perform their assigned jobs properly, was revealed in an FBI tape made at Del Giorno's Ocean City, New Jersey condo (on June 22, 1986). The following dialogue between Del Giorno and Ralph 'Junior' Staino highlights their observations concerning the lack of discipline on the part of new mob members:

DEL GIORNO: These guys, [Nicholas 'Nick the Whip' Milano and Salvatore 'Torre' Scafidi] they're undependable, you know.

STAINO: (Laughs)

DEL GIORNO: No, really, the Whip and Torre are the best kids in the world, but you got to double check with them. That age group lost something. They forget everything, Junior.

STAINO: (Laughs)

DEL GIORNO: Believe me, they do.

STAINO: Because their head isn't on to stay, they're having a good time.

DEL GIORNO: They are...and they're young.

STAINO: They're having a good time. You know, that's all they want to do. They get carried away.

DEL GIORNO: They make me nuts.

STAINO: They never did that before. It's new to them.

DEL GIORNO: They're not responsible, Junior, you know...

STAINO: ...I don't understand people like that. They're just stupid and the greed gets to them. What good is it?

DEL GIORNO: (inaudible) ...All the money in the fuckin' world. What good is it gonna do?

STAINO: What good is it? (Laughs)

THE PERKS

Despite the many examples of "mismanagement of mob activities," as a defense lawyer's assistant bluntly confessed, there were many plusses to be gained by being made a 'blood member' of the mob.

The protection and respect gained from both other family members and those outside the organization became apparent, because of the fears and threats of retribution passed down from above to those who tried to defy the rules.

Although many examples of greed, betrayal and cheating surfaced during the trial, compounded by the confessions of lies and deception of the underlings toward Scarfo, most of the mob retained their loyalty to the family and maintained *Omerta*, even after they were arrested and imprisoned.

If not for Caramandi and Del Giorno, the Scarfo family might still be riding high.

Other advantages of membership in the Scarfo family, according to Del Giorno, were the "opportunity to make more money," than when they were just working as mob associates. Each new soldier was given a partner to help him iron out his problems of pressuring recalcitrant bookies, drug dealers and loanshark clients.

Finally, there was a gigantic tax break for mob members. One rarely paid any federal or state income taxes. Scarfo never declared an annual income of more than $50,000 in recent years, and he declared that the money came only from "fees and consultant work."

Mafia members only paid the state sales tax when they had no alternative, (for example, on restaurant checks, and the purchase of autos). They paid few business or use and occupancy taxes. They did pay local real estate taxes on their personal homes. None paid the Philadelphia wage tax, since they had no weekly pay checks from their employers. The 'laundered' cash transactions, with few bank accounts to show for their weekly activities, provided a perfect cover for the mob's nefarious activities.

I just don't like the wise asses who think they can get away with murder. I hate other people like that — the ones who go elbowing their way through life, thinking the laws are for other people but not for them.

-Al Gregorio[*]

31 THE SINS OF THE FATHERS[†]

AN OMEN

MIDWAY through the trial, Scarfo sustained another defeat when word came through channels on October 17th that the U.S. Supreme Court had rejected his appeal of the May 6, 1987 conviction — without comment — for the attempted extortion of $1 million from Willard Rouse III. This decision closed the book on Scarfo's hopes to be released from his fourteen-year prison sentence anytime soon, no matter what decision would be rendered in the RICO trial. His lawyer, Robert Simone, said disconsolately, "I am disappointed but certainly not shocked."

Scarfo showed no emotional letdown the next day in the courtroom. He sat stoically in his front row seat, with the slight smile of a Buddha.

Meanwhile, the defense attorneys were trying their best to discredit the two government witnesses, Thomas Del Giorno and Nicholas Caramandi, when they each took the witness stand.

[*] Al Gregorio, a fictional New York detective in *The Eighth Commandment* , Berkley Books Inc., New York, 1986, by Laurence Sanders.

[†]Excerpted from "The gods visit the sins of the fathers upon their children," from Euripides' *Phrixus Fragment*, #970 (484-406 B.C.).

'Bobby' Tries to Discredit 'Tommy Del'

When it came time for Simone to stick daggers into Del Giorno during his cross-examination, he hunched over the lectern and spoke loudly and angrily at the witness. He lashed out at 'Tommy Del' trying to impugn the truthfulness of the witness's testimony. Del Giorno, who had been through this 'third degree' ordeal many times before, both in and out of court, maintained his outwardly calm composure.

"Have you been advised to tone down your act for the jury?" queried Simone. "No," answered Del Giorno. "I'm trying to be polite."

Simone then obtained court approval over the objection of the prosecutors — to play a 1985 FBI tape of a quarrel between Del Giorno and his wife, made in his Ocean City, New Jersey home through a tiny wall mike. In the tape, Del Giorno complained that his wife's step-mother should be shot, because she was related to Harry Riccobene, the head of a rival faction within the Scarfo crime family.

His wife, Roseann, replied, "Yeah. You're going to burn in Hell some day, and I'm going to be up there looking down on you."

Del Giorno interrupted saying, "She's related to Riccobene. She should be shot."

"So what?" his wife retorted. "She's related to Riccobene?"

"But she should be killed," answered Del Giorno. "The only reason I don't kill her is because she is related."

"Then why don't you get your machine gun and just kill everybody," his wife said.

"I ain't going to kill nobody," a weary Del Giorno replied.

He told the court years later that he was just trying to aggravate his wife.

'Tommy' Hits Back at 'Bobby'

Del Giorno deftly turned the tables on the chief defense lawyer, Robert Simone, when 'Bobby' zeroed-in on him during his cross-examination. In a series of smart byplays, Del Giorno was able to put Simone on the defensive as Simone tried to attack his credibility.

The wily Del Giorno transformed Simone from defense lawyer into a defendant by linking him to the $1 million attempted extortion of Willard Rouse on the Penn's Landing project, which marked the incident that triggered the beginning of the fall of Scarfo's crime family. From the witness stand, Del Giorno testified (as he had done in four previous trials) that Simone was to get ten percent of the Rouse extortion proceeds. The ex-mob *capo* also noted that Simone became quite nervous after Councilman Beloff's administrative assistant, Bobby Rego, was arrested in the middle of that scam.

Simone kept saying, "This Rego can really hurt me," according to Del Giorno in his testimony. "The way he [Simone] was acting, I thought he wanted me to kill him [Rego]." A second defense lawyer, Oscar Goodman, then jumped out of his seat to defend Simone and the Judge had to order the jury to ignore Del Giorno's remark.

At that moment, two prosecutors, Pichini and Gordon, rose in unison and objected when Simone got back at Del Giorno. They questioned Simone about the alleged Rego conversation.

After a sidebar discussion with the Judge at a corner of his bench out of earshot of the jury, Simone again brought the prosecutors to their feet when he asked Del Giorno, "Isn't it a fact that I never received a quarter of the first $10,000 payment made to the extortionist, Nicholas Caramandi?" Once again, Simone was restrained by Judge Van Antwerpen.

Del Giorno admitted under prior, direct questioning by Gordon that he was next in line to be killed back in 1986, after being demoted because of an argument with Joe Pungitore over his heavy drinking and his problems with the men under his command. He (Del Giorno) also believed that he had sealed his own demise when he 'slipped' and told Scarfo that it was a "stupid idea" to kill Joey Merlino, the son of former underboss, Salvatore 'Chuckie' Merlino.

"I realized after I said it that I had made a mistake because he probably thought I still had some loyalty to 'Chuckie'." After that he began to notice a change in the attitude of his colleagues. "My friends avoided me...they stopped hanging around. That's how it started."

When Joe Pungitore anointed him with a new code name, 'Rudy', Del Giorno sensed that this was some kind of a message marking him next on the Mafia hit list.

Del Giorno also got a big clue when the boss made an unusual decision to allow more than $300,000 to accumulate in the jointly owned pot that they shared in an illegal numbers and sports business. They usually split up the pot when it had reached a much lower figure. "I knew that Scarfo wanted it up there," said Del Giorno, "because if I'd get killed he could split it up and keep my part of it."

A MOB TIFF TURNS COSMIC

Near the end of the long trial, Caramandi related how Scarfo, fearing treason in his family, demoted Salvatore 'Chuckie' Merlino as mob underboss in March 1986, and filled the vacant post with a trusted family member, his own nephew, Philip Leonetti. At the same time, the boss also took down Lawrence 'Yogi' Merlino, Sal's brother, who had been a *capo* in the Mafia family.

But a month later, the tensions between the two warring factions took a 'cosmic turn' when Scarfo told Caramandi that Merlino's daughter had gone to a fortune teller, who said that a "guy named Philip was going to have a problem." Scarfo took this omen as a threat against his nephew and sent for Lawrence Merlino. He delivered this ominous message to Merlino:

"Tell your brother, Sal," said Scarfo, "that I had a dream last night. And in that dream, I dreamed his son's got a problem, his wife's got a problem, his daughter's got a problem and you got a problem."

Fortunately for both sides, nothing came of the proposed violent shakeup and things settled down — temporarily — between the two families.

'THE CROW' DOESN'T CAVE IN

At the end of his long cross-examination, Caramandi admitted under questioning that after the trial, he hoped to write a book about his life in the mob, with the assistance of the *Philadelphia Inquirer* investigative reporter, George Anastasia. He stated that he already had a lawyer and an agent and was seeking a reputable publisher to print the autobiographical confessions of his life of crime and how he became a government witness. The defense used this confession to try and impress the jury that 'the Crow' was just out to make some big bucks from the flipside of his testimony on the criminal revelations of his wrongdoing.

When it came to Simone's cross-examination of Caramandi, 'the Crow' accused Simone of being so close to Scarfo that he could have helped the boss to order Caramandi's murder.

"I know you can't give the order, Bobby," Caramandi said to the shocked defense lawyer, in an attempt to undermine Simone's credibility with the jury, "but you could help give the order."

This line of questioning and cross-examination evolved after Caramandi testified, under questioning by Pichini, that a key reason he had begun cooperating with the government was because he believed that Scarfo had ordered him killed.

Caramandi claimed he had gotten this information from a fellow Mafia soldier, jail inmate, Raymond 'Long John' Martorano, after Caramandi's arrest along with ex-City Councilman, Leland Beloff, for the attempted Rouse extortion.

Martorano said, "Bobby Simone and Nicky Scarfo are selling you down the river [according to Caramandi's testimony]. They are going with Beloff...and then he jumped into the ground twice." This last remark was an explanation of how Martorano had mimicked the fall to the ground of a man who has been shot.

You know what that means?" 'Long John' said to Caramandi, "It means you are dead!"

Later, Martorano's son told Caramandi that he could take his father's information 'to the bank.' "That made me decide [to work with the government]," he told the jury.

Later, during cross examination, Simone got Caramandi to confess that he had wanted Simone to represent him in court, not Beloff, after their arrests in the extortion case.

But Caramandi got back at him, saying, "I learned from 'Long John' you sold me down the river...I know the influence you have with Scarfo. You're not only his lawyer, you're his close personal friend."

Stung by this damaging remark in front of the jurors, Simone sarcastically rebutted, "You're not paranoid, are you?"

Caramandi answered half-apologetically, "I have some degree of paranoia." After laughter erupted in the court, Simone realized that he had lost his argument and quickly turned to other topics.

Responding later to a defense attorney's question about his fear of assassination, Caramandi said, "Yes, I think about it twenty-four hours a day. I'm always worried about the assassin's bullet. I'm not Robocop...[I'm] out there by myself."

WAS 'TOMMY DEL' REALLY ON THE SCARFO HIT LIST TOO?

A critical tape made on August 16, 1986, just before Thomas Del Giorno went under the government's witness protection program, foreshadowed his fears and apprehension about being put on the Scarfo 'hit list.' He felt what happened to Sal Testa would happen to him. In the tape 'Wayne' Grande is heard saying to Del Giorno, "you know, you sound awfully worried."

'Tommy Del' answered, "I'm worried about Joe Pungitore when he came in with Phil Leonetti. It could be the start of something."

Later in the day, 'Wayne' discusses the plight of Del Giorno with Francis Iannarella, when he says, "Faffy, the guy [Del Giorno] just took you the 'fucking down.' He got drunk..."

Iannarella answered, "Ain't nothing going to happen to him yet. It's just a matter of time..."

A SON TURNS AGAINST HIS FATHER

Since the defense chose not to put any of their clients on the stand, they tried to use another tactic to undermine the credibility of Caramandi and Del Giorno. They put Thomas Del Giorno, Jr., 22, the oldest son of 'Tommy Del' on the stand to tell some family secrets that they hoped would pull the rug from under the racketeering evidence against the Scarfo crime family, as spouted by the father.

The son said that his father played golf almost every day while under the Federal witness protection program, ordered him to get a gun for him and hide it at home, and often came home drunk after testifying in court. His surprise unexpected testimony from the defense came on the second and final day of the defense portion of the trial. Young Del Giorno tried to show that his father had lied so that he [the son] could live without fear of retribution from the Mob in South Philadelphia. "I'm doing this for myself," he confessed in court.

Prosecutor Arnold Gordon got Del Giorno, Jr. to admit that he had once accused his father of ruining his life, and even called him a "fucking rat" before leaving his father's secret, government protected home in March, 1988. The young Del Giorno, to make his point, even went so far as to state he never feared the Mafia, only the FBI.

When the son testified that his father told him he was pressured into lying about his role in the mob and the so-called crimes committed by other mob members, the government paraded a whole slew of FBI agents and state policemen onto the witness stand. They all vehemently denied that they had ever told the elder Del Giorno to manipulate or twist his statements or knowledge about the Mob to the court.

"No such agreement ever came to my attention," said Wayne Davis, who had just retired as a Special Agent-in-charge of the Philadelphia FBI office.

They also denied the authenticity of the son's assertion that an oral agreement had been made to the senior Del Giorno in which he would receive another $200,000 bonus — $100,000 from the FBI and $100,000 from New Jersey authorities — as a bonus for lying in court.

The prosecution put several FBI agents on the stand, in rebuttal, to stoutly deny that they had coached the two key witnesses into giving false answers. One irate government agent, Michael Leyden, an eighteen-year FBI veteran, left the stand after shouting his denials of intimidating Del Giorno and Caramandi to tell lies. He remarked in exasperation to a friend in the hall: "The defense knows it doesn't have a case and they will stoop to any subterfuge like this one to try and sway the jury. This maneuver won't work."

TRAGEDY STRIKES THE SCARFO FAMILY

Nicky Scarfo sired three sons, Chris, twenty-six, who stayed out of the limelight running the family cement business at Scarf, Inc. in Atlantic City; Nicodemo, Jr., twenty-three, who spent most of his time in 1988 as an observer attending the various trials of his father with other family members; and Mark, seventeen, the youngest, who stayed away from the trial since he was attending a local parochial high school, although he did attend the trial for one day in October.

Near the final days of the trial, while Caramandi was on the stand facing a grueling cross-examination by the defense concerning his credibility, Nicodemo Scarfo Sr. was told by 'Bobby' Simone during an afternoon recess on Wednesday,

November 1st, that his son Mark had just attempted suicide. The troubled youth had finally buckled under the cruel, relentless taunts of his classmates about the role of his father as the head of the mob, since the story of the trial had been featured for weeks on the nightly TV news programs and newspaper headlines in the press. "He had been subject to teasing by his peers for a long time," explained one family friend.

An obviously despondent Mark had gone up to the bathroom in his North Georgia Avenue house after coming home from school, and hung himself from a rafter with a rope. His mother, Dominique, who rarely attended the trial, found him unconscious. The dark-haired, blue-eyed boy was rushed to the Atlantic City Medical Center at 3:30 PM where he remained comatose. He was pronounced extremely critical by hospital authorities, although a midnight statement noted that Mark's condition had not deteriorated. The next twenty-four hours would be critical.

He did not respond to treatment from the life support system and the next day the hospital announced that he remained "critical, although he is far from brain dead."

There was no suicide note and the only surface injuries were bruises on the boy's neck. A brain scan had been performed, but the results were not disclosed.

Because Mark Scarfo failed to respond to treatment in Atlantic City, the family hired a private helicopter to airlift him three days later to Philadelphia's Hahnemann University Hospital, where he received special care for his comatose condition.

His concerned older brother, Nicodemo, Jr. and a friend, paid Mark a visit in his closely guarded twelfth-floor hospital room, and at 1:00 p.m. got into an elevator to descend to the ground floor.

A lone woman was reportedly in the same elevator, Diane Vanderhorst, twenty-six, who had been visiting her bedridden sister. During the ride down Scarfo allegedly thought the woman was reaching inside her coat for a knife or a gun. He and his friend allegedly then assaulted her, beating her unconscious.

As the elevator door opened on the ground level, a hospital guard, Officer Noble, witnessed Scarfo kicking the limp young woman on the floor. When Noble reached Scarfo's side he asked him what happened inside the elevator. Young Scarfo replied,

"She pointed a knife at me." Then Scarfo and his unidentified friend ran out the hospital's front door. The guard rushed the unconscious woman visitor to the nearby emergency room, and after she was revived and treated for head injuries, she was released. She was not charged with any offense since the police could not find a knife or any other weapon on her person.

Noble told detectives that he recognized Scarfo, Jr. and that he knew the young man had been upstairs visiting Mark.

Scarfo was soon arrested by police in the hospital's cafeteria, and charged with aggravated assault. He was ordered to appear at a hearing in a local court a week later. Meanwhile, Simone had to postpone that assault hearing until March, since he was completely involved with the windup of Scarfo Sr.'s trial.

The crime boss, under heavy guard, was allowed to pay a single visit to his still comatose youngest son, and then ushered back to prison and the courtroom to appear again at his RICO trial.

For weeks afterward, the police were still looking for the unidentified companion of Scarfo, Jr., who was described as a white man, 6'1" tall, with black hair and brown eyes, weighing about 210 pounds.

These two unfortunate Scarfo family incidents demonstrate how the pressures had been mounting among various members of the immediate Scarfo family as the trial moved into its third month.

A frustrated 'Bobby' Simone shrugged his shoulders in despair, saying, "How much can someone tolerate? These things take their toll of innocent people. Wouldn't any son be upset if they saw their father go through this?"

Rumors flew about the courtroom in the ensuing days that Mark Scarfo was *not* a victim of a suicide attempt, but of a revenge murder attempt by followers of the 'Harry the Hunchback' Riccobene faction of the mob. However, the police could find no clues that any second party had a part in the attempted suicide actions by young Mark and so the rumors were soon laid to rest while the family continued their vigil at the bedside of the comatose youth. This served as a tragic shadow over the ongoing trial.

And so to the end of history, murder shall bred murder always in the name of right and honor and peace, until at last the gods tire of blood and create a race that can understand.

-Julius Caesar[*]

32

RICO AND A JURY BURY SCARFO'S CRIME FAMILY

A S the two-month long trial wound down to its final days, one courtroom observer noted that "Nicky Scarfo looked more like a buttoned down, diminutive blue-suited accountant than a vicious mob leader." With his left eye twitching nervously, Scarfo constantly cracked his knuckles as he listened to the damning evidence piled up against him and his family on the multiple counts of criminal conspiracy.

One astute courtroom observer noted as the trial progressed, that its drama and operations had evolved into a 'cottage industry' — consisting of eighteen defense lawyers and three defense 'researchers' and their opposition, dozens of FBI agents, US Marshals, and five prosecutors, who were arrayed against them in the tightly-packed courtroom.

THE GOVERNMENT'S CLOSER

When Lou Pichini, who had spent seventeen years of his life as a career Federal prosecutor, faced the jury for the last time on Veterans Day, November 11th, to sum up the government's case, he asserted that "there were two words that best explained what the *La Cosa Nostra* was all about. They were: Organized Crime." They followed their illegal paths to make money as "modern day outlaws" working to achieve their nefarious ends as "individual

---

[*] George Bernard Shaw's *Caesar and Cleopatra*.

members of crime families" who were part of a "national organization."

Pichini went through a series of earlier taped testimonies, including one made on May 7, 1986, recounting Caramandi's ties with the mob in "Mobster Lament," in which he criticized his fellow mobsters as being paranoid. "They are jealous, vicious and trying to put you in fucking traps."

He then repainted the military sub-structure of the Scarfo family, reiterating the secret 'making' ceremonies, and how each member was expected to touch base with his superiors, as well as to maintain the code of silence.

Pichini related how the "swagger of a mob member's walk" and how the long waiting list of prospective young members, insured a steady supply of new members magnetized by the "lure of the cult." Yet, after they got into the Scarfo family, life in the mob was not all that "attractive and glamorous," said Pichini. "He [Scarfo] took the mob, formerly ruled by Angelo Bruno and Phil Testa, and molded it into his own image. He is a cold-blooded killer, and what he lacked in height [being only 5'4" tall] he made up through his own viciousness. He tolerated no rivalry and turned the Philadelphia *La Cosa Nostra* into a family of mob violence of the worst kind. The hands of Nicky Scarfo dripped blood. Bloodshed was the dubious mark of his reign, a reign of terror.

"The *La Cosa Nostra* came first to its members, even before their own families. They bastardized the word 'family' by calling their own criminal chapter 'a family.' They are bonded together for the wrong reasons, worshipping at the altar of violence and loyalty to the mob. All members must submit to the first commandment of the Mafia — the submission to the boss and his commandments which forced them to turn at times on their best friends and members of their own [crime] family....Their primary pursuit was violence."

Pichini told the jury, "The gun, the knife, the blood are symbols...of the reign of Nicky Scarfo....He turned the Philadelphia *La Cosa Nostra* into a band of urban terrorists and bullies....There's a big difference between mob murders in real life and those shootings that are portrayed in the cinema. In real life, it could take months...and sometimes the victim is never killed."

Pichini then went over each of the RICO counts in the indictment to remind the jury of the overwhelming evidence that the government used, intending to prove the guilt of these men — beyond a shadow of a doubt.

BUILDING UP THE CREDIBILITY OF 'THE CROW' AND 'TOMMY DEL'

Besides highlighting the key tapes, Pichini showed the jurors the blownup photos again, showing both Caramandi and Del Giorno gamboling on the beach at Fort Lauderdale or on Scarfo's yacht back in 1986, just before they switched their allegiances.

Then, anticipating a defense attack on the two key witnesses, Pichini raised his voice and asked the question, "Who is Thomas Del Giorno? Is he a mob impostor who fabricates his stories? Is he a creation of the FBI? The evidence says 'Hogwash to that!'"

Then, lowering his voice, he told the jury: "Let your conscience be your guide. He lived a mob life and then found himself in a courtroom because he has no choice. If he had remained in the mob, he would not be alive. That's why he came here." After finishing with Del Giorno, Pichini asked the second key question to stave off the expected undermining bombardment by the defense: "Who is Nicholas Caramandi?"

"He has a perfect criminal pedigree to be a mob member," asserted the prosecutor. "He led a life of crime, from car thefts to flim-flams to shakedowns and murder....But is Nicholas Caramandi another government witness who is masquerading as a mob member creation of the FBI?"

Pichini urged the jury to remember taped conversations when Caramandi and some of the defendants were talking about shakedowns of Mafia crime victims.

"Those recorded words," Pichini reminded the jurors, "were gathered not when those two individuals were cooperating with the government....They were gathered when they were part of the mob." As he uttered these words, he pointed to the defendants sitting mutely in their chairs.

Pichini reiterated to the jury that the close association Caramandi and Del Giorno had with the defendants was proven by the hundreds of surveillance photos displayed during the trial.

"Keep these pictures in mind when the defendants tell you that the government witnesses are worse than pond scum....The government doesn't disagree or argue about the criminal pasts of Caramandi and Del Giorno, because the criminal past is exactly what ties these individuals together. Crime is the tie, the mob is the bond."

While noting that the mob is made up of people of Italian-American descent, Pichini, who is himself of Italian-American lineage, said, "The members of *La Cosa Nostra* represent a very, very very small percentage of the Italian-American population of this country."

In the back benches of the crowded courtroom where the spectators and family members sat, several relatives of the defendants took umbrage at Pichini's remarks and some complained of his habit of letting the jury know before a recess what he planned to cover next after the court reconvened. "It's like a soap opera," whispered one, "They even tell you what's going to happen after the commercial."

Pichini stood before the jury in the middle of his closing and emptied a large box filled with rifles and revolvers. He dramatically explained that these weapons were used in the nine murders and four attempted murders listed in the Mafia's 'Enterprise' indictment.

"These guns," Pichini said, "represent Scarfo's mentality. They represent how he ruled with an iron fist."

He related how Scarfo's rise to power came in 1981 after mob boss Bruno had been assassinated in March, followed a year later by the killing of his successor, Phil 'Chickenman' Testa. From the late winter of 1981, Scarfo had ruled the mob even after his imprisonment in 1987.

A CLOSING CLIMAX

In his final windup at the end of his nine-hour, two-day long closing, Pichini reminded the jury that they had "been the cornerstone of American jurisprudence....The defendants are entitled to these rights because it is the American system of justice, which is far better than the Mafia system of justice. The U.S. Constitution could not protect the rights of Pat Spirito and the others since the Mafia law decided that the rules were 'Might Makes Right' and 'Violence Will Prevail.' But the U.S. Constitution protects the people and guarantees a fair trial. The Constitution allows for a conviction as well as for an acquittal.

"The government has established proof beyond a reasonable doubt that the U.S. system of law will not bow to intimidation. In the execution of your duty, the jury's strength, independence, and courage should set aside your bias and fear.

"The evidence has shown that the United States system of law will not surrender to violence, bullyism, and intimidation. It's shown that might is not right.

"For the American system to work, there is one word for you to return. There's one word for each defendant on each count on each racketeering act," he said. Then, pointing to each of the seventeen defendants in the courtroom, calling out each man's name and looking them in the eye, he paused and said in a single word, "*Guilty!*"

THE DEFENSE APPEALS FOR JUSTICE

When it came time for the defense to make their last ditch plea on behalf of their clients, Oscar Goodman, representing underboss Phil Leonetti, charged that "Deals have been made with devils." He then ticked off the long list of crimes and lies that Caramandi had confessed to which could have gotten him over 9,000 years in prison to show how the government was unfairly ganging up on his client and the other sixteen defendants.

He concluded, "If you return a verdict like the prosecutors asked for, then you encourage the use of bought and paid for perjured testimony," contending that both witnesses had lied to get money and other rewards in return for their testimony.

His forty-minute summation was intended to lay the groundwork for the other sixteen closing arguments, to show that both Caramandi and Del Giorno were liars, cheaters, thieves and killers who were far worse than anyone ever could be.

"In this case we have a situation that may be a first in the American system of justice; a prosecution case based on deals with felons."

Attorney Goodman shouted, "Caramandi and Del Giorno have broken virtually every commandment ordered by God and every crime known to man. People's freedom and lives are at stake, and they are entitled to have evidence of a quality that is acceptable and not just have this kind of...nonsense."

He also attacked the credibility of former mob associate, Joseph Salerno, now in Federal custody, for his assertion that his client (Leonetti) had killed Vincent Falcone, a cement contractor, while the latter mixed Christmas drinks at his Margate, New Jersey, home in 1979. "I submit that Mr. Salerno is a liar," said Goodman. "Here's a man who participated in a murder, and he wasn't even arrested for it."

In his closing argument, Goodman said, "They will give you the world. They will give you the moon. They will give you the stars [referring to the law enforcement authorities]. Anything you want, you get....They [the government] threw enough mud against the wall and they hoped some would stick against Phil Leonetti, but in his particular situation it doesn't pass muster — not with the kind of testimony you heard from Caramandi and Del Giorno."

"Look what they've done with Caramandi," said Goodman, "the self proclaimed 'shrewd bird'. The government will turn him into a millionaire if he can sell his hoped-for book [of his life in the mob]. But a leopard doesn't change his spots one whit."

HOW THE DEFENSE HOPED TO WIN AN ACQUITTAL

The defense strategy in their closing arguments was aimed at pounding away at the credibility of the two key government informants. Since they chose not to put any of their clients on the witness stand (for fear that they might stumble or otherwise hurt their case under cross-examination by the prosecution), the defense attorneys hit at the two ex-mobsters from all sides saying that the two felons had committed so many crimes and told so many lies that they could not be believed under any circumstances.

One by one, each of the seventeen defense lawyers tried to woo the jury, including one lawyer who set a small model of the brass scales of justice on the jury box railing and then plopped a brick on one side to convey the weight of the presumption of innocence.

None of the defense lawyers tried to undermine the tapes and photos that the government presented as key evidence to justify their arguments.

Defense attorney Willis W. Berry, Jr. gave a hell-fire and brimstone closing argument in which he posed the old question,

"Would you buy a used car from these people?" He contended that both 'turncoats' had been "groomed, fixed-up, dressed and put in condos" and that their testimony had been "nursed, rehearsed, practiced...so that when they testify they will be believable."

Berry, who represented Joe Grande, dramatically used the scales of justice to illustrate his points. He then told the jury that instead of the witness stand, Caramandi and Del Giorno deserved seats in the electric chair. And instead of lawyers, they needed accountants to help them manage their money and other rewards supplied to them by a grateful government.

"They don't need lawyers. They need E. F. Hutton. They figured out how to trick the criminal justice system and trick the government into supporting them. They figured out how to get rich."

Defense attorney Edwin J. Jacobs, Jr., representing former mob underboss 'Chickie' Merlino, made one of the most impassioned pleas to the jury when his turn came during the closing. After arguing that the government had spent enormous amounts of money taking care of both Caramandi and Del Giorno, he pondered the question:

"Did you get your money's worth? Did you get a high quality grade of witness...or did you get things that are shot full of holes?" he asked during his three-and-one-half hour closing argument.

"Where's the proverbial smoking gun in this case?" he asked.

He then tried to point out a few of those holes, such as Caramandi's testimony that his client, Merlino, had given Sal Testa the so-called kiss of death.

"Wouldn't it really be dumb," he suggested, "to give him and the world absolute notice of what was going on?"

He also reminded the jury that the New Jersey State Police had permitted Del Giorno to hire a prostitute while in police custody, to prove the point that "the New Jersey State Police did a real bad job on this guy."

Jacobs noted that Pichini had coined the term "impostor-mobsters" to describe both Caramandi and Del Giorno. "I believe," he said, "that both were pathological menaces despite their protestations of 'I'm only here to tell the truth.'"

Jacobs wound up his closing oration with the conclusion that Caramandi was a "beneficiary of a legal miracle — compounded with the multiple benefits of: a condo, a sauna, a pool, bar, the ocean, and no work, while the government pays to keep him [with a nice nest egg contract] while we work six days a week."

THE LAST OF THE CLOSERS

In the last of the seventeen defense closings, Robert Simone, Scarfo's lawyer, sketched a skewed portrait of an overzealous government that would take any action to get his client, suggesting that this was the reason why the prosecutors had to rely so much on the testimony of the two mobsters.

"How bad do they want Mr. Scarfo?" Simone implored the jury during his one-hour-long closing argument. "It makes me wonder and should make you wonder." But Simone seemed to lose some of the usual punch that he had exhibited during his earlier Mafia trials, as if he was conceding that the overwhelming weight of the government's evidence was just too much to overthrow.

During his rebuttal summation, Arnold Gordon pointed out that the government had no choice in preparing the case, but to rely on the word of the former Mafia men, because they were the ones associated with the defendants.

Gordon told the jury that he would have much preferred having "a Bob Hope or Bill Cosby, with their excellent reputations, as prosecution witnesses," but the sad fact was that "no decent citizen...would know anything about the mob. So, 'the Crow' and 'Tommy Del' became the government's witnesses — out of necessity. They were the only people who can tell you about the mob and how it works since they were inside the organization."

He reminded the jury over and over that photo surveillance which had been shown in court during the trial showed both men in the company of Scarfo and that the long criminal histories of the two did not dissuade the defendants from associating with them before they became government witnesses. Gordon also pointed out that the government backed up the testimony of Caramandi and Del Giorno with recorded telephone conversations between various mob figures, inside mobsters' homes and meeting places, where some of the defendants could be clearly heard talking about extortions, illegal gambling businesses, or other mob related activities.

Gordon said, "The recorded conversations show you that there is a mob, that there are shakedowns and gambling. The tapes, therefore, show that Thomas Del Giorno and Nicholas Caramandi *are* telling the truth about those crimes. *The defense can't get around the tapes!*"

Gordon ended his three-and-one-half hour rebuttal by telling the jurors that, "While all criminal trials are important, this one is particularly important. You can convict seventeen Mafia killers...and end their reign of terror."

Robert Simone, in his last rebuttal, strongly disagreed with the assessment by the government. "This is about the worst level of evidence I have ever seen," he told the jury. "The only reason they get away with it is because there are seventeen defendants and forty charges. Case by case, they [the prosecution] wouldn't stand a chance. Well, with a decent jury, they won't stand a chance either."

He characterized the key government tapes as tainted, and called the jury's attention to several instances in which Caramandi said one thing and then changed his mind.

Simone asserted that, "You will find that the government's case would collapse without the testimony of these people."

Once again, as he had done in earlier Mafia trials where he won acquittals, Simone referred to cases of historical persecution, from the Spanish Inquisition to the persecution of liberals during the McCarthy era in the Fifties, and civil rights activists in the Sixties. Simone then topped off his analogy with this parallel statement: "In the Eighties, we've got the mob and the Mafia. Win at any cost." The prosecution's photos and tapes were aimed at "trying to arouse your passions and your hatred."

The case then went to the jury at 3:30 p.m. on Wednesday, November 17th, 1988, after Judge Van Antwerpen gave them his instructions in the law.

TENSION RISES IN COURTROOM #14B

At 6 p.m., on Saturday, November 19th, after two days of waiting by the prosecution, the defense teams, and the families and friends of the defendants, Judge Van Antwerpen sent a Federal Marshal into the jury room adjacent to his courtroom, high up in the new Federal Courthouse situated across from the

Liberty Bell. He asked them how much longer they wanted to deliberate. The tension rose when they sent back word that they would have a verdict in a few hours.

The delay was due mainly to the complex federal racketeering statute under which Scarfo and his associates were tried. The RICO law required that the jury agree that a defendant had committed at least *two* underlying crimes of murder, extortion, drug distribution, illegal gambling, or loansharking, to justify a guilty verdict.

THE VERDICT

The weary jury of six men and six women, most of whom had been sequestered for two-and-one-half months, came back less than two hours later, having reached a verdict at 7:54 p.m.

They had deliberated for twenty-six hours over three days and were all anxious to get home to their families to celebrate Thanksgiving.

"What is your verdict — guilty or not guilty?" asked Judge Van Antwerpen of the Jury Foreman, referring to the first charge against Scarfo.

"Guilty," asserted the foreman.

For the next forty minutes, the words "guilty" and "proved" rang out for each count against every one of the seventeen defendants while family and friends in the rear benches sobbed quietly and held hands to console one another. Several women left the courtroom in tears, unable to contain their emotions.

Scarfo sat impassively, sipping water from a paper cup as one eye twitched incessantly. Joe Grande twisted a toothpick in his mouth while defendant Sal Merlino smiled wanly.

In a stunning blow to the survival of the Philadelphia Mafia organization headed by Scarfo, the jury found all of the defendants guilty on all counts of the racketeering and conspiracy charges — including murder.

After the verdict was read, law enforcement officers and FBI agents who had been involved in preparing the case and had been attending the trial as observers, stood and applauded the jury for their action. Judge Van Antwerpen then thanked the jurors, most of whom had been sequestered in their hotels as virtual prisoners since mid-September.

"It's sufficient to say you are Americans," he told them. "As long as the American people stay in control of the courts...I don't believe we will go too far wrong." He then personally shook hands with each of the twelve anonymous jurors as they left the courtroom for the last time in the custody of U.S. Marshals. He then revoked the bail of Anthony Pungitore, Jr., the only defendant and reputed mob soldier who had not been incarcerated with the others during the trial because the government had not insisted on it. He and the other sixteen, including Scarfo, were then led away by Federal Marshals.

The trial marked the official end of the seven-year reign of power by the Scarfo crime family over the underworld activities in the Newark, Atlantic City, and Philadelphia triangle of mob rule. All of the defendants faced up to a fifty-five-year maximum sentence in prison.

The verdict came after thirty-three days of testimony featuring more than one hundred witnesses and after the jury had heard almost three hundred FBI and State Police tapes. They included the critical 1977 tape in which Scarfo and three others discussed the election of a *consigliere*. That was the tape in which the late underboss, Philip Testa, actually mentioned the rarely-used code words for the mob, *La Cosa Nostra*.

Eleven of the defendants were recorded on one or more of the tapes, in conversations which backed up the main testimony of both Caramandi and Del Giorno.

Detective Sergeant Edward Johnson, a New Jersey State Policeman, and the first law enforcement official to interview the mobster-turned-informant, Thomas Del Giorno, summed up the feelings of the government's prosecution team as the final curtain was dropped on the two-and-one-half-month-long courtroom drama: "Thank God for the American jury system!"

...If I lived to be seventy-five, I don't think I want no headaches. I'd leave it to the younger generation.

-Nicodemo Scarfo[*]

33

A POST-MORTEM ANALYSIS: WHY THE USA WON

THERE were multiple meanings of this important verdict for the Mafia in America as well as for the Scarfo crime family. For the Scarfo crime family, it signified the virtual wipeout of the entire top leadership. It was the first time anywhere in America that a court decision had established guilt by a sweeping jury verdict of not just the boss and the underboss, but of the second and third echelon *capos* and soldiers as well.

Arnold Gordon, one of the main prosecutors of the Organized Crime Strike Force, summed up the jury decision with these words: "The case helps break the myth of Mafia invincibility."

The lead prosecutor, Louis Pichini, hailed the hard-won victory, stating: "It was an historic prosecution. We salute the jury for their independence and their courage not to surrender to intimidation."

The verdict finally established the credibility of the two key government informants, Caramandi and Del Giorno, whose reputation had been tarnished in earlier trials because other juries had acquitted Scarfo and Company on various drug and murder charges. The tapes and photos backing up the oral testimony of the two ex-mobsters, cemented the jury's feelings about their

---

[*] Then 48 going on 49, on an FBI tape recorded in mid-1980, before the killing of Mafia boss Angelo Bruno, as played to the jury at the RICO trial, October, 1988, Philadelphia, Pennsylvania.

findings of guilt for all of the defendants.

Edwin Jacobs, Jr., a defense attorney, commented to the media, "I think the case was an enormous miscarriage of justice."

Prosecutor Pichini said that "we knew from the start of the long trial that the evidence compiled in the hundreds of court-ordered tapes and photos would go largely unchallenged by the defense. That was a fixed plus for us. What was the unknown quantity was how well the various government witnesses would be able to stand up under the biting cross-examinations of the various defense attorneys. As it turned out, not only did Del Giorno and Caramandi stand up well, but also Norman Lit and Michael Madgin [mob associates now under government protection] under the pressure. None of them cracked under the relentless bombardment...to get them to seriously contradict themselves and undermine our case."

THE KEY ROLE OF THE TAPES IN THE TRIAL

Although no jury member offered any explanation of the main turning points in the case that led to their unanimous decision, it was fairly obvious to most courtroom observers that the use of the government tapes put in evidence during the trial was an important factor in shoring up the credibility of the government witnesses.

Arnold Gordon, one of the prosecutors, argued before the jury on the final day of the trial that "The only people who can tell you about the mob are people inside the mob...and you don't find swans swimming in those polluted waters."

On one of the damning tapes, defendant Ralph Staino, Jr. tells an unidentified man on May 15, 1982, during a phone call: "Bring that money here within an hour or I personally will put your...eye out." They heard other defendants discuss the brutal public beating of a drug dealer who refused to pay the mob the required street tax on his enterprise.

In this August, 1985, conversation, 'Faffy' Iannarella, Jr. boasted that the drug dealer's "got a broken jaw, a couple of broken ribs. He's in hiding." His soldier colleague in crime 'Wayne' Grande echoed, "All South Philadelphia is shaking."

THE SMOKING GUNS

One of the most crucial tapes was made by the FBI listening in on a bug planted on November 4, 1977, to pick up a key conversation between Scarfo and several other high-ranking mob members at the time. Prosecutor Pichini reminded the jury that this key tape "took you into the inner sanctum of the mob — hearing voices from the grave, since two of the four are now dead — Phil Testa and Frank Narducci, Sr.

"That 1977 conversation reflected the calm before the storm, but sent up internal storm warnings about the future leadership of the mob. Angelo Bruno was a bona fide gangster — a throw back to those of yesteryear — who had kept the pieces together until Nicky Scarfo took over," said Pichini. "It is ironic that the voices of the two mob leaders, Frank Narducci and Harry Riccobene, Sr., who were targeted for murder by Scarfo, have now come back to haunt Scarfo as he complains about Bruno's way of heading the mob."

Part of the "Mobster's Lament" tape reads:

PHIL
TESTA: Did you hear anything about the new *consigliere*?

NARDUCCI: He [Bruno] ain't said nothing to us and I'm a *capo*.

SCARFO: And he's the underboss [pointing to Testa].

TESTA: The *capos* are supposed to talk to their men.

SCARFO: And the boss [Bruno] is not a 'shrinking violet' [as he complains about the 'beefs' that he and the rest of the underlings have with Bruno].

TESTA: [twice repeats that the *La Cosa Nostra* has become more critical of Bruno's leadership] He's political. He's not a gangster.

NARDUCCI: He [Bruno] won't get no opposition in the open. But behind [Bruno] is treachery.

SCARFO: I don't know whose idea it was to make this man a *consigliere*.

SCARFO: [later on the 1977 tape] Someone, a kid, tried to kill me.

TESTA: [interrupts and boasts] If I wasn't around a couple
               of times you would have gone.

Ironically, three years later, when Testa became the boss after
the assassination of Bruno, Scarfo became the new *consigliere*.

In a more recent tape made three years later in 1980, Phil
Testa and Scarfo are again conversing about the state of the mob
under the aged septuagenarian, Boss Bruno:

TESTA: I know who's qualified, but he'll never get it. He's
               got smarts. He's not young. How old are you,
               Nick?

SCARFO: Forty-seven going on forty-eight.

TESTA: They [Bruno and Co.] look on us as kids. He
               should quit...He's worrying about protecting the
               cops and the ward healers. A friend of ours has the
               worst of it.

These two conversations made in 1977 and 1980 proved that
Scarfo was a "mobster without a mob" according to Prosecutor
Pichini. Those recorded conversations proved a criminal con-
spiracy did exist under Scarfo and his co-defendants.

On another of the crucial tapes, 'Wayne' Grande could be
heard saying he wanted to "hang with gangsters" — voicing his
ambitions to become a soldier in the mob.

But in the end, it took the two mob members, Del Giorno and
Caramandi, to interpret many of the tapes for the jury, including
the recording about the alleged drug dealer who refused to give
up a slice of his profits to the mob.

In spending a total of fourteen days on the witness stand,
these two men linked Scarfo directly to twelve of the thirteen
murders and attempted murders listed in the broad racketeering
indictment. They painted a lurid portrait of greed, violence, and
betrayal in explaining how the associates of a rival faction in the
mob, under the rule of Harry Riccobene, were stalked and shot,
as well as fellow mobsters within their own Scarfo family circle.

In earlier trials against Scarfo and mob members, government
tapes were not put into evidence and in several of them (eg. the
Sal Testa murder case and the methamphetamine drug trials) the
jury came up with acquittals, in which they obviously did not believe the two ex-mobsters.

Prosecutor Gordon reminded the jurors of the importance of the tapes in his closing rebuttal: "The tapes, the tapes, the tapes," he emphasized. "They can't get around the tapes....It's on the basis of those words — their words — that the government is asking you to convict these people."

THE DEFENSE APPEALS THE CONVICTIONS

In mid-December, 1988, a month after the convictions of Scarfo and sixteen members of his crime family, one of the defense attorneys, Stephen LaCheen, filed a fifteen-page set of post-trial motions on behalf of all the defendants, asking the judge to overturn the guilty verdicts. The motions alleged that "numerous instances of misconduct" where either the conduct of the prosecuting attorneys, or Judge Van Antwerpen had deprived the defendants of a fair trial. Among the accusations were the improper schooling of the two government witnesses, and that they had been allowed to retain deals with the government even after they lied under oath. The appeal also questioned Van Antwerpen's "admonishment of defense attorneys in a voice audible to the jury and by facial expression and tone of voice, which often indicated that objections by the defense counsel were inappropriate and time wasting."

No date was set for the court ruling on the appeal.

A SAD CHRISTMAS AT SCARF, INC.

As Christmas 1988 approached, the Scarfo family hoped to transport the still comatose Mark Scarfo, 17, back home to Atlantic City to be with the remnants of his family. His father had only been permitted to visit him on one occasion, on a pass from his prison cell, as his son lay in a coma in the intensive care unit of Philadelphia's Hahnemann University Hospital. The troubled youth had shown no signs of improvement after his attempted suicide two months earlier.

Meanwhile, Mark's older brother, Nicodemo Jr., 23, was scheduled to face a preliminary court hearing in January, 1989 after his arrest in the same hospital for allegedly assaulting a woman in the elevator as she was on her way down to the street from visiting her patient-sister on one of the upper floors. (He had been under a severe mental strain after seeing his younger brother in a coma a few minutes earlier.)

On February 9, 1989, Dominique Scarfo took her still comatose 17-year-old son back home to Atlantic City. The
prognosis for his recovery was not good.

WHO MIGHT INHERIT 'LIL NICKY'S' MANTLE?

Scarfo had been serving a fourteen-year sentence for masterminding the Rouse extortion plot. After this latest conviction, he
faced up to 55 years on the RICO jury's verdict. It was obvious
that a new leader would inherit the mantle Scarfo had worn since
1981 as the boss of organized crime in the Philadelphia-Atlantic
City-Newark triangle.

But Scarfo, unlike the late Vito Genovese who continued to
run his New York crime family from behind prison bars, did not
have the clout to continue ruling his crime family from jail. Col.
Clinton Pagano, the Superintendent of the New Jersey State
Police, said: "I believe Scarfo's days as a leader of organized
crime are over."

Meanwhile, the Mafia had not gone completely belly-up in
South Philadelphia during and after the trial of Scarfo and his
subordinates. The continued flourishing of loansharking and
bookmaking in the area was a sign that the mob was still in
business.

Many of the older mob members (including some who were
not indicted in the RICO charges) slowly began to view Scarfo as
a ruthless and greedy boss, whose penchant for violence brought
on the slew of federal and state investigations and trials leading in
the end to the demise of his crime family.

"It's his [Scarfo's] attitude, his ruthlessness, his cockiness
and lack of leadership," observed Pagano, "that created the
problems with his family and the law."

One federal source observed that the mob defendants were no
longer harmonious as a group, despite the surface show of
camaraderie during the long trial. "Some of these guys hate each
other," he said. "How do you think the two Narducci brothers
[Frank Jr. and Philip] felt sitting in the same courtroom with the
two accused murderers of their father?"

With the jailing of the top leaders of the mob, it meant that
untrained, younger leadership had to be installed immediately to

take over the remnants of the Scarfo crime family. A similar situation developed in the hierarchy of the five leading crime families in New York — the Gambino, Genovese, Lucchese, Columbo and Bonanno families — when their mob bosses were found guilty on various RICO charges over the past four years. In both New York and Philadelphia, the immaturity of the new leaders caused a myriad of business problems, friction and factionalization among the new members. The old discipline was clearly lacking.

This breakdown in discipline in the crime families generated internal violence since the lucrative narcotics trafficking and its high profits to the pushers provide the seeds for turf wars.

"The young Mafiosos in the Scarfo family...lacked the specialized talents to run the mob actions without continued violence. They have grown up with a different set of values than their elders and are more interested in making money quickly than in honor, respect, and organizational loyalty," said one Organized Crime Strike Force official.

This disintegration in the traditional Mafia personal value system has produced more "turncoats who are willing to cooperate with the authorities to provide critical evidence against their former confederates. The fear of indictments has also now created an uncharacteristic climate of caution on the part of the more experienced mobsters still out of prison.

There were a few other Scarfo family members who were in a position to pick up the fallen lance of leadership, but most were approaching old age. For example, Santo Idone, 68, was the only *capo* identified by the Pennsylvania Crime Commission to escape indictments for his role in the mob. He spent most of his time in Florida, while wrestling with a cloud of continuing federal racketeering investigations into his alleged control of an illegal poker machine network in Delaware County, Pennsylvania.

Alfred Iezzi, 78, a semi-retired former *capo*, was another potential leader as were any one of Scarfo's three uncles: Nicholas, Michael, or Joe Piccolo. Nicholas Piccolo, Scarfo's *consigliere*, though, was 83, Michael was 77 and Joseph was 81. Uncle Nick died on February 14, 1989 and only Nicky Scarfo, Jr. and Phil Leonetti Jr. of the crime family attended the funeral in Seaside Heights, New Jersey.

Albert 'Reds' Pontani, 61, the Trenton-based caretaker of the

Scarfo crime family, did not fare too well himself. He was convicted in a Federal court trial in Newark, New Jersey, on November 9, 1988, after being charged with multi-conspiracy criminal counts of loansharking, drugs and extortion. He faced a
potential life sentence.

The elimination of Pontani as a pinch-hitter to run the remnants of the Scarfo crime regime seriously undermined the capa-
bility of the once-powerful Philadelphia, Atlantic City, Newark
crime network to cooperate efficiently. A vacuum existed by the
end of 1988 in the leadership of the mob that challenged law enforcement officers to find out who was attempting to move in and
pick up the loose reins of Mafia power.

THE SCARFO-RICO TRIAL'S FALLOUT HITS ATLANTIC CITY

The reborn Atlantic City, with its glittering array of hotel-
casinos on the Boardwalk which lured willing gamblers to its
gaming tables, had been declared open territory by the nation's
crime families in recent years. Both Nicky Scarfo and his nephew, Phil Leonetti, enjoyed special access to the huge amounts of
cash made available by extortions from the hangers-on involved
with the lucrative gambling industry.

They had lived there for many years, masquerading behind
Scarf, Inc. Scarfo had developed links to the local government
and organized labor in the area, who were involved directly in
permits, zoning, and construction of the many casino hotels.

Scarfo's influence over the gambling mecca by the sea was
graphically illustrated back in 1984, when former Mayor Michael
Matthews was convicted of extortion and sentenced to fifteen
years in prison for his part in a conspiracy hatched by a Nicky
Scarfo lieutenant, Frank Lentino. Lentino had also been identified as Scarfo's representative to Local #54 of the Hotel Employees and Bartenders' Union.

Scarfo's long dominance of that union led the New Jersey
Division of Gaming Enforcement to successfully defend in court
its right to disqualify all mob-connected persons from holding
office in unions that deal with the casinos.

Most observers of the shifting sands of mob rule in Atlantic
City expected changes before 1990. John Gotti and the other
bosses of the dominant Gambino crime family in New York were
expected to play a more prominent role in the aftermath of

Scarfo's downfall. "Atlantic City is a jewel," said one of the Scarfo prosecutors. "The Gambino family has already made some inroads there."

This expected move by the New York mob was made more evident in the wake of the wholesale conviction of two generations of mob leaders ruling the Atlantic City-Philadelphia axis at the Scarfo trial. Joseph Peters, one of the Scarfo prosecutors, summed it up this way: "We have, in essence, taken the guts out of this family. I don't believe there is enough structure to keep it running. We took down the boss, the underboss, the *capos* and the soldiers."

As one federal agent put it, "Gotti is going to be looking at the labor unions. He's acted friendly to Nicky in the past, and he can go in there now without causing Nicky to lose a whole lot of face."

Evidence and testimony was presented during the trial where Gotti was photographed welcoming Scarfo into a private New York club in June, 1986, at the height of Scarfo's power, along with Leonetti and Scarfo's middle son, Nicodemo, Jr. They had arrived in New York by helicopter, and although they only remained in the Big Apple for part of the day, the meeting with Gotti allegedly led to an agreement divvying up the action in Atlantic City.

In North Jersey, the late mob boss, Angelo Bruno, had had his people running gambling and loan sharking in Newark. Gotti had already taken away control of this operation from Scarfo's minions by mid-1988. This move was a sign that Gotti and his Gambino family *capos* and soldiers would be heading south to Atlantic City before long.

There was also the distinct possibility that the scattered Scarfo soldiers, who were not in jail, would be eventually absorbed into one or more of the New York criminal organizations.

THREE POTENTIAL SCARFO SUCCESSORS STRIKE OUT IN SHORT ORDER

Within twenty-four hours on January 23 and 24, 1989, three area mob bosses and acting bosses had lost their tenuous grip on the tattered remnants of the Scarfo crime family. On January 23, John Gotti, possibly the most powerful active Mafia ruler in

America, was arrested and put in jail without bail for ordering the shooting of John O'Connor, a New York Carpenters' Union labor leader in the restaurant business, back in 1986. Although he was released on several hundred thousand dollars bail the next day, he was ordered to stand trial for the crime of vandalizing the restaurant and the shooting and wounding of O'Connor because he wouldn't pay Gotti a bribe.

On January 24th, Albert 'Reds' Pontani, the acting boss of the Scarfo family since 1987, was sentenced to 30 years in prison by U.S. District Judge Maryanne Trump Barry, in Newark, New Jersey. She rejected the pleas of Pontani's defense lawyer at the pre-sentencing hearing that the Federal government was "just playing games by raising spurious charges" of his client's alleged mob connections with Scarfo.

As if this sentencing on similar racketeering crimes to those sustained by Scarfo and his clan in November had not already sent a strong message to Scarfo and the other incarcerated mob members, Santo Idone, 68, one of the two remaining Scarfo *capos*, who had previously been able to avoid arrest, finally found himself indicted. As the only ranking member of the Scarfo organized crime family in the USA, Idone and three of his associates were charged on the same day with racketeering, conspiracy and extortion in connection with the operation of an illegal poker machine distribution network in Chester, Pennsylvania.

According to the state and Federal investigators, Idone was the Scarfo family's man in Chester, a depressed town located just west of Philadelphia, where gambling, loansharking and the control of illegal video poker machines generated hundreds of thousands of dollars annually.

This latest indictment against Idone marked the climax of the unprecedented three-year onslaught by law enforcement in the Philadelphia area leading to the final dismantling of the once proud and arrogant Scarfo mob organization.

The other Scarfo *capo* not yet in jail was Pasquale 'Patty Specs' Martirano, 59, a fugitive from justice who was reportedly hiding out somewhere in Italy according to law enforcement officials.

"It's been devastated," said Frederick Martens, the executive director of the Pennsylvania Crime Commission, who compared the now-tattered Scarfo organization to a major corporation that had been torn asunder.

Joel M. Friedman, the head of the Organized Crime Task Force in Philadelphia, commented that the arrest of Idone marked the latest part of "a constant systematic approach" to wiping out the Scarfo crime family and shifting the balance in the war against organized crime. Peter Harvey, the assistant U.S. Attorney who prosecuted Pontani, offered this epitaph, when he said: "Between jail and mob-sanctioned killings, the [Scarfo] family has been decimated."

With twenty-eight senior players from the sixty-one members of the Scarfo family being either convicted, indicted or awaiting sentencing, forty-six percent of the organization was out of business, according to a December 1988 report by the Pennsylvania Crime Commission.

MAFIA TURF TURMOIL IN THE WAKE OF SCARFO'S DOWNFALL

"The vacuum that was left by the Scarfo prosecutions generates opportunities for somebody else," said John McGinley, head of the Newark office of the FBI early in 1989.

Organized crime had suffered a body blow all over the country and has become disorganized. With Scarfo out of the picture, a dispute soon arose between John Gotti, 48, and Vincent 'The Chin' Gigante, 61, head of the rival Genovese organization, over how to divide the North Jersey share of Scarfo's rackets empire.

Because Gotti was closer to Scarfo, he was targeted for death by the Genovese mob faction when he tried to encroach on certain areas of North Jersey dominated by the Genovese family *consigliere*, Louis 'Bobby' Manna. Gotti answered this threat against him and his brother by issuing contracts on the lives of Gigante and several other top Genovese family members in a bitter escalation of the blood feud between the two mob leaders.

Neither sought intervention of the underworld's ruling peacemaking body, the Mafia Commission, which led to speculation that the former powerful commission and its control over inter-family feuding, was now a thing of the past.

Col. Clinton Pagano, the head of the New Jersey State Police, summed up the situation this way: "The bottom line is economics. Gotti saw an opportunity on the Jersey side of the Hudson River, an area where the Genovese had long held property rights....And the feud just boiled upward."

Gotti and Gigante presented two sharply contrasting lifestyles as they walked openly about the streets of Manhattan. While Gotti dresses in expensively tailored suits over a turtleneck sweater with his hair neatly trimmed, Gigante prefers to live in the shadows. He is frequently seen strolling the streets of lower Manhattan in pajamas, a bathrobe and slippers. The FBI believes this bizarre getup to be a ruse by Gigante to feign senility in an attempt to thwart investigators. The FBI claims that he walks the streets to conduct business instead of doing it inside his Triangle Social Club on Sullivan Street since he fears that it may be bugged.

On March 6, 1989, six members of the Genovese family went on trial in the Federal District Court in Newark, New Jersey, indicted on fifty-two counts, one of which was the threat to kill Gotti and his brother.

FUTURE MAFIA WIPEOUTS

Since government officials had been so successful in wiping out the hierarchy of the Scarfo crime family and incarcerating the top leadership of that mob, it was hoped that the trial of the key members of the Genovese family and the Gambino family leaders later on, would lead ultimately to further Mafia family wipeouts all over America. The results of the Scarfo Mafia family prosecution will go down in the history books as an important first — a near total victory against the mob in one major region of the country.

Then the body at a point of flat and horizontal extension hit the roof of a car parked in front of the building and the sound it made was as a cannon going off, a terrible explosion of the force of bone and flesh, and what made me gasp was that he moved, the guy moved in that concavity of metal he had made, a sinuosity of bone-smashed inching, as if it was a worm there curling for a moment on the hot metal before even that degree of incredible life trembled out through the fingers.

-E. L. Doctorow[*]

34

A FUNERAL WREATH FOR 'FRANKIE FLOWERS'

THE GHOST OF 'FRANKIE FLOWERS' COMES BACK TO HAUNT 'LIL NICKY'

S CARFO'S troubles with the law were not over, however, as he and his cohorts awaited a long prison sentence similar to that meted out to his pal, 'Reds' Pontani. The Pennsylvania Common Pleas Court trial against Scarfo and eight of his associates had been oft postponed on the grounds of double jeopardy. But they were finally ordered to stand trial on January 24, 1989, by Judge Eugene Clark, Jr. for the murder of Frank 'Frankie Flowers' D'Alfonso.

Clark recognized that all but two of the six present defendants were among the seventeen Mafia members who had been found guilty two months earlier at the RICO trial.

Scarfo and his Mafia associates had originally been charged on July 1, 1987, with conspiring to murder D'Alfonso, and it took over a year and a half to overcome the stalling tactics by the defense to bring it to trial. 'Frankie Flowers' D'Alfonso, who

---

[*] *Billy Bathgate*, Random House, New York, 1989, (with permission)

was once described in testimony as "a major money maker for the mob" had been a close associate of Thomas Del Giorno and Angelo Bruno.

THE FLOWERS TRIAL GETS UNDERWAY AT LAST

In March 1989 the Flowers trial was scheduled to begin. It took three weeks of tedious questioning of 848 candidates before a final jury of twelve people was selected to try the nine defendants accused of conspiring to kill D'Alfonso on July 23, 1985.

The nine defendants were:

Nicodemo Scarfo, age 60;
Frank Narducci, age 34;
Phil Narducci, age 26 (the alleged triggerman);
Joe Ligambi, age 49 (another triggerman);
'Faffy' Iannarella, age 31;
'Chuckie' Merlino, age 48; and his brother
Lawrence 'Yogi' Merlino, age 33;
Nick 'the Whip' Milano, age 27; and
Eugene 'Gino' Milano, age 29.

The reason it took so long to select a jury was due mainly to the excuses offered by members of the jury panels as they took the witness stand for questioning by both the defense and the Commonwealth. Most of them were excused for physical ailments, including pregnancy and drug addiction. One young man became high on the list of unique favorites for dismissal when he strode into the courtroom, but then claimed he couldn't serve on the jury.

When asked by Scarfo's attorney, Simone, why he couldn't serve, he answered: "Death watch," while peering down the line of the nine accused defendants.

"I beg your pardon?" Simone asked.

"Death watch," the man repeated again, implying that he did not relish having to serve on a jury in which he might be forced to recommend a death penalty for the defendants.

"I have no further questions," Simone said curtly.

ONE DEFENDANT DEFECTS AT THE LAST MINUTE

On Tuesday, March 14th, the evening before the murder trial was to start, one of the defendants, Eugene Milano, secretly called the authorities from a prison phone, stating that he wished to cooperate with the law enforcement officials. He agreed to plead guilty to a third degree murder charge in exchange for information he possessed. This would get him a maximum sentence of ten to twenty years compared to his Mafia brethren who all faced life in prison or death on their first degree murder charges. The next morning (Wednesday), Milano rode with the other defendants in the regular Sheriff's van to the courthouse, but then was immediately separated from them on arrival at City Hall where the trial was to take place.

While the other eight Mafia members were waiting in a back room for the court to begin, they noticed that Gino was missing. Because of this unexpected turn of events, the Judge recessed court for the day. Simone announced to the media in the hallway: "Milano is a selfish crumb. It's brother against brother. It's the Civil War. He turned against his own brother [Nick] and the others to save his own life, forgetting the other defendants. He will probably turn state's witness to back up Del Giorno with some more lies. The jury will love him. I believe the Commonwealth hurt their case when he became a 'turncoat.'"

THE TRIAL BEGINS A DAY LATE

On the following day, March 16th, the long delayed trial got under way with an opening argument by Charles Grant, a young Assistant District Attorney who accused Scarfo of being the Crown Prince of the *La Cosa Nostra* in Philadelphia. Grant noticed that after Scarfo became head of the Bruno family, he sent two messages to 'Frankie Flowers' D'Alfonso for not showing enough respect and loyalty to the Mafia hierarchy.

The first message was delivered to 'Flowers', a small shop owner, in 1981. He was severely beaten, resulting in two broken cheekbones, two broken legs, several broken ribs and an injured eye socket, causing him to spend several months in a wheel chair.

Then, four years later, at a gathering of Scarfo family members in a Center City restaurant, the boss gave orders to kill

'Flowers'. This was the second message. The fatal hit took place on a warm, pleasant summer evening, July 23, 1985, as D'Alfonso was walking his dog one block from his home. He had just finished a chat with his old friend, Alex Marsella, at his South Philly deli.

Two men accosted him and shot him at close range in the head and chest. He collapsed on the sidewalk and died instantly. Several guns were found but no witnesses came forward to identify the assailants.*

When it came time for the defense to present their opening arguments, four lawyers, led by Simone, warned the jury that using Del Giorno and Milano as prosecution witnesses could result in "lousing up the government's case, acting like a gun that backfires." He let the jury know that "Del Giorno will have already fleeced the government out of at least $500,000 in return for his services, which would get him a safe trip off the electric chair, and out of jail."

Then the trial settled down to hearing a string of witnesses who described the killing of 'Frankie Flowers'.

THE 'TURNCOAT' RETURNS ONCE AGAIN TO THE STAND

Early in the trial, Thomas Del Giorno returned to the courtroom for one day to testify about the Scarfo-hatched plot to kill 'Flowers'. He told how the late Salvatore Testa and Eugene Milano had given 'Flowers' such a severe beating before the killing that when he was taken to Pennsylvania Hospital for repairs to his broken bones, 'Flowers' lied to the medicos, saying: "I got hit by a car," and they believed him.

During cross-examination on March 22nd by his old nemesis, Robert Simone, he did not buckle under the ruthless questioning hurled at him by Scarfo's attorney. When Simone accused Del Giorno, as he had done in earlier trials, of being tardy in paying his back income tax on his so-called ill gotten gains, Del Giorno

---

* It was not until Del Giorno went into the Federal witness protection program in 1986 that the names of the conspirators surfaced and indictments were issued for the nine defendants. The Flowers trial had to wait until all of the higher priority indictments and trials (RICO, Speed, etc.) were conducted as per negotiated agreements with the various state and federal government prosecutors.

dropped a broad hint to the jury that his opponent owed the government more than he did. Never once during the line of questioning did Simone hint at the fact that he himself owed the federal government $1.2 million in taxes and fines resulting from an earlier trial conviction against Simone.

When Del Giorno explained that after he completed his cooperation with the government as an informant/witness against the Mafia, he would somehow have to find the money to pay his tax debt, Simone interrupted him to ask: "Oh, in other words, there is no 'free lunch,' is that what you're saying?"

"If I don't have the money, I'll make arrangements to pay it back, little by little," shot back 'Tommy Del', "the same way some other people right in this courtroom have."

To this sharp reply, Simone quickly changed his line of questioning to a less controversial area. The jury got the point.

'GINO' MILANO FACES HIS BROTHER

On Tuesday, March 28th, the squat, pudgy Eugene 'Gino' Milano took the witness stand in the first court session after the Easter recess and under the questioning of Assistant District Attorney Brian McMongale he described his life of crime and why he decided to flip to the side of the law. He became a member of the Mafia after participating in the murder of Robert Riccobene and the attempted murder of Frank Martines, crimes for which he had been found guilty.

He expected to serve a long prison term for those crimes but hoped for a shorter term for his 3rd degree guilty plea for the killing of 'Frankie Flowers.' Milano sat in the witness chair, looking straight ahead with his hands clasped in front of him. Only twice did he briefly look over at the defendants when he was asked to identify Scarfo and Sal Merlino for the jury.

When asked the reason for his 'coming over,' Milano answered painfully: "I wanted to go on with my own life. It was not an easy decision because my brother sits over there. I tried to make a deal with the FBI to save my life." Milano, a graduate of South Philadelphia High School, with five brothers and two sisters, served for a time as a Children's Counsellor, but through his friendship with the late Sal Testa, he opted for a life of crime.

In October, 1981, under orders from Sal Testa, he was assigned the chore of beating up the late D'Alfonso, a man he hardly knew. "Sal had a Little League baseball bat and I had a piece of 18" steel. We ran out from behind a van at the corner of 10th and Christian Streets in South Philly, and I hit him all over the face with the pipe and Sal hit him on his lower body with the bat."

"When I hit 'Frankie Flowers' with the pipe, it didn't matter to me whether he was dead or alive. When Sal and I left him there, motionless, he could have been dead, yeh. We then ran down a nearby alley, ditched the bat, pipe and gloves. I did it because I wanted to be accepted by the mob and this was the way to gain their respect."

After that brutal beating of D'Alfonso, Milano was 'made' on Super Bowl Sunday in January, 1982, in Vineland, New Jersey. Scarfo presided at the ceremony. (His initiation into the Mafia was similar to that previously described by Caramandi.)

Milano then related how he had been ordered by his new *capo*, Del Giorno, in early 1985 to join a team of five to wipe out D'Alfonso. The other four Mafia members, picked by Scarfo himself to do the job, were: the two Narducci brothers, Joe Ligambi and 'Gino's' younger brother, 'Nick'. The communication from Scarfo for these five to make the hit was relayed by Del Giorno at the Scarfo family's clubhouse, an old plumbing supply shop located at Camac and Moore Streets in South Philadelphia.

The five attempts, four of them failed, to stalk and kill D'Alfonso were spread out over a period of several months in 1985. The first one took place in early 1985 when the conspirators met in a public parking lot at 9th and Christian Streets with two guns, two ski masks, gloves and an old Ford car with a faked registration so that it could not be traced.

"We had heard that D'Alfonso was going over to New Jersey to attend a funeral of a relative," said Milano, "but after getting into Frank Narducci Jr.'s new Mercedes, we were soon stopped by cops from the Organized Crime unit, so we went back to D'Alfonso's home block to wait for his return. When he did return with his wife and son, we decided not to shoot him there with his wife present, so we called it off."

The second failed attempt as related by 'Gino' occurred "when we received word that 'Flowers' was going to drive up the Expressway to his friend Maggio's house in suburban Gladwyn.

We followed him, but found no safe place to do the job since we didn't know the streets. Besides, it was Easter Sunday (1985) so we came home."

The third attempt was called off when they followed their prey to his son-in-law's house, but when they got there they discovered that Frank Narducci, Jr. was not sitting in the getaway car like he was supposed to be doing.

Following that fiasco, the group of mobsters stalked 'Flowers' for three months in the Spring of 1985. "All five of us followed him almost every day, morning and night." We used the local Pizza Shop, Stewart's Donut Shop and a fruit stand (near the famous Italian Market). We even got the key to the closed fruit stand at night because we could see D'Alfonso's home from there. But then my brother got a subpoena for 'staking' D'Alfonso in late May or early June, so I told Del Giorno." At this stage in the planned wipeout of D'Alfonso, the law authorities were still in the dark.

"He ordered me to tell my brother to stay away from 9th and Christian from then on. We did...and didn't hear about the killing until a month later when I heard it on the TV news that 'Frankie' was dead."

When Assistant D.A. Brian McMonagle showed the witness some small (8"x10") black and white photos of Scarfo crime family pictures, showing both Milano and Del Giorno basking in the sun at the boss's Fort Lauderdale mansion in August 1986 to prove that he was a member of the mob in good standing, the laid back Milano cooly identified his former brethren.

Just before the lunch break and before the cross-examination was to begin, 'Bobby' Simone went over to the witness stand and asked him: "When you told your mother last week that you would never testify against your brother, were you lying to her?"

McMonagle objected and the Judge sustained him, so the question was never answered.

After lunch, Simone tried to undermine the corroborating testimony of Milano that supported Del Giorno's earlier testimony without any major contradictions on the plot to kill D'Alfonso. "Bobby was punching at balloons," observed one veteran news reporter as Milano deftly shunted aside the attempts to make him lose his cool.

The witness did admit to running away and hiding in Pleasantville, New Jersey, after the D'Alfonso murder, since he was a co-conspirator, and also admitted to discussing the case "a little bit" with his brother and others after he was captured and incarcerated in Philadelphia's Holmesburg Prison. While languishing in prison, he also had an opportunity to read the piles of evidence, and confessions of both Del Giorno and Caramandi as well as listen to the FBI tapes.

Under penetrating questions by Simone, Milano finally confessed that his reason for flipping and calling the FBI to make a deal was to save his own skin.

"I tried to get my brother out of the case," he said, "Otherwise it could be life or the chair for both him and me. I'd rather not have to testify against my brother, since I have lost a great deal of sleep over my move. I didn't like beating 'Frankie Flowers', and I take no pleasure in testifying against my brother and the other defendants. But I *want* to be an honest man, which is more important than having to testify here....I always thought it was 'crazy' to do the job on D'Alfonso, but the rest did it because it was mob orders."

THE PROSECUTION AND DEFENSE BOTH REST

After the prosecution rested its case, Mrs. D'Alfonso, the widow of the slain mobster, approached the 41-year-old Assistant D.A. Charles Grant, and accused him during a break of not zeroing in hard enough against the eight Mafia defendants. The confident Grant stood by the bar that separated the defendants and lawyers from the rest of the courtroom observers and gently explained:

"I am not afraid of those guys. They aren't tough guys. They aren't men, but only sneaky cons. They only shoot you when there's two of them going after a victim."

The defense did not put any witnesses or defendants on the stand, but went right into their closing arguments, trying to debunk the credibility of Del Giorno and Milano. Ed Jacobs, Jr., whose client was Sal Merlino, the deposed underboss of the Scarfo family, reminded the jury of the 9th Commandment in the *Holy Bible* : "Thou shalt not bear false witness" — which he claimed both of the two chief government witnesses broke over and over.

"They are polluted, corrupt sources as well as convicted criminals," he said, "and they should not be believed."

Robert Madden, the lawyer for Francis Iannarella, argued that the jury should recognize the reasonable doubt in this case based on the facts that there were no witnesses to identify the persons who pulled the trigger, there were no fingerprints on the guns, no footprints, no fibers from any of the defendants' clothing and finally, no motive.

After each defense lawyer tried to convince the jury, the two big guns took over, the old pro Robert Simone, and the young prosecutor, Charles Grant.

Simone tried to deflect the jury's attention from their main task by imploring them to "think about the true conspiracy in this case in which the local press has shown nothing in the past four years, but Scarfo's face on the TV and in the papers. That is why only a few of you (out of 900) have never heard of Mr. Scarfo."

In his one-hour summation, he reminded the jury that they had been confined to a hotel, and that Scarfo was in jail, while both turncoat witnesses, Del Giorno and Milano, were out of jail. "What an irony that is," he said.

Once again, as he had done in previous trials, Simone characterized South Philadelphia Italian-Americans as the persecuted minorities of the 1980's. He compared the defendants with the persecuted victims of the Spanish Inquisition, the labor leaders of the 1930's, the Japanese Americans who were put into detention camps in the 1940's, the civil rights protesters of the 1960's, and the anti-Vietnam War activists of the 1970's, insisting that the Italian-Americans of South Philadelphia in the 1980's — who are now the objects of contemporary persecution — "just like to bet on ball games and play cards."

In his closing argument Simone suggested that "it wasn't Scarfo who wanted D'Alfonso killed, but rather — like the deaths of the old mob bosses Bruno and Phil Testa — that D'Alfonso's death was against the rules." He speculated that the murder was really Del Giorno's idea in retribution because 'Frankie Flowers' had stolen money from him when they were in the restaurant business together.

"The use of informers rewards crime and the criminals rather than punishing them," he said. "These informers know that nothing is going to happen to them. It causes the police to relax, so they feel they got the case sewed up and they don't need to search for guns and other evidence. Furthermore, Mr. Del

Giorno was a witness who violated almost every commandment that Moses brought down from the mountain."

Simone closed his appeal to the jury by spitting out: "You have all been brainwashed by the press and I look forward to a swift verdict that clears all of the defendants."

GRANT MARCHES TO HIS OWN DRUMMER

When it came to the Assistant D.A.'s turn to give the closing argument to the jury, Charles 'Joey' Grant assailed Simone's arguments and asserted that Scarfo and his seven co-defendants had conspired to murder in the first degree, and that they hunted their prey as a "group of criminals."

In his hour-and-a-half summation, Grant walked behind each defendant and repeated the role that each one played in the stalking and killing of 'Frankie Flowers'. He showed that the difference between the persecution of our labor leaders, Japanese Americans, anti-war activists and civil rights protesters in the past and the defendants was that the former had "laudable and meritorious goals."

Grant belittled Simone for his stretched analogy, saying: "For Mr. Simone in all his pomposity and arrogance to liken this group of criminals and equate them..."

He was cut off by Mr. Simone, who asked the Judge at a sidebar at the Judge's bench to declare a mistrial because Grant had identified the defendants as criminals. The Judge refused the request.

Grant used the defense description of Del Giorno and Milano as ravenous wolves and deftly extended it to the defendants. "Wolves run in packs," he sarcastically said. "Wolves are cowards...and we have all the wolves and the leader right here in this courtroom for the cowardly killing of D'Alfonso." As he walked behind each of the eight Mafia members, Grant reminded the jurors that "wolves seek their security in numbers for their own protection, and rarely do you find lone wolves. But in this case, both Del Giorno and Milano left the pack and they are now rats."

Then he reminded the jurors of the principle that: "when you hunt with the pack, you share in the kill and *also* the liabilities of the conspiracy. It takes more courage to be a 'lone wolf' and tell tales about the pack. Remember, not one of the defense lawyers called Milano a 'liar'."

Grant also reminded the jurors that: "'Gino' Milano found out that this [Scarfo's] family had *more* control over his own life than his real family. Do you ever see any women or children about in the photos? No! So 'Gino' fled from the clutches of the [mob] 'family.' He had gone to college and learned to read and write. He used his analytical processes and God-given intelligence to think that they [the jury] are going to convict me and the others. So he plead guilty."

Grant, a Georgetown University Law School graduate, hit back at Simone on his accusations against the press for crucifying his client. "Look at this headline," Grant said, showing a blown up copy of a May 27, 1981, *Philadelphia Daily News* front page to the jury. It reads: 'A new Don takes over the Philly Mob,' and the lead sentence is: 'The king is dead, Long Live the King!'

"But the new 'King' they were talking about then was *not* Scarfo, but Frank D'Alfonso. They were wrong. It *was* Scarfo who was the new boss...so let's not blame the press."

He then concluded his ninety minutes of histrionics before the jury, with a dramatic closing flourish. "The only way to get them [the mob] is to pluck someone from the inner sanctum (which we did). That's what it's all about."

(This remark was a replay of an earlier semi-humorous pitch to the jury on why he used Del Giorno and Milano as the keys to the prosecution's case. "We'd like to have brought you Jack and Jill from Chestnut Hill," said Grant, "but they don't know about this kind of stuff.")

It was 12:45 p.m. on April 4th, when the courtroom was inching towards a delayed lunch break, that Grant wound down his oratorical summation. Picking up the same murder pistol that Simone had used to brandish in the face of a witness days earlier, the mustachioed prosecutor said: "I did not object when Mr. Simone waved the pistol at a government witness, but remember, the last thing that Frank D'Alfonso remembered in his life was seeing this gun in his face by one of these brigands of death."

The court then recessed until the Judge charged the jury.

THE JURY DELIBERATES OVER A VERDICT

The next afternoon (April 5th), after deliberating for an hour and a half, the jury sent an ominous message to the Judge to explain the difference between first and third degree murder. A half-hour later they signalled that they had a verdict and they returned to a tense packed courtroom. Scarfo pressed his lips together as he and the others awaited the reading of the charges by the court clerk against Frank Narducci, Jr., whose own father was killed in a mob slaying engineered by Scarfo back in 1982.

"Guilty!" said the jury foreman, responding to the first conspiracy charge. He repeated the same verdict on the weapons charge, until he was asked about the murder charge. "Guilty. Murder in the first degree!" he answered. As the subsequent guilty verdicts rang out for the seven others in the caldron-like atmosphere of the courtroom, an eruption soon occurred in the family section.

Women relatives shrieked and cried, with several, like the mother of the two Narducci men, getting up, and running out sobbing from the back of the courtroom. Before she left, Adeline Narducci shouted at the jury: "You're all gonna die. You're murderers."

"Yeah, just like my father died, just like my father died!" shouted sarcastically Gina D'Alfonso, 31, the daughter of the murdered Frank, who sat on the opposite side of the courtroom.

"Fuck your father!" one of the defendants' wives shouted back, and the law enforcement officials quickly moved in to restore order and calm down the combatants.

After the jurors had been polled one-by-one, Gina and her sister, Michele Martines, 29, moved to the front of the courtroom and hugged the two prosecutors, Grant and McMonagle. "Justice has been done, but it took a long time," said Gina. "I wish they would have gotten Nicky Scarfo 40 years ago. My father and everyone else would still be alive."

Outside, in the newspaper-littered hallway, blocked off with yellow police-saw-horses, a distraught Adeline Narducci, the mother of Philip and Frank, Jr., repeated her denunciation of the jury to all who would listen.

"The judge was fair, very fair," she said amidst tears, "but the jurors shouldn't have one night's sleep. The jurors ought to die!"

A happy Charles Grant took a different view, however. "The jurors gave it their undivided attention and found the defendants guilty. The verdict sends a message: 'Don't come into state court thinking you're the mob and you're going to get away with anything.' Those days are over."

A glum Simone intoned later outside the courtroom that: "I don't think I'm going to get much sympathy from a jury that didn't even want to deliberate the case, a case that affects the lives of eight people."

The case was far from over, however. The jury still had one more chore: to recommend either a life sentence or death in the electric chair, according to the statutes of the Commonwealth of Pennsylvania relating to first degree murder convictions.

A TENTATIVE SENTENCE IS REACHED AT LAST

At 2:15 p.m. the next afternoon, June 6th, the defendants marched into the courtroom, smiling and waving at friends and relatives in the jammed courtroom #253, the largest in City Hall. Grant tried to introduce evidence of aggravated assault against D'Alfonso in the form of ricocheting bullets fired at the victim that could have endangered the lives of passersby on the fatal night, which if the Judge agreed, would have justified a death penalty for the defendants.

After listening to arguments from the defense and prosecution, Judge Clark opted for the lesser charge of mitigating circumstances. Police Officer John Finor, a local firearms expert, took the stand briefly in front of the jurors and admitted that the bullets which passed through the body of 'Frankie Flowers' would have been slowed down enough to prevent lethal ricochets.

But he denied 'Bobby' Simone's request to allow the serious illness of Scarfo's long-comatose son, Mark, as a reason for allowing a mitigating circumstance on behalf of his client.

Then the Judge made a decision about the final sentence. "Based on insufficient evidence presented by the Commonwealth to sustain the motion of aggravated assault [with its burden of aggravated circumstances], I will therefore remove the penalty decision from consideration by the jury."

At that moment, the relieved courtroom burst into applause, with hand clapping and shouts from the families and smiles on the faces of the relieved defendants. The Judge broke the pent-up tension when he said, "I will issue a mandatory verdict of life imprisonment with official sentencing to be issued at 9:30 a.m. tomorrow [Friday]."

"Thank you, your honor," shouted several relieved, happy wives, mothers, sons, daughters and fathers of the defendants. Each defendant hugged his own lawyer and others for their representation of their case during the trial. Scarfo turned to Simone, and asked with a half smile and in a voice loud enough to be overheard: "Will I be going to a State or a Federal prison?"

Outside the courtroom, a bitter Simone, with his eyes closed to the bright TV camera lights, expounded: "There is no question in my mind that this was a runaway jury that would have given the death penalty. They were chomping at the bit to put them in the electric chair. The Judge was right to take it away from the jury. The jury really didn't deliberate, unless they did it earlier when they weren't supposed to."

That night, District Attorney Ron Castille disagreed with Simone in a statement to the media, "The Judge made the wrong decision," he said. "It was really an issue for the jury. If the jury would have heard about their past history of violence and death, I'm sure they would have easily given them the death penalty which they deserve."

One of the jurors, Arthur Tribble, 60, agreed with the D.A.'s assessment. "During our deliberations of the defendants' guilt or innocence, everyone was in accord for life imprisonment," he said angrily. "Simone is a liar! I do not appreciate him saying that we were a runaway jury. We were not a runaway jury....It does not take intelligent people long to sum up evidence and what was presented to them. The concern for our personal safety did not affect us. No one feared anything."

The other jurors declined to comment.

CHARLES GRANT, A RISING STAR IN THE PHILADELPHIA LEGAL WORLD

District Attorney Ron Castille gambled in May, 1988, when he assigned young Grant to prosecute the D'Alfonso case, after the stunning acquittal of Scarfo and his clan in the Sal Testa case, which many courtroom observers attributed to the haughty and icy demeanor of Homicide Chief Barbara Christie who prosecuted that trial. Castille had known that Charles Joseph Grant had the rare combination of affability, skill and charm to work a jury, to conduct himself with poise before the Judge, and not to buckle under the acidic barbs of 'Bobby' Simone.

The dapper, well-dressed Grant had risen fast in his profession. The only child of a Connecticut couple who divorced when he was a child, Grant grew up with five stepbrothers after his mother remarried and for awhile with his six stepsisters born to his father's second wife. Graduating from Ohio University with a B.A. in creative writing, Grant first headed for New York City where he thought he was "going to become a famous writer."

But after teaching English to cadets in the New York Police Department, he decided that this route to fame and fortune would be too slow, so, looking for a new profession, he accepted a scholarship to Georgetown University Law School in Washington, D.C. He soon realized that he had made the right move. "I was born to this stuff," he said after his greatest courtroom victory. "I like the pressure because you have to perform. Grace under pressure — that's the classiest thing you can have."

Fresh out of law school, he first accepted a job as deputy attorney general in the U.S. Virgin Islands and then moved to Philadelphia's Homicide Division of the D.A.'s office in 1981. Common Pleas Judge Lynne M. Abraham, a distinguished jurist in the local court system, noted to me: "Every time he appeared before me in court, I had him marked for bigger things in his future. He was far superior to most of the Assistant D.A.'s who prosecuted cases before my bench."

Having served as a top prosecutor for 15 years, Grant has been giving serious thought to exploring a new career, possibly in broadcast journalism, where many observers feel he would be a natural. "This criminal thing is getting a little stale for me. I'm tired of talking about dead people and dealing with the families of dead people...yet I might be reluctant to miss the drama of the courtroom. It's very dynamic. People are always changing, the situation is always changing. Every courtroom is different," he said in a personal interview.

The flamboyant and crafty Grant knew from the beginning that his twin hopes for victory would come down to jury selection and his closing arguments. That is why he and his co-counsel Brian McMonagle chose a predominantly black jury of men between the ages of 40 and 60. "These are the people," he said, "who were least likely to know a lot about the Mafia" and not at all coincidentally — most likely to identify more closely with

Grant's black skin color.

Insisting on brevity, Grant kept the central issue of the murder case — and not the peripheral Mafia connections — in front of him at all times. He knew he was pitted against the highly-polished tactics of Robert Simone, and did not respond to the latter's volatile attacks until it came time for his own closing.

"I was waiting for the end," said the cocky Grant. "I didn't forget one thing; I was just storing them up one at a time. When I play chess, I'm not going to march down the middle of the board and knock your king down. I like to come from the angles, lull you into relaxing, and then come in and whack your head off."

And that's just what he did in the 'Frankie Flowers' trial. His tactics worked to perfection.

THE JUDGE MAKES IT OFFICIAL

At 10 a.m., Friday, April 7th, Judge Clark made a short statement to the eight defendants jammed in front of his bench with their lawyers behind them. "This is group therapy," several shouted in unison.

Clark responded, "This is not the final sentence, which will have to wait until post-trial motions [set for July 26, 1989] have been denied or settled. Since each of you have been found guilty of first degree murder, I must impose a mandatory sentence of life in prison, but I will hold that in abeyance until the other sentences [RICO, which could bring an expected 40-year Federal jail sentence] are imposed. I will order a mental health examination for all, and give your attorneys three weeks to file supplemental motions."

The trial was finally over and the clerk recessed the court by 10:15 a.m. The defendants hugged their lawyers one more time and then trooped out — back to Holmesburg Prison. As he was led away from the courtroom, Scarfo waved to his son, Nicky, Jr., and his sister in the back of the courtroom and said with a sheepish grin: "God knows where I'll be."

Outside, in the hall, a happy D.A., Ron Castille (running for re-election as an unopposed Republican candidate in a Democratically-controlled city) expounded enthusiastically on the meaning of the court decision for the TV cameras, radio, tape recorders, and press scribes:

"This was a victory in the war against organized crime. It's V-M day in Philadelphia — Victory against the Mafia. It's a great day for law enforcement. We will fight all appeals. The Mafia is decimated as far as the *La Cosa Nostra* is concerned, and we will keep these men in jail. Grant did a great job prosecuting the case. We were disappointed that the Judge took the decision away from the jury, but we're happy for the conviction and the life sentences. The only way they can get out of jail now is a commutation by some Governor, but no governor would dare let them go with their past histories of violence....There are some fringe Mafia players left out there, but we and the Federal law enforcement officials will be watching them."

While Castille was speaking, the defense lawyers and the defendants' families walked over to the nearby swanky Four Seasons' Hotel for a victory celebration. The only thing they had to celebrate this time, however, unlike the orgy a year earlier when a similar crowd of Mafia members' families held a wild party after their acquittal in the Testa murder case, was that the lives of their menfolk had been spared.

THE REAL MEANING OF THE VERDICT

For the *first* time in modern American organized crime history, a mob boss had been found guilty of murder in the first degree. All others had either been assassinated, died in bed, or convicted of lesser charges of racketeering, income tax evasion, drug running, extortion or loansharking. Not since the late Lewis 'Lepke' Buchalter* was arrested on a murder charge in 1939, had a Mafia leader been so charged and convicted. 'Lepke' was the boss of Murder, Inc. which was associated with the Mafia but he was not a blood member of the mob. He was executed in 1941.

So, for the first time in half a century, a crippling and final blow to the Scarfo crime family came from a relentless and multi-pronged legal attack against its bloody roots that spanned a decade of pursuit by law enforcement officials in two states and at three levels, Federal, State and Local.

Although Scarfo had relished his role in the spotlight as a Lit-

---

*A contemporary of 'Lucky' Luciano, Meyer Lansky and Vito Genovese

tle Napoleon-type gangster who had established himself as a mob
boss like no other in America, his days of glory were now over.
Despite thousands of indictments and hundreds of convictions
around the country against other Mafiosi leaders and subordinates, this was the *first* time that a Mafia Don, the boss himself,
had been convicted of murder.

The shootings and murders that marked Scarfo's short reign
of power were in sharp contrast to the rather violence-free 20-
year rule of his immediate predecessors, Angelo Bruno and Phil
Testa. Ironically, the murder of 'Frankie Flowers' D'Alfonso
was the last in a line of brutal killings that, at that time, seemed to
solidify Scarfo's exalted power base.

But this last in a line of what Del Giorno later called a series
of "senseless killings," echoed the prophetic 1987 report of the
Pennsylvania Crime Commission, which predicted that these
murders would eventually bring down the mob boss.

"Scarfo's failed leadership was directly related to his uncon-
tested reliance on indiscriminate use of violence," the commission
noted. "His exercise of naked, brutal power destroyed whatever
loyalty he may have fostered in his subordinates and caused some
to look to law enforcement for protection."

As the crime commission so accurately predicted two years
earlier, Scarfo's maintenance of control over his crime family
through fear and violence led to his own downfall. "Scarfo has
proven to be an ineffective and bumbling leader," the 1987 report
also noted. "He has spent nearly one third of his limited five-year
reign incarcerated. Historically, it is unheard of for a mob boss
to spend that much time in jail. Assuming that he is convicted
and sentenced to a long jail term, this will effectively end his
reign as the Philadelphia [mob] boss."

The commission's prediction came true, not once, but twice.
Once for a RICO conviction in 1988, and once for first degree
murder in 1989.

Through his "ruthless, vicious and violent terrorization," as
Frederick Martens, the Executive Director of the Pennsylvania
Crime Commission, put it, Scarfo went too far. Eventually, as
Federal prosecutor Lou Pichini observed, "If you live by the
sword, you die by the sword." And that's what Scarfo did to
himself and his crime family. 'Lil Nicky's' career as top boss of
the old Bruno family was fraught with the seeds of self-destruc-

tion brought on by the blood feuds and ever shifting alliances.

The last act in this semi-classical tragedy featured the switch in loyalties of 'Gino' Milano, who Simone labeled a "crumb," for taking the stand against his own brother. The defense didn't believe that this 'turncoat' could help the prosecution's case, and they did not ask for a new jury, which they could have done. But this miscalculation boomeranged, because 'Gino' was believable, testifying against his own flesh and blood. The defense had been caught in a Catch 22 situation, since they knew that any delay in the start of the trial and the long and harrowing process of selecting a new jury, would give Grant and the prosecution more time to rehearse and prep Milano.

In the end, Milano turned out to be a cool and effective backup witness to Del Giorno, because he did not appear to be rehearsed, nor did he make any attempt to dramatize his reluctant role in the planning and stalking of D'Alfonso. Neither did he wilt under the stilettos thrown at him during the cross-examination by the defense.

"They really didn't really know 'Gino'," remarked a source close to the case. "Scarfo really didn't know him well. 'Gino' didn't like a lot of those guys. He was close to the late 'Salvie' Testa, his friend, and Testa was the one who taught him about the ways of the Mafia."

· In his recent best-selling crime novel, *The Seduction of Peter*,[*] Lawrence Sanders had one of his characters ask the question: "You know the three biggest money makers in the world, don't you? General Motors, the Mafia and the Vatican. The mob has the smallest gross income of the three, but when it comes to net profit — *mamma mia* !"

For Nicky Scarfo, his money-making days via the elbow, street tax, bookmaking, drug pushing and loansharking pipelines are now over. There are no more *mamma mia* days of exultation and frolics at Casablanca South in the Florida sun for 'Lil Nicky' and his soldiers and *capos*; now there are dark cells behind prison bars.

[*] Berkley Books, New York, 1984.

Democratic contrivances are quarantine measures against the
ancient plague, the lust for power. As such, they are very necessary
and boring.

-Friedrich Nietzsche

35 THE FUTURE OF ORGANIZED CRIME AS A POWER IN AMERICA

WILL repeated prosecutions and prison bars put the Mafia out
of business? Not so, say most law enforcement observers
who feel that something more is still needed to eradicate this cancer in our society. The RICO law is helpful, in that it not only
allows prosecutions against criminal organizations, but also provides civil action to seize their assets whether it be cash, cars or
mobsters' homes.

THE DECLINE OF THE MAFIA IN PHILADELPHIA

In a press interview, Carl P. Brown of the Pennsylvania
Crime Commission interpreted the late 1980's setback of the
Mafia in the Philadelphia area as being indicative of what was
going on nationwide. He noted that by early January, 1987, at
least eight Mafia leaders had been convicted in New York of
racketeering and sentenced to prison terms ranging from 40 to
100 years. He also observed that top Mafia leaders in Cleveland
and Kansas City had also been successfully prosecuted in recent
years. So what happened in Philadelphia was not unique.

But Brown warned that current successes did not mean that
organized crime's activities or influence would end in the USA.
The continued prosperity of organized crime and new gimmicks
attempted by the younger members or retired mobsters to seize
control of the leaderless families should keep the local, state and

federal investigators ever vigilant to prevent further outbreaks and to prevent the blatant resurrection of the Mafia.

GOTTI LOOKS TO THE FUTURE OF THE MAFIA

Shortly after he became boss of the Gambino crime family in New York, John Gotti was heard on tape (played in a courtroom in December, 1987) predicting to an associate that if he was lucky enough not to go to jail, that he would be able to build a strong organization that could last 30 years.

"The law is going to be tough with us," said the only New York-based Mafia crime leader to escape imprisonment after the 1987 spring trials, "If I can only get a year run without being interrupted...to put this thing together...[then] they could never break it...[or] destroy it. Even if we die, [it] would be a good thing. It's a hell of a legacy to leave!"

THE IMPACT OF THE FEDS' MOVES AGAINST THE MAFIA

Rudolph Giuliani, the crusading former U.S. Attorney for the Southern District of New York, who had been successfully orchestrating the recent major anti-Mafia court suits, put it bluntly: *"The Mafia will be crushed!"* He took as a personal affront the damage done to law-abiding Italian-American citizens like himself by the negative image that the Mafia has created in the minds of the general public.

C. Robert Blakey, a Notre Dame law school professor who helped draft the 1970 RICO statute as the major prosecutional tool now being used against organized crime, echoed Giuliani, when he remarked: "It is the twilight of the Mob. It's not dark yet for them, but the sun is going down."

John Hogan, the Chief of the FBI's New York office, insisted that, "We are out to demolish a multi-headed monster and all its tentacles and support systems and followers. They are bleeding and demoralized."

Many cynics believe that these grand goals expressed by law enforcement officials can never be achieved, but they have admired the tenacious determination exercised by the current crew of prosecutors around the country in the struggle to bury the Mafia and its camp followers.

Over the past five years, federal attorneys, the FBI and organized crime strike forces have put together a series of RICO cases that have had a startling impact on the national and regional hierarchy of the Mafia. The successful prosecutions have included the convictions and jailings of mob bosses in New York, Chicago, Milwaukee, Boston, New Orleans, Kansas City and Philadelphia. 1987 was called the "worst year for the Mafia" in the words of Rudolph Giuliani. With the court battles won in most cases, the Mafia became severely crippled in its ability to yield its formerly awesome power of intimidation and shakedowns of both legitimate and illegitimate business operations.

In a September, 1986, cover story on "The Mafia on Trial" in *Time* magazine, the editors concluded that: "The combination of prosecutorial pressure and the slipping of family ties may be feeding upon itself, creating further disunity and casting a shadow over the Mob's future. Certainly, when the old timers go to prison for long terms, they lose their grip on their families, particularly if ambitious successors do not expect them to return. Younger bosses serving light sentences can keep operating from prison, dispatching orders through their lawyers and visiting relatives. They may use other, less-watched inmates to send messages. Prison mail is rarely read by censors."

Most observers of the workings of the mob feel that the clannish Italian-American communities in our big cities have grown away from their immigrant beginnings. The Mafia is no longer replenishing itself with younger blood the way it did in the '20's through the '50's. But the Mafia still acts like a bloodsucker to milk not only the manufacturer, but ultimately the consumer.

The old techniques of law officers around the country "just helped to speed the succession along," said Rudolph Giuliani. The new approach appears to be striking the Mafia on all fronts to "peel their empires" down to the roots, Giuliani insisted. "It is not an unrealistic goal to crush them!"

THE LAST GASPS OF THE AMERICAN MAFIA FAMILIES

Joel Friedman, the head of the Philadelphia Organized Crime Strike Force, summed up the motivation that will keep some form of underworld crime organization alive. "As long as there is human greed you are going to get organized groups preying upon society," he said. "But I think you can shift the equilibrium in favor of society and a free form of government, and that we've done [in our victorious court cases.]"

In April 1988, FBI Director William Sessions summed up the successes of the federal and state war against the Mafia since 1981 in testimony before a U.S. Senate Subcommittee. He noted with pride that 1,000 members or associates of the Mafia had been convicted and sentenced to prison.

"The hierarchies of the five New York *La Cosa Nostra* Families have been prosecuted and similar prosecutions have crippled the LCN hierarchies in Boston, Cleveland, Denver, Kansas City, Milwaukee, New Jersey and St. Louis," he said in a report submitted to the Senate's Permanent Subcommittee on Investigations. Prosecution of the Scarfo organization on the RICO charges was still pending when he made his assessment.

He stated that in New York, unlike Philadelphia, the indictments, arrests and prison terms of thirty mob officials in several crime families did not have the disruptive effect on the day-to-day operations of organized crime there, as it soon would have in Philadelphia following the late-1988 RICO convictions. This statement was based on the fact that the Bonanno family had a reputed 100 members, while the Genovese and Gambino families each contained 250 to 300 members.

In the business which the organized crime families dominated, i.e., bookmaking, drug distribution, loansharking and gambling, the front line operations are usually carried out by non-Mafia mob associates. These types of illegal underground businesses would continue to operate whether or not the Mafia soldiers were there to collect their weekly street tax to help sustain the health and welfare of the members of various crime families, and to pay their defense lawyers.

In the wake of the sentencing of Pontani, Scarfo's once mob heir apparent, U.S. Prosecutor Peter Harvey observed: "I think you'll see a number of independent operators, loan sharks, narcotics dealers and bookmakers surfacing. But at some point, they will ultimately affiliate with another crime group. They have to. They need the muscle...for their own protection and to eliminate competition."

IS THE MAFIA IN A PERMANENT ECLIPSE?

In recent years there has been a plethora of evidence that the twilight of the gangsters and their Mafia families is upon us.

"Contrary to popular mythology," wrote Jacob Weisberg in a recent *New Republic* essay on "The Mafia and the Melting Pot," "*La Cosa Nostra* has never been a centrally directed conspiracy, here or in Italy. It can easily survive decapitation....The Mafia kingpins are adept at conducting diplomacy from prison cells.

"In fact, the Mafia is showing symptoms of internal maladies far more dangerous than its current legal tribulations." According to Weisberg, some of these symptoms are the lack of respect for the aging mob leaders around the country by the young, the growing number of dissident members who are breaking the Code of Silence, the independence of the younger mobsters both inside and outside the Mafia, and the inability of the older leaders to keep up with societal change.

According to a recent New York City Police Department report, the average age of local Mafiosi is over sixty. To some observers, this fact can be interpreted as a sign of terminal anemia. By 1950, there were signs that the Mafioso's traditional function was beginning to change. Wealth alone, rather than the traditional Mafia enterprises, began to confer honor and respect, reflecting deeper changes in Italian-American society. Throughout the 1950's and 1960's, crimes of honor, most notably murder, declined precipitously in most cities, except in the Philadelphia area where the Mafia infighting ascended to a new high in the late '60's and '70's.

Often the Mafioso's role in the decade of the '60's became more and more that of "a common criminal, a modern urban gangster who had neither popular roots nor popular backing, occasionally supported, sometimes tolerated, and sometimes suppressed by the authorities," so wrote Pino Arlacchi in his book, *Mafia Business: The Mafia Ethic and the Spirit of Capitalism.*[*]

As the Mafia became 'marginalized,' it sought refuge in new ways of making money, i.e., in construction, control of roofers, truckers, and trash handlers, unions, credit and politics.

In the '70's, a new Mafia began to emerge, an entrepreneurial one, which tried to regain its lost place in society by the only measure left open to them: capital accumulation. Mafia violence reasserted itself nationwide in the '70's. The Mafia applied new methods of moneymaking with a strange mixture of entrepreneurial innovation and old Mafia methods, according to

[*] Verson, New York, 1987.

Arlacchi's thesis. The discouragement of non-Mafia competitors gave the Mafia firms immediate access to new financial capital.

HOW THE MAFIA COULD BE CONFRONTED BY THE LAW

Although Arlacchi's book was mainly an analysis of the Sicilian and Calabrian Mafia, this sociologist, who teaches at the University of Calabria and serves on Italy's anti-Mafia Commission, holds views which may profitably be applied to the American scene. Already, the American Mafia had achieved one leg up on the old country counterparts by moving into such areas as labor racketeering, with its domination of the construction industry, for example, in many large urban areas.

Arlacchi invoked Professor Joseph Schumpeter's classic notion of animal spirits to prove that there is an aggressive, irrational element in all capital accumulation, whether it is made by the Mafioso entrepreneur or a capitalistic-oriented businessman.

But there is a significant difference between the typical capitalist and the Mafia-type criminal. The former does not gun down his competition, while the latter seems to have no qualms about it. Arlacchi feels that the only way to attack organized crime in America or anywhere in the world is to recognize it for what it has become and not approach it by traditional means.

His prescription is two-fold: (1) that we attack the Mafia from an international base and (2) that we think in terms of the underlying economic structures — the banks, markets and accumulated capital. He recommends seizing illegally obtained assets which will deprive the Mafia and its sister organizations of their reason for being, and erecting barriers between "clean" and "dirty" capital by regulating offshore banks that have been used to launder money.

In his late 1987 sensationalistic TV documentary, "The Sons of Scarface" (*Tribune Broadcasting*), Geraldo Rivera noted that the Sicilian and Italian-dominated mobs have been yielding their hard won turf to leaner, and sometimes meaner, violent mobs based in South America and Asia.

One of the reasons for this shift was the fact that the old Southeast European-rooted mobs never adapted very well to the exigencies of the drug trade, which has become the most important and lucrative form of contemporary criminal activity in recent years, dwarfing traditional Mafia enterprises of extortion, robbery, protection, etc., in the amounts of violence and money that it generates.

THE CHINESE CHALLENGE THE MAFIA

Nature and politics abhor a vacuum. This truism applies to the control of underworld economics both here and abroad. During the pre- and post-World War II years, the various Mafia families carved out their territories, running their illegal multi-billion-dollar enterprises for years until they were caught up in the coils of the law.

One branch of illegal activities, drug importation and distribution, particularly the control of the heroin and cocaine traffic, had been the almost exclusive preserve of the Mafia for generations. But following the major prosecutions in 1986-87 of mob leaders in New York by the Federal government, a decline in the Mafia's traditional grip on the drug traffic became apparent to Federal law enforcement officials, particularly in the New York area.

A new ethnic element began to surface as they moved in to grab a substantial slice of the heroin imports: Chinese-Americans. This new group of traffickers began to dominate the business by flooding the Northeast American drug market in 1987 with huge shipments of Southeast Asian heroin, or "China White," which is among the world's purest forms of this high-priced drug.

The smuggling of multi-million-dollar packets of this substance into the U.S. by plane and ship from North Burma via Thailand had suddenly become noticeable to Federal narcotics agents as they trailed sophisticated and bold Chinese criminal organizations which had formerly been active in prostitution and extortion, but had played second fiddle to the Mafia organizations in the imported drug business. Law enforcement agencies had previously concentrated on the Mafia since they lacked sufficient information about the Chinese elements.

Early in 1987, Federal drug agents had already noted that Chinese criminals had become the dominant force in the city's multi-billion-dollar heroin industry. But since then, law enforcement officials had become increasingly alarmed by the rapid growth of sophisticated Chinese criminal activities in other underground operations.

As the organized Chinese crime operations expanded in New York in the latter months of 1987 into extortion, prostitution, loansharking, gun smuggling, murder, and illegal drugs, federal law enforcement agencies began to take even more notice with this movement into the vacuum created by the decline of the Mafia. It became evident that Chinese organized crime had spread well beyond the confines of Chinatown in Manhattan, and there was a fear that eventually this new element "could achieve as much wealth, power and influence as Italian organized crime has had over the last half century," according to Peter Kerr, a *New York Times* research reporter.

Because of this expansion, the Administrator of the Federal Drug Enforcement Administration (FDEA), authorized the agency's New York office to double the number of agents in 1988 to pursue the Chinese criminals who had moved into new rackets.

"Chinese criminals are the No. 1 emerging organized crime group in New York — not just in drugs, but in many, many things," said Janet Goldman, a senior special agent with the Federal Immigration and Naturalization Services. "Their activities are no longer limited to Chinatown. It has spread to the five boroughs, Long Island and upstate."

Although crime in Philadelphia's burgeoning Chinatown appeared to be well under control in early 1988, there was no question that criminal elements in that section of town were intent on trying to imitate their New York brethren ninety miles to the North.

In Hong Kong, which is being returned to Mainland Chinese control by Great Britain in 1997, young Chinese entrepreneurial criminal elements see the USA as a continent fertile with opportunity to spawn their illegal activities. With the Chinese population swelling in the big cities from both Taiwan and the mainland, and the Mafia losing its grip in the U.S., the members of the Chinese secret societies, or "triads" have migrated here, using their contacts with one another to start up new criminal enterprises.

Although they are still not as active or as flamboyant as the Mafia families, they are making inroads into the rackets, often creating new alliances with the aging Mafia. For example, Chinese operators of gambling houses in New York have recently entered into agreements with the Mafia in Chinatown to operate bookmaking operations on horse racing. The Chinese operators of one bookmaking operation in a restaurant located near an Off Track Betting office are known to be paying a protection fee to the Italian-American Mafia figures who still dominate the sports bookmaking industry.

But with increasing talk and restlessness among younger and bolder Chinese criminals about the Mafia being vulnerable, this element has already replaced many Mafiosos in selling Southeast Asian heroin directly to the drug pushers in the poor neighborhoods.

Between August and the end of December, 1987, it was estimated that the share of New York City's illegal heroin market, controlled by Chinese Mafia-type criminals, had risen sharply to between sixty and seventy percent, up from a mere forty percent in mid-year. Since New York is the central hub of this drug traffic — with spokes fanning out to Boston and Philadelphia among other cities — it is not too difficult to perceive the switch from Italian Mafia control to Chinese control of the rackets for the rest of the twentieth century and beyond.

Following a similar pattern to the Mafioso in past decades in this century, the younger Chinese criminals have disregarded warnings from their elders that the drug business is too dangerous. They do not stay away from this lucrative business, just as Scarfo's boys could not resist the temptation to muscle in on a sure thing.

One New York Chinese person familiar with the doing of the younger ethnic criminals in his Chinatown sector commented: "The youngsters think they are aggressive and tough, and a lot of Italians are getting old. The latter can put people in cement, but we Chinese can shoot them out on the street."

If the past patterns hold true, there is reason to believe that the new ethnic mobsters coming from Asian and Hispanic roots will ultimately decline only when they begin to blend in and become accepted by the general society. As law enforcement has become more sophisticated with its legal RICO weapons and its electronic bugs and video tapings, it makes it more difficult for the old-time mobsters and even the new ones to continue with their old fashioned methods, ignoring the law.

What the law enforcement officials have yet to learn is how

the new Asiatic and Hispanic criminal cultures operate, as contrasted with the methods of the old style Mafia. To penetrate them now before they are assimilated will require government crime fighters to take heavy doses of foreign languages, sociology and psychology.

Barbara Christie, Philadelphia's Chief of the Homicide Unit in the District Attorney's Office, commented: "Maybe we will have to start some in-house seminars for our surveillance officials in Spanish and Mandarin so that they will understand what is going on in the conversations between the new type of drug dealers when they bug them for information and evidence."

PROOF POSITIVE OF THE CHINESE AMERICAN, SOUTHEAST ASIAN DRUG TAKEOVER

On February 20 and 21, 1989, Federal agents and the New York City police seized more than 800 pounds of heroin in Queens, New York, confiscating over $3 million and arresting 19 people linked to a major Southeast Asian heroin network. The city and the Federal authorities noted that this was the "largest drug seizure yet made in the United States."

Working under the code name, "Operation White Mare," more than 100 FBI agents and city police officers raided three locations, culminating an 18-month international investigation involving police agencies from New York City to Hong Kong. However effective this raid was, it did not end the heroin drug trafficking in the New York area but only served to jack up the prices.

Andrew J. Mahoney, the U.S. Attorney for the Eastern District of New York, declared in a *New York Times* article that these raids greatly hurt a Chinese heroin ring operation in the city and its environs, causing them to lose $1 billion worth of the drug, $3 million in cash and the arrest of 45 figures worldwide linked to the ring.

The head Chinese Mafia figure to be arrested in the sweep was Fok Leung Woo, a 71-year-old Chinatown liquor store owner and former Chairman of the Chinatown Democratic Club. Since the Italian-American Mafia figures were in eclipse, New York City law enforcement officials estimated that half of New York's 250,000 heroin addicts had been supplied by the new Fok-led mob.

Mahoney concluded that "this case, along with some other cases, is clear proof that the Chinese are responsible for seventy to eighty percent of the heroin that is smuggled into New York." The officers involved in the undercover operation had found most of the heroin packed into hollowed-out rubber wheels, packed in over 250 crates and driven from Los Angeles in rental trucks. Of the 31 drug pushers charged in the conspiracy to import heroin, fourteen were already discovered to be in jail in various cities running from Detroit to San Francisco to Singapore.

A new Oriental Mafia was rising from the ashes of the old Italian-Sicilian Mafia in urban America to rule the underworld.

THE BLACK MAFIA TRIES ITS WINGS

With so many members of the Italian-American Mafia in the Philadelphia Atlantic City area either in jail or indicted, it was obvious to law enforcement officials that some group would try to muscle in on the territory formerly dominated by Scarfo and his crime family.

Just before Thanksgiving time in the late fall of 1987, Willie Byrd, a special agent in charge of the Southeast region for the Pennsylvania Crime Commission, noticed a pattern of groups of young Black males driving around in jeeps and BMWs and dealing drugs, primarily cocaine. They called themselves the Junior Black Mafia or the Young Black Mafia, and they brazenly challenged the Jamaican drug dealers in Southwest Philadelphia to control the lucrative territory in that area of the city.

Other informants corroborated Byrd's observations, and linked three convicted drug dealers to the newborn organizations. One of them, Michael Youngblood, who recently surfaced as a federal informant, had previous ties with the Scarfo crime family.

The rising cast of characters has adopted such high-style symbols of their gangs as diamond encrusted rings with the initials JBM (Jr. Black Mafia) and other names like the Shower Posse, Dog Posse and the Dunkirk Boys, as they have spread throughout the West, Southwest and Germantown] sections of Philadelphia.

The growing violence involving a Jamaican drug ring that allegedly has netted $100,000 a day in Philadelphia has alarmed police since there have been over thirty homicides in the past few years that investigations have shown to be directly related to the gang-drug wars between the Jamaicans and native Black Americans for control of the turf.

Informants have placed the numbers of gang members at somewhere between fifteen and fifty, with many members having no previous criminal records.

It has been difficult for the law to obtain the names of the new cocaine, heroin and other drug dealers who have recently surfaced in what is now loosely recognized as the new Black Mafia.

But what is known to the law is that newly inducted members have begun to take on the trappings of successful upwardly mobile, young urban professionals. They wear expensive clothes, frequent fine restaurants and trendy clubs and drive high-priced (but not flashy) autos with fancy stereos.

"They're entrepreneurs," said a Philadelphia Police Department investigator, "and they believe in displaying the trappings of their success. That's why we are seeing the jewelry and the cars. It's awareness and status in the neighborhoods. They take the position that it's no use to be successful if no one knows about it."

According to police observers, at least one meeting took place at a clubhouse in South Philadelphia in February 1987 between remnants of the Scarfo organization and members of the new Junior Black Mafia. Because of increased police surveillance, however, several members of the JBM have melted down their diamond identification rings and medallions so they would not be so easily recognized.

"We don't want to create a Mafia mystique with this new group like we did with the Italians...," said Officer Martens from the Pennsylvania Crime Commission, "but we also don't want to ignore what's going on now and in the future."

The emerging Black Mafia, along with the rising Asian and Hispanic gangs profiting from the burgeoning drug rackets, has presented new challenges to law enforcement officialdom. Unlike the *La Cosa Nostra*, which communicated with one another through hand signals, winks, and code words, the new Black, Hispanic and Asian Mafia members have been operating mainly in their own ethnic communities, masked in the secrecy of their own cultures and languages.

THE FBI'S ASSESSMENT OF ORGANIZED CRIME IN THE LATE '80'S

The current FBI Director, William S. Sessions, was optimistic when testifying recently before a U.S. Senate investigations subcommittee on organized crime, when he said that, "it would soon be possible to remove [organized Mafia-type] crime as a significant threat to American society." But his FBI Executive Assistant Director, Oliver Revell III, warned that "emerging criminal organizations, such as Asian gangs, financed by huge profits from drug trafficking, gambling, loansharking and extortion," may soon step in to fill the void created by the neutralization of the *La Cosa Nostra* families.

It is these new underground families, still veiled in a cloak of silence much like that of the Mafia families, that will bear watching in the future. With the twilight of the Italian-American mob families, brought about by national and local prosecutions of the leaders and soldiers of the Mafia, the pastures for these new elements of organized crime appear ready for cultivating.

In time, these embryonic groups may possibly present a far more serious challenge to officers of the law than did the once powerful dinosaur — known as the Mafia.

Frederick T. Martens, the Executive Director of the Pennsylvania Crime Commission, in presenting the annual report of his group to the people of the Commonwealth in mid-April 1988, noted that these new crime groups are at the beginning of their growth, like little entrepreneurs in the business world on their way up.

"There's going to be a shakeout, violence is going to be used. Better products are going to be used. And in the end, there's going to be a merger, and a bigger, more sophisticated organization — unmatched since the early days of the *La Cosa Nostra*."

Understanding these groups is a must for society, he pointed out, adding: "We don't want to be in the same boat we were forty years ago as far as the LCN was concerned. It took us forty years to understand *La Cosa Nostra*. Our concern is to be ahead of what's coming. *I don't think we are.*"

THE PENNSYLVANIA CRIME COMMISSION SPEAKS OUT IN 1989

A year later, on April 25, 1989, the Pennsylvania Crime Commission issued its annual report. The ninety-two pages documented how organized crime in Philadelphia continued to expand beyond the old Italian-American-dominated Mafia monopoly, which had been so severely decimated after the arrests and successful convictions of Scarfo and the leading members of his crime family.

Martens pointed out at the time the report was issued that: "There have always been other groups. To believe that taking Scarfo out is going to knock out organized crime is to have a distorted view of what organized crime is.

"Part of the problem of why we sometimes don't look at these other characters is that their names don't end in a vowel. We've got an erroneous belief, for example, that Blacks can't be involved in organized crime....The history is totally opposite of that. They've been involved for 40 years."

Martens stressed that the older Black and Chinese crime organizations have institutionalized their operations, avoided publicity and seldom resorted to violence. The newer groups, however, attracted by quick profits generated by the crack and cocaine trade, are more transient, more prone to violence and involved in ever-shifting alliances.

Based on the PCC's report, here is a listing of the four major (non-Mafia) organized crime groups in Philadelphia and their status as of 1989.

The Junior Black Mafia: Bullets and violence have become the main calling cards of this group of young mobsters who had established their own narcotics network in sections of the Northeast, Southwest, South, West Philadelphia and Germantown sections of the city.

"This JBM is intent upon establishing itself as a respected organization in the Philadelphia criminal underworld," the commission report concluded. They also noted, however, that this brazen attempt to take over the shattered turf of the Scarfo mob will most likely "be stifled by the same traits that hampered and eventually crippled the Scarfo LCN family — an unusual high visible profile and a penchant for violence."

"They're essentially cowboys," Martens commented.

The Jamaican Posses: The Jamaican immigrant criminals, who dubbed themselves posses, operated in several sections of the city, where they had established gatehouses. These locations were fortified drug distribution centers from which cocaine and crack were sold. "Police officials have expressed concern over the cold-blooded ruthlessness that characterizes this group," the commission report noted.

Asian Organized Crime: In contrast to the high-profile, flamboyant emerging crime groups like the JBM, a well-established and generally low key organized crime operation flourishes in Chinatown, according to the commission. Alliances have been forged there, according to the PCC investigators, between community business and benevolent societies — known as the *tongs* and organized street gangs.

Some of these new gangs, called 'The Flying Dragons,' 'Ghost Shadows,' and 'Tung On Boys,' provide security for the illegal gambling casinos that have been linked to the *tongs*. The gangs also are engaged in the usual extortion, narcotics trafficking and prostitution.

The report listed the names of seven massage parlors or health clubs located in Chinatown, most of which were part of a nationwide prostitution ring. Asian women, working as prostitutes, travel a circuit that includes New York, Houston, San Francisco and Boston — as well as Philadelphia.

Black Numbers Rackets: The largest numbers operator in West Philadelphia, according to the commission report, is James W. Nichols, who was arrested in 1988 on bribery and racketeering charges. Nichols, 66, allegedly heads an organization employing more than 40 illegal number writers and grosses more than $10 million annually.

The commission investigators called Nicholas one of the traditional, old-time Black rackets operators (like the late Angelo Bruno of the Mafia). They seldom attract attention to themselves, preferring to operate through a network of illegal 'banks' and 'lead houses,' grocery stores and taverns. Martens claimed that men like Nichols make up part of the social fabric of many Black communities. "They're institutions," he says. "They've been there for years, from one generation to the next."

The commission described other players in the African-American illegal numbers operations as "an industry to which there are few new entrants and in which most bankers have long established careers." Although the investigators noted that illegal lotteries have often been considered a benign example of street crime, the revenues generated were "often used to finance other criminal activities," like drugs.

And drugs, the report stated at the outset, remain the "number one organized crime problem in Pennsylvania."

The mantle of drug pushing in Philadelphia in the late '80's has passed from the hands of Nicky Scarfo and his Mafia mobsters to the new wave of Black, Chinese and Hispanic mobsters who appropriated the turf of the incarcerated Mafia boss.

Organized Crime is a society that seeks control of the American people and their governments. It involves thousands of criminals, working within structures as complex as those of any large corporation, subject to laws more rigidly enforced than those of legitimate governments. Its actions are not impulsive but rather the result of intricate conspiracies, carried on over many years and aimed at gaining control over whole fields of activity in order to amass huge profits.

-The President's Commission[*]

36

THE RICO SENTENCES OF THE SCARFO CRIME FAMILY

DURING a nine-day period, between May 1-11, 1989, Judge Van Antwerpen sentenced the eighteen convicted Scarfo family members who had been found guilty of the 40 RICO counts on November 19, 1988. Starting with Joe Ligambi, a family member who pleaded guilty to one count of illegal gambling before the RICO trial began, the Judge heard pleas, two every day by the defense and the prosecution. The defense argued for reduced prison sentences and the prosecution argued for the maximum 40-year sentence.

Ligambi, who had been sentenced to life in prison just a month before for his role in the 'Frankie Flowers' D'Alfonso murder, was sentenced to a modest three-and-a-half year prison term.

In the afternoon of May 1, before a packed courtroom of family members of the other defendants, Van Antwerpen listened

[*] On Law Enforcement and Administration of Justice, Task Force Report: Organized Crime #1 (1967).

to arguments concerning the fate of Anthony Pungitore, who was described by his defense attorney, Stanley Weinberg, as just a "marginal or bit player" in the mob. The onlookers knew that the Judge's sentence would set a pattern for future mob members' sentencing as he moved up the ladder of the hierarchy to the last family member to be sentenced on May 11, Nicodemo Scarfo, Sr., the mob boss.

THE SENTENCING OF ANTHONY PUNGITORE, JR.

Pungitore, age 34, brought in a priest and some friends who begged the Judge for compassion and a chance for a new life. He nervously read a short statement to the court, saying: "I give my word that I will never be in this or any other courtroom again in my life." He told the Judge that his only hope was to get out of prison in time to marry his girlfriend and leave Philadelphia to start a new life elsewhere. His girlfriend sat somberly near his father, Joseph 'Blond Babe' Pungitore, also a 'made' Mafia member, in the back of the courtroom.

David Fritchey, the Special Attorney of the U.S. Organized Crime Strike Force, contended to the court that, "Where all three members of the same family, representing two successive generations, are... soldiers in the Mafia, it is difficult to conclude other than that Anthony Pungitore, Jr. grew up and became precisely what he was raised to be." Prosecutor Fritchey pointed out that Pungitore had helped to stalk Robert Riccobene, before that mobster was killed and that he had fired shots into the cafe where Harry Riccobene was severely wounded.

In a memo to the court in the Government's Pre-Sentencing Memorandum, the five government prosecutors stressed the conclusion made by the 1986 *Report to the President and the Attorney General* by the President's Commission on Organized Crime that "Although the [Mafia] soldier is the lowest-ranking formal member of the organization, he nevertheless is a considerable figure on the street, a man who commands respect and fear."

Pungitore knew this fact when he became a member of the mob. The Philadelphia Organized Strike Force's Memo went on to say that:

Membership in the Mafia involves the adoption of a perverted value structure and contempt for the law, that, unfortunately, appears to be deeply ingrained in the Pungitore family. The defendant was apparently raised with these aberrant values and adheres to them. The RICO offenses for which he was convicted were not impulsive acts of an immature youth, but rather the product of the considered judgment of a man who sought a career in the major leagues of crime. His crimes were not fleeting acts done in the heat of passion, but methodical, calculated acts, involving tactical planning and coordinated execution, that were conducted over the course of months. At no time before or since his conviction has he shown any degree of remorse or acceptance of responsibility for his criminal conduct. He has done nothing to sever his ties with *La Cosa Nostra* and appears to be hopelessly and inextricably bound to it. Given his background and his demonstrated behavior, Pungitore's capacity for rehabilitation appears to be nil.

After considering the appeal of Pungitore's defense attorney and priest for leniency, Judge Van Antwerpen told the defendant that "in the final analysis, I had to consider the seriousness of what you've done."

He then sentenced the convicted felon to 30 years in a Federal prison — 20 years on one count and 10 years on another, to run consecutively, plus a $10,000 fine.

Joel M. Friedman, the Attorney in Charge of the Philadelphia Organized Crime Strike Force, commented outside the courtroom that, "Society is entitled to the protection of the laws and the message sent today was that "society will not tolerate those who join criminal organizations!"

Outside the courthouse, it started to pour, marking the beginning of a continuous rain of long prison terms on the convicted Mafiosis caught in the web of the RICO conspiracy of their own making.

THE SENTENCING OF NICHOLAS VIRGILIO AND JOSEPH GRANDE

When it came time to sentence the gaunt, craggy faced 'Nick the Blade' Virgilio, age 61, the defendant approached the bench and in a booming bass voice declared that the prosecution witnesses had lied and that his trial in the fall of 1988 had been a "gross travesty of justice, an orgy against the lady called 'justice'.

"This might be the real reason why she's [Justice] blind-folded. I was innocent before the trial started, I was innocent during the trial, and I remain innocent of all these charges."

His speech dominated the day, particularly when he denounced the jury as "ignorant..." and "the most stupidest," and accused the prosecution of being "part of the conspiracy of lies."

Virgilio went on to characterize prosecutors David Fritchey, Louis Pichini, Arnold Gordon and Joseph Peters as the "Four Horsemen of the Apocalypse" — the symbolic characters cited in the Book of Revelation in *The Holy Bible*, who were given the power to bring war, pestilence, death and famine.

He said that the four prosecutors, who were sitting behind him as he spoke, would be disbarred for their complicity "in the conspiracy of lies."

Virgilio then asked Judge Van Antwerpen to sentence him and his co-defendants to the same sentences that are given the government's 'turncoat' witnesses, Thomas Del Giorno and Nicholas Caramandi, who were awaiting sentencing on a variety of charges.

"If the court doesn't do this, maybe they should close the courts of this country because maybe justice doesn't exist here, only hypocrisy," he said.

Prosecutor Fritchey, however, reminded the Judge that Virgilio had killed two people long before he became a mob member and that the jury had convicted him of killing the Somers Point, New Jersey, Municipal Judge Edwin Helfant, after Virgilio became a Mafia member.

Defense Attorney Stephen Patrizio argued that Virgilio had already served sentences for two earlier killings, which he claimed his client had committed in self-defense, but the Judge was not moved by Virgilio's pleas. "It appears that we are dealing with a career criminal incapable of living in society," he said.

He then remanded him to the custody of the U.S. Attorney General to be incarcerated in a Federal prison for 40 years.

A few hours later, the Judge read the touching letter of Janice Grande, the wife of Joseph, 29, the next mobster to be sentenced. She wrote: "Please, your Honor, give my daughter a chance to know her father. I love my husband very much and it has been very hard to be away from him. Please, your Honor, let us be a family. Please don't let our lives end like this!" But the Judge sentenced Grande to 40 years also.

THE SENTENCING OF RALPH STAINO, JR.

Then it came time to sentence the well-tanned 'Junior' Staino on May 3, before another packed courtroom lined with his daughters, grandchildren and his wife, Lillian 'Tiger Lil' Reis prsent. Courtroom observers were anticipating that something out of the ordinary might happen with the appeal of Staino, now 57, and the self-proclaimed 'Poet Laureate' of the mob.

They were not disappointed when 'Junior' took the podium and sobbed openly as he professed his love for his wife and family. The handsome Staino, who had been inducted into the Mafia at the advanced age of 54 and still looked like Marlon Brando in his heyday, soon lost his grip after telling the Judge that he had been with *one* woman for 35 years. He started to cry and so did his wife. Staino sat down, slumped in his chair, dabbing his eyes, as his attorney, Michael Pinsky, finished reading his short statement.

"Please find it in your heart to show leniency," Pinsky read from 'Junior's' notes. "I know I did wrong in my life...I'm very sorry."

But Prosecutor Fritchey reminded the Judge of how Staino had been heard in phone conversation secretly taped by the FBI threatening to "rip out someone's eye unless a certain extortion payment was made...fast." After that conversation, the prosecutor reiterated how Staino turned to a colleague and said: "Ooh, I loved it!" He also recalled that the FBI had found $100,000 in cash hidden behind a wall in Staino's home in South Philadelphia and that he had a net worth of more than $2 million.

The Judge whacked Staino with a 33-year prison sentence, which drew a sarcastic retort outside the courtroom from his companion of 35 years. "I think this guy's name should be 'hangman judge' I think his name should be Roy Bean."

Reis told reporters that, "We still love each other today as much as we did 35 years ago, [despite his one indiscretion with a Dominican woman who gave birth to his baby]."

But that was not all for Staino. A few hours later, District Judge Thomas O'Neill, Jr., who had presided over his Speed trial in 1988, seemed to take some pity on the convicted defendant. Staino explained in front of him, with a choking voice, that, "I wouldn't know how to import or distribute P2P....The money that the FBI found in my home was legitimate money that came from the sale of property back in Italy of my deceased father. I am truly remorseful for participating in these crimes. I made mistakes...but if I'm fortunate enough to get out, I will move from Philadelphia."

But like the others before him, he was *not* given the opportunity to sever his ties with the Mafia.

Judge O'Neill refused to impose a consecutive sentence of 33 additional years on Staino, which the prosecution had asked for, but instead sentenced him to another 12 years which would run concurrently with the 33-year sentence imposed earlier in the day by Judge Van Antwerpen. He also ordered Staino to pay an additional $200,000 fine, a penalty he could have escaped if he had chosen to stand trial with Boss Scarfo on the same charges earlier in 1988.

THE SENTENCING OF SAL SCAFIDI

In the afternoon, Judge Van Antwerpen sentenced another mob soldier, Salvatore Scafidi, who had been inducted into the mob at age 24, to 40 years in prison before a near-empty courtroom. Unlike Staino, Scafidi remained silent, with his attorney, Christopher Furlong, weakly suggesting that his client had gotten into trouble because he had been attracted by the elevated position that mobsters enjoyed and had gotten caught up in an "us against them" mentality. You can't imagine what it might be like growing up in that particular neighborhood," Furlong stated. "They had their own lifestyle that had apparently been handed down from generations."

THE SENTENCING OF THE NARDUCCI BROTHERS

The next day, the Judge sentenced Frank Narducci, Jr., age 34, to 35 years in prison, and his stoic younger brother, Philip, age 26, to 40 years, for their mob roles, particularly in the murder of 'Frankie Flowers' D'Alfonso, for which they had previously received life sentences in state court. It was apparent that both would be spending the rest of their lives behind bars, unless some future governor pardoned one of them, which seemed remote in light of their multiple crimes.

Outside the courtroom, Sharon Wohlmuth, a photographer who had been employed by *The Philadelphia Inquirer* since 1975, was accosted by a stocky, 6'3" male friend of the Narducci's. He kicked her on the right thigh, while a woman grabbed her camera before she could take a picture, and then threw it into the street. Wohlmuth was taken to the nearby Hahnemann University Hospital for treatment of her leg injury and was then released. She was unable to identify her assailant.

THE SENTENCING OF JOE PUNGITORE

Joe Pungitore, age 32, who could have been sentenced to the maximum 60 years for his crime, represented the most heart-rending appearance of the entire group when he appeared for the last moment in the Mafia limelight. Before another packed courtroom, containing his girlfriend and thirty character witnesses, including a priest and a 26-year-long domestic house servant, Pungitore read a short statement in a cracking voice. "I would like to be able to go home some day and see my family, get married and have children." His sobbing girlfriend and somber-faced father sat a few feet away on the benches reserved for family. "I will raise them away from Philadelphia. I have matured, your Honor, during my last two years in jail."

Then, in a choking, half-audible voice, he said: "Your Honor, you will never see me in front of you again....I promise." Then he sat down.

Prosecutor Fritchey agreed that Pungitore had admirable qualities and could have made a positive contribution to society. "He is intelligent and has leadership ability. He could have made a successful businessman, perhaps even head of a company...[or] a Captain or Major in the Army. But the only army he ever served in was Scarfo's army and he followed the boss's orders," said Fritchey. "I feel he is the greatest loss [of the eighteen convicted Mafia members] to society....But he chose the wrong path and it is now society's loss and Joe Pungitore's loss. He has maintained his fealty to the mob and if and when he is ever paroled, he can go back to the street as a mob leader."

He then pointed out to the court how Pungitore lured his best friend, Sal Testa, to his death in the candy store, and how he shot and killed the mob captain, 'Chickie' Narducci, Sr., in 1982, the father of the two Narducci brothers.

Stephen LaCheen, Pungitore's defense attorney, tried to convince the Judge in a 30-minute plea, that his client might not have committed all those crimes and that the murder victims were not the most upstanding members of society themselves.

"I do not mean that they derserved to die," LaCheen implored. "We are not talking about babies...We are not talking about satanic murders. We are not talking about murdering police officers."

But the Judge was not moved. "A murder is a murder is a murder," he told the defense attorney.

In a pre-sentencing memo, Joseph Pungitore's organizational vision was laid out in an intercepted telephone conversation of January 21, 1986. There, speaking to one Michael Esposito, who was identified at trial as one of Pungitore's associates in loansharking activities, Pungitore explained his plans to build a large crew of associates, in what a prosecution staffer labeled his "'I have a Dream' tape":

> I wanna build up where this year I pick up three, four guys. Next year I pick up two, three guys, and in fucking ten years I got fucking two hundred guys around me...And this guy makes ya make four hundred, this guy makes ya make three hundred, ya know what I'm saying? That's the way ya do it.

Pungitore then went on to criticize the current Philadelphia Mafia hierarchy for being too abusive and greedy in dealing with actual and potential associates:

> These guys, they fucked their way to the top. Ya know what I mean? And then when they burned everybody out, they blew what they got, and they got nobody. Nobody wants to do nothing with them 'cause they fucked everybody....That ain't the way to treat people. They abused the image of who they are. That's the worst thing, that, that's your number one mistake....I know I'm right. Ya know I'm right? Because my father is sixty-five and Freddy's seventy-five, and that's what they told me, and they did well.[*]

---

[*] 'Freddy' is an apparent reference to Alfred Iezzi, Pungitore, Sr.'s *capo* in the Philadelphia Mafia family.

After examining the arguments from both sides, the Judge sentenced Pungitore to 40 years in prison.

THE SENTENCING OF SALVATORE 'WAYNE' GRANDE

In the afternoon, before another thinned-out courtroom, Sal Grande, age 35, killer of young Testa, was characterized by Fritchey as a man who "was deeply into violence, and deeply into intimidation." Rehabilitation would be difficult, he said, since he had neither filed nor paid any Federal income tax return between 1981 and 1986.

"It's pretty clear in this case, which family came first for 'Wayne' Grande. It was the Philadelphia *La Cosa Nostra* family, not his own family," said Fritchey.

The Judge returned a sentence of 38 years in jail, after which Grande turned around to face his tearful wife and family, saying bluntly, "See you later," as he was led away by the U.S. marshals.

THE SENTENCING OF CHARLES IANNECE

After a brief two-day weekend respite, the convicted defendants once more trooped into Courtroom #15B beginning with 'Nicky Crow's' former partner, 'Charley White' Iannece, age 54. The prosecutor reminded the Judge that Iannece had shot to death mob captain Pasquale 'Pat the Cat' Spirito in 1983 and helped to dispose of the body of the slain *capo*, Sal Testa. Fritchey reminded the court that the defendant had not violated the Mafia's oath of silence and had remained loyal to the Mob organization.

While the curly haired Iannece stood before the bench, staring straight ahead, the Judge sentenced him to the maximum 40 years in prison. He showed no visible reaction as he was led silently out of the courtroom.

THE POSTPONED SENTENCING OF LAWRENCE 'YOGI' MERLINO

A major break in the dike of *omerta*, the Mafia's Code of Silence, occurred on the afternoon before the slated court appearance of Lawrence Merlino, 42. He joined mobsters Del Giorno, Caramandi and Milano. The brother of the demoted *capo*, 'Chuckie' Merlino, who had yet to be sentenced, informed the court through his new attorney, Nino Tinari, that he wished to cooperate with the law enforcement authorities. He became the fourth mobster to come across the bridge into the Federal Witness protection system in exchange for damaging inside information on mob activities.

Prosecutor Arnold Gordon informed the Judge that Tinari needed more time to prepare for the expected reduced sentencing and the request was granted. When Scarfo's attorney, Simone, heard that Merlino had defected, he shrugged his shoulders and said: "Nothing surprises me anymore, but I will be surprised if a new informant [of the remaining four to be sentenced] would come out of the woodwork."

The government hoped that Merlino would be able to provide some much needed information about the dark recesses of mob-related construction activity in Atlantic City where both Scarfo and the Merlinos lived. Merlino was known to be connected to two companies, Nat-Nat, Inc. and Bayshore Rebar Inc., which were both involved with construction and union activities.

Nat-Nat, a concrete reinforcement construction company involved in a business similar to Scarf, Inc., earned about $1.3 million from publicly funded projects between 1981 and 1986, and $686,000 between 1979 and 1986 for work on eight hotel-casino projects, according to a 1987 report for the New Jersey State Commission of Investigation.

In that same report, the commission also stated that Bayshore Rebar had done similar construction work at Atlantic City casinos. So Merlino's sentencing, set for May 9th, was delayed for a time until the government could analyze his information.

THE SENTENCING OF FRANCIS IANNARELLA, JR.

When it came time to sentence 'Faffy' Iannarella, age 41, Robert Simone served as pinch-hitter for the defendant's regular attorney, Robert Madden, who was defending another client in Newark, New Jersey. Simone got the Judge to concede that some of the money which the prosecution claimed had been garnished by the defendant during his career had been attributed to a crime for which Iannarella had been acquitted of all charges.

Consequently the Judge suggested using language that said the defendant received substantial sums of money during his shakedowns as a *capo* in the mob.

The defendant, dressed immaculately in an attractive gray suit and black loafers, chose not to make any statement to the court.

Prosecutor Fritchey, on the other hand, lambasted the defendant for his conviction on 18 RICO acts, including participating in five murders as a Mafia killer in which he was the shooter in two. He also pointed out that his federal income tax returns for the years 1981-85 only showed him declaring annual totals between $15,000 and $21,000.

"Although he served in the U.S. Armed Forces in Vietnam, honorably," Fritchey told the court, "when he got out, he had a more distinguished record in the service of one of America's most significant domestic enemies, the Scarfo-led Mafia, in which he swore to break and ignore our laws. He was vicious, brutal, greedy, ambitious, ruthless and violent as he stepped over the bodies of his victims as he climbed up the ladder of the mob hierarchy. Iannarella is a savage animal and if he is ever paroled he will return to the street as a mob leader. He should receive a consecutive full prison sentence to the life sentence already meted out to him by another Judge."

Simone jumped up in rebuttal and told the Judge: "That was an outrageous statement that Mr. Fritchey made referring to the defendant's military service. How dare he detract from Iannarella's army record and medals that he earned in Vietnam. That inference should be stricken from the record."

A solemn and chastened Iannarella limped noticeably as he approached the bench for his sentencing. The Judge gave him the maximum 45 years, but denied Simone's motion that it run concurrently with his life sentence for the D'Alfonso murder. He added a modest $150 assessment but no fine. Then a smooth Iannarella turned to his family and friends in the audience, and waved without speaking to them, after which he was handcuffed and led away.

Outside the courtroom, a sarcastic Simone commented to the media in his own brand of black humor, "Now that the four turncoats are free maybe they are on the verge of starting a second mob in Philadelphia." But those four were *not* free and would be sentenced in the near future.

THE SENTENCING OF 'CHICKIE' AND 'CHUCKIE'

Mob captain Joseph 'Chickie' Ciancaglini, age 54, who had been in prison on other racketeering charges since 1983, appeared for his sentencing on the RICO conviction just two days before he was to have been paroled for earlier racketeering convictions. Dressed in a white, black and turquoise running suit, the barrel-chested Ciancaglini stared straight ahead, as Prosecutor Fritchey depicted the felon as an old-school mobster who had come up through the ranks during the placid rule of the late Angelo Bruno. He was a "breath of fresh air...and is a man who could have been boss. I think it is safe to say that if he made boss in 1981, instead of Scarfo, that the judgment day for the mob might not have come so soon."

Defense Attorney, Nicholas Nastasi, tried hard to persuade the Judge to impose a sentence that would let Ciancaglini return to his family one day, since he had been in prison for all but 19 months of the 11-year-long mob conspiracy in the RICO case.

"He alone among the defendants occupies the position of having been incarcerated, not only for the majority of the time of the events in this indictment, but continually for an uninterrupted period of time after his appeals were exhausted," said Nastasi, who also pointed out that his client was a model prisoner.

Fritchey admitted that the man was a "charming and likable person" but that he was "also ruthless." As Judge Van Antwerpen imposed his sentence of 45 years, Ciancaglini's wife, Maria, blinked back tears as her husband was led away by marshals — to spend at least the next 30 years behind bars.

In the afternoon, the gaunt former underboss, 'Chuckie' Merlino, age 49, who had been demoted to a lowly soldier in 1986 by Scarfo, appeared in court wearing a dark suit. The sad-faced Merlino chose not "to exercise his right of elocution" according to his attorney, Edwin Jacobs, who noted later that his client had taken the news of his brother Lawrence's cooperation with the government very badly.

Fritchey said that Merlino faced up to 218 years in prison for his conviction on the multiple crimes and that he served as the acting boss of the mob while Scarfo was incarcerated in a Texas prison between August 1982 and January 1984. And even though he was demoted after Scarfo's return, "Merlino remained dedicated to the evils of the *La Cosa Nostra*, so the government asks for the full maximum sentence of 55 years."

As Merlino stood quietly before the Judge, Van Antwerpen gave him 45 years behind bars to be served consecutively to the life sentence that he had received for his part in the D'Alfonso murder, plus a $250 special assessment . His daughter called out softly from the family section: "Goodbye Dad," as her father was led away from the limelight for the last time.

THE SENTENCING OF PHIL LEONETTI

The last day of sentencing witnessed the appearance of the Mafia underboss, 'Crazy Phil' Leonetti, age 36, in court, wearing a dark blue sweater and gray slacks.

The Judge, as he had done with previous defendants, denied all pre-sentencing motions by the defense.

A well-tanned Oscar Goodman, who had flown in from Las Vegas to make one last dramatic court plea for his stoic client, told the Judge that "25 years ago, when I started practice, I was impressed with the late eminent Federal Judge, Learned Hand's observation of the crime of 'conspiracy where the prosecution used conspiracy as a dragnet to sweep all the fish into the net.'

"Today, Phil Leonetti is caught up in a modern dragnet of RICO, the act which has been termed 'the darling of the prosecutorial nursery,' which is why he stands before you. But times change," commented Goodman, "in an era of electronic surveillance. In the old days, Thomas Del Giorno and Nicholas Caramandi were not given 'passes' for testifying against their former colleagues.

"Also in the old days, there were no double jeopardy exceptions. But today, under RICO, the government was able to try my client again for the Testa and Falcone murders, for which he had been acquitted in state courts in New Jersey and Pennsylvania.

"This is his first felony conviction," intoned Goodman, "He has been in the legitimate concrete business in New Jersey but because of his birth and the fact that he loves his uncle who raised him in part, he is here. Law enforcement made it impossible for him to make a [straight] living. That is a shame and a black mark on the law. He still says that he is not guilty on any of these counts and asks for probation so that he can be with his family of his wife and two teenage children."

After he finished his short plea, the Judge noted that Leonetti had indeed been convicted once before, back in 1975, of a misdemeanor and had paid a $100 fine.

Prosecutor Fritchey opened his summation with a repeat of a

tape made over a decade earlier of Leonetti speaking with Joe Salerno Jr. about the Mafia's role in the murder of New Jersey Judge Edwin Helfant. "This is *who* we are and this is *what* we can get away with."

"That day is past," said Fritchey. "Today [May 11, 1989] is 'Judgment Day.' He has been convicted of 21 racketeering acts under RICO by a jury picked in part by the defense. The 21 acts for which Leonetti was found guilty included four murders, four murder conspiracies, one count of gambling and 15 acts of extortion.

"In a state court, he would have been eligible for three life terms for these crimes, plus an additional 75-150 years in prison."

Fritchey pointed out that being found guilty of these crimes under RICO was not a case of double jeopardy, since these violations were a "predicate act" that flouted the rights of others under the protection of the U.S. Constitution. The Prosecutor noted that Leonetti had been made a *capo* by his uncle at the age of 28 in 1981 and promoted to underboss five years later in 1986 at age 33.

"The Philadelphia Mafia family has an important position in the Mafia's ruling National Commission," said Fritchey, "according to U.S. Government surveys, Leonetti was being groomed to succeed Scarfo as a future boss. He is an intelligent and able young man, but under the influence of his uncle, Nicodemo Scarfo...[became] a vicious, ruthless, cold-blooded Mafia killer!"

Despite the fact that he was fairly tried by a jury of his peers, and with a competent counsel, Fritchey also noted that "Goodman's attacks on the government witnesses were positively savage. But the jury believed the government witnesses. The government views Leonetti as extremely dangerous. It is unfortunate that as a young man, Leonetti took that wrong course in life, so the government asks for the maximum sentence of 45 years."

The Judge denied Goodman's plea for reasonable alternatives, like probation, and sentenced Leonetti to 45 years and an assessment of $150.

His look-alike son waved silently to his father, and the senior Leonetti waved back without speaking as he was led away out of the rear of the courtroom.

Outside the chambers, Goodman stated that he had been

hoping for probation and then said, "There is a pattern of racketeering activity in the sentences being handed out inside" (an obvious reference to the Judge's stiff sentences).

Joel Friedman, the head of the Strike Force, observed that: "It's great to be a piece of history," on behalf of his five-member team who won the biggest case in his office's operations as an adjunct to the U.S. Attorney's Office.

THE SENTENCING OF THE BOSS

The courtroom was packed on the afternoon of Thursday, May 11, for a half hour before Scarfo entered the courtroom. His mother, Catherine, and son, Nicodemo, Jr., who was one week short of his 24th birthday, sat quietly in the middle of the family section.

Scarfo wore an expensive blue black business suit with a white shirt and a red, white and blue print tie as he sat down in his chair rocking slowly after smiling and waving confidently to the audience of family and friends.

The courtroom grew so crowded that FBI agents, state police, office secretaries and other law enforcement officials took up seats in the jury box. Another 50-60 curiosity seekers were locked out of the courtroom.

Sixteen minutes later, at 1:41 p.m., the bailiff called out "All rise," as Judge Van Antwerpen entered the dais under the American eagle scroll on the wall above his chair. He announced that he had denied all post-trial, pre-sentencing motions on the 32 RICO counts which Scarfo had been convicted of back on November 19, 1988, and then asked the defendant's attorney, Robert Simone, if he wished to make a statement.

Simone walked up to the bench, and in a short three-minute, low-key pitch to the Judge, said: "I recognize that mere words cannot undo the deeds and misdeeds of the defendants, the prosecution and the jury's actions. Mr. Scarfo has asked me not to make any plea on his behalf. But the thing that upsets me the most are the last two counts regarding his drug conviction — when another jury found him innocent earlier on the same charges. The only evidence in that ['speed'] case was three sentences uttered by Thomas Del Giorno. Everyone knows that Scarfo did not use drugs or condone selling them.

"I should like to repeat the words of Oscar Wilde [the British dramatist] that 'those involved in punishing criminals do more harm to society than the criminals themselves.' The last thing that Mr. Scarfo wants here is a speech by the prosecution. But I recognize that the starving press needs to be fed to contaminate future jurors."

Prosecutor David Fritchey, heeding the gentle goad by his opponent to keep it short, rendered a six-minute closing, noting that he and the other four prosecutors had a total of 72 years of prosecutorial experience between them and that they all agreed that this case was the "most fiercely litigated, and well tried case in our collective experience in court."

"Despite the qualifications of the defense attorneys to offer a case to get their clients acquitted, the evidence was there and Scarfo and the members of his family were all convicted. What's to be said of a man convicted of eight murders and nine attempted murders plus other crimes?

"He faces a total of a maximum of 55 years," the Prosecutor told the court, "which seems inadequate based on his record. He was the boss of a family of violent criminals. A Pre-Sentence Memo to the court read:

> NICODEMO SCARFO is a remorseless and profoundly evil man. His life has been committed to the Mafia and all the negative values it represents: greed, viciousness, treachery, deceit, and contempt for the law and the rights of others being prominent among them. As boss, he served as the catalyst to make an already violent organization even more violent. Additionally, he aggressively recruited many new members into the organization, all of whom were first steeped in the new tradition of blood and violence he imposed. Had these young Mafia killers not been convicted with him, they would, could have attempted to impose a reign of terror on this region for decades to come. That was Scarfo's vision. Fortunately, his vision has been destroyed....SCARFO should be incarcerated for the remainder of his life. He should never again be free to prey upon society." (POSF)

Fritchey concluded his brief remarks by saying: "I look at something positive to say about the man. He undoubtedly saw the handwriting on the wall when Del Giorno and Caramandi agreed to cooperate with the government. He could have fled, but he did not. He stood his ground.

"And when the aging Nicholas 'Nick the Blade' Virgilio called us — the four members of the Prosecutorial team — 'the Four Horsemen of the Apocalypse,' he forgot to mention that in the *Bible* they represented the symbols of the end of the world. But now it's the end of the mob's world.

"He rejuvenated the mob and made something fearsome even more fearsome," Fritchey observed. "He even had his own City Councilman, Leland Beloff, whom he owned body and soul and then extorted Willard Rouse III, which was a fatal mistake. When Del Giorno and Caramandi agreed to cooperate, they decided that they feared Scarfo more then the spectre of imprisonment.

"Maybe 'Nick the Blade' was right, that we are the Four Horsemen. But the end of the mob family is not complete although it is severely crippled. The boss, two underbosses, several *capos* and one third of his soldiers have been convicted, and of the two *capos* left, one has fled the country and the other is under indictment.

"That this end has come about," Fritchey concluded, "is a tribute to the zeal of law enforcement officials in New Jersey [and] Pennsylvania, on...the state, local and federal levels. In a larger sense, this has been a victory for society as a whole. This group of criminals is *not* above the law, even though he once profited handsomely, but we now ask for a full 55-year conviction."

Simone made a brief rebuttal, asking the Judge to not impose a consecutive sentence on his client since he did not give the eight mobsters convicted in the 'Frankie Flowers' murder the right to appeal.

Before the Judge imposed his final sentence on the boss of the Scarfo mob family, he told the court that "Prison wastes lives, but in this case I feel that I have no choice. This is the City of Brotherly Love, not a city of murder."

Nicodemo Scarfo, Jr. sat impassively, chewing gum and looking up at the ceiling as the Judge sentenced his father to the full 55 years to be served consecutively with the previously imposed life sentence. He also added a $500,000 fine, since he felt that "Scarfo had the ability to pay that amount based on trial testimony."

The Judge made the point that his sentence was to be served in addition to the 14-year term that Scarfo was already serving for the $1 million Rouse extortion conviction. 'Lil Nicky' didn't show any outward sign of emotion when he heard the sentence, other than to shake Simone's hand and wave briefly back to his mother and son.

The defendant was given ten days to appeal the sentencing under Federal Rule #32-82, and Simone assured him that this action would be taken.

But as Joel Friedman, the head of the Philadelphia Strike Force, noted: "This is a victory for society over those who would try to destroy the system. We will now approach other organized crime groups with the same dedication."

Outside the courthouse, in the shadow of Independence Hall, where both the Declaration of Independence and the U.S. Constitution were written, Fritchey, with the others of the 'Four Horsemen' repeated a digest of his remarks to a crowd of TV, radio and press reporters who were unable to get inside the packed courtroom.

The wheels of democracy, as President Lincoln once said, move slowly, but somehow they wobbled straight. And that is what happened after almost three-and-one-half years following Scarfo's arrest as he stepped off a plane bringing him up from Casablanca South — that he would never see again.

Prosecutor Louis Pichini summed up the significance of the convictions after the session this way: "The community should roundly applaud the court because justice has finally been done. The public has witnessed a rare and historic event — the complete dismantling of an organized crime family."

The late head of the New Jersey State Police Organized Crime Bureau, William Sullivan, who watched Scarfo's rise to power through most of the '80s, rendered this apt one sentence description of the mob boss: "He's a homicidal maniac."

Scarfo's indiscriminate use of excessive violence and murder to settle any score and to avenge any slight, had finally taken its ultimate toll. In destroying his enemies, real or perceived, Scarfo destroyed his own organized crime family — and in the end, himself.

'TOMMY DEL' GETS FIVE

On June 8, 1989, the diminutive Thomas Del Giorno, the first Philadelphia mobster ever to break *Omerta* appeared in a packed Federal courtroom for a 90-minute hearing regarding his final sentencing concerning his 1986 guilty plea on racketeering chages. After listening to a bevy of FBI agents, local, state and Federal prosecutors present glowing accounts of the cooperation given by the star anti-Scarfo informant, U.S. District Judge Louis C. Bechtle gave Del Giorno a five-year (out of a possible 20-year) prison sentence for his confessed crime.

After the sentencing, Joel Friedman, head of the U.S. Organized Crime Strike Force, explained that since Del Giorno had already been in custody for two-and-a-half years, he was already eligible for parole consideration since he had served a third of the sentence. Friedman stopped short of a complete endorsement of Del Giorno, however.

"We do not vouch for the character of Thomas Del Giorno," he said. "But of paramount importance in the sentence today is society's interest in rewarding cooperation...and encouraging others like [him] to come forward."

FBI Agent Klaus Rohr, who supervised the squad responsible for organized crime investigations in the Philadelphia area, testified that Del Giorno had jeopardized his life when he dared to break the Mafia code. "I think it would be foolish to buy life insurance on Thomas Del Giorno," he said. "The only way he's going to stay alive is to remain in hiding for the rest of his life....At all times, he's imprisoned by the idea that *La Cosa Nostra* is looking for him."

This thought was echoed by Defense Attorney Gerard Egan, who concluded: "It would be suicide for Mr. Del Giorno to ever engage in any other illegal conduct for the rest of his life....He will never be totally free regardless of the time he spends in prison. He will be in his own prison. Every day of his life he will have to look over his shoulder."

CARAMANDI WAS NOT SO LUCKY

On July 26, 1989, Judge Fullam sentenced Nicholas Caramandi to eight years in prison. He said that 'Nicky Crow' had been living "The Life of Riley" during his three years with the FBI, and really deserved 20 years.

A 'TOMMY DEL' SEQUEL

After a month of secret negotiations, the last nail in the coffin of the Scarfo crime family was driven home, when 36-year-old Phil Leonetti, the Number Two man and underboss, agreed to cooperate with the Federal government in return for a lessening of his 45-year RICO sentence. Leonetti, Scarfo's nephew, caved in in late June, 1989, at the same time that Del Giorno was receiving his five-year sentence, reduced as a result of becoming a government witness. When Robert 'Bobby' Simone told Scarfo that Leonetti had agreed to become a cooperating federal witness, the mob boss was both "surprised and embarrassed" at the turnabout. Meanwhile, Leonetti was being debriefed by federal authorities on a wide range of subjects including: Atlantic City politics, casino construction, zoning variances, casino union activities, and the relationship of the Scarfo crime family to the New York Gambino family, headed by John Gotti. He thus became the fifth member of the mob to break the code of silence.

Who would be next?

On the following page is a chart summarizing the sentences of the convicted members of the Scarfo Mafia family.

The Summary of Final Sentencing by Federal Judge Franklin S. Van Antwerpen, in the United States District Court of the Eastern District of Pennsylvania.

re: THE UNITED STATES OF AMERICA

v

NICODEMO SCARFO, ET AL

Criminal Action (RICO) #88-00003-1-19

Date of Sentencing	Name of Defendant	Sentence
5/1/89	Joseph Ligambi	3 1/2 yrs (plea bargain) (plus$150-$250 assessment)
5/1/89	Anthony Pungitore, Jr.	30 years + $10,000 fine (plus $150-$250 assessment)
5/2/89	Nicholas Virgilio	40 years
5/2/89	Joseph Grande	40 years
5/3/89	Ralph Staino, Jr.	33 years + 12 years for 'speed' conviction
5/3/89	Salvatore Scafidi	40 years
5/4/89	Frank Narducci, Jr.	35 years
5/4/89	Phillip Narducci	40 years
5/5/89	Joseph Pungitore	40 years
5/5/89	Salvatore Wayne Grande	38 years
5/8/89	Charles Iannece	40 years
5/9/89	Lawrence Merlino	(sentence postponed — plea bargain opted to cooperate at the last minute)
5/9/89	Francis Iannarella, Jr.	45 years
5/10/89	Joseph Ciancaglini	45 years
5/10/89	Salvatore Merlino	45 years
5/11/89	Philip Leonetti	45 years (to be reduced because of cooperation)
5/11/89	Nicodemo Scarfo, Sr.	55 years plus $500,000 fine

Epilogue

THE IRONIC PARALLELS BETWEEN THE MAFIA AND THE IRAN-CONTRAGATE CONSPIRATORS

There are several not so strange parallels between the underworld illegal business operations of the Scarfo-Mafia family, known as "The Enterprise" and the Iran-Contragate operations, also known as "The Enterprise," which were conducted clandestinely in the basement of the White House by Lt. Col. Oliver North and his co-conspirators.

Both operations were conducted in secrecy, with the latter protected by the umbrella of the CIA and the National Security Council for a time. Both operations flouted the U.S. Constitution and the rule of law. Both were based on a series of lies and the concealment of information. Both the Mafia and the Iran-Contragate co-conspirators were interested primarily in pursuing the motives of personal self aggrandizement. Both organizations practiced buccaneering dictatorial methods based on the belief that the ends justified the means.

A generation ago, the CIA made alliances with the then Mafia dons, Johnny Roselli, Santos Trafficante, Tony Calvalcante and Sam Giancana, to try to wipe out Fidel Castro soon after he assumed power in Cuba, and our nation's moral fiber has suffered for that ill-fated attempt ever since.

Both the Mafia and the Iran-Contragate crowd practiced secretive means of ducking their accountability to the government until criminal indictments were handed down and the slow processes of court cases were undertaken to bring them all to the bar of justice.

Appendices

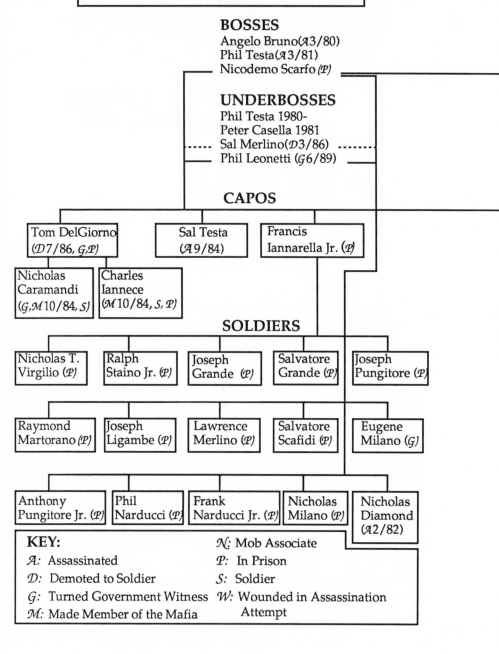

"THE ENTERPRISE"
THE ORGANIZATION OF THE
PHILADELPHIA—ATLANTIC CITY
MAFIA CRIME FAMILY (1980-1989)

BOSSES
Angelo Bruno(*A*3/80)
Phil Testa(*A*3/81)
Nicodemo Scarfo *(P)*

UNDERBOSSES
Phil Testa 1980-
Peter Casella 1981
Sal Merlino(*D*3/86)
Phil Leonetti (*G*6/89)

CAPOS

Tom DelGiorno
(*D*7/86, *G,P*)

Sal Testa
(*A*9/84)

Francis
Iannarella Jr. (*P*)

Nicholas
Caramandi
(*G,M*10/84, *S*)

Charles
Iannece
(*M*10/84, *S, P*)

SOLDIERS

Nicholas T.
Virgilio (*P*)

Ralph
Staino Jr. (*P*)

Joseph
Grande (*P*)

Salvatore
Grande (*P*)

Joseph
Pungitore (*P*)

Raymond
Martorano (*P*)

Joseph
Ligambe (*P*)

Lawrence
Merlino (*P*)

Salvatore
Scafidi (*P*)

Eugene
Milano (*G*)

Anthony
Pungitore Jr. (*P*)

Phil
Narducci (*P*)

Frank
Narducci Jr. (*P*)

Nicholas
Milano (*P*)

Nicholas
Diamond
(*A*2/82)

KEY:

A: Assassinated
D: Demoted to Soldier
G: Turned Government Witness
M: Made Member of the Mafia

N: Mob Associate
P: In Prison
S: Soldier
W: Wounded in Assassination Attempt

CONSIGLIERES
Nicodemo Scarfo
Frank Monte(*A*5/82)
Nick Piccolo
Tony Caponigro(*A* '80)

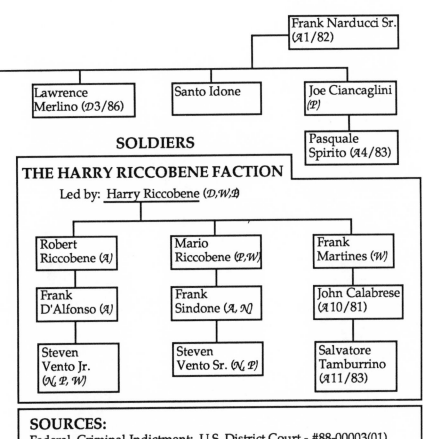

Frank Narducci Sr.
(*A*1/82)

Lawrence
Merlino (*D*3/86)

Santo Idone

Joe Ciancaglini
(*P*)

Pasquale
Spirito (*A*4/83)

SOLDIERS

THE HARRY RICCOBENE FACTION
Led by: Harry Riccobene (*D,W,P*)

Robert
Riccobene (*A*)

Mario
Riccobene (*P,W*)

Frank
Martines (*W*)

Frank
D'Alfonso (*A*)

Frank
Sindone (*A, N*)

John Calabrese
(*A*10/81)

Steven
Vento Jr.
(*N, P, W*)

Steven
Vento Sr. (*N, P*)

Salvatore
Tamburrino
(*A*11/83)

SOURCES:
Federal Criminal Indictment: U.S. District Court - #88-00003(01)
Philadelphia, PA. (6/13/88)
RICO Trial Testimony of 'Nicky' Scarfo & Mafia Org.(9/88-11/88)

A Glossary of Mafia Jargon*

A reader of the nine trials involving Mafia figures in the pages of this book may require a special "mob dictionary" to properly understand the peculiar terms and jargon used on wiretap tapes and by various witnesses. This is an alphabetical listing of the unique Mafia language that will *not* be found in any standard dictionary.

We have to thank three Mafia informants, now under Federal witness protection custody, Nicholas Caramandi, Thomas Del Giorno and John Pastorella (a friend of the mob) for supplying us with these terms and their particular meanings:

All of them	When a hand was raised by Nicholas Caramandi with one finger pointing up and six zeroes (circles) made with two other fingers to a Rouse official, the signal meant the total shakedown was $1 million.
Banged	To let oneself become too drunk on alcohol or drugs.
Barons	Certain district council persons in Philadelphia (term used by Robert Rego).
Beefing	A disagreement over a mutual problem.
Bomb Squad	A name adopted by Charles Iannece, Nicholas Caramandi and Ralph Staino, Jr. to describe their shakedown crew and to characterize the trio's strongarm tactics to collect money for the mob.
Blunt of it	To take the headache of having problems dumped on a Mafia soldier.

---

* As used by the Scarfo *La Cosa Nostra* Family

Bothering	Pressuring someone for money, union dues, or payoffs.
Bugged	Being wired to record a conversation with another.
Business	To do = to extort money for 'protection.'
Capo	A captain in the mob; middleman between the soldiers and the bosses.
Capo Regime	The boss and underboss who made up the leadership of the Mafia hierarchy.
Casablanca South	Nicky Scarfo's beachfront home in Fort Lauderdale, Florida.
Coca Cola	Cocaine
Consigliere	A counsellor in the mob below the boss.
Deal	A piece of money, crooked business, extortion.
Elbow	A percent of extortion money set aside for the *Capos* and Bosses.
Emergency	If mob member didn't do what he was asked, he would be killed.
Extras	A lump sum payment from single extortions or shakedowns that sometimes ran as high as $25,000.
Flim-Flam	A crooked deal, racketeering.
Funny Guy	One who is 'bothered' by a demanding 'message' to perform.
Good Faith Money	Substantial payoff (usually $50,000 to $100,000)
Heat	Pressure from law and legal officials.
Hot Dog	Small amount of money paid in a shakedown.
Hustle	Illegal commercial transaction for profit.
Kilo	2.2 pounds of heroin or coke (cocaine) worth anywhere from $175,000 to $250,000.

Kings	Bob Rego's description of Mayors (Goode, Green, Rizzo, et al)
LCN	*La Cosa Nostra* (*aka* the Mob, Family, Mafia)
Loan Shark	Mobster who loans money at exorbitant interest (usually 25% per week).
Made	The process of initiating a new member into the mob.
Mafia	(see LCN) The mob, almost always Italian-Americans.
"May I burn like the saints in hell if I betray one of my friends"	Oath of new Mafia members stated orally while holding a burning piece of tissue paper during 'making'
Message	Order from *Capo* or Boss, or from Soldier to victim.
Mouthing off	A Mafia member or associate's criticism of the mob hierarchy who had been accused of boasting about his own muscle power to others.
Oil	P2P (Phenyl 2 Propanone) used to manufacture methamphetamine.
P2P	(see OIL above)
Paranoid	Mob members' fear of being spied upon by the law.
Pop	To kill (Nicky Crow's term)
Power	Feeling of new mob member after he is made.
Problem	There is a contract to terminate the individual's life who is told that he has a 'Problem.'
Put me in	Request of a fringe candidate to become a mob member.
Put one in traps	To try to catch a member or other person doing something wrong.
Right Thing	To play ball with Mafia or face a serious 'problem'.

Scam	A shakedown, scheme used by racketeers and the mob.
Shakes	(aka Shakedown or Tribute Payment) The so-called 'street tax' form of extortion imposed by the Mafia on the illegal businesses operated by drug dealers, bookies, et al.
Shore	Atlantic City, Scarf Inc. (Scarfo's headquarters), Longport, New Jersey.***
Soldiers	The privates, workers in the Mafia, who report to *Capos* .
Speed	Slang for methamphetamine.
Street Tax	Payoff by illegal bookies, drug dealers, loan sharks to the mob (LCN) to continue their business.
Test	Prove loyalty to mob by carrying out a mission.
"That guy's hungry up there. He only makes $300 a week"	A description of Bob Rego, Beloff's assistant in Council by Nicholas Caramandi.
The Little Man	Reference to the shortness of Scarfo by mob figures.
This Guy	Usually a referral to Nicky Scarfo by 'Nicky Crow'.
This Thing of Ours	The real meaning of LCN.
Underboss	The chief deputy to the top boss of the mob (in recent years, Phil Leonetti, Nicky Scarfo's nephew).
With	(to be) = Description of friends of the mob who do business with the Mafia, but are not members.
Whack it up	To divide up extorted money (N.C.)

Why the American Mafia
Adopted the Name 'La Cosa Nostra'
(Our Thing)

On June 9, 1985, Aniello 'Neil' Dellacroce, an underboss in the large Gambino crime family, discussed the problem of taped-phone and room-bugged conversations among mob members, which the Federal prosecutors were using to prove that certain members were conducting illegal activities. In a court-authorized bug planted in his Staten Island home, Dellacroce is overheard talking to John Gotti (then a *capo* and later the boss of the family, just six months later) and Angelo Ruggiero, a lifelong friend of Gotti's. On the tape, the three men refer to *La Cosa Nostra*, "which the Justice Department claims is the name adopted by the American Mafia"[*]

Lecturing Ruggiero about his obligations to obey the then Gambino family boss, Paul Castellano (who was to be assassinated six months later), Dellacroce says: "You see, that's why I says to you before, you, you don't understand *Cosa Nostra*."

Gotti joins in, "Angelo, what does *Cosa Nostra* mean?"

Dellacroce interjects, "*Cosa Nostra* means that the boss is your boss. You understand. Forget all about this nonsense.... Angelo, if you refuse to obey the boss, it could ignite a war [within the family]. A lot of other fellas'll get hurt."[†]

---

[*] Raab, Selwyn, "Running the Mob," *The New York Times Magazine*, April 2, 1989, p. 71
[†] Ibid.

Bibliography

I.   **Transcripts** — Federal District Court and State Common Pleas Court (and FBI Tapes) 1/87 through 11/88 of eight Mafia trials (all covered in toto by the author)

1.   First extortion trial of Councilman Leland Beloff and Robert Rego (3/23/87 - 4/6/87) Federal Court (Hung Jury)

2.   Nicodemo Scarfo Extortion Trial (4/28/87 - 5/6/87) Federal Court (Guilty Verdict)

3.   Second Extortion Trial of Beloff and Rego (6/22/87 - 7/2/87) Federal Court (Guilty Verdict)

4.   Methamphetamine Drug Trial of Scarfo and Co-Conspirators (4/4/88 - 4/21/88) Federal Court (Acquittal)

5.   Sal Testa Murder Trial (5/88) State Court (Acquittal)

6.   Ralph 'Junior' Staino 'Speed' Trial (7/88) Federal Court (Guilty Verdict)

7.   RICO Trial of Scarfo and 16 Mafia Family Members (9/88 - 11/19/88) (Guilty on all counts)

8.   'Frankie Flowers' D'Alfonso Murder Trial (3/89 - 4/89) State Court (Guilty)

II. **Periodicals**

Cox, Donald, "The Beloff Jury: Ignorance is Bliss," *The Welcomat*, Philadelphia, Pennsylvania, April 8, 1957, p. 1.

Del Guirdice, Marguerite, "Winning Through Elimination," *The Philadelphia Inquirer Magazine*, February 16, 1983.

Fried, Stephen, "Who the Hell is Leland Beloff," *Philadelphia Magazine*, June 1987, pp. 79-159.

Kerr, Peter, "Chinese Crime Groups Arising to Prominence in New York," *The New York Times*, January 4, 1988, p. 1.

Mallowe, Michael, "Arrivederci Nicky — Goodbye Mr. Scarfo," *Philadelphia Magazine*, May 1988, pp. 106ff

Marriott, Michel, "Heroin Seizure at 3 Queens Sites is Called Biggest US Drug Raid," *The New York Times*, February 22, 1989, p. 16A.

McFadden, Robert, "The Mafia of the 1980s: Divided and Under Siege," *The New York Times*, March 11, 1987, p. 1.

Raab, Selwyn, "Investigators Say They're Ready to Topple New Mafia Chiefs," *The New York Times*, December 12, 1988, p. 3B.

Time , "The Mafia on Trial" (Cover Story) *Time*, September 29, 1986, pp. 17-24.

Weisberg, Jacob, "The Mafia and the Melting Pot," *The New Republic*, October 12, 1987.

III. Books on the Mafia of Recent Vintage

Alexander, Shana, *The Pizza Connection*, Weidenfeld and Nicholson Co., New York, 1988, 442 pp.

Arlacchi, Pino, *Mafia Business: The Mafia Ethic and the Spirit of Capitalism*, Verson, New York, (translated) 1987, 239 pp.

Blumenthal, Ralph, *The Last Days of the Sicilians*, Times Books, New York, 1988, 354 pp.

Davis, John, *Mafia Kingfish, Carlos Marcello, and the Assassination of John F. Kennedy*, McGraw Hill Publishing Co., New York, 1989, 580 pp.

Goode, James, *Wipeout, Listening in on America's Mafia*, Fireside Book, New York, 1988, 201 pp.

Mills, James, *The Underground Empire: Where Crimes and Governments Embrace*, Doubleday and Co., New York, (Dell Paperback) 1987, 1165 pp.

Pileggi, Nicholas, *Wiseguy: Life in a Mafia Family* , Simon and Schuster Inc., New York, (Pocket Books, paperback) 1987, 256 pp.

Scheim, David, *Contract on America: The Mafia Murder of President John F. Kennedy*, Shapolsky Publishers, New York, 1988, 480 pp.

IV. TV Documentaries

Rivera, Geraldo, *Sons of Scarface: The New Mafia*, (a two-hour documentary on the present state of organized crime in America shown over an independent national network on August 17, 1987)

V. Interviews by the Author

Robert Rego, Maryann Mongaluzzo (juror in first Beloff trial), Lou Pichini, and various relatives of the trial defendants, *et al*

Chapter Notes

KEY TO PRIMARY AND SECONDARY SOURCES OF INFORMATION USED IN THE 36 CHAPTERS

(See accompanying Bibliography for details of annotated references, which are listed chronologically within chapters and not necessarily in their order of appearance)

ABBREVIATIONS OF PERIODICALS AND REPORTERS' INITIALS TO IDENTIFY SOURCES

A.P.	Associated Press
D.B.	Dan Biddle, Pulitzer Prize Reporter, *The Philadelphia Inquirer*
E.L.	Emilie Lounsberry, Federal Court Reporter, *The Philadelphia Inquirer*
FDCTT	Federal District Court Trial Transcripts (7 trials covered in this book)
FBI	Federal Bureau of Investigation
NR	*The New Republic*
NYT	*The New York Times*
PDA	Philadelphia District Attorney
PDN	*The Philadelphia Daily News*
PI	*The Philadelphia Inquirer*
PIM	*The Philadelphia Inquirer Magazine*
PM	*Philadelphia Magazine*
TMTT	Testa Murder Trial Transcripts (1 trial in Pennsylvania Common Pleas Court)
USA	US Attorney (Eastern District of Pennsylvania)
USNWR	*U.S. News and World Report*
USOCSF	US Organized Crime Strike Force (attached to Justice Department

FEDERAL AND STATE INDICTMENTS USED IN THE RESEARCH AND WRITING OF THIS BOOK

1. Vote Fraud:
   U.S. vs. LELAND BELOFF, DIANE BELOFF, MARGARET COYLE and CHARLES POLLAN, 84-454, 10/28/86
2. Extortion (Rouse):
   USA vs. LELAND BELOFF, ROBERT REGO, NICHOLAS CARAMANDI, aka 'Nicky Crow,', 86-453, 10/27/86 (superseded on 1/5/87 USA vs LELAND BELOFF, ROBERT REGO, NICODEMO SCARFO, and CHARLES IANNECE)
3. Drug - 'Speed':
   USA vs. NICODEMO SCARFO et al, US District Court, E. District Pennsylvania, #87-00258, 6/27/87, 95 pp.
4. Drug - 'Speed':
   USA vs. RALPH STAINO, JR., US District Court, #87-258, 6/17/87, 35 pp.
5. Testa Murder:
   THE COMMONWEALTH v. N. SCARFO (and 8 other Mafia members) Information Sheet, (no indictment) 7/1/87, 1 p.
6. RICO:
   USA vs. NICODEMO SCARFO (and 18 others) US District Court #88-00003 (01) 6/13/88, 91 pp.

CHAPTER 1: THE BLOODY MAFIA WARS OF THE 20TH CENTURY

TIME , 8/29/86 (see Biblio)

McFadden, R. NYT, 3/11/87 (see Biblio)

Lubasch, Arnold, "Prosecutors Say Mafia Infiltrated 3 Industrial and Teamsters' Unions," NYT, 4/29/87, p. A 33

Raab, Selwyn, "Link is Sought Between Gotti and S.I. Body," NYT, 5/1/87, pp. B-1-3

Rivera, Geraldo, Network TV program/Mafia, 8/11/87 (see Biblio)

Raab, Selwyn, "Many New York Builders Accept the Mafia (Willingly), NYT, 9/9/87, pp. 1-9

Weisberg, J., NR, 10/29/87 (see Biblio)

Suro, Robert, "338 Guilty in Sicily in Mafia Trial, 19 Get Life Terms," NYT, 12/18/87, pp. 1-7

Lubasch, Arnold, "Inside the Mob: Agent Recalls Games of Wits," NYT, 1/26/88, pp. B-1-4

Epstein, Aaron, "A Rat Tells Senate Panel of Mafia Code," PI, 4/30/88, p. 1

Carpenter, Theresa, "The Mob Within the Mob," (Review of two books on the Mafia - (see Biblio), NYTBR, 8/11/88, p. 12

CHAPTER 2: THE 20-YEAR REIGN OF MOB BOSS BRUNO

Anastasia, George, "Behind Bruno's Slaying: The Tale of a Triple Cross," PI, 3/12/89, pp. 1B-4B

Mallowe, Mike, PM, 5/88 (see Biblio)

CHAPTER 3: THE RISE OF 'LIL NICKY' SCARFO

Del Guidice, M., PIM, 2/16/83 (see Biblio)

Gruson, Lindsey, "Jailing of Crime Figure Called Telling Blow to Mafia in Philadelphia," NYT, 1/19/86, p. 10

Biddle, Dan, E.L., "Scarfo Arrested at Atlantic City Airport," PI, 1/9/87, pp. 1-16A

E.L., "Scarfo Fails in 2nd Bid for Release," PI, 2/11/87, pp. 1-8A

Mallowe, Mike, PM, 5/87 (see Biblio)

Woostendick, John, "Behind Bars With Scarfo: Holmesburg's Little Big Man," PI, 11/22/87, p. 1A

E.L., "Prosecutor: Mob Contracts were Put Out on Informants," PI, 6/2/88, p. 4B

CHAPTER 4: THE MAKING OF A MAFIA MEMBER

FDCTT (Trials of Scarfo, Beloff, et al - 1987-1988) see Biblio

TMTT (Testa Murder Trial - 1988) see Biblio

CHAPTER 5: THE CROWNING OF THE BARON OF SOUTH PHILLY

Editorial, "Tiptoeing Around Beloff," PI, 1/19/87

Lopez, Steve, "Conversation with Diane [Beloff]", PI, 2/16/87, p. 1B

E.L., "Beloff Moves to Bar Tape of Conversation with Female Friend," PI, 2/18/87, p. 3M

Lopez, Steve, "A Story That's Beyond Belief," PI, 2/18/87, p. 1B

E.L., "Memo: Beloff Asked Scarfo to Help Rego," PI, 3/31/87, p. 2B

Mallowe, Mike, "Who the Hell is Lee Beloff?" PM, 5/87 (see Biblio)

CHAPTER 6: THE PRICE OF THE CLOSING OF ORIANA STREET

Bissinger, H.C., Marimow, William, "Beloff Accused of Extortion Bid in Rouse's Penn's Landing Project," PI, 6/28/86, pp. 1-6

Nussbaum, Paul, "South Philadelphia Politicians Will Watch Case Closely," PI, 6/28/86, p. 7A

Goldwyn, Ron, "Beloff Aide: Business as Usual," PDN, 7/1/86, pp. 5-16

Maryniak, Paul, "The Shadow World of Bobby Rego," PDN, 9/30/86, p. 5

Schneider, Howard, "Beloff Had Me Fired, Woman Tells FBI," PDN, 10/31/86, p. 3

Maryniak, Paul, "Mystery Woman, Dating Cost Me My Job," PDN, 10/31/86, p. 3

Cox, Don, "Act Now!" (Letter to the Editor), PI, 11/17/86, p. 12A

CHAPTER 7: THE FREEBIE APARTMENT

FDCTT (Rouse Extortion) 3/23/87 to 4/3/87

E.L., "Beloff Hires Las Vegas Attorney," PI, 12/19/86, p. 13B

Sutton, Wm. Jr., "Council Limits Beloff," PI, 1/13/87, p. 1B

Sutton, Wm. Jr., "Council Takes Steps to Handle Beloff's Bills," PI, 1/16/87, p. 14A

Sutton, Wm. Jr., "Beloff Thanks His Supporters on Council," PI, 3/20/87, p. 14B

Locy, Tony, "Beloff Trial Ties Crooks to Pols," PDN, 3/28/87, pp. 4-16

CHAPTER 8: THE MILLION DOLLAR SCAM AT PENN'S LANDING

FDCTT (Rouse Extortion Case) 3/23/87 to 4/3/87

Guthman, Edwin, "City Council's Course is Clear on Beloff Charges," (Op/Ed Page), PI, 6/29/86, p. 7C

Marimow, Wm. K., "In Beloff Case, Probers See Mob Moving into Politics," PI, 6/29/86, pp. 1-12A

Infield, Tom, "Denying Involvement, Beloff Says: 'There will be Better Days.'" PI, 6/19/86, pp. 1-10A

Sutton, William, "Special Council Session Set for Bills Stalled by Beloff," PI, 6/29/86, p. 10A

Sutton, William, "Penn's Landing Bills Clear Council After Being Held Up Earlier by Beloff," PI, 7/8/86, pp. 1-8A

Infield, Tom, Sutton, Wm., "Beloff Case Dismissed Pending Grand Jury," PI, 7/9/86, pp. 1A-6A

Sutton, Wm., "Beloff Dismissal Not Unusual Step, Official Says," PI, 7/10/86, pp. 1B-4B

E.L., Bissinger, H., "The Undercover Figure in the Beloff Case," PI, 10/30/86, p. 1B

Anastasia, George, et al, "Two From Mob to Aid Probe of Scarfo, Sources Say," PI, 11/15/86, pp. 1A-7A

CHAPTER 9: THE GOOD GUYS MAKE A MOVE

Gruson, Lindsey, "Philadelphia Councilman and Others Indicted in Extortion Case," NYT, 10/29/86, p. 16A

Locy, Tony, Jim Smith, "FBI: We're Building a Case Against the Mob," PDN, 10/29/86, pp. 3-10

Infield, Tom, "A Feisty Beloff Declares His Spirits are Good and He's Ready to Fight," PI, 10/30/86, pp. 1-19A

Clark, Robin, "Beloff Steps Down as head of Council's Labor Panel," PI, 10/31/86, pp. 1B-2B

E.L., "Crime Figure Pleads Guilty to Conspiracy with Beloff," PI, 12/24/86, pp. 1A-9A

E.L., Dan Biddle, "Scarfo Approved Extortion Plan, Indictment Says," PI, 1/10/87

Anastasia, George and Biddle, Dan, "A Long List of Violations for Scarfo," PI, 1/10/87

Goodman, Howard, "Beloff Backers Easy to Find in South Philadelphia," PI, 1/11/87, p. 10A

E.L., "Ruling is Delayed in Beloff Tape," PI, 2/29/87, p. 2B

E.L., Biddle, Dan, "Rego, Beloff Expected to Profit, Developer Says," PI, 3/26/87, p. 4A

Anastasia, George, "Mob Informant Pleads Guilty," PI, 3/28/87, p. 4B

Locy, Tony, "Witness: 'They're Our Judges,' Beloff Said," PDN, 3/28/87, pp. 6-36

Biddle, D., and E.L., "A Key Issue Emerges in Beloff Trial," PI, 3/29/87, pp. 1E-8E

CHAPTER 10: THE SKUNK OIL SCAM

Locy, Tony, "Informant Talks of Law and Order," PDN, 11/17/86, p. 8

Locy, Tony, "Federal Informant Links Beloff to Skunk Oil Plot," PDN, 2/24/87, p. 3

E.L., "Beloff is Cited in 'Skunk Oil' Trial," PI, 2/25/87, pp. 1B-8B

CHAPTER 11: THE UNITED STATES VS. BELOFF AND REGO

FDCTT (Rouse Extortion Case) 3/23/87 to 4/3/87

E.L., "Beloff Trial Set to Start Tomorrow," PI, 3/22/87, p. 1

E.L., "Only Three Jurors Selected as Beloff Trial Begins," PI, 3/23/87, p. 1B-2B

E.L., "Beloff Jury Complete for Extortion Trial," PI, 3/24/87, pp. 1B-6B

E.L., "Mob Informer Ties Beloff to $1 Million Extortion Plan," PI, 3/28/87, pp. 1-6

Meltzer, Mark, "PNB Tightens Check Policy in Response to Beloff Incident," PDN, 4/1/87, p. 3

E.L., "Beloff Signifies He Was in Deal, FBI Agent Says," PI, 4/1/87, pp. 1A-4A

E.L., Biddle, Dan, "Hand Signal One of Several Issues Crucial in Beloff Case," PI, 4/2/87, p. 6B

E.L., "On Stand, Beloff Denies all Charges," PI, 4/2/87, p. 1B

Locy, Tony, "Memory of 'Nicky Crow' Makes Rego Weep," PDN, 4/3/87, pp. 5-39

Biddle, Dan, E.L., "Rego Takes Stand, Blames Plot on Caramandi," PI, 4/3/87, pp. 1A-9A

E.L., Biddle, Dan, "Beloff Extortion Case Goes to the Jury," PI, 4/4/87, pp. 1A-6A

E.L., D.B., "Lawyer Comes Home in Defense of Beloff," PI, 4/5/87, pp. 1B-6B

Locy, Tony, "Beloff Jurors Resume Deliberations," PDN, 4/6/87, pp. 2-28

Fix, Janet, "In Wake of Testimony, Banks Checking Their Policies," PI, 4/6/87, pp. 1E-8E

E.L., D.B., "Beloff Jury Hits Dead end," PI, 4/7/87, pp. 1A-18A

E.L., D.B., "Juror: Most Were Ready to Convict Beloff and Rego," PI, 4/8/87, pp. 1B-2B

D.B., E.L., "Why a Verdict Escaped Jurors in Beloff/Rego Case," PI, 4/12/87, pp. 1E-4E

CHAPTER 12: THE CLEANSING OF THE CITY COUNCIL

Gallagher, Maria, "Four, Maybe Five, Challenging Beloff," PDN, 7/21/86, pp. 3-12

Infield, Tom, "Beloff Picks a Successor, But Says He is Counting on Acquittal and Re-election," PI, 12/18/86, p. 16B

Infield, Tom, "Tayoun Set to Announce Council Bid," PI, 1/22/87, pp. 1B-4B

Infield, Tom, "Beloff Has Largest Campaign Fund," PI, 2/3/87, p. 2B

Goldwyn, Ron, "Dems Stick With Beloff for Council," PDN, 3/13/87, pp. 5-25

Sutton, Wm., "Primary Nod for Beloff," PI, 3/13/87, pp. 1B-6B

Infield, Tom, "Beloff Foe Quits Race: Clears Field," PI, 3/18/87, p. 3

Sutton, Wm., "Beloff Dominates Issues in District's Three Way Race," PI, 4/15/87

Grace, Joe, "Beloff Finds Comfort in Fireside Chats, with Pals," PDN, 5/20/87, p. 5

Infield, Tom, "Beloff is Defeated in Three Way Race," PI, 5/20/87, pp. 1A-9A

D.B., E.L., "They Played Key Roles in the Beloff Trial," PI, 7/5/87, p. 5C

CHAPTER 13: 'LIL NICKY' IN THE HALLS OF JUSTICE: THE U.S. VS. NICODEMO SCARFO

FDCTT (Rouse Extortion Case/Scarfo Trial) 4/27/87 to 5/6/87

E.L., "Scarfo Ordered Held Without Bail Pending Trial," PI, 1/16/87, p. 1A

E.L., Tulsky, Fred, "U.S. and Castille Split over How to Try Scarfo," PI, 3/20/87, pp. 1A-17A

D.B. & E.L., "In the Shadows in the Beloff Trial," PI, 4/1/87, pp. 1B-2B

Tulsky, Fred, "U.S. Attorney Uncooperative on Scarfo, Castille Tells Meese," PI, 4/3/87, pp. 1B-2B

Locy, Tony, "Jury: Scarfo Rites in Blood," PDN, 4/10/87, pp. 3-30

Daughen, Joe, "It All Began with Bug on one Mobster's Pad," PDN, 4/10/87, pp. 3-29

Price, Debbie, "Slain Judge Put Price on Own Head," PDN, 4/10/87, p. 29

Cooney, Tom, "Jersey Rounds up the Usual Suspects," PDN, 4/10/87, p. 28

Anastasia, George, "A Broken Vow Broke the Case Against Organized Crime," PI, 4/12/87, pp. 1E-2E

U.P.I., "Secrecy Sought for Jurors," PI, 4/12/87, p. 4B

E.L., "Scarfo Jurors to be Unnamed, Judge Rules," PI, 4/15/87, pp. 1B-7B

E.L., "Role Seen for Dennis in Scarfo Trial," PI, 4/24/87, p. 3

CHAPTER 14: THE SECOND TIME AROUND FOR BELOFF AND REGO

E.L., "New Trial Refused in Beloff Case," PI, 7/28/87, pp. 1B-2B

CHAPTER 15: THE SENTENCING OF NICKY, LEE AND BOBBY

FDCTT (Vote Fraud Trial) See Biblio - 11/16/87 to 4/22/88
E.L., "Ex-Aide of Beloff May Take Stand," PI, 6/6/87, pp. 1B-2B
Anastasia, George, "Scarfo's Assets are Targeted," PI, 7/5/87, pp. 1B-7B
E.L., "The Judge Who Will Sentence Beloff, et al," PI, 8/2/87, pp. 1B-4B
Ditzen, L. Stuart, "Beloff is Sentenced to 10 Years," PI, 8/6/87, pp. 1A-8A

CHAPTER 16: LAST GASPS BEFORE THE PRISON GATES CLANGED SHUT

E.L., "Beloff and Rego's Extortion Conviction Upheld," PI, 4/1/88, p. 6B
E.L., "U.S. Asks that Beloff and Rego Start Sentencing," PI, 4/5/88, p. 1B
Slobodzian, Joe, "Partners in Crime Go Separate Ways to Jail," PI, 4/27/88, pp. 1B-2B
E.L., "Scarfo Conviction Upheld in Rouse Extortion Attempt," PI, 6/30/88, p. 7B
E.L., "Rego Pleads Guilty in Drug Case," PI, 7/6/88, pp. 1A-10A
D.B., "Top Court Spurns Extortion Appeal," PI, 10/18/88, p. 3B

CHAPTER 17: VOTE FRAUD IN THE NURSING HOMES

FDCTT (U.S. vs. Leland Beloff, et al) see Biblio
Weiner, Tim, et al, "Beloff Said to be a Focus of FBI Election Probe," PI, 4/30/86, p. 1
E.L., "U.S. Says Beloff Suggested Ways to Sign Ballots," PI, 1/29/87, pp. 1B-2B
Cass, Julia, "Shots Fired into Car of Witness in Beloff Case," PI, 8/14/87, pp. 1B-2B
Cass, Julia, "Co-Defendant Files a Guilty Plea in Beloff Case," PI, 8/15/87, p. 3B
E.L., "Diane Beloff Defends Self in Vote Fraud Case," PI, 8/19/87, p. 1
E.L., Beloff's (Vote Fraud) Trial in Delay," PI, 8/20/87, pp. 1-8
Locy, Tony, "Diane's Dilemma: Dump Lawyer or Dump Hubby," PDN, 8/20/87, p. 2
E.L., "Beloff's Trial Postponed Indefinitely," PI, 9/9/87, p. 4B
E.L., "U.S. Describes Vote Rig Boast in South Philadelphia," PI, 11/17/87, pp. 1A-18A
E.L., "South Philadelphia Democrat Gets Three Years in Vote Rigging," PI, 11/24/87, p. 3A
Warner, Susan, "Beloff Pleads Guilty: Gets 3-Year Term," PI, 4/23/88, p. 2B

CHAPTER 18: THE 'SPEED' (P2P) CONSPIRACY

FDCTT (The Speed Trial, US vs. Scarfo et al) See Biblio - 11/30/87 to 12/12/87

E.L., "Scarfo Charged as Drug Lord," PI, 6/19/87, pp. 1-20

E.L., "Indictment in Scarfo Case Revised," PI, 6/3/87, p. 1B

Anastasia, George, "Scarfo Family Reported Run by Reputed Trenton Mob Figure," PI, 10/5/87, pp. 1A-8A

Locy, Tony, "Not Far from Home," PDN, 10/30/87, pp. 5-14

E.L., "Request for Anonymity on Scarfo Jury Rejected," PI, 11/17/87, p. 1

CHAPTER 19: THE SPEED TRIAL: FROM START TO FINISH

FDCTT (see Biblio)

E.L., "Drug Trial Begins for Scarfo," PI, 11/30/87, p. 1B

E.L., "Six Jurors Picked for Scarfo Drug Trial," PI, 12/2/87, p. 1B

Anastasia, George, "Tapes Show Jurors Confused About Sequesteration Issue," PI, 12/4/87, p. 34

E.L., "U.S. Informants are Assailed by the Scarfo Defense," PI, 11/5/87, p. 1B

E.L., "Scarfo Said to be Drug Profiteer," PI, 12/6/87, pp. 1B-6B

E.L., "Drug Scheme Outlined," PI, 12/8/87, pp. 1B-2B

E.L., "Defense Asks Scarfo Dismissal," PI, 12/10/87, pp. 1B-2B

E.L., "Witnesses Cast as Liars by Defense in Scarfo Trial," PI, 12/12/87, pp. 1B-2B

CHAPTER 20: SCARFO, THE 'SPEED KING' IS VICTORIOUS

E.L. & Anastasia, George, "Scarfo Acquitted in Drug Trial," PI, 12/13/87, pp. 1A+

A.P., "Reputed Mob Leader is Acquitted in Philadelphia," NYT, 12/13/87, p. 41

CHAPTER 21: THE MAN WHO GOT TOO BIG FOR HIS BRITCHES

TMTT (Testa Murder Trial) 4/5/88 to 5/10/88 (See Biblio for ref.)

Tulsky, Fred, et al, "Scarfo Held in Slaying of Testa," PI, 4/11/87, pp. 1A-6A

E.L., "Ex Mobster: Defendants Upset by Testa Plan," PI, 4/26/87, p. 1B

Slobodzian, Joe, "Informers as Witnesses Can be Risky," PI, 5/15/87, p. 1B

Goldman, Henry, "Scarfo Faces Trial in Testa Kill," PI, 5/15/87, p. 1

Goldman, Henry, "Bail is Sought for Scarfo and Seven Others in Murder Case," PI, 5/22/87, p. 6B

Tulsky, Fred, "Scarfo and Associates Denied Bail in Testa Case," PI, 5/29/87, p. 4B

E.L., "Sweeping Charges Target Scarfo," PI, 1/12/88, pp. 1-4

Anastasia, George, "Jury Selection to Begin in Scarfo Trial," PI, 2/7/88, pp. 1B-8B

Anastasia, George, "Prosecution Says Sal Testa Victim of Organized Crime Killing," PI, 2/9/88, p. 6B

Anastasia, George, "Secrecy of Scarfo Jury at Issue," PI, 2/11/88, p. 10B

Caba, Susan, "Outside Jury Sought for Scarfo Trial," PI, 2/20/88, pp. 1A-4A

Caba, Susan, "Scarfo Jurors to be Chosen From Philadelphia," PI, 2/25/88, pp. 1A-4A

Anastasia, George, "Reputed Mobster Pontani Ordered Held Without Bail," PI, 3/1/88, p. 3B

Johnson, Tyree, "Scarfo Trial Costs Top $100 Gs," PDN, 3/2/88, p. 3

Anastasia, George, "In Court Drama, Simone Plays to Audience of Jurors," PI, 3/30/88, pp. 1B-2B

Caba, Susan, "Trial of Scarfo in Testa Slaying Gets Underway," PI, 4/6/88, pp. 1B-2B

Locy, Tony, "Love Lost to Life Lost, Testa's Last Six Months," PDN, 4/7/88, p. 10

Caba, Susan, "Word Was 'Salvie's Gotta Go,' Ex-Mobster Recalls," PI, 4/13/88, pp. 1A-6A

Gallagher, Maria, "Scarfo's Lawyers Put Accuser on the Hot Seat," PDN, 4/14/88, p. 5

Tulsky, Fred, "Witness Says Testa Slaying Defendant Killed Second Man," PI, 4/16/88, p. 3B

Chapter 22: The Body Near a Lovers' Lane Sandpit

TMTT (4/5/88 to 5/10/88) Testa Trial

Caba, Susan, "Scarfo's Defense Attacks Ex-Mobster's Character," PI, 4/14/88, pp. 1B-6B

Lopez, Steve, "Bumbling Boys of South Philadelphia" (column), PI, 4/14/88, p. 1B

Caba, Susan, "Scarfo Trial Turns into Verbal Battle," PI, 4/15/88, pp. 1B-6B

A.P., "Mobster's Body Found in Bag," NYT, 4/16/88, p. 3B

Chapter 23: The Ghosts of Past Mafia Murders Come Back to Haunt 'Lil Nicky'

TMTT (4/5/88 to 5/10/88)

Chapter 24: The Commonwealth of Pennsylvania vs Nicky Scarfo et al

Caba, Susan, "In Scarfo Trial, Ex-Mobster Testifies About the Mafia," PI, 4/12/88, p. 1

Caba, Susan, "Witnesses Are Called to Bolster Caramandi," PI, 4/21/88, p. 4B

Gallagher, Maria, "Lawyers Question Del Giorno on Son's Arrest," 4/26/88, p. 10

CHAPTER 25: THE SAL TESTA MURDER CASE

TMTT (4/5/88 to 5/10/88) See Biblio

Caba, Susan, "City's Toughest Prosecutor Pushes Limits," PI, 3/29/88, pp. 1B-2B

Caba, Susan, "Their Days on Court in Scarfo's Corner," PI, 4/17/88, pp. 1B-6B

Caba, Susan, "In Scarfo's Trial, Opening the Door to Past 'Bad Acts'," PI, 4/30/88, p. 8A

Caba, Susan, "Scarfo Cleared in Testa Slaying," PI, 5/11/88, pp. 1A-8A

CHAPTER 26: THE ORGY AT THE FOUR SEASONS HOTEL

E.L., "Defense Raucously Toasts the Jury," PI, 5/11/88, pp. 1A-8A

Locy, Tony, "Joyous Relatives Mob Hotel Bar," PDN, 5/11/88, p. 4

Heine, Kurt, "Nicky and His Eight Buddies Win a Big One," PDN, 5/11/88, p. 5

Caba, Susan, "No Proof, A Scarfo Juror Says," PI, 5/12/88, pp. 1A-20A

E.L., "For the Jury, It was a Most Trying Six Weeks," PI, 5/12/88, p. 20

CHAPTER 27: WHEN A DIARY BECAME A SMOKING GUN

FDCTT (Staino 'Speed' Trial) 7/11/88 to 7/15/88

Gallagher, Maria, Smith, Jim, "Staino Nabbed in Caribbean," PDN, 1/14/88, p. 3

E.L., "Evidence Seized About Arrest to be Used in Staino Trial," PI, 7/12/88, p. 3B

E.L., "Informer Says Lawyer 'Close' to Being in Mob," PI, 7/13/88, p. 3B

E.L., "Beloff's Wife Makes Guilty Plea," PI, 7/26/88, pp. 1B-2B

E.L., "Staino Convicted in Mob Drug Trial," PI, 7/16/88, p. 3B

CHAPTER 28: NICKY TRIES TO PREVENT HIS OWN WATERLOO

FDCTT (Scarfo-RICO Trial) 9/28/88 to 11/19/88 (see Biblio)

E.L., "In the Scarfo Jury Pool: A Reluctance to Serve," PI, 8/15/88, p. 11B

A.P., "20 Acquitted in U.S. Trial Tied to the Mob," PI, 8/26/88, pp. 1A-4A

E.L., "Mob Informant Spotted by Defendant's Relatives," 8/31/88, pp. 1B-2B

Locy, Tony, "Feds Hope to Demob Scarfo and Army of Pals," PDN, 9/9/88, p. 6

E.L., "Trial to Begin for Scarfo and 16 Others," PI, 9/11/88, pp. 1B-9B

Clark, Robin, "Jury in Trial of Scarfo and 16 Known to be 'Firm but Fair'," PI, 9/24/88, pp. 1B-2B

E.L., "A Jury Chosen to Consider Scarfo's Fate," PI, 9/28/88, pp. 1A-20A

E.L., "Lawyers Open Trial of Scarfo," PI, 9/29/88, pp. 1B-2B

E.L., "A Consig Discussed on Tapes," PI, 9/30/88, pp. 1B-6B

E.L. & Clark, Robin, "Scarfo Spoke to New York Mob, Agent Says," PI, 10/1/88, pp. 1B-4B

Wines, Michael, "Thornburgh Seems Prepared to Shut Anti-Mafia Units," NYT, 3/19/89, pp. 1-26

CHAPTER 29: NINE PLUS FOUR EQUALS THIRTEEN (MURDERS, THAT IS)

E.L., "Photos Introduced in Scarfo Trial," PI, 10/6/88, p. 3B

E.L., "Plan to Kill N.J. Judge Detailed," PI, 10/4/88, pp. 1B-4B

E.L., "Government Begins Presenting Evidence in Slaying of Narducci," PI, 10/5/88, p. 3B

E.L., "Scarfo Trial Focuses on Faction's Feud," PI, 10/6/88, p. 2B

E.L. & Clark, Robin, "Murders and Misses Detailed by Del Giorno," PI, 10/11/88, pp. 1A-8A

Locy, Tony, "Witness Guarded, Testimony..." PDN, 10/11/88, p. 13

E.L., "Del Giorno Tells of a Difficult Killing," PI, 10/12/88, pp. 1B-6B

E.L. & Clark, Robin, "Del Giorno Recounts the Clues that 'Scarfo Wanted Him Dead'," PI, 10/14/88, pp. 1B-2B

Locy, Tony, "Simone Jumps to His Own Defense," PDN, 10/14/88, p. 8

E.L., "Simone Suggests Witness is Lying for Government," PI 10/15/88, pp. 1B-4B

E.L. & Clark, Robin, "A Witness Recounts Scarfo's Chilling Words," PI, 10/26/88, pp. 1B-6B

E.L. & Clark, Robin, "Caramandi Tells of Hits and Misses," PI, 10/28/88, pp. 1B-6B

E.L. & Clark, Robin, "Caramandi on the Mob: 'They are Paranoid'," PI, 10/29/88, pp. 1B-2B

E.L. & Clark, Robin, "Caramandi Tells of Life in the Mob," PI, 10/29/88, pp. 1B-4B

Clark, Robin, "Caramandi: A Mob Tiff Turns Cosmic," PI, 10/30/88, pp. 1B-3B

E.L., "My Whole Life's Been Crime," PI, 11/1/88, p. 1B

E.L., "Del Giorno's Son Focus of Testimony in Mob Trial," PI, 11/11/88, pp. 1B-4B

CHAPTER 30: 'THE ENTERPRISE': HOW THE MAFIA RAN ITS BUSINESS

FDCTT (Scarfo-RICO Trial) 9/28/88 to 11/19/88)

Gabor, Andrea, "The Long Arm of the Law on Wall Street," USNWR, 9/26/88, p. 24

Anastasia, George, "Today's Mafia Means Business," PI, 9/13/88, pp. 1F-8F

Locy, Tony, "He Writes Lyrics, Trial Hums Along," PDN, 10/6/88, p. 8

E.L., "Former Bookie Tells Scarfo Jury of Mob Partnership in Business," PI, 10/18/88, p. 3B

E.L., "Mob Figure Describes Shakedown," PI, 10/19/88, pp. 1B-2B

E.L. & Clark, Robin, "Loan Shark Tells of Mob Dealings," PI, 10/20/88, pp. 1B-6B

Clark, Robin, "Witness Ties a Scarfo Co-Defendant to Drug Trade and Murder Attempt," PI, 10/21/88, p. 7B

Clark, Robin, "One Man's Success and Dreams of More," PI, 10/21/88, p. 7B

CHAPTER 31: THE SINS OF THE FATHERS

FDCTT, (Scarfo-RICO Trial)

CHAPTER 32: RICO AND A JURY BURY SCARFO'S CRIME FAMILY

FDCCT (RICO) 9/28/88 to 11/19/88

D.B. et al, "With the Depletion of Scarfo Ranks, Power May Shift to Sedate Type," PI, 5/10/87, pp. 1B-6B

E.L. et al, "Scarfo, Jr. is Charged in an Assault," PI, 11/5/88, pp. 1B-2B

E.L. & Clark, Robin, "U.S. Closes With Tales of Mob Killings," PI, 11/12/88, pp. 1B-4B

E.L., "Defense Closings Begin," PI, 11/13/88, pp. 1B-4B

E.L., "Government Case Tainted, Scarfo Jury Told," PI, 11/16/88, pp. 1B-6B

E.L., "In Mob Trial, Defense Pounds About Informants' Testimony," PI, 11/16/88, p. 6B

E.L., Clark, Robin & Cipriano, R., "Scarfo and Associates Convicted," PI, 11/20/88, pp. 1-22, 1F

CHAPTER 33: A POST-MORTEM ANALYSIS: WHY THE GOVERNMENT WON

Clark, Robin, "Tapes Turned the Tide in Government's Case," PI, 11/20/88, pp. 1-22

Anastasia, George, "Control of Mob a Wide Open Question," PI, 11/20/88, pp. 1F-4F

Daughen, Joe, "Mob Loses Strength Of Its Convictions," PDN, 11/21/88, pp. 4-21

Anastasia, George, "Dismantling Philadelphia Mob," PI, 1/29/89, p. 3F

Anastasia, George, "N.Y. Feud Could Lead to Mob War, Investigators Say," PI, 3/5/89, p. 25A

CHAPTER 34: A WREATH FOR 'FRANKIE FLOWERS'

FMTT (Flowers Murder Trial Transcripts) Pennsylvania State Court - Common Pleas, 3/89

Caba, Susan, "848 Candidates Later, the Scarfo Jury is Complete," PI, 3/14/89, p. 4B

Caba, Susan, "A Defendant in Scarfo Trial Defects," PI, 3/16/89, pp. 1A-24A

Moran, Edward, "Scarfo Stunner, Pal 'Flips' to Other Side," PDN, 3/16/89, p. 6

Anastasia, George, "Prosecutor Says Scarfo Ordered Hit," PI, 3/17/89, pp. 1B-6B

Caba, Susan, "D'Alfonso Slaying is Relived," PI, 3/18/89, pp. 1B-4B

CHAPTER 35: THE FUTURE OF ORGANIZED CRIME AS A POWER IN AMERICA

Arlacchi, P. (See 1987 book in Biblio)

Kerr, Peter, "Chinese Now Dominant in N.Y. Heroin Trade," NYT, 8/9/87, pp. 1-20

Weisberg, Jacob, (see Biblio), NR, 10/12/87

Raab, Selwyn, "Gotti's Swagger is Bolder as His Reputation Grows," NYT, 10/22/87, pp. 1B

Buder, Leonard, "Gotti on Tape: Tells of Plans for Future," NYT, 12/3/87, p. 1B

Kerr, Peter, (see Biblio), NYT, 1/4/88

Raab, Selwyn, (see Biblio), NYT, 12/12/88

Raab, Selwyn, "The Odd Old Man on Sullivan Street, New Mob Power," NYT, 2/3/88, pp. 1B-2B

Anastasia, George, "Police Investigation Reports a Jr. Black Mafia," PI, 3/18/88, pp. 1B-6B

Cusik, Fred, "Report: War Between City Drug Gangs Likely," PI, 4/13/88, pp. 1B-2B

Goodman, Howard, "Report: Organized Crimes Change Face," PI, 4/12/88, pp. 1A-10A

Anastasia, George, "Dismantling the Philadelphia Mob," PI, 1/29/89, op. cit.

Marriott, M., (see Biblio), NYT, 2/22/89

Anastasia, George, "Organized Crime Has Many Faces, Panel Says," PI, pp. 1B-10B

CHAPTER 36: THE RICO SENTENCING OF THE SCARFO CRIME FAMILY

Main Sources: U.S. Government Sentencing Memorandums vs. the 18 convicted Mafia defendants in the RICO trial ending on November 21, 1988, U.S. District Court, the Eastern District of Pa., (#s 88-00003-1 through 88-0000s-18) May 1, 1989, Philadelphia, Pa. (by the U.S. Organized Crime Strike Force).

Anastasia, George, "Little Nicky's Big Mistake," PIM, 5/14/89, pp. 15-33

'Lil Nicky' Scarfo: The Rap Sheet

October 2, 1980 — Acquitted in New Jersey Superior Court along with two associates of murder in the 1979 slaying of Atlantic City cement contractor Vincent Falcone

April 9, 1981 — Convicted of illegal possession of a firearm, a federal charge. Served 17 months of a two-year sentence.

May 6, 1987 — Convicted of conspiracy to commit extortion, in federal court, in connection with the attempted $1 million shakedown of developer Willard G. Rouse 3d. Sentenced to 14 years in prison.

December 12, 1987 — Acquitted, along with four associates, of federal drug charges.

May 10, 1988 — Acquitted, along with eight associates, of murder in Common Pleas Court in the 1984 killing of Salvatore Testa.

November 19, 1988 — Convicted, along with 16 associates, of federal racketeering charges under the RICO statute. Awaiting sentencing.

April 5, 1989 — Convicted in Common Pleas Court, along with seven associates, of first-degree murder, conspiracy and weapons offenses in the 1985 slaying of Frank 'Frankie Flowers' D'Alfonso. Sentenced to life in prison.

May 11, 1989 — Sentenced to 55 years in prison with a $500,000 fine for November 19th RICO conviction.

INDEX